MY BABA AND I

Dr. John S. Hislop

PUBLISHED BY
Birth Day Publishing Company
San Diego, California, U.S.A.

DISTRIBUTED BY
SATHYA SAI BOOK CENTER
OF AMERICA
305 W. FIRST STREET
TUSTIN, CA 92780, USA
714-669-0522

By the Same Author

CONVERSATIONS WITH BHAGAVAN SRI SATHYA
    SAI BABA

Special thanks goes to Lila Youngs. Not only is Lila a meticulous proofreader, but she is also an editor par excellence. With unerring judgment she pointed out areas for improvement in the writing, and in the context, style, and grammar.

Contents

Author's Preface

Three years ago, I told Baba that a new book was ready, and I asked if it should be published now or ten years from now. Why I put it in that odd way, I don't know, but Baba's response was immediate, "Ten years from now!" So I put the manuscript aside. Last year, however (1984), Dr. Sandweiss brought surprising news. Baba had said to him, "Print Hislop's book now." Dr. Sandweiss responded, "But Swami, you said it was not to be published for ten years." Baba's answer was, "The ten years is up!"

A couple of months later I was in India and asked Baba if Dr. Sandweiss had understood correctly. Baba said, "Yes." I then said that I was unsure about a title, but I thought I might call it, "Experiences with Sri Sathya Sai Baba." Baba said at once that such a title would not do. Then, a moment later he said, "This will do. Use the title, 'My Baba and I.' Here, I will write it for you." And he then proceeded to write the title on a slip of paper — which slip of paper I am treasuring, needless to say!

To me, as well as to many hundreds of thousands of people in North and South America, Europe, Africa, Australia, New Zealand and Asia, Sri Sathya Sai Baba is considered to be an Avathar: Divinity in human form. His wisdom, the love which is so strongly felt when one is in his presence, and his awesome power over the natural elements and human circumstances contribute to the extra-ordinary veneration in which he is held and to the almost irresisti-ble attraction felt by people of all ages and races when they see him, or begin to give close attention to, his teachings and to his life.

Often, people ask about Baba's personal life-style, and about how his educational and other projects are financed. A number of years ago certain devotees organized a Trust which is administered by the State Bank of India. The Trust provides the finances for the Sai work. At Puttaparthi, the village where Baba was born and which is now the site of the Sri Sathya Sai Institute of Higher Learning and of his schools from kindergarten through junior col-lege, Baba lives in one small room with very little furniture. He eats sparingly, sleeps very little (if at all), and shows no interest in personal possessions. All objects used by him, including cars, are supplied for his use by a very limited number of long-time devotees. Attempts by other people to provide things for him are unsuccessful. Transportation, a small private room, a few simple ankle-length robes, and food sparingly served meet his needs. Beyond that, he requires nothing for himself. Baba's entire life is selfless service to his devotees and to all people everywhere.

This book is divided into four sections: four areas of interest, and an epilogue. An apology is due from me to the scholarly readers of the section devoted to the principal teachings of Baba. Every quotation should be referenced, but in this there is a prob-lem. Over the years, as I studied, it was for my own interest and without any thought of writing a book. When I read something that had a strong impact on me, I would copy it on a slip of paper, but never bothered to jot down page and volume reference. To now attempt to reread the many thousands of pages to try to find the reference for each quotation is not a project that I can take on. I hope my apology will be accepted.

By his discourses, writings, and interviews, Sri Sathya Sai Baba inspires those people who turn to him. He encourages inter-ested men and women to change from the living of an ordinary, conventional life to a life based on spiritual values. Individuals, who have come to have a feeling of great confidence in Baba's wisdom, tend to become acquainted with each other, and find it of mutual benefit to meet occasionally, usually weekly, to discuss the Sai teachings and to plan service activities in the particular community where they are living. These Sai devotee groups now exist in many parts of the world.

The limitation of the writer himself prevents a full exposition of the teachings of Sri Sathya Sai Baba. A final and complete account will need to wait until his mission unfolds itself over the ensuing years. Baba has said, "My life is my message." His devotees take this to mean that Baba's message to those whom he addresses as "Embodiments of the Divine," is not limited to his words of wisdom, but will be complete and will be deeply understood only when considered in the context of his full life of compassion and selfless service to all mankind.

Baba has, however, clearly set forth the means for peace and happiness in the world in the following verse:

"When there is righteousness in the heart,
There is beauty in the character.
When there is beauty in the character,
There is harmony in the home.
When there is harmony in the home,
There is order in the nation.
When there is order in the nation,
There is peace in the world."

To Sri Sathya Sai

And to all those who with
divine discontent seek
to be free.

Materialized crucifix, story page 17.

HAPPENINGS

Our First Meeting with
Sri Sathya Sai Baba

My wife and I first heard of Baba in 1968 through a description of him given to a friend of mine by a lady who had visited India. She had brought back some sacred ash (vibhuti), a beautiful ring as a gift to her from the miraculous nature of Baba, and she had many fascinating stories to tell. One special remark struck fire. The lady said she had felt a change in her character while with Baba, and the change persisted even after she returned home. This statement had a strong impact on my mind. Could there be a man, was there a man living today whose being was so subtle, so powerful, so mysterious, so divine that he could change the human heart?

If it were indeed true that such a man lived in today's world, then nothing else in my life could equal the urgency of seeking him out. I prayed that through his grace and kindness, he might touch my dry heart and make it alive and vibrant again.

My wife and I heard the story of Baba on a Monday, and the same week we were aboard a plane to India.

I should not imply that my faith was able to keep up with the eager rush of my heart, but my intellectual doubts, which had gained considerable strength during the journey, were unable to survive even the first meeting with Baba. In his presence, doubt is like very shallow water in the burning sun — in no time at all it disappears.

3

There is nothing in Western tradition to prepare a person for his first meeting with Baba: He comes to the room of our small foreign group, sits on the floor with us, and invites us to express our spiritual doubts. We see before us what appears to be a man of brown skin, slight in build, with a mass of darkest brown hair with golden highlights framing his face. We are naturally as observant as possible when we meet this extraordinary being of whom we have heard such strange stories. All senses are alert. Our minds and our intelligences tend to be wide awake. We note that he has sensitive features which quickly reflect changes in mood and in thought. He has a sweet and loving smile — like that of an innocent and affectionate child. His eyes are dark brown, soft and melting, and sparkle with intelligence and humor. His voice is sweet and tender like that of a mother; sometimes gay with laughter and wit like that of a friend and companion, and at other times stern and serious like the voice of a father. The movement of his body as he sits, arises, and walks about is graceful and flowing and extremely light. His hands are wonderfully expressive.

There is a faint perfume in the air, which my wife says is jasmine. Yet Baba does not wear perfume — this I know from close members of his staff who sleep in the same room. Yet, wherever he is, there is perfume in the air.

One would need to be very negative to be other than captivated and delighted by the first impression of Baba. But, as we sit close to him, we quickly realize that here is far, far more than an elegant and charming Indian man. Our perception deepens, beyond the senses, and we become aware of a subtle yet total beauty that has quietly filled the room. Our critical, questioning mind stops its restless activity, and we experience an upflow of happiness. All care drops away. Remembrance of the world and its problems falls away from consciousness. Only our happy blissful state in the present is real. Although Baba is talking, one is surrounded by quietness. In that peaceful state of being, one's awareness deepens without effort. And now, like a faint breeze, there is a movement in the heart, a perception that some aliveness, something unknown is in the heart. In a moment, the realization comes that a current of love is moving in my dry heart, and then it was clear that the source of the current of love was Baba — nay, more, that the sweetness of Baba himself was there, with life, in my heart.

How could Sri Sathya Sai Baba, a stranger never seen before, come into the heart of a mature man and bring about a change from within, a change from which there is no turning back? Surely, the Divine is the only Stranger who can do this.

The happiness that has come with Baba's presence becomes still more intense when he answers questions and speaks of matters spiritual. The depth and wisdom of his words carry such a thrill of truth that it almost seems that one's consciousness cannot bear the intense joy that fills heart and mind. Whereas the senses report that Swami is a man, the more subtle levels of perception are not satisfied with that explanation. The deeper awareness only serves to sharpen the question, Who is Baba? How can one ever penetrate such a mystery and know the truth?

God is all-pervading, but, yet, we have some scientists who assert, "We have searched all outer space, we have looked for Him on the moon; no, He is nowhere to be found. He does not exist." They do not know what to seek and where, still, they have the impudence to assert that it is not found. Is God an occupant of an identifiable body or form. Has He a habitation and a habiliment that is traditionally His? God is all this and more; He is in all this and beyond. He is the inner motivator of the very scientist who "denies" Him! Man himself is God; all matter, even in the moon, is suffused with the Divine Presence. To search for God with the instruments in the laboratory is like trying to cure pain in the stomach by pouring drops into the eye! There is a technique and a special instrument for that purpose which the past masters in that science have developed and spoken about. Equip yourselves with a clear eye through detachment and love, sharpen your sense of discrimination so that it has no prejudice or predilection, then you can see God in you, around you, in all that you know and feel and are.
– Sathya Sai Baba

From Age 16

Each and every one of us is unique, Baba has said this is so. To realize happiness, which is ever new from moment to moment, we must strive to realize our own uniqueness. This means that each of us must start from where he is, and the story of each person's search will be his or her own, until finally one's uniqueness is realized as That without a Second, the Divine Indivisible Supreme Absolute.

Each person's journey will be his or her own search, and something about my own search should be told, I believe. This book is (for me) a serious appraisal of Sri Sathya Sai Baba and his teachings, and the reader should be able to judge my bias when I speak of Baba, for each mind has some bias, at least that is my experience.

For myself, the inquiry started at age 16. Our Episcopal church had a play for its young people, and I had a part. In the midst of the play, a thought struck me with great force. I thought, "These church people do not know what they are saying. Someplace in the world there must be someone who knows the truth and is able to directly say from that truth." From that moment, the direction which my life would take was known to me, and whenever I would hear of a person who was said to know the truth of life, I would drop everything and go to him. I caused my saintly

Mother and Father lost sleep, for regardless of what job I had, I would leave it and go. The final conclusion: *that I myself must find the truth within myself* was, to be sure, a concept totally unknown and far distant when I started my inquiry.

The first sign-post came to my notice in Tahiti, where as a young lad of 18, I had gone for a year of adventure. A man I met there, the Reverend Arthur deVere Anderson, told me about Theosophy, and as soon as I returned home I joined the Society in Los Angeles. At the time, I had the feeling that the only thing of value to be done in this world was service to humanity. I said this to the Society President. Very soon he told me that the way I could start such a career had opened. I could go to Ojai, California and help Fritz Kuntz, who had just come from India as Field Secretary of the Order of the Star in the East. This was an organization formed by Dr. Annie Besant in order to launch the career of J. Krishnamurti as "World Teacher." Work assigned to me in the Ojai Valley included operating the pump installation which took water from the river and pumped it up to the orange groves and houses which comprised the estate, Arya Vihara, the Ojai home of Dr. Besant and J. Krishnamurti. After a few months, they told me I could stay at Arya Vihara, and I was there whenever they were there for the two years, 1925 and 1926. Dr. Besant said I should stay and manage the ranches and farmlands, but I decided I had better finish school and I went back to college. For years thereafter, I would leave school or job to go to J. Krishnamurti Camps in the U.S. and Europe. I met my wife, Victoria, at such a meeting. At that time, Krishnamurti and Dr. Besant were giant figures who filled the horizon, and it seemed to me that they and they only had found the truth of life. I feel eternally grateful to Dr. Besant and to Krishnaji for their great kindness and great patience with an undisciplined young man. But wisdom was not born in me as a follower of Krishnamurti.

The next sign-post, to my mind, was Yoga, and my wife and I looked to yoga for an insight to truth. We met Swami Yogananda and would drive into Hollywood each week to listen to him and talk with him. We took lessons whenever we could find teachers of good reputation, like Swami Vishnudevananda and Iyengar (in Europe), and Dr. Roman Ostoya, the "Russian White Yogi," who once was buried under the baseball field at Inglewood, California for two weeks, emerging unharmed by virtue of yogic power. But in yoga, we did not find our way.

All this time we were, to be sure, exploring the literature which had emerged from spiritual disciplines the world over, but we knew that writings, no matter how noble their source and their subject matter, could not be the finality — direct knowing from the depth of experience was necessary.

The next opening in experience for us was the coming to America of Maharishi Mahesh Yogi. We met him at his first talk in a room at the Friar's Club in Hollywood. He had just arrived from Hawaii, which was his first stop after departing from India and Burma. My wife and I liked him at once. We found him to be sincere, with strong personal force, and with a great background as the favorite disciple of Sri Swami Brahmananda Saraswati, Shankaracharya of Jotirmayapithan in the Himalayas. Swami Brahmananda Saraswati was a Siddha (i.e. having yogic powers) and a master of Sri Vidya discipline. He was famous for his combining of the Bhakti and Advaita systems. Mahesh Yogi was an adept at a form of meditation designed to carry the consciousness of an individual to the source of thought, which would be the universal source of manifestation, the Undifferentiated Divine. His vision was that since it was demonstrably true that the peace of a person in deep meditation would spread its influence to persons close to the meditator, then if millions of people around the world would engage in deep meditation, this could lead to the birth of true world peace. This idea appealed to me greatly, and I became the first president of the Mahesh Yogi American organization, and the first person in America, other than Maharishi himself, to initiate others into the secrets of this meditation. It was obvious, of course, that meditation teachers would have to be working worldwide if people were to be meditating world-wide, and Mahesh Yogi, therefore, drew up a plan for an Academy for meditation teachers to be established high up in the Himalayan Mountains, close to Tibet, in a valley called Uttar Kashi, the Valley of the Saints. I told him that I would get the land and build the Academy. By that year, 1958, I had my doctorate from UCLA, had resigned from an academic career after ten years as a college teacher, and was in business. I was the Vice-President of a large corporation and was earning an astounding amount of money, yet the old tend-

ency to leave all was as strong as ever, and I left the job and went
to India.

In Uttar Kashi, an ideal site for the Academy was found by
virtue of a peculiar circumstance. On the way up to the high Valley
of Saints, a police officer was sitting next to me, and I asked him
why he was going to Uttar Kashi. He replied, it was to investigate a
man named Hislop who was suspected of being a CIA agent. I
convinced him that I was not an agent, and to celebrate he suggested that we have tea at a small mountain village stopping point.
I knew better, but was afraid to refuse, and the anticipated disaster
from dirty food soon arrived. By the time we reached Uttar Kashi,
I was deathly sick and was unable to leave the small ashram where
Maharishi had arranged for me to stay. Yet, time could not be
wasted, and on the third day, I engaged a guide and forced myself
to climb a nearby mountain and start looking for an Academy site.
After a while, we came to an abandoned farming terrace, and I
was so sick I could not force myself to another step, so I slumped
down and lay flat on the ground. I had not been there for more
than a moment or so when something very strange came about. A
subtle current of strength came into me, seemingly up from the
ground into me, and after about five minutes I was able to jump
up, not just improved, but fully well and as strong as though I had
never been sick. I thought, "This terrace must be a sacred place;
the land for the Academy is found!" I wired Maharishi, who was in
Europe at that time — and my wife was also there. She, Maharishi,
another lady, and a devotee who owned a Rolls Royce car had just
finished touring Germany in the Rolls, helping Maharishi while he
gave a series of lectures on his meditation, initiated new meditators, and described his vision of world peace. I had the Uttar
Kashi land surveyed and went to Lucknow to see the Prime Minister and ask him to release the land, for it was under the control of
the State Government. The Prime Minister informed me that he
would gladly do so, for he himself planned to retire to Uttar Kashi
to finish out his life as a yogi. He said to return in a month and all
would be ready. To wait out the month, I went to Burma and
entered the Buddhist Pagoda of Thray Sithu U Ba Khin, about
which Maharishi had told me, in order to learn and practice Vipassana Meditation — in which there was a deep experience and to
which I would later return.

At month's end, I again visited the Prime Minister of Uttar Pradesh, only to hear of a disaster. The Communist Party in the Government had accused the Prime Minister of planning to aid Hislop, a CIA agent who was masquerading as a student of yoga, and place Hislop in a sensitive listening-post close to the Tibetan border. The communists were almost successful in unseating the Government, and the Prime Minister was unable to release the land. I was puzzled about the CIA label which was attached to me as soon as I arrived at Rishikesh and arranged for transportation to Uttar Kashi. Now, after the event, I realize it must have come from the President of India. When I arrived at New Delhi, I had phoned the President and arranged for an interview to tell him about Maharishi's plans for the world and especially for an Academy in the Himalayas. The interview was most sympathetic, but in his mind, the President must have had a doubt and must have given an order that I should be investigated.

I then went to London and informed Maharishi of the turn of events. He said he would go to India at once and have a try at getting the land in Uttar Kashi. He did not succeed, but the Government, to please him, gave him the present Academy site, across the Ganges River from Sivananda's ashram at Rishikesh, where the Ganges emerges from the Himalayas to begin its long course across the plains of India to the Sea.

On trips back and forth to Uttar Kashi, I would stay for a day or so with Swami Sivananda at his Rishikesh ashram. Sivananda was a famous yogi, known around the world. The present-day yoga master of Canada and the Bahamas, Swami Vishnudevananda, was Sivananda's pupil. Swami Sivananda was a yogi with Siddhi powers. One practice of his was to tap with his fingers on every letter sent from the ashram. Upon receiving the letter, even in America, one's fingers would burn like fire, thus reminding one there was something beyond the usual in a relationship with Sivananda. I found that if the letter were placed on the ground and covered with sand for a moment — whatever caused the burning sensation would disappear.

Upon my return to Los Angeles, friends and myself continued to build the Mahesh Yogi organization. Charles Lutes, the current American President, was active in this work. For our first National Convention, we took over the principal hotel on Catalina Island,

off the California coast. An event which occurred there, terminated my relationship with the Mahesh Yogi organization. I was
myself doing quite well with the meditation (which is now named
Transcendental Meditation), but I was telling those persons whom
I initiated that the meditation would lead to the goal of life, Liberation, Self-Realization, Union with the Divine. The two weeks at
the hotel would be free from responsibilities for me, since
Maharishi and Charley Lutes could run the convention. I decided
to stay in my room, do nothing but continuous meditation from 3
a.m. until I fell asleep at night, and see if I would be able to know
directly that which I was telling the people whom I was initiating
into the meditation. After several days of the 3 a.m.-to-bedtime
meditation, waves of bliss started to sweep through me. They were
so intense, I could hardly bear them. But, at the same time a deva-
stating realization struck me — "This sensation was being experienced in the nervous system of the body — it was not the Divine
Bliss which the ancients have described as 'that peace which
passeth all understanding.'" At this moment, I realized that in my
work, I was a perfect example of "a blind leader," and especially so
when I initiated people into meditation. I went at once to Maharishi's room, resigned, and returned to the mainland.

   The next move of my wife and myself was to return to Burma
to further explore the Buddhist Vipassana meditation. The Vipassana meditation was an experience which my critical mind could
not deny. Since the reader may be interested, and since I was
strongly influenced by the Buddhist way, I will briefly describe the
discipline. It is said to be the very discipline which the Buddha applied to himself under the Bodhi Tree when he gained Release, and
it was being taught now only by Thray Sithu U Ba Khin, who had
himself learned it from a meditation master deep in the jungles of
Burma. Of the many ways to approach the "destruction of the
mind," this version of Vipassana meditation was said to be the
most difficult, yet the most efficient. When the renowned Burmese
"liberated while yet alive" monk, Way Bu Sayadaw, reached an
obstacle in his meditation which he was unable to surmount, he
came to U Ba Khin for instruction in the traditional way of the
Buddha and, with this, he overcame remaining obstacles and
gained Release. U Ba Khin himself had taken the vow to become a
Buddha in distant, distant time and was thus deliberately holding

back from the path of full Self-Realization. All this we heard from U Ba Khin at various times over a period of years. I had an opportunity to meet and speak with Way Bu Sayadaw and was deeply impressed with him. Vipassana meditation, which aims directly at Release, is in the tradition of Theravada, or Southern Buddhism.

The meditation of Mahayana, or Northern Buddhism was different from the Theravada approach. I first learned of this from the Dalai Lama when I visited him at his home in Upper Dharmasala, and from Trungpa Rimpoche when he was in Scotland. He is quite famous now. At that time, friends in England had just bought a large house and estate in Scotland for Trungpa Rimpoche as his "Tibetan Monastery" in Europe. He was, according to Tibetan history, the sixteenth-time-reborn Abbot of a group of six Tibetan monasteries, had escaped the Chinese invasion, and was found by an English woman who took him to England and enrolled him in Oxford University. When I asked him about his many rebirths, he told me of the most recent. When he died, the senior monks went to visit the head monk of their tradition — there are several monkish traditions in Tibet — and said their Abbot had died. The head of the Order then went into deep meditation and told what he saw. He saw the reborn baby, its parents, and their village, their neighbors, and the dog of the house. But its geography, the place of the village on a map was not seen. Word of this was then sent throughout Tibet. At length, replies came that the description was recognized, and the location of the village was given. Next came the visit. The visiting party included some monks closely related to the dead Abbot and some monks who were strangers. The party carried a number of artifacts, some of which had belonged to the dead Abbot and some of which had not. The visiting monks seated themselves in front of the baby and spread out the array of artifacts. The test was that the baby must point at once to the monks he had known before death and to the artifacts which had belonged to him. This test was immediately and successfully passed by the baby. The monks than asked the parents if they would give their Abbot to them to be educated and trained for his high office. I asked Rimpoche if, as he was growing up, he remembered the past. He replied that he did often remember, but his tutors would tell him that it was just a dream and he should forget it and pay attention to his lessons. We stayed with Rimpoche in his house in Scotland for a month, taught him to drive a car, became well-acquainted with him, and met him again some years later in California.

Thus, when I first went to U Ba Khin, I had some idea of the Buddhist way, but had no prior knowledge of what I would experience in Vispassana meditation. In fact, an important aspect of the meditation is that one should have no prior knowledge; for the experience should not be imagined by the mind, which is very powerful and will project its concepts. The experience should be unanticipated, new, and totally surprising. In this way, the Meditation Master could judge if the pupil was making genuine progress.

There were a series of meditation caves — for darkness and perfect silence — beneath the Pagoda. Each pupil would be alone in a cave. Work started at 5 a.m. and continued until 9 p.m., with a one-hour break for lunch. The first task was to concentrate the attention at the juncture of the nose and the upper lip and become aware of the breath as it entered the nostrils with the in-breath and as it left the nostrils with the out-breath. When the mind wandered away, it was just to be noted that it had wandered away and then calmly brought back to attention. My wife's progress was faster than mine, and it took me a week before the mind settled quietly at the juncture of nose and lip without wandering away. After a few days' work, the mind becomes aware of a spot at the juncture of nose and lip that is either very hot or very cold. Faster progress is then made because the mind can hold to this sensation.

When he saw that my mind was quiet, U Ba Khin called me into the Pagoda under the central dome and spire. It was said that herein one was sheltered from the subtle influence of outside tensions and forces. He told me to concentrate my mind as per my practice. Then he said, "Move your mind to the top of your head." At once I felt like ants were crawling there, and involuntarily raised my hand to feel the area. U Ba Khin then said, "No, don't do that, we will start again." Then he told me to move my attention down my face. With this, the sensation, which was now one of burning, followed my mind. Then I was told to return to the cave and work with the sensation until I could place it in every part of my body. This sensation is named "Anicca" (pronounced, Annaysa), and is said to be the direct perception of the arising and the disintegration of the most subtle particles which form the physical mass of the body. It is the direct perception that the body is temporary and therefore not one's reality. The disintegration of each particle is atomic, and therefore, the sensation of burning heat. Some pupils, whose bodies are lodged with impurities, cannot bear the agony of the burning and must stop and leave. After a number of days of this, all impurities are burned away and the Annica can be freely moved throughout the body. The ability to sweep Anicca throughout the body still remains with me.

When the Meditation Master sees this, he takes the next step. He told me to concentrate on the chest area. After two or three days of this, Annica, which at first was felt throughout the chest area, narrowed down until there was no sensation in the entire body except for one small spot at the center of the chest and which seemed to be no larger than the head of a pin. When the Meditation Master saw this, I was again called into the Pagoda. I was told to concentrate again until I felt only the pin-point of Annica. U Ba Khin told me then, "I will say, 'Give me your mind.'" No sooner were the words out, then an ice-cold breeze entered into me at the back of the neck, and in surprise, I raised my hand there. U Ba Khin said, "No, don't do that. We will try it again." This time the cold breeze entered me from all around my neck (at least that was how it felt it was happening). I felt cool and delightful and as light as a feather as the cool, delightful sensation spread throughout the body. I was then told to return to the cave and practice this until it was under my command.

But away from the cave I could never do it except once — after stopping off in Rome, I went into an ancient Catholic Church, concentrated my mind and was again filled with that cool, delicious lightness. My wife, however, is much better than I and can do this "drop into the transcendental state" as it is called.

I thought, then, that this work with the Buddhist way was surely the path to Liberation, to Truth-Realization, to the goal of life. And my wife felt the same.

But then, after working in the Pagoda for two or three months each year over a period of six years, we heard of Sri Sathya Sai Baba. I was fascinated and had to see for myself, and my wife, who could not bear the climate of India, agreed to go because of her foot. In Switzerland, the previous year, at a J. Krishnamurti Camp, she had fallen and broken her foot. When we returned to

California and the cast was removed, the foot had set in a badly twisted way and the doctor told her she would be like that for the rest of her life and would always use a cane. When it was said to us that Sri Sathya Sai Baba could change a person's life and it would never change back again, she thought to herself, "Perhaps my foot, then, can also be changed!" And, sure enough, Baba looked at it, not even touching it and told her the foot would be all right. And so it was. Gradually it changed by itself and, in some months time, was as good as new and has been like new ever since.

The Buddhist way was a way of the intellect and the mind. And despite my great appreciation and gratitude for having found the discipline, I felt that my heart was dry; that I had a dry Western heart with little love left in it. We had begun to realize, also, that the Vipassana discipline could be dangerous for a life in the world and that to pursue it properly one should become a monk as in the time of the Buddha. But this was not possible, for Burma had closed its borders to any long stay for foreigners. These considerations were hazy and not in our thoughts to any serious extent, but perhaps they were there to keep our minds open.

Upon meeting Baba, I knew at once, without doubt, that for me here was the true source of wisdom. The circumstances of our first meeting with Baba were fortunate. Now, people by the tens of thousands are always around. But in January, 1968, there were fewer than a dozen foreigners in the Prasanthi Nilayam Ashram, which is located next to the village of Puttaparthi, Baba's birthplace. At that time, there were only a few rooms for visitors — probably less than half a dozen. We were given two rooms — one for the ladies and one for the men. As soon as we were settled, Baba came to visit us, and returned to visit us each day, often twice a day, staying for an hour or so each time. My wife and I were scheduled to stay for ten days and then continue on to Burma. It is difficult, and probably impossible to express in words the effect upon myself of that first meeting with Baba. My entire being was profoundly affected and changed. Immediately, Baba became the center of my life and has remained so. In his presence, at that first meeting, the world fell away from me, my entire consciousness was drawn inward and, at a most subtle level of awareness, Baba appeared in my heart as love. Love was unmistakable and that

Baba was this love was equally unmistakable. It seemed to me that only God Himself could enter my heart as love and, since then, this feeling of the Divine Presence has never changed. About how others view Baba, I am afraid I am totally indifferent, for there is no way I can deny my own direct experience. I became an instant devotee of the divine Baba and happily remain so. I found to my great surprise that although I had always used an intellectual approach to spiritual life, the devotional path was at once very natural to me as soon as I encountered Baba. What the future holds for me, I do not know. Nor do I think very much about it. To the extent that my attention can stay with this moment, conscious of the immediate Presence of the ever-loving, ever-caring Lord; to that extent, thoughts of the future are not a worry or a bother to me.

He is in you, and it is God that has prompted you to project Him into the outer world, as this idol or that image, to listen to your outpouring and give you peace. Without the inspiration, solace, and joy that He confers from within, you will be raving mad, as one who has lost his moorings and is tossed about, rudderless on a stormy sea. Hold on to Him in the heart, hear Him whisper in the silent words of counsel and consolation. Hold converse with Him, guide your footsteps as He directs, and you reach the goal, safe and soon. The picture before which you sit, the flowers which you place on it, the hymns you recite, the vows you impose on yourselves, the vigils you go through — these are activities that cleanse, that remove obstacles in the way of your getting aware of the God within.
— Sathya Sai Baba

The Crucifix

The crucifix was created by Baba on a most auspicious day, Mahasivaratri. Baba had reached a decision to halt the yearly public viewing of the birth of the lingam as it flashes from his mouth and comes to rest in his hands, cushioned by a silk handkerchief. Although that public portion of the holy festival of Mahasivaratri was now terminated; nevertheless the lingam would be created by Baba each year again and again, for it is a principal sign by which we may know the Avathar. In respect to the oval, egg-shaped lingam which Baba produces from within his body on Mahasivaratri night, he says, "It is not possible for you to understand the divine purpose and gauge its potential or to know the significance of its manifestation. In order to bear witness to the fact that Divinity is among you, it becomes necessary for me to express this attitude of mine. Otherwise the atmosphere of hatred, greed, envy, cruelty, violence, and irreverence will overwhelm the good, the humble, and the pious. The lingam is a symbol of the beginningless and endless, of the infinite . . . it is the most fitting symbol of the Omnipresent, Omniscient, and Omnipotent Lord. Everything starts from it and everything is subsumed in it."

We may also know the Avathar by the sixteen signs that accompany him: creation, preservation, dissolution, knowledge of incarnations, special Grace and the power to bestow it; each of these in the past, present, and future, thus totalling fifteen, with the sixteenth being Paramatma, the Divine, resident in the heart of each being. To these sixteen signs of the divine incarnation of the Avathar, Baba adds another sign, which he terms the most significant of all — divine love, universal and impersonal, yet personal.

The lingam has been seen by the writer a number of times. On the occasion of one Mahasivarathi night, I was sitting quite close to Baba. When the moment came, I saw a flash of gold come from his mouth and saw the lingam caught in the silk handkerchief held by his hands. It was of gold. How an object that size came up Sri Baba's throat cannot be explained. At another Mahasivaratri, the lingam was translucent, and there was a clearly visible flame in the center of the lingam.

The evening before the Mahasivaratri Day of 1973, we were told to be ready in the early morning for a trip; and that when the cars were loaded and ready we would know the destination. Swami had decided that only a handful of people would be with him when the lingam became manifest.

Our destination was the Bandipur Game Sanctuary in Bandipur Forest, several hours away in Mysore State. We arrived at the Forest resthouse in the early afternoon. The next morning we returned to our cars, and, guided by the Forest people, took various winding roads hoping to come upon one of the Forest's wild elephant herds. As we moved through the trees and the open areas, in our minds we were hoping for a replay of the dramatic and fascinating encounter between Baba and a wild elephant herd which had taken place some years before when Swami and some devotees had made a holiday expedition to the Game Sanctuary. This time, however, the elephants remained in their secret places and not even one was seen. But the drive through the hills had another and more important objective. Swami intended to find a correct site where we could gather at dusk for the sacred event of the lingam birth. It was on this great and most mysterious occasion, unknown and beyond imagination to the world at large, that the crucifix came into being.

As we crossed a bridge above a sandy, dry riverbed, Baba indicated that this would be the place. He said we would all return here just at dusk, and this we did. The cars halted at the side of the road, and we started to climb down the bank to the sandy river bottom. I was beside Baba. As we passed a bush, Swami broke off two twigs, placed them together and asked me, "What is this, Hislop?"

"Well, Swami, it is a cross," I answered. Baba then closed his fingers over the twigs and directed three somewhat slow breaths into his fist, between thumb and forefinger. Then he opened his hand to reveal a Christ figure crucified on a cross, and he gave it to me.

He said, "This shows Christ as he really was at the time he left his body, not as artists have imagined him or as historians have told about him. His stomach is pulled in and his ribs are all showing. He had no food for eight days."

I looked at the crucifix, but found no words. Then Baba continued, "The cross is wood from the actual cross on which Christ was crucified. To find some of the wood after 2,000 years took a little time! The image is of Christ after he died. It is a dead face."

I noticed something odd and asked, "Swami, what is that hole at the top of the cross?" Baba replied that the cross had been originally hung from a standard.

We continued down to the river bed, and Baba seated us in a rectangle, with himself at the head. It could be seen that Swami's body was already in labor, and the group at once started singing bhajans (sacred songs of devotion and praise to Divinity). This continued without interruption until the lingam came out from Baba's throat and was caught by him in a silk handkerchief. After the lingam had been admired by everyone, Swami put it aside. He then raised a small heap of sand in front of his knees, and with his finger sketched an outline on it. Then in a moment or two, he dug his hand into the sand and brought forth a silver flask filled with amrith. Then he moved his hand and created a small silver cup. Everyone, from his hand, was then given a portion of the amrith, nectar of the Gods. How delicate and delicious was the taste! It is unique. There is no other taste to compare to it.

Within a few weeks we were back at our home in Mexico and were soon to witness an amazing series of events in relation to the crucifix. The cross is so small that the details on the figure of Christ escape the eye. A friend, Walter, came down to our home and took some color photographs of the crucifix. The over-all length of the Christ figure is only one inch, and Walter was to make some enlargements to bring out the detail. When he mailed us a sample of the prints, my wife and I were astounded. I wrote to him and said that if the pictures were seen around the world, they would create an art sensation. I am sure it is the greatest sculpture of Christ every made. In my estimation, it is the most extraordinary object Sri Sathya Sai has ever created for the joy of his devotees.

A few weeks later, Walter and his wife returned with color enlargements of the cross. These, along with the actual cross, were spread out on the dining room table, next to large french windows overlooking the sea. The time was about 5 p.m. The details revealed by the photographic enlargements were so extraordinary that all persons present were concentrating on this amazing vision of Christ, and on the mystery and wonder of Sri Bhagavan. On this afternoon, the sky along the Mexican coast was clear and peaceful. But suddenly, without any warning, there was a loud crash of thunder and as our eyes turned to the windows, lightning flashed from a dark cloud where a moment before there had been only clear sky. A violent wind rushed through the house, causing windows and doors to open and shut with such force that glass was in danger of shattering. The curtains were flying in all directions. We were much startled by this turn of events, but my wife at once, said, "It is 5 p.m., the time Christ died on the cross, and what is now happening is described in the Bible." She later brought a Bible and we looked until we found the pertinent paragraph, which said that at the moment Christ gave up His life, a violent storm arose with lightning and thunder, and winds rent the curtains of the temple. We concluded that we had witnessed a wonder totally beyond our power of imagination. Before our eyes had occurred nothing less than a recapitulation of events related to the crucifixion. The following day newspapers in San Diego carried a brief story commenting on the sudden and mysterious storm that had arisen without warning on the Mexican coast, near Ensenada. We and our friends concluded that this recapitulation of an event which had taken place some 2,000 years ago upon the crucifixion of Christ, implied a great power connected in some way with that small cross and Christ figure materialized by Baba. A year or so later I sent a description of the event to Dr. Eruch B. Fanibunda for his book, *Vision of the Divine*. He showed the memo to Baba. After reading the memo, Baba said the event had occurred as described and that the significance attributed to it was correct.

It might be thought that the story of the cross was now complete, but there is still a sequel. In 1975, I made an unannounced trip to India to consult with Baba about arrangements for a visit to America that we hoped he would undertake. Swami had not been informed of my visit and was away on tour when I arrived. On that day he was having lunch with a few senior devotees and he said, "Hislop arrived in Bangalore just now and is waiting."

One of the men at the table (who later told me of the scene) remarked, "You made a crucifix for him."

Baba replied, "Yes, I made it for him. And when I went to look for the wood, every particle of the cross had disintegrated and had returned to the elements. I reached out to the elements and reconstituted sufficient material for a small cross. Very seldom does Swami interfere with Nature, but occasionally, for a devotee, it will be done."

Base your action on knowledge, the knowledge that all is One. Let the action be suffused with bhakti; that is to say, humility, love, mercy, and non-violence. Let bhakti be filled with knowledge, otherwise it will be as light as a balloon which drifts along any current of air, or gust of wind. Mere knowledge will make the heart dry; bhakti makes it soft with sympathy, and karma gives the hands something to do, something which will sanctify every one of the minutes that have fallen to your lot to live.

— Sathya Sai Baba

The Weeping Saris

Can saris[1] weep? Is it conceivable that saris, inanimate objects made of cloth, can weep, can shed tears as real as the tears that flow from one's eyes? Yes. It is so. Along with other men at the Dharmakshetra in Bombay, I saw it. I was the first of the men to notice. The four rejected saris were in a box on a table. I looked down and saw water seeping from the box and called it to Baba's attention. He removed the cover and we all crowded around to look. Water was coming from the edges of the saris. I said, "Swami, there is no water here. We have been standing around this table for almost an hour. The table has been perfectly dry."

Baba replied, "They are weeping because I rejected them."

I said, "Swami! Weeping! Do you mean to say that inanimate cloth has feelings?"

Let Baba tell the story from here. It was included as part of a discourse at Prasanthi Nilayam and is printed in Vol. VII of *Sathya Sai Speaks*:

Nothing ever happens, without proper reason, however accidental or mysterious it might appear. The

1. The traditional length of cloth, Indian ladies, from centuries past, have wrapped about themselves as garments.

roots go deep and are out of sight. I was telling Hislop, in Bombay, at Dharmakshetra, the same thing. The bridge towards Sri Lanka was being built over the straits, so that Rama and his army could march across to the realm of the demon King, Ravana, where Sita was interned. The valiant monkeys were plucking mountains and leaping vast distances in space with those peaks hoisted on their shoulders, so that they could be thrown into the sea to create a passage for Rama! The monkeys had formed a queue all the way from the Himalayas down to the southernmost point, where the bridge was fast coming up. When the causeway was completed, word went fast along the queue that no more hills were needed, and each monkey placed on the ground, wherever it stood, the hill it had on its shoulder at the time.

One hill, however, did not sit quietly. It started bewailing its fate! 'Why was I removed from where I was and why am I now refused? Alas! I was elated that I was destined to serve a Divine Purpose; I was overjoyed that the armies of Rama, and Rama, himself, would walk over me. Now, I am neither there, nor where I was!' It shed profuse tears. News reached Rama, and his compassion was great. He sent word that in his next Avathara, when he would come again upon his mission in human form, he would certainly bless the sorrowing hill. This very hill was the Govardhana Peak which Rama (as the boy, Krishna) lifted on his finger and held aloft for a full seven days, in order to save the cowherds of Gokul from the deluge of rain that Indra dared inflict on them!

I related this story to Hislop when he asked me whether inanimate things, too, had emotions and feelings of disappointment and despair. The occasion at Dharmakshetra was: I asked that about a hundred saris be brought, so that I could select some for distribution to the women workers at Anantapur who are helping build the Sathya Sai College there. I selected 96 and asked them to return 4 to the shop. I kept the 4 aside and the 96 were placed in my room. Later, when I passed the table on which the four discarded saris were kept,

(Hislop was standing by the side of that table), it was
noticed that the cardboard box which contained the four
was dripping tears! The saris were weeping that they
could not get appreciation from me and were declared
unfit. Yes! They *had shed* tears! You may ask whether
this is ever possible. I answer, there is nothing in this
world which has no heart, which is incapable of feeling
joy or grief! Only, you must have the eye to see, the ear
to listen, the heart to respond.

When, in the Dharmakshetra in Bombay, Baba had finished
telling us the story about the mountain peak in the time of Sri
Rama, some ten thousand years or more ago, and of the Govardhana Peak in the time of Sri Krishna, some five thousand years
ago, I exclaimed, "Swami! The self-same drama that occurred in
the time of Rama and again in the time of Krishna was played
again here today in this very room!"

Baba replied, "Yes. And with the self-same Rama and the self-
same Krishna here again today in this very room!"

As was the case with the rejected mountain peak, the rejected
saris received the compassion of the Lord, and they were presented
to the ladies in Baba's party to be used by them. In fact, my wife
received one of the saris, and the sari receives plenty of appreciation from her!

The morning shadow moves in front of you. However fast you
run, you cannot catch it, on plain or mountain. Or, the shadow
may pursue you and you cannot escape from it. This is the
nature of desire. You may pursue it or it may pursue you — but
you cannot overcome it or catch it. Desire is an insubstantial
shadow. But turn desire inward, towards spiritual treasure, then
it yields substantial results.

                          — *Sathya Sai Baba*

A Mirror of the Moon

Early on the morning of Dec. 8, 1973, Swami departed Prasanthi Nilayam for Brindavan. After an hour or so of driving, he directed the three accompanying cars to turn off the road to a clearing in an uninhabited area of the forest. Everyone got out. Baba was in a delightful mood, moving about among the party and cracking jokes with the men.

Beside the picnic area was a wood-apple tree with a few large wood-apples in view in the upper branches. The men tried to knock some of these to the ground by throwing stones, but without success. One small wood-apple, about two inches in diameter, did fall to the ground, and Baba picked it up.

Holding the small wood-apple between thumb and forefinger against the morning sun, Baba said, "Here is the moon." Then he closed the small object in his hand for a moment, and when his hand opened, the wood-apple had disappeared, and in its place there was a most extraordinary object.

The object was a translucent disk (of stone?) thin at the edges and thicker at the centre. It reflected light in a brilliant way, and throughout its body there was a puzzling variety of modifications. There were dark areas of uneven shape and size; there were short and longer veins of luminous mineral-like materials of all shades

25

of color; there were specks and dots of color that reflected brightly in the sunlight. The total effect of the disk was one of great beauty.

Everyone gazed at the object with intense interest and wonderment. Holding the disk to the sun, Baba said that it was the moon in miniature, comprised of the moon's matter; that it was a "mirror of the moon." Nobody understood what he meant, and we started to ask questions. At length, we understood that the two-sided disk was an accurate miniature in stone and minerals of the two sides of the moon.

It was as if one were to photograph the moon as it is seen from Earth, and then to journey to the opposite side of the moon and photograph that side. Each side photographed would appear on a photographic plate as a circular disk. Thus, one side of the translucent disk created by Baba mirrored one side of the moon, and the other side of the translucent disk mirrored the opposite side of the moon. The darker, unevenly shaped areas on the disk were the very large features of the moon's surface; the brightly reflecting specks and dots were individual mountains and smaller mountain ranges; the shorter and longer veins of brilliant vari-colored minerals were additional features of the moon's landscape.

Indeed, the visual modifications to be seen in the disk were so complex that we did not readily understand them. Baba said that the mineralized appearance of the luminous features of the disk were in fact moon minerals, that they could be seen in the disk because it was thin and therefore translucent, and that the same mineralization was in the moon itself. The miniature moon was exact and fully accurate, and were there to be a photographic enlargement, scientists would at once recognize all the landscape features with which they were familiar.

Baba told us that he would not give the miniature moon to anyone, and that the disk would be returned from where it had come. He did not describe that source and nobody asked him.

At this point, food taken from the cars was ready, and a delicious breakfast was served by the ladies of the party. I had the moon-disk in my hand, so I put it in the pocket of my jacket and kept it there. After breakfast, with a smile, Baba held out his hand, and I reached in my pocket and returned the moon-disk to him. He again held the disk up to the sun, and all along the edge of the disk there was a rich golden light. Baba said, "See, there is the sunrise!"

After we had all admired the golden light, Swami again closed his hand, the moon-disk was gone, and in its place was the original small wood-apple. Baba tossed it to me, and it is at our house as one of the objects in the shrine room.

By this time, a few strangers had appeared from somewhere, and Swami gave them the remaining food. The ladies tidied up the picnic ground, we all returned to our cars and resumed the drive to Brindavan, thoroughly pleased by the breakfast picnic with Baba.

Have no thorn of hate in your mind, develop love towards all. Desire is a storm, greed is a whirlpool, pride is a precipice, attachments is an avalanche, egoism is a volcano. Keep these things away so that when you recite the name of God or do Meditation, they do not disturb the equanimity. Let love be enthroned in your heart. Then, there will be sunshine and cool breezes and gurgling waters of contentment feeding the roots of faith.

— Sathya Sai Baba

The Resurrection of Walter Cowan

Resurrection, the rising again from the dead, is something which all Christians have heard of, and because it is a sacred story we tend to believe it — if we have not been pounded by doubts from agnostics, atheists, humanists, and people who, in general, hold to reason and logic more than to faith. And, stories of resurrection in recent times come from people who are not viewed as "establishment" and the stories are not, therefore, given serious attention. Mostly, what has been said above refers to the western world. The same structure of belief and disbelief about resurrection is not the norm in India, and this story is about events which occurred in India, although Walter Cowan and myself were born in the West.

Walter died in his room at the Connemara Hotel in Madras. He and his wife, Elsie, had arrived there on December 23, 1971 to see Baba, who himself was in Madras to preside at an All-India Conference of Sai Organizations.

Early on the morning of December 25, a rumor quickly spread that an elderly American had died of a heart attack. My wife, Victoria and I immediately thought of Walter. We went to the hotel and found Elsie there. Walter had fallen to the floor in the very early morning hours. Elsie had called Mrs. Ratanlal whose room was just down the corridor. The two women managed to lift

Walter to the bed, and he passed away in Elsie's arms a few minutes later. An ambulance was called, the body was taken to a hospital, pronounced dead upon arrival, placed in an empty storage room, and covered with a sheet to await daylight and decisions about the funeral.

Elsie and Mrs. Ratanlal had already been to see Baba when we arrived. He had told them he would visit the hospital at 10 a.m. The two ladies were ready and waiting to join Baba at the appointed hour. They did go to the hospital, but Baba had arrived earlier and had already departed. To the joy of the ladies, but also to their their total amazement, they found Walter alive and being attended to. Nobody saw Baba with Walter, nor has Baba chosen to say how or why Walter was resurrected, but on returning to the devotee family who were his hosts, Baba told the people there that he had brought Walter back to life.

Walter's own story throws some light on what happened, and later on, I was a party to a fascinating episode; for Walter's life continued to be in danger and, in fact, Baba told me that Walter died three times and had to be returned to life three times.

Walter described his experience. He said he realized that he had died and that he had remained with the body in the ambulance, looking at it with interest. Then Baba came and together they went to a place, which seemed to be at a great height. There they entered a conference room where people were seated around a table. There was a presiding chairman who had a kind face and who spoke in a kindly way. He called for Walter's records and these were read aloud. The records were in different languages and Walter did not understand what was said until after some time when Baba started to translate. Walter was surprised to hear that he had occupied a lofty status in various times and cultures and had always been dedicated to the welfare of the people. At length, Baba addressed the person presiding and asked that Walter be given over to Baba's care, for Baba had work for Walter to do. Then, when Baba and he departed the room, Walter felt himself descending towards a place where his body was, but felt great reluctance. In terms of direct experience, he had realized that he was not the body, and he had no wish to be subject again to bodily anxieties and miseries.

After hearing Walter, I asked Baba if Walter were just imagining the incidents. Baba replied that it was not imagination. The events were real. They had occurred in Walter's mind and Baba himself had guided the thoughts. I then asked if everyone had a similar experience at death. Baba answered that some people had similar experiences and some did not. Several years later I brought up the question again. Baba answered that the corpse was common to all, but beyond that there was no common experience.

The day after Walter returned to life was one of high interest for me. Sri Appa and I accompanied Baba to the home of a devotee. From there we went to a meeting of lady members of the Nigara Sai Samiti where Baba was to give awards and speak. Sri Appa and I were sitting on the platform, just a few feet from Baba, and were able to observe him closely. He made the awards and gave a spiritual discourse, all without any break or any moment of hesitation. From that meeting, we were to go to the home of a devotee for lunch. As soon as we got in the car, Baba turned to us and said, "While I was talking in the meeting, Mrs. Cowan called me. I at once went to the hospital and did what was necessary. Mr. Cowan's health had taken a bad turn for the worse."

So, even while busy on the speaker's platform, Baba had gone to the hospital, and had done what was necessary. But, to the eyes of Sri Appa and myself, Baba had continued in action and speech on the platform for the whole time without any break or hesitation whatsoever. How does one explain this mystery?

When we arrived at the devotee's house for lunch, Baba turned to us and said, "You will not be able to join me for lunch. Take this vibhuti to the hospital, give Mr. Cowan some in his mouth and rub the rest on his forehead and chest. If you will walk to the corner there, you will find Mrs. Hislop in a taxi. She will take you to the hospital."

Now the fact was, that my wife had been following in a car. However, she had taken great pains to stay out of sight, but her effort was to no avail for, as usual, Baba knew everything. When we reached the hospital with the vibhuti, Mrs. Cowan said, "Walter took a very bad turn just a little while ago. I thought he was dead, and I was terrified. I at once called Baba in a loud voice. Now, Walter seems a little improved. When I called Baba I felt his presence at once." At the hospital, Elsie experienced exactly what Baba had told Sri Appa and myself in the car.

Other instances of Baba's powers of resurrection are known to other devotees. The Raja of Ventagiri told me of his experience when, some twenty or so years ago, he witnessed Baba's resurrection of a man dead some six days in whom body decomposition was taking its normal course. About these mysteries, one can make no comment; they are outside the customary human experience.

Detachment, Faith, and Love — these are the pillars on which Peace rests. Of these, Faith is crucial. For, without it, Sadhana (spiritual practice) is an empty rite. Detachment alone can make Sadhana effective and Love leads quickly to God. Faith feeds the agony of separation from God; detachment canalises it along the path of God; Love lights the way. God will grant you what you need and deserve; there is no need to ask, no reason to grumble. Be content, be grateful whatever happens, whenever it happens. Nothing can happen against His Will.
— Sathya Sai Baba

Touring with Baba

Every trip with Baba has the excitement and romance of a grand expedition. It is as though one were in the company of a magnificent emperor touring his domain, or in the immediate party of the most glamorous and famous movie star of all time. As his car moves along the road, farmers working in the fields abandon their work and start running to intercept the car. How can they know who is in the car? There has been no notice, and in those earlier days the car was just an ordinary sedan. Does the subtle power and beauty of Baba's presence alert the farmers? Or are they drawn to Swamiji outside of their own volition, as iron filings are drawn to a magnet? I never cease to be astonished and deeply affected when I see it happen.

As the car comes to the villages along the road, it seems as though an advance agent has been there broadcasting the news of Baba's itinerary. There must surely be a few people who remain at work and in their houses, but it appears that every man, woman, and child is at the roadside waiting for Baba. The people surge into the road and the car must slow to a crawling pace. Hands and faces are pressed against the car windows, anything to catch a glimpse of the divine personage. As the car reaches the village limits and picks up speed, the villagers do not fall away, but on the

32

contrary, start running to remain close to Baba to the last possible moment. How do the villagers know? Nobody has informed them. Surely, somehow or other there must have been a rumor, but if so, how could it spread so far and so quickly?

When the car arrives at a large town or at a city, great crowds assemble; enthusiastic, tearful, and yearning of heart. No matter to which household Baba pays a visit, multitudes are gathered and are waiting for his arrival. As long as Baba remains there, the civic authorities have to contend with the problem of a massive traffic congestion. But many of the police are also devotees, and it is hard for them to be stern with the people. The mood is not one of curiosity, but of wonder, awe, and devotion. All eyes are riveted on Baba whenever he appears. People are overcome with their emotions; they dissolve in tears and prostrate themselves in honor of Sri Baba and in wordless petition for his grace. It is an extraordinary scene and an experience that is unique.

In western countries now, God is denied, and man is relying on himself. He exaggerates his own intelligence and sense of adventure and prides himself on the advance he has made through science and technology. But, intelligence without equanimity is filling mental hospitals. Peace is fleeing from the hearts of men and women; social harmony is becoming a distant dream, international concord is a mirage pursued by a few. Man travels to the moon, but does not explore his own inner levels of consciousness, and understanding them, cleanse them and control them.

— Sathya Sai Baba

Baba in Havana, Cuba

Baba sent a message at lights-out time, 9 p.m., that we should be ready at 5 a.m. to ride with him on his return to Bangalore. The departure was confidential and not a word was to be said to anyone. We were elated, as may be imagined. This was our first invitation.

At 4:30 in the morning we were ready, and with our small amount of luggage walked towards the driveway. Our first surprise was to find a line of cars in the lane leading to the outside road, obviously prepared to get behind Baba's car at the very moment of his departure. But how could this be? Nobody was supposed to know. Puzzled, we continued to the Mandir (i.e. the temple) where we were to meet Baba. Another surprise! The entire area in front of the Mandir was filled with people sitting on the ground, in silence — no conversation, not even whispers. This was to be a secret departure?

Similar happenings were experienced a number times subsequently, and finally we were able to understand. It could not be otherwise. The question, "When is Swami leaving?" is in everyone's mind as soon as the function which brought Baba to Prasanthi Nilayam is over. The alarm, "When is Swami leaving?" is a daily event thereafter. Someone may observe a package being transferred to the shed where Baba's car is stored and a rumor cir-

culates. That is enough. Then the game starts. Every hour, from 3
a.m. onward, will have its group of supporters and so at every
hour people are ready and waiting.

On this particular day, it was 9 a.m. before Baba departed.
Soon a signal was received that he was ready. He came from the
Mandir, paused briefly to survey the assembled devotees, and the
trip to Brindavan started.

Baba is cautious in driving, often instructing the driver, but
nevertheless traveling at high speed on open stretches of the road.
This puts considerable stress on the drivers of the cars following
him. But Baba himself is relaxed and totally at ease, smiling sweetly and talking in a most kindly voice. Victoria had wanted an
opportunity to ask Baba about an incident in her childhood and,
securing his permission, she told this story.

It was at the family home in Havana, Cuba. There was a large
walled garden, as is typical of Spanish houses, with interior doors
opening to it. Victoria was about a year old; her mother was teaching her to walk. She toddled into the garden from the room where
the family was gathered, and then stopped. For, there in the corner
of the garden, a man was standing against the wall. She said,
"Dada" (Daddy) and took a few steps forward, but then turned
towards the room behind her, much puzzled, for she had just left
her father in the room. Turning back to the garden, she saw that
the man was still there.

At this point in the story, Baba interrupted and said, "Yes,
yes, I was there. I was standing against the wall like this." Swamiji
then stretched out his legs, crossing one over the other. Then he
continued, "I had a cloth around my head like this." He illustrated
by moving his hand around his head, "And I had a cloth around
my waist." And, indeed, that was what Victoria had seen. She had
never told anyone, nor even thought about it again, but the incident was engraved in her memory, and it came to life in a most
unexpected way many years later in the house of a friend in the
Ojai Valley. The friend was much interested in India, having at
one time been the secretary of Paul Brunton, the famed author of
several books about esoteric India. Victoria's attention was caught
by a picture in a book. Pointing to it, she exclaimed, "Who is that
man? I know him." The friend replied, "That is Sai Baba of
Shirdi." In this way, Victoria learned that as a very young child, she

had had the Darshan of Baba in the form of Sri Shirdi Sai, and it was this she wanted to verify in her conversation with Baba.

Fascinated with Baba's reply, Victoria started to respond to his statement about his presence in the garden in Havana, but he held up his hand for silence. He seemed to listen for a moment, then said, "Stop the car. One of the cars following us has had a tire puncture."

By this time, the caravan had fallen behind us and was not visible. We waited, not breaking Baba's silence. Then, looking behind, we saw one car rapidly approaching. The driver reported, "The car just behind me had a puncture, and I hurried ahead so as to tell Swami. The other cars are waiting there."

Well, what happened then was that Swamiji made room for one of the individuals from the stranded car, other cars took the rest of the people, leaving the driver of the taxi to fix his tire, and Victoria's great opportunity to have a further confidential and intimate conversation with Baba had come to an end — as all things eventually do!

When a tree first shoots forth from the seed, it comes up with a stem and two incipient leaves! But, later, when it grows, the trunk is one, and the branches are many! Each branch may be thick enough to be called a trunk, but one should not forget that the roots send food as sap through one single trunk. God, the same God, feeds the spiritual hunger of all nations and all faiths, through the common sustenance of truth, virtue, humility and sacrifice.

— Sathya Sai Baba

The Double Halo

Baba was at the Dharmakshetra in Bombay. It is built on a
small hill and includes, among other structures, a medium-sized
building which serves to house some of the devotees in Baba's
party while he is there. In addition to sleeping rooms, there is a kit-
chen and a dining room. The front area of the structure has two
banks of sleeping rooms divided by a central plaza. The ladies of
the party use one bank of rooms, and usually there is just a curtain
across the doorways except during sleeping hours. The men have
the same situation in the opposite bank of rooms. As is well
known, Baba is almost invariably in a light-hearted mood, and he
freely enters both sections of the building talking to, and joking
with his devotees. His private quarters are in the principal building, some hundreds of feet away.

One day, after lunch, he came to a room on the men's side. I
had just arrived from America about three days before, and had
had an interesting experience at the mid-day meal. It was always
my intention to dedicate the food of the meal to Baba before taking the first bite. But resolve though I always did, invariably I
failed, and a portion of the meal was eaten before I recollected
that I should have dedicated the food to the Lord. My reaction was
always just as predictable – I was furious at myself. At this par-

ticular meal, Baba was sitting at his individual table as usual and
the rest of us were sitting in a row on the floor. As the first bite of
the food was on its way to my mouth, I suddenly recollected my
duty. Putting aside the food for a moment, I silently dedicated it
to the Lord, and then I thought, "Thank God! Finally I remembered!" I then opened my eyes and Baba was looking directly at me
and laughing. With Baba, one might as well shout as think. He
hears or knows thoughts just as clearly as I hear the spoken words
of a person sitting next to me; or, better said — he knows everything since he transcends both time and space.

When after lunch Baba went to a room on the men's side, I
noticed and followed him, as did the other men. Baba took an easy
chair against the inner wall of the room, the rest of us sat in front
of him, and a conversation started. At the first opportunity, I
began with my deplorable custom of questioning Baba. Because I
see him as no other than the direct personification of Divinity, I
am intensely one-pointed towards him and especially so when
speaking with him. Questions and answers were traded back and
forth between us for a while, and my attention was riveted on
Baba. I soon noticed something which to me was extraordinary in
the extreme. A golden light encircled his head. It was not like the
halo seen in artist's drawings. The strong golden light — as if one
were looking at a sheet of pure gold that was illuminated in some
fashion or other — came from his scalp, up through the hair, and
extended about 12 inches from his head. The edge of the light was
not even, but was somewhat irregular. When he moved his head,
the halo of gold moved with the head, and this natural movement
revealed a second extraordinary situation. Against the wall, behind
Baba's head, there was a round disk of gold, whose diameter
appeared to be somewhat smaller than the halo. This circle of gold
was quite even around its edges, but the truly amazing feature was
that it remained stationary — when Baba moved his head, this second and perfectly round disk of gold remained on the wall without
in any way moving. Needless to say, my gaze was absolutely glued
to Swamiji. During this time I continued my questions and he
answered.

After I had asked Baba a final question, there was a brief
silence. Then one of the men said, "Hislop, why are you staring
like that at Swami?"

Without turning away from Baba, I explained. Baba then said, "What Hislop sees is correct."

The questioner then said, "Well, how is it that we do not see it?" Baba replied, "It is always there. Anyone can see it at any time. Only an intensity of interest is required."

Baba's visit with us was then concluded. He arose and left the room.

Unfortunately, there was no opportunity to ask about the stationary golden circle, and to this day I have no information or understanding about it.

You may say that progress is possible only through My Grace, but though My Heart is soft as butter, it melts only when there is some warmth in your prayer. Unless you make some disciplined effort, some Sadhana, Grace cannot descend on you. The yearning, the agony of unfulfilled aim, that is the warmth that melts My Heart. That is the anguish that wins Grace.
— Sathya Sai Baba

Baba Protects Our/His Home

By mid-1976, four houses on our hill, Loma De Carmen, had crumbled away and had fallen down the several hundred feet to sea level, and seven more houses, including ours, were in immediate danger.

The community, Villa De San Miguel, is about 100 miles south of the U.S. border. The Mexican part of the coast is called Baja California. Our house is on a hill with a grand view of ocean, islands, and coastline, to the South and West, and to the East, a panoramic view of the inland mountains. We had built it as a house for Baba in the western world, and much care had gone into its planning. The floor-to-ceiling arched windows were all guarded with iron, which is advisable here, and 48 Om symbols had been worked into the design of the iron grills, which were white like the house itself. But now, suddenly, its destiny was uncertain. It would soon be destroyed, according to the Mexican geologists and engineers. Crevices, appearing in the land, were described as being hundreds of feet deep, extending beneath the sea floor. In fact, the first slice of the hill to fall had pushed up a portion of the sea floor to a height of some 20 feet above the surface of the water. The forces of nature in movement on our hill were very powerful indeed.

My wife, Victoria, was afraid and much worried. Yet, at the same time, she could not believe that Baba would allow "his" house to be destroyed before he had even paid a visit to it! These were the two currents of feeling and thought opposing each other in her consciousness. She tried to organize a group meeting of the people living on Loma De Carmen so that we could all join together and make a prayer to Baba to save our homes. But the different families had their own ideas about Divinity, and this plan of Victoria's did not meet with success.

Right in the midst of this difficult time, when any day might be the day our house might tumble down the hill to the sea, I was scheduled to tour the Sathya Sai Baba Centers in the Mid-West, the deep South, and the East Coast. It seemed heartless to leave Victoria alone to face the trouble, but we were both of the same mind — that Baba's work comes first, so off I went. It was to be a three-week trip, and I could not be in touch by phone, for the Mexican Government had not (and still has not) extended phone service to San Miguel.

Travel, Sai meetings, and conversations with Sai devotees kept me busy day and night, yet although I had a strong trust in Sri Sathya Sai Baba, I could not help but worry as to how Victoria was getting along with the danger and the situation. So it was with a keen and somewhat anxious anticipation that I approached San Miguel upon driving home from San Diego when my tour was completed. As my car came over a rise in the highway, before it dips down to the beach and San Miguel my eyes were watching for the top of the hill to come into view, for our house could then be seen — if it were still there! Yes, it was there!

When I greeted Victoria, she told me that two more houses had partially fallen, two to the north of us. I then asked about our situation. In reply, she led me to the terrace and pointed to the reason why our house was still standing, totally untouched by the trouble. Left to herself while I was away, Victoria continued to pray to Baba, but she also moved into action. From her treasured collection of Sai photos, she had taken one and fastened it to a window facing the sea. It was that picture of Baba so familiar and dear to many of us, where he is standing, smiling, with his hand raised in a gesture of blessing, palm outward. Now he was there, facing the sea, hand raised with his palm to the sea. Smile and gentle eyes were to the sea, but the raised palm seemed to say to the sea, "Thus far, my child, but no further!"

Whatever the reason, and for ourselves we think of no reason other than Sai, the house stands solid and unharmed to this very day. The earth continues to move in portions of the hill, inevitable damage follows, but the Sai home remains unchanged, still waiting to welcome a visit from our beloved Baba.

You sit in Meditation for ten minutes after the evening Bhajan session; so far, so good. But, let me ask, when you rise after the ten minutes and move about, do you see everyone in a clearer light as endowed with Divinity? If not, Meditation is a waste of time. Do you love more, do you talk less, do you serve others more earnestly? These are the signs of success in Meditation. Your progress must be authenticated by your character and behavior. Meditation must transmute your attitude towards beings and things, else it is a hoax. Even a boulder will, through the action of sun and rain, heat and cold, disintegrate into mud and become food for a tree. Even the hardest heart can be softened so that the Divine can sprout therein.
— Sathya Sai Baba

Baba Knows Our Mexican Gardener

In our neighborhood at Villa de San Miguel in Mexico, there is a young Mexican man who does gardening. He is poor, and also unfortunate; for he has the habit of liquor. He married a nice local girl, and a baby had been born just before we left on a visit to India.

While we were away, we had arranged with this young man to visit our house once a week to water the flowers in the garden.

During the course of an interview granted to us by Baba, on the day of our departure from India, he turned to my wife and said, "About that servant of yours."

My wife said, "But, Swami, we have no servant."

Baba said, "Yes, but there is a man watering the flowers. Take this and give it to the baby." Then, he moved his hand and there appeared a medallion on a chain, which he handed to my wife.

My wife exclaimed, "How wonderful! It is a lovely baby, and he is a nice man."

Baba responded, "No. He has very serious faults."

Sugar Candy

My wife and I were with Baba to bid him goodbye, for we were returning to America. After some time, when the personal interview was over, he said, "I want you to give this to Mr. and Mrs. Cowan."

He moved his hand in the mode he has adopted to create objects, and there appeared a white, soft mass about the size of half of a closed fist. He extended his hand and showed it to us. "It is sugar candy," he said. Then, in a childlike voice of wonder, "Look, you can still see the process of creation."

In the palm of his hand there was water slowly disappearing into the mass of sugar candy. He did not explain further, but I took it to mean that the movement of creation was from the subtle to the gross — space, air, fire, water, and earth.

By the time we arrived in California, the sugar candy was quite hard and brittle. Needless to say, Mr. and Mrs. Cowan were overjoyed by this mark of Baba's attention to them and his remembrance of them.

Master of Time and Space

One evening in 1973, we left Brindavan about 8 p.m. to return to Bangalore. There were five of us in the taxi, plus the driver. The Bangalore road is only two lanes. Some miles from Brindavan we overtook a bus. Although the driver of our taxi saw some lights ahead, he estimated there was plenty of time to pass the bus. He could not have been more mistaken — the lights ahead were of a car moving at a very high speed towards us.

At this point in time and space, the simple action of passing a bus had escalated into a situation of terrifying potential, that of a fatal head-on collision. In this particular area, the layout of the road was also deadly. The road was under repair, and there was a high bank of dirt and rocks covering the side of the road. Thus, there was no possibility of the oncoming car being able to swerve off the road. We, too, could not take evasive action, for the bus was on our left and the road-repair material on our right, and by this time the oncoming car was directly in front of us. A foolish driver in that car and an equally foolish driver in our taxi! Of course, at the time of the impending crash, there was no time for this analysis; the incident sort of exploded upon us without warning. The lights of the oncoming car now struck directly into the windscreen of our taxi. The cars could not have been more than a

45

second or so apart. We were stunned. Not one of us recollected Baba or called him. We felt we were as good as dead, and we instinctively tensed for the crash. But at that very moment something happened that was without rational explanation. At one moment the two cars were upon each other, about to be smashed in a fatal head-on collision. The very next moment, the oncoming car was behind us, and we were continuing to pass the bus with a clear road ahead. Looking backward, we could see the receding red tail-lamp of the other car. There was no crash. There was no lapse of time; there had been no possibility of a last-moment maneuver.

The next day we drove out to Brindavan as usual about 8 a.m. so as to be waiting on the veranda for Baba to appear for morning Darshan. As soon as he came into the room, I touched the Lotus Feet and said, "We want to thank Baba for saving our lives last night."

Baba smiled and said, "Yes, that was a close one. You were so shocked that not even one of you called for Swami! But, Swami saved you anyway." Then he turned to a group of men and in Telugu told them the entire story of the incident.

I then said, "Swami, you must have altered time and space in order to save us." Baba just smiled and did not answer.

In 1978, I happened to meet Joe King, one of our fellow taxi passengers. It was in New York, where he lives. He asked, "Were you ever able to figure out what happened that time in the taxi?"

I smiled, shook my head, and said, "No."

Choosing a Cow in Bangalore

One morning, while the Second International Conference was still in the planning stage, Baba took three of us with him in the car on a drive to Bangalore. We were going to inspect a site for the Conference as suggested by some members of the Central Trust. It was their recommendation that Bangalore was a more convenient site for the Conference than were other possibilities in Madras, Bombay, or Prasanthi Nilayam. A potential site in Bangalore was a large park-like property on the eastward boundaries of the city, which included buildings suitable for large gatherings.

The proposed Conference site was inspected. Baba noticed everything about it, but made no definite comment. Upon leaving the area, we drove to the home of a devotee where Baba had accepted an invitation to lunch. Lunch with Swami at the home of a devotee is always a grand occasion which remains alive and treasured in the memories of the family and which becomes a principal highlight in the family tradition. Usually, a few close friends have been invited by the host, to their extreme delight. Other friends and acquaintances suffer a sharp disappointment, but it is clearly impossible for the host to agree to all requests. Naturally, the ladies of the household are thrilled to the tips of their toes and they have been vastly busy with the preparations.

47

After a correct and ceremonious welcome has been tendered to Baba, he usually retires to the family quarters for an intimate conversation with mother, children, and close relatives. The devotees who are travelling with Swami stay in the salon in quiet conversation. Before long, Baba and the family members join the other guests, and soon the lunch is served. Baba sits at a small table and is served by the hostess; the guests sit on the floor and are served by family members.

After lunch, Baba engages in some conversation with the guests, and then speaks separately again with the family. Perhaps some two hours have now passed since we arrived at the home. Farewells are made, and we are once more in the car.

The next destination, it transpires, is a large house in one of the city's suburbs. The purpose of going there is unknown to me. I could see that the house had a courtyard, and in this courtyard are cows. There are a number of cars parked in the street, and our car has to stop some distance away. Baba steps from the car and moves towards the house. I ask one of the men of our party what is going on. The reply is that the owner of the house is a cattle dealer and that Swami intends to purchase a top quality milk cow to add to the dairy herd either at Brindavan or at Prasanthi Nilayam. No sooner does Baba leave the car, however, than people start running toward him from all directions. He calmly returns to the car and we drive away. However, instead of departing, we circle the block and drive slowly past the house; Baba glancing into the courtyard as we pass the gate. Then the car heads back towards Brindavan.

I ask if Baba will return again on another day to select a cow. The reply to my question is that he has already selected the best cow. "But how could that be?" I said, "He did not even go to the gate, much less inspect the cows."

"A glance was enough," replied my informant, "Swami has chosen the best cow. The owner will deliver it to Brindavan."

Baba's Miracle of Life

While asleep in Brindavan in the month of October, 1978, without any prior warning to me, the prostate suddenly closed off the urethra. What happened then was agonizing, but nevertheless most comical. When Baba came down from his apartment, about 8 a.m., I told him that the urethra was closed and that already the bladder was very swollen. He smiled, said not to worry, and gave me vibhuti. About 11 a.m., he returned from inspecting some new construction and as he came to the veranda, both Dr. Goldstein and I approached him saying that my condition seemed to be serious. Baba came up to me, looked in my eyes, patted me on the head and said not to worry, it was just the heat. Then at 4 p.m., when Baba usually came down after rest, I did not wait, but sent a note upstairs that the situation was steadily getting worse and that now severe pains were moving back and forth throughout my body. Baba came down immediately. In the group of devotees waiting for him, there were, as usual, several physicians, including Dr. Goldstein from California. Without any discussion, Baba told the doctors to take me at once to the hospital and operate if necessary.

Now the comedy quickened. We got into several cars and went to Baba's hospital for women in Whitefield. The Medical Officer-in-Charge, Dr. Mrs. C. Rajeswari, made an examination room available, and the assembled doctors tried some 20 or more times to insert various sizes of catheters into the bladder, but with total failure — all they could draw was a bit of blood.

By now I was in agony, although I bit my tongue and kept silent. It was the immediate decision of the doctors that an emergency opening would have to be made through the wall of the abdomen. But at this a big argument arose as to whether the operation (which was an emergency move and could have been done simply and quickly in a few minutes) should be at Whitefield or at Bangalore. Since there was this difference of opinion, it was decided to consult Baba, and some of the doctors went to do this. They returned without a firm decision and again the topic was argued. Again a group returned to Brindavan for further consultation. Believe it or not, there were no fewer than three such trips! On the final trip, Baba was impatient and told them that since they could not agree, they had better take me to Bangalore.

By the time I was on the operating table in Bangalore, it was about 8 p.m. Swami sent two of his college students to stay with me, and needless to say they were superb. My condition by that time can be imagined. Although I continued to bite my tongue and keep silent, I was in such agony that I did not know where I was or what I was doing. The emergency job could have been done in five minutes at Whitefield, but instead, four hours of this! And still the comedy went on.

At Bangalore, the job was botched by the resident surgeons; heavy infection set in, and in three days Baba ordered me back to Brindavan. He then searched out India's best surgeon for prostate operations.

After examining me, the surgeon saw that the situation was so bad there was practically no chance of survival, and why should he unnecessarily preside at a fatality. But Baba persuaded him, saying that he would take care of everything, and a date was set for the operation. Baba then went to Prasanthi Nilayam after having delayed his trip until arrangements were complete, saying that he could attend to my difficulty just as well from there.

Baba arranged for the operation at the Whitefield hospital, the Sri Sathya Sai Hospital for Women and Children. The care was magnificent, and the multi-hour operation took place in the modern operating theatre with many devotee physicians and sur-

geons in attendance. The entire inside of my abdominal cavity was
filled with virulent infection, and the tissues were so rotted that
standard operating procedures could not be used. The principal
surgeon, Dr. Bhat, who had not met Baba prior to this, said that
he was calm and confident and in retrospect found this surprising
in the circumstances. The lady doctors said that certain characteristics of the operation procedures indicated to them that Sri
Baba was there and in charge. I was told later that from deep
anesthesia I twice said that Baba was there and that I was talking
with him. After the operation and until I was discharged, the care
that I received from the lady doctors and staff resident at the
hospital was wonderful, and this daily care was continued by the
male doctors when I returned to Brindavan and until I was on my
feet and healed enough to travel.

Why the big comedy in the whole affair? It took me some
time to figure it out. We all knew that Baba could have corrected
the entire matter by his Grace when I first reported the trouble.
Why the long and agonizing delays? Why the deadly complications
at the Bangalore hospital?

When Baba returned from Prasanthi Nilayam, he visited our
cottage almost daily. Once he described the entire operation, including my comments under anesthesia. He said that the odds had
been against me, that he had been there throughout the operation,
and that had the trouble struck me at any other place in the world,
I would not have survived. Finally, at the time of another visit, I
told Baba that I had figured the matter out. My conclusion was
that I had come to the end of my natural life, Baba had let me go
down to the final step, and at the last moment, he had reversed my
natural death by giving me rebirth. Baba smiled and confirmed
that what I said was true; he had given me new life.

After returning home to Mexico in January, some continuing
complications arose which took me into a Mexican hospital and
then an American hospital. Baba sent word to not worry, that
these were just rebirth pains.

Gita, Her Destiny
Is To Be a Human Person

Very likely all of Baba's devotees know about his pet elephant, Gita, either by directly observing incidents in which she partakes, or by hearing stories. She is very much attached to him, and he is most kind to her.

On the occasion of festivals and celebrations, Gita is a proud, stately, and magnificently decorated member of the ceremonial procession, calling to mind the pomp and circumstance of India's imperial past. When the celebrations are at Brindavan, Gita will walk the long miles from Prasanthi Nilayam, taking a number of days for the journey. Once she arrives at Brindavan, Gita usually stays for a time in the compound; a member of Baba's sub-human family of buffaloes, cows, deer, monkeys, dogs, birds, and cobras. She is playful and good-humored except when impatient for Baba to appear. One game she very much enjoys is playing with an old tire from an automobile. College students who happen to be in the compound, will play the game with her for a while. They roll the tire full force toward her. She trumpets and, very friskily for an individual of her weight, she chases wildly after it, kicking it and scampering around it.

I learned about Gita's destiny one day at Prasanthi Nilayam. Gita's home is at the Gokulum, Baba's dairy farm which supplies

pure milk both to the Ashram and to the adjoining village of Puttaparthi. The Gokulum covers several acres. It has modern sani-
tary sheds for the cattle, houses for the workers and their families,
a park, and a wonderful statue of Sri Krishna with a cow. The
statue of Sri Krishna is especially admired by visitors. It was made
to Baba's specifications, taken to his quarters, and painted by him
before being installed at the Gokulum. The cows at the Gokulum
are wonderful in themselves. They are the finest cattle available in
India and are prize winners in the quantity and quality of milk
produced.

On this particular day, I had been fortunate to accompany
Baba in the jeep on the short drive to the Gokulum which he visits
almost daily. He knows every cow as an individual, greets each
one, strokes it, and speaks to it. The cows, of course, know him
and come forward to be greeted. Such a visit to the Gokulum is
always a happy occasion, and the beauty of the fine animals is a
pleasure to see.

The inspection of the cattle over, we were ready to leave. I got
into the jeep first, as is protocol, so that when Baba gets in the
driver can immediately put the car in motion. But now, Baba
delayed getting in, for Gita had become aware of his presence and
was hurriedly coming toward him. Baba waited for her, stroked
her trunk, spoke to her, and gave her bananas, which someone had
provided. Then he moved to enter the car, but Gita made a noise,
and he turned toward her once more, stroked her, and spoke to
her again. "See," Baba said to me, "She is crying. She is saying,
'Swami don't leave now, stay longer with me.'"

And, sure enough, as I looked at her closely, large tears were
indeed rolling from her eyes. The car got underway, and I said to
Baba, "Swami, people say that, in her former life, Gita was an
Indian Princess, so devoted to Baba that she took birth as an
animal so as to be close in this way to yourself. Is this true?"

Baba replied, "Not so. Gita has never been human, but her
next birth will be as a human being."

Three Rings and Prema Sai

I showed the broken setting to Baba and asked if he would fix it.
"Yes," Baba said, "but do not take the ring to a jeweler.
Swamiji is the jeweler." But he did not fix it at that time.

My wife and I returned to America, and now, a year later, we
were again in India. The ring was still broken; it had not been fixed.
Then, one evening on the veranda of Swami's house at "Brindavan,"
when the room was filled with college boys waiting for evening bhajans, Baba turned to me and told me to give him the ring. He examined it and gave it to the students to pass around. As soon as the
ring had returned to him, Baba blew his breath upon it, and at once
a new ring appeared. Baba smiled at me, but did not give me the
ring. Instead, he passed the ring again to the students. When the
ring returned, Baba placed it on my finger. It was a totally different
ring. Not heavy gold, like the others, but light in weight, with
filigree around the setting and down along the band. The setting
held a light blue stone with a small but beautiful portrait of Baba.

Careless man that I am, the ring did not stay intact for long.
The stone in the ring broke loose and soon fell out of the setting. I
put the ring on a chain around my neck to be there until we would
be in India again.

On the next trip, whenever I was in Baba's presence, I wore

the empty ring, touching my nose quite often so that it had to be seen. The other people there joked that Baba had given me the perfect ring, because I could, in my imagination, fill any portrait of him into the empty setting.

At length I gave up, afraid to say outright that I had again broken Baba's ring, and I replaced it on the chain around my neck. One evening with Baba, at Bhajan time in the glassed veranda at Brindavan, he looked at me and said, "What is that bump under your shirt, Hislop?"

He knew full well what it was, of course, but I at once brought it out and said, "It is my ring, Swamiji. Broken again."

"Give it to me," Baba commanded, and I quickly did so. He examined it and said, "These stones are no good." And he threw it back to me. Then, in his familiar gesture, he blew on empty thumb and forefinger, and I could see the shine of gold, but not the ring. Again, to tease me, he started it around the room on the side away from me, but at length it returned, and he gave it to me.

The new ring was a marvel, a creation of great beauty. It was heavy. It must have contained at least three ounces of gold. The band was wide and heavy and supported a thick gold disk from which arose a portrait of Baba in bold relief, head to chest, all one unit of solid gold. That night, at home, my wife and I admired the ring and felt much joy. Lucky we did, for the ring had a life of one night only.

The very next morning when the College boys gathered on the driveway outside the veranda to greet Baba as he came downstairs, and as we formed a circle around him, he said, "Give me the ring, Hislop." He carefully examined it then said to me, "What do you want, a picture of Swami or a picture of Prema Sai?" (Prema Sai will be the third embodiment of this triple Avathara).

What a problem Baba gave me with that question! I simply could not answer, so I did not. He then moved around the encircling group showing the ring to everyone. Returning to where I was, he again said, "Well, Hislop, what will it be? Swami or Prema Sai?"

Imagine, please. Baba I love with all my heart, and he was there before me. Could I say, "I prefer Prema Sai over thyself, dear Swami?" Never! So I turned political man for a moment and said, "Let it be thy will, Swamiji."

Very well," he said, "so let it be Prema Sai. You already have Swamiji."

The boys pressed close around him, almost touching him and leaving me hardly any room to see. He held the ring, folded it back into his palm, as though what was to happen was too precious for open display, blew the creative breath three times through the thumb and forefinger, opened his hand, and there was Prema Sai! The ring itself was a silver color, that unique 5-metal alloy particular to India. The stone was a cameo of Prema Sai, the loving Lord of Creation, destined to appear on Earth a few years after the death of the Sathya Sai body. It was a brownish stone, highly glazed, sculptured in profile, the bridge and length of the nose visible with a suggestion of the arch of the left eye. It was a noble head with shoulder-length hair, mustache and beard; the head resting on, or emerging from, a lotus flower. His countenance was tranquil, peaceful, majestic.

Baba said, "He is only now in the process of birth, so I cannot show more of him. This is the first time he is shown to the world."

The boys were very excited and at once brought up cameras to take photographs. But I hid the ring and asked if Baba gave his permission. He replied, "No. No photographs."

Wherever I go, devotees ask to see the ring — to see the face of Prema Sai. In a year or so, those devotees who had seen the ring sometime earlier, said something surprising on seeing it again. They said, "It is turning. The whole nose can be seen now."

My reply was always, in truth, that I could see no change. But they said, "You see it every day and do not notice."

Nevertheless, I put it down to imagination and the enthusiasm of those who were looking at the ring. That is, until this year (1980). One day, at a devotee meeting, I was showing the ring, and I looked at it carefully. It struck me, "It is different! It is changing!"

Now the entire nose is there and visible, whereas at first the entire nose was not visible — or better to say the nose merged into the edge of the stone and did not appear to be fully visible. But now there is a space between the nose and the edge of the stone. Moreover, a portion of the left eye can be seen and also a portion of the left cheek. We can hardly wait to see it a few years from now. What will it be in ten years? In twenty?

It seems to me that I must be very careful of the ring. I only wear it now at gatherings of Sathya Sai devotees. At other times, it sits securely in the prayer room alongside the holy crucifix that Baba created several years ago.

Sai Krishna

In a way, this story was not completed until November, 1975.

A number of years ago, I was in Baba's car. He was in the rear seat with two persons. I was in the front seat with the driver. We were on our way to Puttaparthi. Driving in the car with Baba as a passenger is a fascinating experience; not only is there the thrill of being close to him, but sometimes he will give one the opportunity to ask questions. At times he engages in animated conversation in Telugu with his companions; and at times he remains silent, making the characteristic gesture with his hand that seems to indicate that he is giving attention to beings quite invisible to us. And very often, he sings bhajans with everyone in the car joining in the chorus (except me, who has a musical voice akin to the crow). The net result of all this enthralling activity is that my neck is constantly being twisted in order to see what is going on in the back seat. Baba understands my plight, but does not advise me to desist; he allows me the liberty to turn around. Of course, I do not stare all the time. I look only as long as I dare, and then I turn to the front again. So, my looking at Baba is intermittent, back-and-forth.

At some point in this journey, perhaps about half-way, Baba was talking, and I turned to look. My breathing stopped and I was transfixed! I could not credit my eyes. His devotees see Baba's face as beautiful indeed, although the chief impression I receive from his features is that of power and majesty.

What transfixed my movement and stopped my breathing now, was his face . . . The Baba I knew was not there! Instead, there was a face of the most extraordinary beauty — quite different in shape and cast from the features of our beloved Sai. The charm was so great, so poignant, that my heart seemed to twist, almost as though it were in pain. Never in my life, not in photos, nor in paintings by great artists have I seen a face of such exquisite beauty. It was beyond imagination and concept, totally beyond experience.

And his color was blue. Not just blue, not the blue with which artists paint Sri Krishna, but a deep blue like the velvet blue that sometimes can be seen in a dark sky, like a blue that I have at times seen from the deck of a ship thousands of miles from shore on the Pacific Ocean. I do not know how else to describe it.

I could not take my eyes from Baba's face. At length I caught myself and turned away. But, at once, I looked again, and the same beauty, surely not of this world, was still there. This continued for at least fifteen minutes. The two men sitting with Baba were beginning to look at me with somewhat puzzled expressions, for my staring was different from what they had become used to.

After a few miles, Sri Vittala Rao (on Baba's left) asked me, "Hislop! Why were you staring at Swami like that?"

Instead of answering, I directed a question to Baba, "Swami, what was that blue colour?"

He replied, "Oh! That? Whenever there is something of unfathomable depth, it appears to be deep blue."

That was the end of the conversation about the incident. Naturally, the thought had come to mind that maybe this was Lord Krishna, but, neither then, nor at any time in connection with this experience did I ever say the name, Sri Krishna, to Baba.

There the matter rested until November, 1975. It was before people started to arrive in multitudes for the Birthday. Baba's schedule was still somewhat free and he was taking me with him in the jeep, and so on . . . and probably that was why I was invited into the interview. An army man and his family had come from Assam. They were devotees, but this was their first time to actually see Baba. Often people wait for months for an interview, but this family was called as soon as they arrived. I was seated on the veranda of the mandir and saw them go into Baba's room. No sooner had they entered than he motioned to me.

There were mother, father, son, and daughter. Baba spoke to them in English, most lovingly. He knew everything about their lives, and it was evident that he was an intimate member of their household.

After a while, Baba asked me, "Hislop, tell them some experiences."

I complied and, after mentioning some incidents, I told the same story, just now related in these pages. But not even then did I mention the Sri Krishna name. The man was deeply impressed and words broke from his lips, "Oh! That had to be Lord Krishna!"

Baba smiled and said, "Yes, that was Krishna; not the Krishna pictured by artists and imagined by writers. I showed Hislop the real Krishna."

The military man said, "Oh! How I want to see Krishna!"

Baba smiled again and said, "Wait. Wait."

There is a sequel to this story. About a month later, in December, in Brindavan, I was talking with Baba, and I brought forward the names of some famous saints and gurus of the past. He said some things about each of them. Then the idea struck me that, wonderful though it must have been to know those great personages and to learn from them, yet the present day was the first time since the time of Sri Krishna that one could have God Himself as Guru. So I started to say, "Swami! In the thousands of years of time since Lord Krishna . . ."

Baba interrupted me before I could say another word and exclaimed, "Time since Krishna . . . ? I am Krishna! Where is Time?"

I folded my hands and bent low to him and said, "Well, Swamiji, this is the best of all times to be born!"

Baba replied, "Yes. The most fortunate of all times. Even more fortunate to be born now than during the Krishna Avathara."

Once before, within my hearing, Baba declared himself as Lord Krishna. This story has been told in detail elsewhere in these pages. It happened in the Dharmakshetra, in Bombay, and came about as part of the extraordinary drama of "the weeping saris" to which a few of us in the room with Baba were the fascinated witnesses. I had exclaimed that this had to be the re-enactment on this very day, of the famed drama of the mountain that had occurred in the Avatharas of Sri Rama and then of Sri Krishna. Baba had replied, confirming the statement. He said, "Yes, and it is the self-same Rama and the self-same Krishna here again today in this very room!"

In the light of what has been recited in the preceding pages by me as a direct witness and participant, we need never look back with even the slightest tinge of envy to those fortunate people who lived during those wonderful days of the Krishna Avathara. Because, indeed, every time that we have the joy of looking at our beloved Sai, we *are* gazing directly at Sri Krishna. In ages to come, the rich experiences of our days will be told and retold as the wondrous story of the Sai Avathara.

When the Name is pronounced by the tongue, and the Image is adored by the mind, these should not degenerate into mechanical routine; the Meaning of the Name and the Content of the Form must, at the same time, inspire and illumine the consciousness. Escape the routine; involve yourselves in the attitude of worship, deeply and sincerely. That is the way to earn peace and contentment, for which all human activity ought to be dedicated and directed.

— Sathya Sai Baba

For This, One Cannot Look to Baba

One of the puzzles about Baba is his position on criticism. At times, he has made kind remarks about me, directly to me, and also to other people. This is very pleasant, but at the same time I know only too well that I am a faulty man. And, as all men know, if they ever lose sight of their imperfections, then their good wives stand ready to correct them and bring them back to the true facts of their human nature.

But to be informed that one is imperfect is not the same as knowing exactly where the fault is. It stands to reason that while family and friends may point out personality aspects that annoy them, yet they may miss the genuine faults that prevent one from realizing the final or ultimate truth as to who and what he really is. But there is a person presently alive in this world who sees me through and through, and that one is Baba. With this in mind, when I was alone with Baba, and there was an opportunity, I asked him, "Swamiji, if my essential nature is bliss and freedom, there have to be some big faults that prevent me from realizing my essential nature. Please point out my big faults to me. That would be a great help and I would very much appreciate it."

In response, Baba smiled, shook his head in negation and said, "No. No. Just continue as you are doing."

61

What could I do? It would not do to press the question, so I had to abandon what would have been the perfect way to pinpoint my principal faults. Why would Baba not tell? One has to suppose that it would not be of real benefit to me if he told me. Perhaps the deep and vital faults have to be found by oneself.

Let the petty wishes for which you now approach God be realised or not, let the plans for promotion and progress which you place before God, be fulfilled or not; they are not so important after all. The primary aim should be to become Masters of yourselves, to hold intimate and constant communion with the Divine that is in you as well as in the Universe of which you are a part. Welcome disappointment, for they toughen you and test your fortitude.
— Sathya Sai Baba

The Heart May Be Open and Free

A highly valued facet of Sri Sathya Sai Baba, at least it is so for me, is that one can love him with all one's heart, without fear and without restraint. Every person wants to love greatly, with an open heart, but experience has made us afraid.

We may observe how natural it is for young children to love wholeheartedly. With what richness and sweetness do very young children embrace parents, brothers, sisters, and close playmates! How much joy there is for an adult when a child of three or four years embraces him with the sweetest of smiles and says, "I love you, I love you."

It is the river of love rushing from the open heart of the child that makes the child so incredibly sweet and so overflowing with bliss. It is this rich treasure of love and affection that touches even the dullest adult and makes him share the child's bliss for a moment or so.

But, as each of us leaves the innocent open-hearted years of early childhood, something very sad and tragic happens. Worldly experience invades the shelter of early years, and the heart suffers betrayal and rejection. One loves someone and love flows to that person. But, if the response is indifference, or a harsh word, or outright rejection, then the resultant hurt may be deep and agonizing.

The child tries again and again, and here and there he is hurt again and again. In time, a natural self-protection arises and the child's love is qualified with caution.

A person learns that when he loves, he is unprotected; love destroys his self-protection and makes him vulnerable to suffering. With each year of worldly experience, additional self-protective factors come into one's life. Ambition, business cares, competition, gratification of the senses, greed, resentment, hatred, jealousy — the whole range of narrowing tendencies exert more and more influence on body, mind, heart, and intelligence. The open, natural heart-expansion of early childhood is by now a thing of the past.

Is not this obstruction of the flow of love a fundamental reason why the life of an older person is often dry and joyless?

In this modern society, a dry and joyless life is the general experience. Witness the frantic search for distraction and pleasure the world over. An almost universal prayer arises from adult persons caught up in today's culture: "O Lord, may there be a new season of Spring in my heart. May the river of Love flow deep and strong again in my heart."

Here, to me, is one of the most wonderful miracles of Sri Sathya Sai Baba. The fettered heart, turning to Baba, can break free from all its bondage. Seeing him, being sure that he will never betray, is a most wonderful feeling. With joy, the heart responds to this trust. With each day, love for Baba grows stronger. He is divine Mother and Father to his devotee. One may love him without reserve, without guard, without fear, however guarded one may still be with fellow human beings. Of course, one's outward behavior with him must remain strictly disciplined.

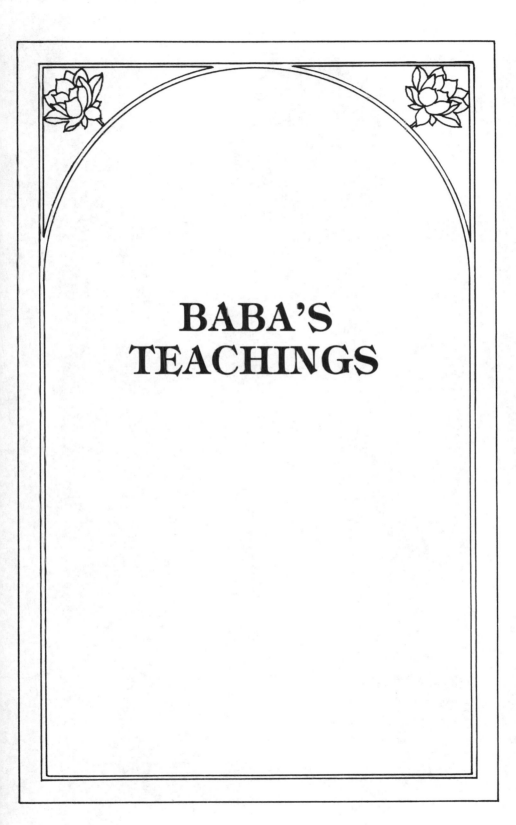

BABA'S
TEACHINGS

Become as a Little Child

It is not possible to hear Baba's discourses or to read anything of his without observing that he constantly speaks of love. He says, "Love cannot be disregarded." His devotees are told, "Love is the Royal Highway to God." His teaching proclaims, "God is love, and love is God." He addresses audiences as "Embodiments of Love." He says that when Self is realized, the love which is Self is not different from the love which is God.

It is the experience of mothers the world over that very small children, if loved and protected, are themselves embodiments of love, and this gives great joy, without end, to mothers. Love is the genuine spontaneous nature of the small child. That this spontaneous and natural love becomes modified by the worldly nature of the child as it grows older and as the world becomes part of its consciousness, does not negate the fact that the child's spontaneous nature shines forth as love.

The devotee of God must become as a little child, with God as Divine Mother and with the fullness of love flowing from the devotee's unguarded heart to Divine Mother. This open, unrestrained and unmodified love, spontaneously embracing Divine Mother, is devotion to God. The little child, when its being is love incarnate, shines with happiness, and one can see that in love the child is in ecstasy. Thus, the joy, the ecstasy, the happiness for which we long and for which we would willingly pay any price, will naturally be ours when, with an open and unguarded heart, we merge in love with God. Baba tells us there can be too much love between persons and that too much love between persons becomes destructive, but that love for God is totally without danger and may be totally unrestrained.

To know our Self is to be our Self. To know God, one must be God, not just an observer of Him. Like can merge with like, but unlike cannot. Fire merges with fire but does not merge with the ocean. Baba patiently explains that God is love and that if we would know ourselves as God, we must know ourselves as love. Only in love are we God and thus merged in Him.

Since we have the interest to transform our worldly life into spiritual life and remove that veiling which obscures our truth, we pay close attention to what Bhagavan Baba has to say about the significance of love. How does the heart rekindle, or release from constraint that flame of pure love which was oneself as a little child? Bhagavan Baba assures us that it is never too late to turn, in love, to God who ever resides in our heart. Baba says that although Divinity remains in the background, leaving the stage to our ego, Divinity is ever ready to respond if called upon.

Although Baba advises that it will be beneficial if we open our hearts to God and love Him without restraint, it does not mean that our family and those people very close to us will be denied our love. Baba points out that we now have a myriad of loves for various people, objects, and pursuits. He advises that we may gather all these streams of love together into a full and strong river of love and love God with that fullness of love. To explain this, Baba uses the simile of a tree in our garden. We notice that its leaves are shriveled and dry, and we at once feel compassion. We put garden hose in place and direct a spray of life-giving water to the leaves, but they do not respond; they do not benefit from the water. However, if instead of spraying the leaves with water, we give water to the roots of the tree, that life-giving water quickly finds its way to trunk, branches, leaves, flowers, and fruit. Similarly, if we gather together all our loves and love God with the fullness of love, then our family and friends will naturally and inevitably receive the love they need.

The pure spontaneous love that was oneself as a little child has not been destroyed and taken from us by the world; it is obscured only by Maya, by our worldliness. The shadow of the world will not remain, if we give heart and mind to Baba and to his divine teachings.

Let Me tell you one thing: However you are, you are Mine. I will not give you up. Wherever you are, you are near Me; you cannot go beyond My Reach.
— Sathya Sai Baba

The Inner Voice

A doubt may arise: "Baba is far away in India and I am unable to talk with him. How am I to know God's 'inner guidance'? Is not an 'inner voice' doubtful? People have even claimed the 'inner voice of God' as the reason for harmful actions."

The question was directly put to Baba as follows, "Baba says that conscience is God's voice. But how could that be? Millions of people have been killed in religious massacres, and the 'inner voice of conscience' tells the persons doing the killing that what they are doing is right."

Baba replied, "Not so. In such cases an idea or concept from outside has been accepted. If the individual would stop, discard all ideas and concepts from other people, turn inward and ask his conscience, a true answer would be forthcoming."

In addition to the reply of conscience, when we put aside all ideas and concepts, we are given any number of additional clues as to how our life can be as God wills. The divine Avathar tells us that God is love, that we must act in love and not act from anger, envy, pride, lust, greed, and delusion. He says, "See good. Do good. Be good." He advises friendship with the holy, compassion for the afflicted, rejoicing in the joy of the virtuous, and being alive to our own present faults with less emphasis on the shortcomings of others. Thus, we are not lacking in guidelines as to how we should live. Still further, when we have faith in Baba and dedicate our life to his divine wisdom, our impulses come to be self-correcting. As our practice of spiritual life goes on, we find that we are unable to engage in bad actions. If there is an initial impulse for a harmful action, something arises within us, and there is no possibility of going ahead with the harmful impulse. The inner latent Divinity becomes patent as conscience, guiding our life and our actions.

However, even though we carefully look at our lives and acknowledge divine guidance to be there, it is still possible to find ourselves with problems about which we are uncertain, or puzzled. If and when this is the case, Baba says that we may be quiet for a while, think of him with all intensity for ten or fifteen minutes and then put our question to him. He assures us that before long our mind will be clear, and we will know what is best to do. This is the actual experience of earnest devotees of Sri Sathya Sai; one's mind does become clear and doubts are resolved.

As we live our days in the practice of Baba's divine teachings, he says we must learn to have confidence in our inner Self and in our good common sense. Let us not find ourselves in the position illustrated by the plight of the reverent pastor of a church in the hill country. He had placed his life in God's care. A great storm broke over the hill country. Extraordinarily heavy rains fell on hill and valley, the river rose high beyond all limits and the pastor's church was carried away in the flood. He found sanctuary for himself on the roof of his church. First, a man on the shore cried out that he would save the pastor by throwing a rope to him. The pastor's reply was, "No, thanks. God is my Savior and God will save me." Then two men came in a boat with the same offer and received the same reply. Later on, just before the final disaster, some people in a motor launch approached with the intention of saving the pastor, but he again gave the same reply. After the final disaster, the pastor appeared at the pearly gates of heaven to seek admittance, and he complained to the guardian angels that God had deserted him in his hour of need. The angels, somewhat taken aback, replied, "But Pastor, we did send help to you. Right away we sent a man with a rope, and after that we sent two different boats!" In this same context, Baba once remarked, "First there must be common sense, then comes Divine Sense."

Baba's advice as to how we may lead a spiritual life is revealed by him in clear words in his teachings. We need not yield to doubt and misunderstanding. Baba says in plain words how to conduct our lives, and he is ever available as the Inner Voice of conscience, if and when we are in trouble and doubt.

The age span 16-30 is crucial, for that is the period when life adds sweetness to itself, when talents, skills, and attitudes are accumulated, sublimated, and sanctified. If the tonic of unselfish service is administered to the mind during this period, life's mission is fulfilled — for the process of sublimation and sanctification will be hastened by this tonic. Do not serve for the sake of reward, attracting attention, or earning gratitude, or from a sense of pride at your own superiority in skill, wealth, status, or authority. Serve because you are urged by Love. When you succeed, ascribe the success to the Grace of God who urged you on, as Love within you. When you fail, ascribe the failure to your own inadequacy, insincerity, or ignorance.
— Sathya Sai Baba

God, Himself, Is the Only Reliable Guru

We complain that we do not actually experience divine bliss as a constant of our daily life even though divine bliss is said to be the truth of oneself. Baba acknowledges this difficulty and says that ignorance of self, of one's true nature is almost universal. He says that just as a person who is caught in quicksand is best helped by another person who is on firm ground, the individual who longs for happiness is best helped by one who is himself firmly established in ever-constant divine bliss. The one who is able to help is named the Guru, in the tradition of India.

Baba goes on to inform us that in this age, which is marked by a deterioration of self-discipline and righteous behavior, God, Himself, is the only reliable Guru and, if appealed to, God will answer from within the heart of the devotee, or will cause an embodied guru to appear in the devotee's world. If called upon, God will lovingly guide the devotee.

That Baba does indeed guide his devotees is my own constant experience. How can I describe the course of my life with Baba? Perhaps a start could be made by mentioning some of the ways in which Baba is found to be unique, at least within the limits of my own life-experience.

Baba demonstrates again and again that nothing is concealed

73

from him, that in fact he can give an immediate true answer to any question in any field of knowledge — spiritual or mundane. Even specialists bow to him because of his superior knowledge in their fields of expertise.

Baba is not separated from his devotees by physical distance. Though he may be half-way around the world in India, engaged in actions there, does not prevent him from being with us here. So many times has he appeared to my wife and me in our house in Mexico or when we were away from home in our car — and this has been the experience of devotees in many countries.

Nor, is there ever any doubt as to his instructions to me, his devotee. The mind moves to him, or develops a thousand ears to hear him. I do not know how it happens, but my mind is in the shape of his teachings.

There are only twenty-four hours in the day, and the physical and mental energy of an ordinary guru can reach far, perhaps very far, but a limitation soon appears. Is there a person on this planet who can perceive, experience or even project a limitation for Baba? Where is the limit of his influence in India? Already the educational system has been changed, and the lives of countless numbers of people have been changed, and Baba still has many years to live. And now people in other parts of the world are bending towards Baba. Who can project a limit? And, beyond the boundaries of eye and ear, where is the limit for Baba? For years, we have known of his dominion over the elements; and, if asked, Baba may calmly respond that the entire cosmos is his.

People learn of a guru and come to him. A certain number of disciples can use up a guru's time and have direct contact, help, and advice. But that is the limit. Where is the limit for Baba? At one and the same time, in various regions of the world, great numbers of people experience direct contact and direct help from Baba by means of inner hearing and intuition, by dreams, by visions, by manifest appearance, by leading events, and — very rarely — letters and telegrams. Yet, to watch him day by day in close contact, as I do because I have entry to his house, he ever appears relaxed, even apparently wasteful of time by engaging in light-hearted conversation with visitors and college students. Not only is Baba's advice and help received at so-called out-of-the-ordinary levels of consciousness, but he also grants hundreds of interviews. And, he is as kind and patient and attentive to the last person of the day as to the first person.

People say that in their first interview, Baba not only knows their thoughts and about incidents long forgotten, but also intimately knows about their home, their work, and equally knows about every member of the family. It is evident to people that Baba has been a member of the family from the first days.

This Chapter must come to an end, but cannot terminate without mention of a factor which is so strange that it is beyond comparison. That is; the rescues. Many hundreds of people, including my wife and myself, have experienced a rescue by Baba. At a point where death is a second or so away, Baba will intervene and save the devotee. And, often, Baba, himself, appears and is *seen* doing the rescue. The pages of Baba's journal, *Sanathana Sarathi*, have recorded many a first-hand account of rescues by Baba, and I have wished that someone with access to the historical file of past issues of *Sanathana Sarathi* would bring together in one volume these first-hand accounts. What a joy such accounts would be to the growing number of Sri Sathya Sai devotees, worldwide.

Baba, ever constant in his Being, will and does respond to our prayers, and will and does guide not only his devotees, but all devotees of God wherever they are. The total impact of the extraordinary capabilities and actions of Baba, and the endless extent of unseen actions that must be inferred from around-the-world reports, is that Baba is no other than the Divine Unlimited Energy, manifest in human form — at least that is my conviction. I am Baba's devotee, and that fact is basically the story of the course of my life since meeting him.

Because he is ever illumined, having the limitless power and energy of the Divine Omnipresent Creative Energy, Sri Sathya Sai Baba is called the Avathar of the Age. We may challenge and test Baba's teaching in any way we see fit. Some faith and some concentration are required at the beginning: then make the test. Let us have faith, try Baba's teaching, and we will know for ourselves the bountiful good fortune of knowing him.

Self-Inquiry

Self-inquiry is not a regular practice for most of us. It requires a change from our present way of being so involved with the world that we never take the time to ask ourselves about ourselves. The dictionary tells us that "to inquire" means to seek to learn by asking, to make investigation. The meaning of "self" is given as a person or thing referred to with respect to individuality, one's nature, character, etc. Self-inquiry, then, is to investigate a person (oneself) with respect to individuality, nature, etc. This definition will serve to get us started.

For example: we visit a medical clinic, have tests, and report the results to our family, "The doctor examined me and said I am strong and healthy." Sometime later, we become ill and complain to our family, "My body hurts all over." If then we were to stop our ordinary routine for a moment or so and wonder, "Why do I perceive myself in two different ways? When I went to the doctor, I referred to the body as myself, and now I refer to the body as a possession of mine, as 'my body.' Is this just a minor variation of the way I talk, or is it something significant which I should look into?" — in that moment of asking about ourselves, we would be engaging in self-inquiry. If our interest were touched deeply enough, additional questions might arise, such as, "Can 'I' actually be separate from my body in the sense that although the body might be destroyed, 'I' am not thereby destroyed? If the body is not 'me,' how did it come into my possession? If I had any say in the matter, no doubt I would have asked for a better and more beautiful body! If indeed the body is mine, and not just assumed to be mine, what is my responsibility to it? And, further, who is this 'we,' this 'I' who at one and the same time claims to be the body and to be the owner of the body."

In this way, self-inquiry may start. Or, any incident may spark the beginning of self-inquiry. In any event, we are most firmly told by Sri Sathya Sai Baba that self-inquiry is essential if we choose to become free of illusion and delusion and their accompanying miseries. Baba says, "We are not body, mind, intellect, senses. They are manipulated by us. The day we recognize this differentiation and live in that knowledge; from that day, we become aware of our reality and our goal."

At present, many of us are intensely interested in the world. Because of our interest in the world and because of our desire for the things of the world, we are attached to the world and powerfully fascinated by it. But it is we who become fascinated with the objects and experiences of the world; it is not that the world captures us and holds us as its prisoner. Of the two, the world and us, Baba tells us that it is ourselves upon which all depends, and of the two it is ourselves who are all-powerful and truly fascinating. Self-inquiry is a method to see the obvious truth of this and act on it right away.

That which we are able to observe belongs either to the world outside our skin, or to our inner world, so we feel: "I am observing all this." Self-inquiry means to search out this "I" who feels he or she is the observer of all this, to inquire, who am "I" really? What am I really and truly? Does this subtle subjective observer have a ground or source? About this, the sage Ramana Maharshi observed, "The 'I' thought cannot be the totality of the individual for it perishes daily in deep sleep, but there is no break in the continuity of one's Being."

Unless we know the answers to such inquiries, and until we realize and take our stand in the truth about ourselves, our decisions and actions have the terrible potential of being dreadful mistakes. It is because of this that Baba says, "So long as one does not know who he is, he cannot escape these sorrows. As long as one does not realize the presence of God in everything, one cannot escape this sorrow. As long as one does not understand that to be born and die is for one purpose only — to understand the nature of Atma (i.e. the Self), one cannot escape this sorrow."

The formal question, "Who am I?" although helpful, is not essential. There can be a direct and immediate realization of the Self as indicated many centuries ago by the Self-Realized sage, Astavakra, in response to the question of King Janaka as to how he might be free. The sage replied, "O King, know the Self as pure consciousness, the unaffected witness of the phenomenal world and you will be free."

If we were to have it in mind to follow Sage Astavakra's advice as given to King Janaka, the initial step, to know oneself as pure consciousness, is not difficult. The difficulty is to be *established* in that pure consciousness. We, as complicated adults, intent on realizing the absolute truth, are worlds away from the young children we once were. Great changes have come about in our lives, but despite these great changes, our consciousness has not changed one iota during the years. Feel the way into consciousness, and it will be realized that at a very deep level of our being, nothing which has happened, either outside the skin or within the skin, has had the slightest effect on that beingness — it remains untouched and unchanged. This part of Sage Astavakra's advice will be easy for anyone. The difficulty arises within the mind which will not be content. The point of deep awareness is quickly abandoned because of our fascination with the phenomenal world. About this, Baba informs us that for consciousness to remain firm in non-differentiation into identity and object, the mind must immolate itself in total surrender to the deep undifferentiated state; to the Divine. There must be that final moment of total surrender to God. That crucial moment of total surrender, and what follows, seems to be very much an individual affair. For instance, Baba tells the story of King Janaka; that immediately following his full, never-deviating Self-Realization, he returned to his throne and continued to rule his kingdom. The great Self-Realized saint, Sri Ramana Maharshi, on the contrary, after that crucial moment of surrender to truth, which came in a flash while he was still a young active boy, retired to the pit of the temple at Tiruvanamalai and remained there, absorbed in the Self for many, many months before he would even speak to another person.

The ultimate subjectivity is our Self, and all that is not Self is objective. The status of non-self, of "object" must be assigned to everything in life about which we can say, "Of this I am aware, I have a feeling about it, I am thinking of it, I am the witness of it, but it is not I, for when it has changed or gone, I remain, and I know what has come into the place of that which is gone." In self-inquiry, we do not pause to investigate that which we perceive as being non-self. We simply say, "Not this. Not this," and continue onward. It is said that whatever changes and becomes other than what it was, cannot be the true, eternal Self of which sages speak. We cannot, therefore, accept anything which is subject to change as being our ultimate, ever-constant Self.

Some great philosophers hold that even "I," the witness, is constantly changing, that both observer and observed are changing every moment and therefore "permanent and eternal" is a phrase without meaning. They are correct as far as they go, no doubt. But Baba, and also the ancient rishis say that the state of witnessing is not particularized into a "witness" and that if full and complete attention is concentrated on the "I," that while "I" will indeed change, losing name, force, and form, it will merge thereby into the "Absolute" which cannot be described in terms of categories of any type, including those of "eternal" and "temporary." Baba tells that this non-categorized Absolute is his reality, and our reality also, if we choose to realize it.

Once self-inquiry is underway, we find ourselves more alert and less liable to be acting without really knowing what we are doing. Not that we are setting goals, it will just naturally happen that we are less "sound asleep" than was the case in the past. Baba has said that to be "awake" throughout the day is real meditation. Sooner or later, as we become watchful, the very powerful question of "Who and what am I," whether expressed in those particular words or not, will occur to us with great intensity. This is the significant beginning; awareness becomes a deep self-inquiry.

The question, "Who am I?" is widely known and is freely bandied about in conversation. It has become a worldwide saying because it was the central point of the teaching of the great saint of Arunachala Hill at Tiruvanamalai in southern India, Sri Ramana

Maharshi. But it is also the pertinent question put to us by the blessed Avathar, Sri Sathya Sai Baba, as well as by great seers and sages of past ages about whom we may read and study. "Who am I?" is, perhaps, the most vital question which can arise in the life of any one of us. Not that the question is necessarily phrased in those particular words. However, to know the question and to repeat it is one thing. To actually penetrate deep within one's consciousness and put the question, is quite another thing.

Whenever our self-awareness is sufficiently deep to actually have the intense feeling, "Who am I?," then what is the mode, how is it done, what next?

In discussing spiritual matters with interested people, it will be found that most devotees pose the question, "Who am I?" and look for an answer to the question. The question is taken to be a way to get from oneself the deepest knowledge about oneself. For this reason, devotees will often express uncertainty; that is, the question has been deeply and most sincerely asked, but there has been no definitive answer, and the Self is not realized. The solution to this puzzle is quite plain, but apparently hard to come by. People read and reread about "Who am I?" but do not notice the explanation of the question. The fact is, there is no duality of questioner and answer. The answer is the questioner. This means there is no answer in the customary question and answer dichotomy. Actually, the question, "Who am I?" is only a means we have elected to use in order to focus total attention upon the feeling, "I." All other content is dropped from consciousness and every iota of burning interest and concentration is focused on "I." The goal of the chase is to free our awareness from every attachment or interest or concept or activity other than the concentrated attention upon the feeling, "I." The goal is, to be, for an instant, totally unencumbered; the goal is, to be, for an instant totally without borders, totally vulnerable to the truth of oneself.

If that be the case, then why fasten attention upon the "I" of immediate awareness, which certainly will be the empirical "I" of our ego-self? The answer, again, is very plain. We are chasing hard upon the trail of that "ultimate I," that ultimate "something or other" about which we can make no projection. And, that "I" which we are presently holding to, is the best clue we have. Upon that clue we concentrate. Let us see where it will lead us! The self-proclaimed "I," under intense scrutiny, will yield to the subtle reality which is its ground. But now words are no longer meaningful, any attempt at description would be false. From this point, each of us must go alone, naked of ideas and words.

In Baba's divine teaching, he again and again tells us the practice of self-inquiry is vital to spiritual life. Self-inquiry is the flash of total consciousness. Its practice can be engaged in at any time. People engage in self-inquiry in order to realize the truth of Self once and for all, and thus be free of doubt. No philosopher, or sage or writer claims credit for discovering self-inquiry. Just as small creatures arise spontaneously within a mass of rotting flesh, self-inquiry arises spontaneously within the pain of human sorrow. The modes of self-inquiry are as varied as the individuals within whom the urge to inquire arises. The text and chapter of self-inquiry is more easily come upon in the East than in the West, but the urge to know what one naturally is, stripped naked of all that can be discarded, is strong and alive to inquiring minds the world over.

Remember that with every step, you are nearing God, and, God, too, when you take one step towards Him, takes ten towards you. There is no stopping place in this pilgrimage; it is one continuous journey, through day and night, through valley and desert, through tears and smiles, through death and birth, through tomb and womb. When the road ends, and the Goal is gained, the pilgrim finds that he has travelled only from himself to himself, that the way was long and lonesome, but, the God that led him unto, was all the while in him, around him, with him, and beside him!
— *Sathya Sai Baba*

Karma

In India, people use the word "Karma" when referring to an action which will not be complete until its energy has been totally expended in the consequences of that action. Baba informs us that the impending consequences of an action in innumerable past lives is an enormous karmic force. He says that our present birth came about because of that karmic force and, until we can get free from the entangling web of action and reaction, our karmic destiny will continue through aeons of time, until eventually, we do get free.

Our world is afloat on a vast sea of information, but information is raw data only; it is the distillation of that information which yields knowledge. In the most ancient of times, the distillation of information by saints and sages yielded a supreme elixir of knowledge about human life; the knowledge of how to free oneself from the endless turning of the wheel of action and reaction. For, until that was done, one could not know what was contrived, transient, and therefore, unreal; and what was uncontrived, eternal, and real. As it was in the past, so it is now: the only knowledge worthy of the name is that elixir of knowledge of how to escape from the prison of action and consequence. Without this, the information we gather each day, is an ocean into which we are sinking, and in which we will die, as ignorant and helpless in death as we were at birth.

Today, this day, that precious elixir of knowledge is ours if we are sufficiently awake to reach out and take it. This precious knowledge is available to us in the teachings of that extraordinary being, the divine Sri Sathya Sai Baba. Full release from the turning of the wheel of birth, death, and rebirth may be ours now, in this brief lifetime, now that we know of Baba; and if we have the good sense to pay careful attention to his teachings and the will to take appropriate action. However, if we, by our carelessness and inattention, gloss over this extraordinary and unique opportunity, who can say to what distant shore we will be carried by the hurricane of karmic consequence readying itself to manifest as another of our continuing existences?

The doubt may arise, what is done is done, and the force of bad action will work itself out. How can it now, after the event, be erased? Baba gives an answer which applies to all persons, of all ages, of all races and nations. He says that a seed will not germinate when it is covered with too much earth. In the same context, the seeds of wrong behavior will not germinate and grow into painful events of our life, if the seeds are covered deep with loving service to those who are in need of sustenance, courage, love, and help. He is saying that a lifetime of good deeds will cover a multitude of past sins. Constant work in loving service to others, covers the seeds of past sinful and harmful actions, so they die away and do not grow into a new round of misery.

A question often put to Baba is, "But how about the total of our impending karma? Can the burden of impending karmic consequence, both good and bad, be instantly burned to a crisp and thus be done away with in a flash, as it were?" The answer seems to be, "Yes, it can, but it is not likely." To this question, Baba has given the same answer a number of times. He says that nothing in creation, including the unspent reaction-energy of past action, can withstand the force of God's Will. But it is not likely that the Divine will totally eliminate karma from the life of a person. For Baba has said that people learn through action and its result, and that if he made a practice of cancelling out karmic consequence by a mere act of will, it would negate progressive evolution. In ordinary language, it is to say that if the rules of the game are broken, the game is over . . . there is no longer a game, the game being "progressive evolution." Baba has pointed out,

however, that when the empirical self — the person, the ego — sur-
renders to God in the final moment of Self-Realization, all karma
is transcended. The body of the liberated one may continue to live
out the life-span and act like other people; but consciousness,
which in the moment of liberation abandons its particularity, no
longer identifies with the body. There is unimpaired freedom at
that moment. This should not be taken to imply, however, that
there is no way-station between the full suffering of karmic consequence and full release at the moment of God-Realization. If, in
devotion to Him, we dedicate our life to God, praying that His
Will be done, He softens the due consequence of our past actions.
Inconveniences there will be, "accidents" and illness there will be,
but major disasters do not touch us. This is the long-term experience of Sai devotees. Baba explains it in terms of medicine stored
in the medicine cabinet. The consequence of our action is the
medicine. Everything changes, in time, in this manifest world,
and, in time, the potency of the medicine stored in the cabinet is
reduced and does not have its full impact, even though we eventually take it. For his devotees, for those persons surrendered to
God's Will, Baba "ages" the medicine of karmic consequence, and
thus softens its impact.

To the question, "May we know total freedom from all
karma?," Baba's answer is "Yes." Total freedom from ignorance
and untruth about oneself, grants freedom from all karma. That
divine freedom is at hand for us; let us be wise and accept it.

Reincarnation

Rebirth (reincarnation) is a concept known to almost everyone nowadays. It is known to people in most parts of the world,
but there is no general agreement as to exactly what it means, or to
what aspect of the human person it might apply. Is rebirth
uniform for everyone, did it have a beginning and does it have an
end? Can willpower or certain practices modify rebirth? Is there
rebirth for lower forms of life and higher forms of life (if there be
such), or is rebirth a concept only? The topic is of deep interest,
and an entire series of questions about rebirth may arise in the attempt to find the truth of the matter. The Buddha explained his
experience of rebirth in great detail, and these descriptions have
been translated into many languages. Baba confirms that rebirth is
a fact in the empirical world. But although he explains how it plays
a vital role in the life of creatures on planet Earth, he does not go
into detail about the mechanics of how it takes place, except to say
that what follows death is not uniform, that the corpse is common
to all, but there is no uniformity beyond that.

Rebirth is a concept which is related to the concept of progressive evolution. Progressive evolution is said to carry each specialized manifestation of universal consciousness through a long, long
evolutionary journey until finally the particular merges into the

universal and realizes that it is the universal. If looked at from the human time-frame, the length of the evolutionary journey boggles the mind. Baba says that the journey starts when life is particularized as granite. The journey is from granite to vegetation, to animal, to human, to super-human, to cosmic, to Divinity; and the journey is completed in the realization of the Absolute Unmodified Divine Principle — the Divine Creative Energy. Comprehension of universal progressive evolution cannot be jammed into the confines of a time-frame able to be comprehended by the mind, so we can safely disregard all that and examine what Baba says about how the human person is affected.

We can quickly get to the heart of the matter with Baba's statement that the consequence of good and bad deeds is the only luggage carried from death to rebirth. In fact, good and bad actions are the cause of rebirth and, further; they determine the kind of life into which one is born and the kind of nature and character one finds oneself having. But we need not worry, for Baba assures us that the binding power of our deeds can be overcome by turning to the practice of spiritual life and praying to our Lord for His Grace. He says, "Do not think or worry about death and birth, or the joy and sorrow which accrue to you — they are relevant only to the body. Therefore, you should not brood about things which are natural, like birth and death, joy and sorrow. One day or other, everything existing in the world will have to undergo modifications. Seek out the Divine, and, while discharging your duties, keep that Divinity always in view."

Baba, in divine love for us, shows us exactly how we may be free from the monstrous core of good and bad deeds which follow us, until we waken and give some intense examination to our predicament. He tells us that if we will study his teachings and put them into practice, there is no need whatsoever to have any worries. The spiritual practices he tells us to engage in will lead to happiness and to that peace which passeth all understanding; to joy in the eternal now and total freedom from the past.

It is said that the idea of reincarnation was included in early Christian writings, but was deleted at a later date. Certainly reincarnation is not uniformly taught in Christian churches today. Nevertheless, many westerners wonder if the concepts of action, consequence, and rebirth might not explain the seeming injustice evident in both world affairs and in individual lives. If we push someone, for example, and get pushed in return, action and its consequence are evident, and most of us would not cry, "Injustice." But if a kind-hearted, innocent person is crushed by misfortune after misfortune, while at the same time a person of evil action and character gains fame and fortune, we tend to cry, "Injustice!" But according to the concept of reincarnation, apparent injustice ceases to be that when the time-frame is widened. The "good" person is now experiencing the results of past bad actions, and the "evil" person is now experiencing the results of past good actions.

Like the illustration of "push and get pushed in return," most of the events in our life are the consequence of present action, according to Baba, and it is only major deeds which carry their seeds of consequence to subsequent births.

Much of what we experience can be seen as the consequence of present action. The illustrations are endless: take driving lessons and become a good driver; go to the gym and become stronger; love others and treat them with kindness and consideration and (in general) receive kindly treatment in return. The "in general" exception is mentioned because of a possible karmic relationship with certain people — the "push" we gave them may have been a serious action in a prior life, and we may be about to get "pushed" in return. The complications and cross-currents of action and consequence are not clear and evident to most of us, fortunately for us. We are not fully happy with our actions in this life — think of the intolerable burden it would be if we had to agonize over the actions of innumerable past lives.

Action and consequence appears to be a cruel revolving wheel from which there is no escape, since each reaction in its turn is also an action with further consequences. The wheel is the symbol the Buddha used to picture the endless sequence of birth, life, death, and rebirth. The Buddha pointed out that Release could be achieved by a deep and intense realization of the Four Noble Truths and their unremitting practice, such practice being more likely to result in Release if one became a detached monk, engaged in spiritual discipline in cave and forest.

Baba, the blessed Avathar of this age, out of the depth of his limitless knowledge, tells us that in this age we may be released from birth, death, and rebirth by spiritual discipline and the fullness of our devotion to God, even though we remain in family and society. The spiritual discipline appropriate to this age is explained in Baba's divine teachings. The priceless secret of Release is to render unto God that which is His — and everything is His in the final analysis. Baba tells us to abandon the notion that we are acting in order to enjoy the fruits of action, and instead, dedicate the fruit of every action to God. God will then, Himself, be the Doer of the action and will graciously assume the burden. We, no longer grasping the role of doer, no longer reap the consequences; God, as the Doer, takes the fruit of the action. Baba tells us, "Both the Jnani (i.e. one who is free from rebirth) and the Agnani (i.e. one who is ignorant of what must be known) will have desire; desire for the other world and the burden of past karma, all in equal measure. Only, the Jnani will not have the consciousness that he is the doer. So, he will not be bound. The mind is the cause of bondage (i.e. bondage to the cycle of birth, death, and rebirth) as well as liberation. The mind is the cause of everything."

There is a simple and effective way to begin detachment from reincarnation.

This simple way is to do good to others, to do good for others, instead of aiming always at gaining benefits for ourselves. Baba points out that just as a flower-seed covered with too much soil will not germinate; the seeds of our past bad actions will not germinate if covered by good deeds. The common saying is, "Good deeds cover a multitude of sins."

We do not know directly for ourselves that reincarnation exists — even our so-called visions of the past are but thoughts existing at this moment, for a brief moment, then disappearing. We have to take the information about reincarnation, in faith, from someone we trust. For many of us, Sri Sathya Sai Baba is trustworthy — he is ever poised and balanced in truth, needs nothing from us, and has no cause to deceive us, nor advantage to gain from us. He says, in effect, "True, you do not know for yourself. Faith and trust come first in spiritual life and experience follows. Plunge into spiritual discipline with faith and by this you will find your own truth and you will know fully all that is worth knowing."

Is reincarnation true or not? If, in faith, we accept it to be true and then engage in the appropriate action, where can be the

harm? To love God with all our hearts and to do good for others —
where can the harm be in loving God and in doing good actions?

A puzzle remains — "Who" or "What" reincarnates? Is it this
changing personality which reincarnates? That seems unlikely. But
if we look to Baba, he provides an answer. He says, "What is this
'I' whose limit is the body, but which is distinguished from the
body? There is no soul other than it, and if it is done away with,
only the non-dual spirit remains. What is distinctive of the human
is the causal body which persists until Release."

What Baba is saying is that as long as we do actions in order
to gain their fruits, we are fully involved in and are part and parcel
of that process. Therefore, we must experience the consequences
of the process whether they are happy consequences or painful
consequences. We have attached ourselves to that process and are
identified with it — its life is derived from our energy and when we
cease to provide energy, the process will not continue. The Buddha
said that the "karma" which we experience is like a string of beads
trailing along with us — the beads do not follow us, we pull the
beads behind us and keep them with us. The moment we cut the
cord which pulls the beads, we are free of them. When we remove
ourselves from the throne of the doer, which we have usurped, and
let God, the rightful King take His throne, we are at once released
from the burdens of kingship.

If we surrender our minds to God, accepting Baba's statement
that all is God, then the identity of the actor is shifted from "ourselves" to God, and what is done is His doing. We then feel the
care-free bliss of Release, and we have by that transcended the
periphery of the personality.

This release from ego-identity and the surrender to God of the
idea of separateness from God can be done — in fact, Baba says, it
is possible at any moment. As soon as the stormy clouds of ignorance are swept away, God, our own Self, will shine forth. Baba
has clearly said that this flash of truth can be instantaneous. If our
ignorance is deep-rooted and stubborn — as is almost always the
case — and we do not know instantaneous Release, nevertheless, we
can know and be convinced of its possibility by virtue of practice.
Nobody can prevent us from accepting that whatever we are doing
is being prompted by the Divine — which is our innermost Reality.
We can cross out the "I am doing," yet action will still continue.

Yielding the feeling and the claim "I am acting" to God, who is the source of man and world and hence is the true Actor, we can accept whatever comes to us as His Will, no longer making distinctions such as "I want" or "I do not want." Baba puts it very simply when he says, "The road to happiness lies not in doing what you like, but in liking what you must do."

Detachment is possible, and it is the way of Release. Baba assures us that while the beginning of rebirth cannot be perceived, yet it can come to an end. Further, Baba says that in this very lifetime rebirth may come to an ending.

Baba's use of the word, "Release," is identical with the use of such terms as God-Realization, Self-Realization, Enlightenment, Liberation, Freedom from Bondage, Freedom from Birth and Death. Baba describes "Liberation" as follows: "When the entire creation in and around him becomes a blissful love and light-emitting experience, then the Sadhaka loses the limited consciousness of his individual entity, transcends the peripheries of personality to experience at all times through all his senses the Blissful Immanent Divinity which was always latent in himself."

Life is a pilgrimage, where man drags his feet along the rough and thorny road. With the Name of God on his lips, he will have no thirst; with the Form of God in his heart, he will feel no exhaustion. The company of the holy will inspire him to travel in hope and faith. The assurance that God is within call, that He is ever near, nor is He long in coming, will lend strength to his limbs and courage to his eye.
— Sathya Sai Baba

If All Is God, Who Does Evil?

Newspaper headlines, T.V., and radio insistently call our attention to evil in the world. Critics say, "Bad news sells, good news does not sell." Evil actions brought to our attention, although not experienced by us directly perhaps, are deeply troubling. As one talks with people, questions often arise as to, "Why Evil?" We hear that only God exists, that all is God, and the thought may occur to us, "If all is God, then God must be the Doer of evil as well as of good." But this thought, although apparently logical, seems beyond belief — it cannot be possible, we feel, for one is advised to love God with all one's heart.

The concepts of reincarnation and action/reaction provide an explanation of *why* a person may be on the receiving end of evil, but they do not provide an explanation to account for the one who does the evil. The reason as to why a person performs an evil action is not clear despite the many explanations which are brought to our attention and which range from the genes and/or "unconscious" infantile trauma to the evils of capitalism and/or excess sugar in the diet. Published research supports each explanation, but still we are not satisfied, and questions about evil continue to trouble us. Nor are we satisfied with the explanation that two principles are at work — the Divine Indivisible Supreme Absolute, and the principle

91

of evil personified as the Devil — for despite this time-honored solution we continue to look for more light on the topic.

Explanations are also put forward to indicate there is no actual need for a second principle (the Devil). For instance, the God-Realized saint, Sri Ramakrishna, responded to a question as to why God allowed evil in His world. He said that God created the world in play, as it were, and, without villains, there would be no drama. Sri Ramakrishna's explanation is a description of the "mechanics" of the drama but still leaves the question, "Why does God, Who is love and mercy incarnate, allow evil in His world?"

Masters of divine wisdom reply to questions according to what the questioner is able to understand. But if replies do not satisfy, we have to dig deeper, if we are at all resolute. In his discourses, Baba has declared that God Himself does not do evil, that God is Love only, and that evil actions are ego actions.

If questions and doubts still remain, one must look to oneself and plunge even more deeply into the matter. A first question could be: has one, in the past, engaged in some action which now would be regarded as an evil action; an action which one would not repeat? If so, why would one do such an action in the past and why would one not do it now? The answer is that one acted unwisely in the past instance, because the action seemed justified according to one's judgment at that time. And one would not repeat the bad action now, because one knows better now.

But why did one not know better in the past, at the time of the evil action? The answer is that one's intelligence and feelings at the time were overshadowed by wrong notions about the world, other people, and oneself. In other words, one was under the sway of ignorance and identified with ideas appearing in the mind and with passions which agitated the emotions, and therefore acted unwisely.

But Baba assures us that one's innermost or essential being is Divinity Itself. How then, could the Divine (my Self) engage in bad actions? Yet, the fact is, one did so. One could properly ask — "Why did *I*, the Divine, engage in bad (or evil) actions?" If the correct answer to this question is seen, it will also be the answer to the more general question, "Why does God allow evil in the world?"

Evil in the world can continue only as long as individuals continue to do bad actions, for evil actions come from individuals; it is individuals who do the evil. Of course, people will continue to suffer through disease, accidents, and natural disasters, but we do not regard these as evil actions for they are due to natural conditions. For instance, wild animals will attack because that is their nature.

It might be said that not only tigers, but people also attack because of their nature. This is certainly true and from this arises the label, "evil person." But not everybody has such a nature, so we must look to the particular individual concerned for an explanation. Baba has said there are no "evil" persons, but there are evil actions. So the question will need to be, does the person do evil actions because of an evil nature, or is he said to have an evil nature because he does evil actions? If the latter is the case, there can be change, and Baba's remark indicates the latter case is the correct one. In this context, if a person can see why he, himself, does an evil action, then the entire field will be illumined. An action is regarded as being evil if the motive is evil. For instance, one person tortures his victim to satisfy hatred, or in revenge, or to enjoy the suffering of the other. Baba says that such evil action comes from the ego, the "ego" being the feeling: "I am that entity which is born, fears, enjoys, suffers, and dies."

If one alertly watches himself in action, he can observe that a bad or evil action takes place in the light of one's ideas and concepts about himself and about other people. These erroneous ideas and concepts constitute the "veil" of ignorance which hides one's *true* nature, which Baba says is Divinity Itself. If a person is willing to calmly consider Baba's teachings, which he explains in his discourses and which are reviewed in some detail in the pages of this book, he will find that wrong notions, which one has held for all of his or her life, will fall away and one will cease to do bad actions — there will no longer be a base for evil actions. This direct experience will give one the direct knowledge of how evil comes into life and how evil may be overcome. If we clearly see this in ourselves, we will be able to give a true explanation to others when they bring up the question, "How can there be evil in God's world?"

A person who has realized God as the Reality of his or her life is no longer under the illusion that the body is his or her true self. Such a person has realized that God, the inner Self, is the Source of happiness and he no longer mistakes the body and its actions as the source of happiness. Such a person is no longer ignorant about the role of the body and no longer gives authority to body desires. Being no longer ignorant about this vital point, such a person no longer engages in sinful actions. The possibility that every individual in the world could be at the point of wisdom at one and the same time is improbable; for if Sri Ramakrishna's statement is correct, God's play would then be over and there would no longer be the drama of human life. Even at a mundane level, a universal change would be unlikely, for "every fruit on the tree does not ripen at the same moment." But if one is able to see in himself the basis for evil actions, he will know how evil comes to be.

It is oneself, the aspect of God manifest as a human person, who does evil because of the veiling power of ignorance. It hides one's true nature, just as a small transient cloud hides the blazing sun. A slight wind will blow away the cloud hiding the sun, and the practice of the divine teachings of Baba will disperse the ignorance hiding the truth from oneself. That accomplished, no more evil will come into the world from oneself.

About evil in God's world, one must be very careful. Baba tells us there is God only. Accepting this, we will, for instance, realize that God is manifesting Himself as the tiger according to tiger tendencies. Likewise, the human body manifests God according to its tendencies. The tiger cannot transcend its tiger-tendencies, but the human being, Baba assures us, can transcend his or her tendencies. Baba advises, "Do not think that you are human and that you have to reach the state of the Divine. Think rather that you are God, and from that state you have become a human being. As you think this way, all the attributes of God will manifest in you. Know that you have descended from God as human beings and that eventually you will go back to your source."

Caution has to be used in worldly matters, and we have to treat the beings who populate this world according to their status and their actions. It would not be good sense, for instance, to go up to a wild tiger and give it a hug! From tiger-God it is best to keep a distance. Likewise, with human persons, whose status of wisdom we do not know, we must be alert and watchful. Baba says, "Let hearts be together, but keep bodies separate."

Even though we work our way through the puzzle as to how evil actions may come about, although all is God, and even though we understand that effects are brought about by causes, yet our understanding may be shaken by the impact of large-scale sufferings, such as genocides and famines which cannot be alleviated promptly because political considerations dictate to the contrary. Here, we feel, suffering is so vast in its extent and depth that surely God's love for His human family will move Him to intervene. To secure an answer here, it would be best to question Baba directly, and this was done by Sri R. J. Karanjia, the senior editor of *Blitz Publications*, Bombay. Sri Karanjia asks the questions and Baba answers:

Q: The critics of Swamiji ask why Sai Baba does not help people in distress by bringing rains in times of drought or creating food where there is famine by means of his Sankalpa Shakti. Cannot an Avathar help humanity to control the natural forces and prevent calamities like earthquakes, floods, droughts, famine, and epidemics?

BABA: This is precisely what I am doing by incarnating the indwelling God in man to overcome such calamities. There are two ways in which an Avathar can help people: an instant solution as against a long-term one.

Any instant solution would go against the fundamental quality of nature itself as well as the Karmic law of cause and effect. Most people live in the material world of their desires and egos which is governed by this law. They reap the fruits of their actions. This brings about their evolution or devolution. If the Avathar intervenes to instantly solve their problems, it would stop all action, development, even evolution. This solution can be ruled out because it totally negates the natural laws.

The other and more effective alternative presents a long-term solution whereby the Avathar leads the people themselves to a higher level of consciousness to enable them to understand the truth of spiritual laws so that they may turn towards righteousness and steadfastly work for better conditions. This will relate them back to

Nature and the Karmic law of causation. They would then transcend the cycle of cause and effect, in which today they are involved as victims, and thereby command and control the natural forces to be able to avert the calamities you mention.

Q: You mean that you are presently raising the consciousness of mankind to a Godlike condition to enable them to command their own destiny?

BABA: Exactly. They would become shareholders of my Sankalpa Shakti (divine power, universal energy). I have to work through them, rouse the indwelling God in them, and evolve them to a higher Reality in order to enable them to master the natural laws and forces. If I cure everything instantly leaving the people at their present level of consciousness, they would soon mess up things and be at one another's throats again, with the result that the same chaotic situation would develop in the world.

Suffering and misery are the inescapable acts of the Cosmic drama. God does not decree these calamities, but man invites them by way of retribution for his own evil deeds. This is corrective punishment which induces mankind to give up the wrong path and return to the right path so that he may experience the Godlike condition of Sat-Chit-Ananda — that is, an existence of Wisdom and Bliss. All this is part of the grand synthesis in which the negatives serve to glorify the positives. Thus death glorifies immortality, ignorance glorifies wisdom, misery glorifies bliss, night glorifies dawn.

So, finally, if the Avathar brings the calamities mentioned by you to an immediate end, which I can, and do, when there is a great need, the whole drama of creation with its Karmic (universal inescapable duty) law will collapse. Remember these calamities occur not because of what God has made of man but really because of what man has made of man. Therefore, man has be *unmade* and *remade* with his ego destroyed and replaced by a transcendent consciousness, so that he may rise above the Karmic to command.

Q: So your objective can be summed up as a brotherhood of humanity to be achieved through the doctrine of love?

BABA: Yes, what else can save the world from thermonuclear fires? Everything points to the terror of that conflagration coming; and my mission is to pre-empt the fires by reestablishing Dharma and the spiritual law of one God, one Religion, one Language embracing one Humanity.

I preach only one religion of love for all, which alone can integrate the human race into a brotherhood of man under the fatherhood of God. I know only one language — of the heart — beyond the mind or intellect relating man to man and mankind to God, thereby creating mutual understanding, cooperation, and community life in peace and harmony. On this basis I want to build one humanity without any religious, caste, or other barriers in a universal empire of love which could enable my devotees to feel the whole world as their own family.

Q: Well said, Baba — but wouldn't this dharma with its Hindu orientation conflict with the established religions?

BABA: No, it will not do anything of the kind because my objective is the establishment of Sanathana Dharma which believes in one God as propitiated by the founders of all religions. So none has to give up his religion or deity, but through them worship the one God in all. I have come not to disturb or destroy but to confirm and vindicate everyone in his own faith.

Q: But how will that prevent a nuclear holocaust?

BABA: By removing all causes, sources, barriers,and provocations of class, caste, creed, colour, and race, and replacing the existing hate and violence with love and nonviolence. I expect to provide humanity with an evangel of peaceful cooperation to replace the present escalation to death by co-destruction.

R. K. Karanjia: Thank you, Swamiji. I am all the more grateful to You because I really did not expect You to answer the whole long list of my questions.

In the course of his discussion with Sri Karanjia, Baba informed us that although His hand may not be visible, the Divine does intervene at certain times in the affairs of men and, further, the Divine also intervenes before the event to keep mankind from totally destroying man and other life forms as well. Baba further pointed out that if the Divine were to bring all suffering and inequality to an immediate halt, the same conditions would quickly arise again, and that a permanent change can take place only when mankind raises its consciousness to a higher level than is now the case.

The child has its tongue and the mother has hers. The mother keeps the child on her lap and pronounces the words so that the child may learn to speak. However busy the mother's tongue may be, the child has to speak through its own tongue. The mother cannot speak for the child and save herself all the bother! The Guru, too, is like that. He can only repeat, remind, inspire, instruct, persuade, plead; the activity, the disciple must himself initiate. He must jump over the stile himself. No one can hoist him over it!

— Sathya Sai Baba

Sadhana, Our Spiritual Practice

Baba tells us, "In all the universe there is no other planet that has human life or a similar life form. All life may aspire to human birth, but only through human birth may God be realized. Here and now is the opportunity to realize the absolute goal of life."

If, for reasons known only to Baba we have turned in faith to him, and if we are determined to put aside untruth, come what may, what are we waiting for? This is where most of us find ourselves. We are told that we are the Divine; but as we do not, without hesitation or delay, realize ourselves as the Divine, then what to do?

The "What to do?," the path to God-Realization, is called "Spiritual Practice." In India, it is named, "Sadhana."

God is Truth, and we aim to know Him as the Truth. In order to know truth, we must stop believing untruth. If every untruth is put aside, if everything which is subject to modification and therefore not eternal is rejected, then if anything remains, we can at that time ask ourselves if the goal stands revealed. That which never changes, which is the same tomorrow and forever, can be believed. It can be relied upon, it can be loved and trusted without fear of betrayal, it can be extolled without end; it is the ever-constant firm foundation and is thereby named Truth.

Baba tells us that God is that Truth, that He is real, omnipresent. He is the One named in all faiths and religions, and we ourselves are no other than He. Thus, by the declaration of the all-wise, all-knowing Baba, we may know that our Self is the goal of our spiritual practice, and that the pathway to God-Realization is the pathway from ourselves to our Self. The pathway is within this "fathom-long frame," it is not a pathway to be found in the outside world.

Who is to point out this inner pathway to truth? Who is to guide us, who will be a true "Guru" to us? To these questions, Baba answers, "Today there is only one true Guru, and he is God. Call upon God." If our call is loving and sincere, He cannot withstand our call. It is said that there is one who is more powerful than God, Himself, and that one is His true devotee. God cannot withhold His Grace from His true devotee. Let us take even one step towards Him, He will take many steps towards us. Baba tells us this, and we may believe him. We may start our spiritual practice with full confidence, without worry or fears, but with joy and enthusiasm.

God is Love, and divine love is forever. Hatred, anger, lust, envy, and their brood are ego interests and are not forever. If we aim to put aside that which may exist for the time being, but which is transient in nature and therefore cannot be relied upon, how do we proceed? The most direct answer, one which comes from Sri Sathya Sai as well as from Krishna, the Avathar of the last Age, is to love God with all one's heart. Surrender every action to Him, the inner Charioteer of our lives. Keep the thought of Him present in the mind always, and be carefree and happy. The Lord will take care of us, and in due course, when our minds and hearts are purified, He, the Lord, will bestow wisdom upon us and will bring an end to the age-old round of birth, death, and rebirth with its accompanying misery. Were the spiritual practice impossible for us, the teaching would not be given.

When God is the beloved of our heart, we will always be thinking of Him. If we love beauty, God is the archetype of all beauty; He is the most beautiful of the beautiful. If we love to be loved, then God's love for us is sweet beyond measure. If we love truth, then God is the very foundation of truth and wisdom.

The question may arise, "Where is God?" The answer is that He will graciously take up residence wherever we think Him to be.

For some great devotees, the question is, "Where is God not?"
Wherever they look, God is there. Draupadi was once in great peril
and she urgently called upon the Lord to save her. He did so, but
not until after some delay. She reproached him, "Lord, I called
you, why did you take so long?" Krishna in turn asked, "Where
did you look? From where did you call me?" She answered, "I
called you from your residence in your capital city." Krishna answered, "Oh, that is the reason! I had to come from there to here.
Had you called me from your heart, where I am always, I could
have saved you without this delay!"

Baba assures us that God is indeed that close to us. He is
always in our hearts and is always our true Beloved, even if we deny
Him and even though we may be allowing ourselves to be fascinated
with the transient objects and persons of the world outside us.

For ourselves, we may find one spiritual practice to be more
attractive than another. For this reason, Baba says, "Do not condemn the many gurus. I am in each one." That is, if we turn to
God in any form, He will respond according to our ability to
receive. At one time, early in our search for truth, in our Sadhana,
we might adopt a spiritual practice which later would be a quite
inadequate, or even quite wrong. For those devotees of God who
turn to Him as Sri Sathya Sai, the Avathar of the Age, Baba
teaches a number of ancient spiritual practices, any one of which
we may adopt according to its appeal to us, and any one of which
will safely carry us to the infinite subtlety of the Lord, who is the
final Truth, resident everywhere. If we turn to Baba and pray to
him, he will most graciously be our guru and he will guide us and
protect us.

Wonderful spiritual practices are revealed to us by the divine
Baba. We may adopt one only, or several combined, according to
our delight, and with total safety. Their practice will be our Sadhana. Each of these marvelous and beautiful ways of Sadhana is as
practical today as it was in the most ancient of times. Each will
safely take us on the inner path to the realization of Divinity. And,
each is a path of happiness, for our guru will be the beloved of our
heart, our divine Baba. These wonderful and enlightening spiritual
practices are described in this book.

The Divine Name

What Baba says about removing illusion from mind and heart may surprise us, because it sounds so simple, and yet it is said to be totally effective. Sri Sathya Sai, at 14 years of age, told family members that his life in the family was ended, and that he would now fully engage himself in the work for which he had come. In his first discourse he declared, "O ye seekers! Worship the feet of the Guru with all your mind; you can thus cross the ocean of grief and joy and birth and death." The meaning is that if we adopt the practice of repeating, with love, that name of God which is most dear to us, and simultaneously visualize, with love, the particular form bearing that divine name, this practice alone is sufficient to clear our minds and hearts of impurities, and thereby we will fully realize the truth of our inner selves.

This practice of repeating the divine name gives joy at the start; joy continues with the practice, and the culmination is Liberation — God-Realization. The practice is simple, needs no explanation, and Baba tells us that its effect is sure. However, our minds are accustomed to explanations and this explanation is given. The significance of the divine name, which is a spiritual practice, is that we thereby keep ourselves in the divine presence of the Lord, and in His immediate presence nothing which is evil can survive. Tendencies, which spring up from delusion and desire, have their growth and sustenance in ignorance and cannot survive and grow in the pure light of Divinity. Bad tendencies are likened to a ferocious all-consuming fire which dies down without struggle when fuel is no longer fed to it.

In order for the practice of the repetition of the divine name to have its effect, it must be started and then continued. To illustrate the need to start and to continue, Baba tells the following story: At dusk, a traveler came to a large forest which he needed to cross through without delay. With him, he had only a small lantern whose light did not extend beyond a 3-foot radius. Yet the forest was dense, dark, and threatening with unknown dangers. Intimidated, the traveler sat down at the base of a tree and began to weep. Soon, a party of travelers came from the depth of the forest and, seeing the man weeping, stopped and asked about his trouble. After hearing him, they said, "But Sir, a lantern which throws light even two feet ahead is sufficient to pass through this dark forest. But you must rise, carry your light, and walk forward." The forest is the dark, unknown course of our life, and the lantern is the little, small name of God. But by taking that little name and walking forward with it, we will safely pass through the forest of life.

Baba tells us that name and form are not separate, that when God is given form, the form is accompanied by His name. And, conversely, where His name is said, the name is accompanied by His form. Name and form together are God manifest in the full light, glory, and power of Divinity. Thus, by repeating His name with love; God, who is love, responds. He is called and He comes to us, happy and loving, and willing to walk with us and be our divine companion. In addition to the repetition of His name, by also visualizing the accompanying form, which we love, we give added scope for an outpouring of devotion to our supreme Lord.

God is pure light. He has been held to be so throughout the ages. We, living our days in that pure divine light, will not be able to hold on to our bad tendencies even if we wanted to do so. Bad tendencies are as flowers which grow in the darkness — they cannot survive in the pure light of the Lord; they will diminish and disappear. Our good tendencies give us no trouble, for in the presence of the Lord, they will not develop into a big ego.

Along with our tendencies, the ego, which is constructed of

our tendencies, will also finally humble itself at the feet of the Lord. Heart, then totally purified, is fit to realize its truth, its inherent unity with God. It will seem extraordinary to our complicated minds that such a *simple practice* will purify our life and make heart and mind fit for enlightenment, make us fit for release from the entangling web of opposites, of likes and dislikes, and make us fit to fully be the eternal undifferentiated Divinity. Baba declares this to be the power inherent in the spiritual practice of the divine name.

Repetition of the divine name with visualization of the divine form was known in the early days of the Christian era. Baba has said that Jesus advised his devotees to adopt the practice. Some years after the death of Jesus, Christian mystics were told by their preceptors, "Collect your mind, constrain it to enter the heart with the breath and keep it there, but do not leave it idle, instead give it to the prayer, 'Lord Jesus Christ, Son of God, have mercy upon me.'" Thereafter, the mystic, whether in the monastery or wandering throughout the land, would constantly visualize the form of Jesus and repeat the name, suffusing it with his love for Jesus.

The supreme value of the divine name was known also to the disciples of Muhammad. When questioned by a devotee, "What if the heart is blind?" Muhammad replied, "For everything there is a polish that taketh away rust, and the polish of the heart is remembrance of God."

For some of us, the practice of the repetition of the divine name may seem a bit dry at first. But that is inevitable if the heart itself is a bit dry. Pay no attention to this. Continue the practice and very soon love will accompany the sacred name.

There may be a doubt, "How can I be repeating the name and visualizing the form when I am engaged in some task? It would be inattention to my work, and that would not be good." To explain this point, Baba tells the following story. A certain king had a heavy burden of state and was unable to find a competent minister. He turned to God in prayer. God appeared and asked, "What do you want?" The King explained that he was in dire need of a good servant, for his kingdom was getting out of hand. God then granted the King's wish, but warned him, "The servant will be efficient, but if you fail to keep him busy, he will turn upon you and destroy you." The King gave no weight to this. However, the servant had boundless energy and intelligence, and one day the King realized with a shock that the work was almost completed. He then remembered God's warning, and in panic again turned to God in prayer. God appeared and said, "Well, what is it you want now?" The King explained, and God in His mercy advised him, "I will save you. Do this: Instruct the servant to build a wall twenty feet high. Then, when he has no task to accomplish, have him climb up and down that wall until you have another task for him."

The servant is the mind. The wall is the name of God. When the mind is idle, put it to work repeating the sacred name of God; for if left idle the mind will surely destroy us. When we must do work, we address Baba and say, "Lord, I dedicate this work to you." Then, we go ahead giving full attention to the work. Baba assures us that work in his name is tantamount to repeating the name. When the work is done, then return the mind at once to the repetition of the sacred name.

A question may arise: which name and form of God to use? Since God is held to be one and indivisible, although diverse in name and form in the minds of people, He is fully manifest in any name and form which we attribute to Him. Baba's suggestion is, "Take the name and form of God which is most dear to you." If at present the devotee does not cherish any of the historical names and forms of the Divine, the name and form of Baba may be chosen. In this case, the name used may be "Om Sai Ram" or "Om Sri Sai Ram."

Whatever name of the Divine is chosen, Baba suggests that the form to accompany that name be deliberately created. The name of Jesus, for instance, is best accompanied by the mind making its own form of Jesus rather than picturing a form taken from a painting of Jesus or a statue. *Baba tells us that when the mind creates God's form, then the mind itself becomes that form, and God Himself will fill that form of Himself with His Divinity.*

Baba informs us that this age, which is named Kali Yuga, is considered to be low and gross, but that, in fact, it is the best of all ages for the devotees of God. We have Baba's assurance that in this Kali Yuga any person who gathers his or her will and energy into a one-pointed attention to the divine name and form can thereby penetrate the veiling of the Divine and gain Release, Liberation, and the realization of his or her ultimate truth.

Meditation

Meditation, as a practice having to do with the inner world of a person, is now familiar to millions of people in the West. Baba defines meditation in this way, "Correct meditation is the merging of all thoughts and feelings in God. Persons adept in this meditation are very rare — most people go through the external exercises only. So they are unable to win Grace."

People usually speak of meditation in terms of a place for meditation, how to sit, what to do, and for how long. This is only the beginning. The fruition of meditation is what is called "Sahaja Vastha"— all actions originating from the consciousness of God rather than from the mind of the individual.

Sitting meditation is the beginning only. Baba tells us that alertness and watchfulness of our inner drama should be the all-day discipline of the person who is determined to live a spiritual life.

Meditation represents the construction of a boat, so to speak, which will be able to carry us safely across the turbulent sea of the experience of our lives to the other shore. The "other shore" is Self-Realization, God-Realization, Liberation, Release, Enlightenment, Nirvana — all such words have the same meaning. They mean the merging of the particular into the Absolute.

It is quite important to have in one's mind that meditation

means the *merging of the particular into the Absolute*. Baba states, "When existence is Absolute, it is all right. When it is particularized it is wrong. That is the whole truth."

Merging into the Absolute means clearing away the veil of ignorance which is the delusion of the dual existence of the differentiated particular versus the One Absolute. Thus, the practice of meditation is not really practice for a new achievement, even though it involves action with a particular end in view.

This *merging* of the apparent and describable particular into the invisible and indescribable Absolute could never take place unless the particular was essentially the same as the Absolute. For instance, a ring made of pure gold can be thrown into a melting pot with an idol of pure gold and they will merge because the different forms and functions of the ring and the idol are finally irrelevant, for the two are actually one and the same pure gold. Baba says that the particularized individual and the ultimate Absolute, the Lord, differ only in name, form, and function. Otherwise there could be no merging, and meditation would not be a viable concept.

The *merging* of the particular and the Absolute — the individual with God — can be done, and from ages past into the present day, its reality and its value have been demonstrated in the lives of great saints. The Absolute, manifest in the particular, is witnessed in the life of the Avathar. In him, the twin facets of the particularized individual and the divine Absolute are united, and this is witnessed by all persons who may be privileged to approach the blessed Avathar, Sri Sathya Sai Baba.

With the above mentioned considerations in mind, it will be evident that the word, "meditation," includes any means whose end will be the disappearance of the delusion that God and the essence of oneself and the essence of the world are in reality other than the same. The perfection of meditation is referred to as *Samadhi*.

What are the various true meditation techniques? A few are known, and no doubt there are others being quietly practiced in the context of the various cultures and various religions and faiths. But this lifetime of ours is too brief to uncover, explore, and test the many excellent meditation techniques before choosing one and adopting it for our own practice. Our available years merge into each other with shocking velocity. Thus, it is only good common sense to concentrate our attention and limited time on the meditation advice of he whom we regard as the Supreme Guru, the supreme knower, our beloved Sathya Sai.

Baba advises that the supreme meditation is devotion to God and direct union with Him through love. The love in us and the love that He is, are one and the same, regardless of the form love presently takes in our life and regardless of the function to which we presently apply that love. This way of rending the veil of delusion is fully dealt with in other pages of this book. But suffice it for the moment to say that this way of merging the particular into the Absolute does not mitigate the value of traditional meditation techniques.

Baba tells us how to do the best of all sitting meditations, and also gives us a very firm, even a harsh warning of some dangers.

First the warning. Throughout the ages, many ways to meditate have become known and have been practiced. No doubt each was successful in its day and no doubt an endless succession of human beings have used those meditations and have managed to become free of delusion and illusion. But "in its day" is the important phrase. "In its day" essentially means the availability of a living guru knowing fully the particular meditation, himself fully Self-Realized through that meditation, and thus fully competent to safely guide any of a great variety of individuals to the fruition of that meditation. Baba does not condemn any of the ancient meditations, including those which have persisted in the knowledge of people to this very day. He does not say that these meditations are bad or wrong. But what he most emphatically does say is that today not even one of these ancient and potent meditations has a living guru fully competent to guide its practitioners. The guides are not Self-Realized in the meditations they teach; they do not know the meditation fully in its every aspect.

A few practitioners of meditation may be calm people of good common sense and no difficult tendencies, and these few may be able to practice any meditation and stay out of trouble for the time being. But in meditations full of power and unknown potentials, the meditators are moving along a very tight and narrow path, so to speak. To lose balance in meditation and fall away has disasterous consequences in the life of that particular individual. Baba comments, "You have only a few years of life remaining. Why take these risks?" His advice about spiritual life is, "Start early, drive carefully, arrive safely."

For people who are determined to stay with meditations already in practice, it would be good to dedicate that action to Baba and pray for his guidance and protection. We have that right, and if Baba is approached with love and faith, Grace will not be withheld.

Baba tells us that in this day and age God is the only genuine and safe Guide. He says that in this day and age there is only one good and safe sitting meditation; and that is the ancient meditation upon light. It is called "Jyoti Meditation." It is safe, effective, its practice will be successful, and Baba tells us that he himself will be our inner guide in the meditation, if we will but call on him.

To begin the Jyoti meditation, one first prays to the Lord to accept and guide the meditation. One should sit in a comfortable position, with spine straight, and gaze steadily through partially closed eyes at the flame of a candle. Continue until the breath is calm and slow. Continue until the flame of the candle (the Jyoti) is firmly visualized in the mind when the eyes are closed. Move this pure flame, which is now firmly visualized, to all parts of the body. Wherever impurity is touched by the Jyoti, the impurity vanishes, for it cannot survive in pure light. Now move the light away from the body; first to family members, then to friends, acquaintances, enemies, and finally let its benignant quality bless the entire universe. Bring the Jyoti back to the body and emplace it in the heart. Sit quietly for a few moments, offer a prayer of gratitude to the Lord, and then carry on with daily affairs.

A good practice, recommended by Baba, is to enshrine in the Jyoti that form of the Lord which is most dear to you. The first two steps of the Jyoti Meditation just described are named concentration and contemplation. They are preliminary and the only steps which can be guided by the mind.

Contemplation is moving the Jyoti from the particular to the universal. The Jyoti is moved away from the particularity of the body to others, both near and far. The limitation of one's body falls away from consideration, and one's attention expands without limit until it encompasses the entire cosmos. In his meditation, the great Swami Vivekananda was heard to exclaim, "Where is my body? I cannot find my body." Such was the expansion of his previously limited self.

To start the meditation by gathering one's normally fragmented attention into one unitary concentration, an object of concentration is needed to serve as a focus for the mind's concentration.

This first step is a common factor to meditation techniques. In Buddhism, for example, more than 40 acceptable objects of concentration are named and described. Baba informs us that the Jyoti is the best object of concentration.

The third and final step in the meditation practice occurs when the particular is lost in the Universal, the individual self-identification falls away, and only God *is*. This third stage of the meditation practice is above the senses and the mind and cannot be reached through the mind's volition. It comes only through the Grace of the Divine. With the practice, mind and heart become purified; mind is not wandering from thought to thought and desire to desire, but is alert and concentrated. Then, in a flash, the time is ripe; the meditator, the meditation, and the object of concentration vanish and God alone *is*. Only this final stage is called Meditation. After a time, the habitual mind re-identifies itself and the meditation is ended.

Baba tells us there are some circumstances which are helpful to a smooth start to the daily sitting meditation. The early morning hours from 3 a.m. are good, for all is still and quiet then; but these hours are not possible for everyone, and they are not essential to meditation. One should not sit directly on the ground, but should arrange for some insulation of the body from currents which naturally move in the earth. It is well to be in a room where there are not extremes of temperature, and a light woolen shawl is convenient for throwing around the shoulders. The meditation should be at the same time and place each day. Swami jokingly says that it is more convenient for God if He knows the time and place of the appointment. If away in travel, continue the meditation at the same hour and, in imagination, feel that you are seated in the accustomed place. As for length of time allocated to the meditation practice, there is no set time, but twenty minutes to half an hour would be appropriate for beginners.

From ages past, spiritual aspirants have been advised to adopt the practice of meditation. Baba comments, "The mind is prone to gather experiences and store them in memory. It does not know the art of giving up. Nothing is cast away by the mind. It does not have even a short interval between one thought and the next. And in the continuous succession of thoughts there is no order or relationship. Meditation is the name for a period of rest we provide for the busy and wayward mind."

Our Pure Mind

The word "mind" and its adjective "pure" are verbal symbols which represent something of a certain quality, but neither of the two refer to anything which can be measured and thus given a standard definition to which everyone could turn. When we talk about a pure mind, we are speaking of that which is subjective, and we cannot be sure that we all attach the same meaning to those words. Yet, something real is meant.

How can we agree as to what is meant by a pure mind? Our options are not many. We can study what great seers and sages say. We could get a number of opinions from a variety of people and try to arrive at a common denominator. Or, we can make the assumption that really we know what we are talking about when we refer to a pure mind, even though it is subjective and not measured or precise.

Would we agree that an agitated mind is not what is meant by a pure mind? I believe we would agree. Suppose there is a mind of which we become aware because of a flow of clear, precise, logical thinking. We might admire such a mind, but I doubt if that is what we mean by a pure mind. How about the quality of thoughts as a determinant of a pure mind? That some thoughts are impure almost everyone would agree. But not all thoughts are impure.

111

There are loving thoughts about some of our co-inhabitants of planet Earth, there are sensible and more or less neutral thoughts about many topics, and there are devotional thoughts about sacred matters. But all thoughts are born from some concern or other which might or might not be totally pure; they persist for a few moments and then they die. We might call certain thoughts wonderful and pure at their birth; but in their death there is disintegration and its by-products, one of which would be that the pattern of the mind has been influenced and modified by the thought to some minute degree. By the term "a pure mind" I doubt if we mean a mind that is pure in part or for a certain time only.

When we say "a pure mind" surely we do mean a mind that is pure in itself and not pure because of something else. We call the sun pure light because it *is* light in itself. Would we not mean it in that way when we speak of a pure mind? For the moment, at least, it seems to be that when we use the words a pure mind, we do not mean pure because of any particular kind of thoughts. It appears that we may mean a mind that is pure because *it has no thoughts at all.*

A mind without thoughts! What is a mind like which is without subtle thoughts or gross thoughts or any kind of thought? From time to time we experience that state of mind. To many people, perhaps to all people, there comes a moment or so, now and then, when thoughts slow down almost to nothing or stop entirely. People say that in those moments they feel peaceful and happy. When there are no thoughts, one is in a peaceful state, and that peace is felt as happiness. But thought-free peaceful moments do not last very long with most of us. A multitude of concerns are waiting to disturb us. Quickly there are thoughts again in the mind. So when we say "a pure mind" it is doubtful that we mean a mind which cannot but think about concerns. And there are certainly innumerable very urgent concerns every day which we cannot reasonably ignore.

When we thus inquire into what is meant when we speak of a pure mind, we appear to have a dilemma, for a mind which accommodates thought cannot be considered "pure." Yet, inevitably, concerns do arise in daily life, thought is provoked, and the mind becomes agitated. At this point it might appear that "pure" and "mind" may not fit together. Purity itself is real to us, for we know that a little child or a superior person can be "pure at heart," "pure of motive" and so on. And, mind itself is real to us, for we note that what we call mind in ourselves is seen to be operative in other people also. Could it be that because mind is vulnerable to thought we will need to compromise our topic and speak of "our more or less pure mind?"

Perhaps so, but there are still possibilities to be explored. Could the mind be eliminated? Could we live as an intelligent flexible human being without a mind? Or, is there a mind whose silence is so firm and strong that no concern could ever break into that silence; and, without thought, how could there be even that minimum action which is necessary to preserve life?

I believe we would admit that our knowledge is not so complete that we can always and immediately give correct answers, especially about something as intangible as the mind. I believe most of us would have to admit that some aspects of our life are not yet totally clear to us. Many of us, perhaps most of us, could not say for sure that the mind can or cannot be eliminated, that we could or could not live effectively without a mind, or that there could or could not be a mind which is pure — a mind which is firmly and forever silent. Those areas of knowledge are not within our present experience, and to try to reach conclusions without first having some experience would be speculation only and not valid reasoning. What we need is to experience further, then draw some reasonable conclusions.

At this point in the inquiry, as to what we mean by "a pure mind," we find ourself in a dilemma because of limited experience. It would be good to turn to Sri Sathya Sai for information about the mind and for advice as to how we may have a direct and deep experience which would allow us to break out of our dilemma. Those of us who have listened to Sai, and talked with him, know that he is immensely wise and that no person has been able to frame a question to which Sai cannot give an immediate and correct answer.

Sri Sathya Sai provides us with information about the mind which we would be hard put to find elsewhere. He tells us that purity, wherever it may be, is divine love not particularized by notions of self. From notions of self there arises the concept of "yours" and "mine." From the feeling of "mine," desire and love for the objects of desire arise, concerned thoughts are then formulated, and this flux of desire and thought is referred to as "our mind." Baba tells us that when desire for objects and the pleasurable stimulation of experience is eliminated, thought subsides. He tells us that true, pure, and direct communication from one person to another is through silence, not through a mind agitated by limited thoughts which are then set forth in limited words. To explain this, the example of the sage, Dakshinamurti, is cited. Through silence, Dakshinamurti conveyed the absolute pure and perfect knowledge of liberation to his disciples. In the disciples there was direct seeing; just as when we see a mountain, we know that a mountain is seen without having to resort to thought and reason.

However, it cannot be denied that mind, or at least the potential of mind, does indeed exist. Sai himself says that a pure mind is an aspect of Divinity and is, therefore, in itself, divine love and divinely peaceful. When notions of self and the concerns of desire fall away, mind is none other than the Divine Itself. To speculate, then, that a mind which is pure and which is not agitated by patterns of thought cannot thereby meet the challenges of daily life,would be to say that the all-powerful Divinity cannot effect His will. Such a viewpoint would not be tenable, since neither the reality of our being nor the immeasurable energy and activity of the universe are dependent upon the agitated and transient flux of thought and desire which we call "our mind."

If we were willing to concede the possibility that Divinity might not be foiled, so to speak, by the non-existence of that flux of desire and thought which we believe to be our mind, we might then ask Sai to advise us how we might quiet our mental agitation.

It must be quite evident to us that if our life continues as it is now, our mind will continue as it is now. Baba confirms that this is indeed true; a pure mind represents a fundamental transformation. For our life to reach its inherent destiny, as a flower blooms in due course or as a fruit ripens in season, our notion of limited self must surrender to the inherent divinity of the pure mind. Baba likens the situation to the well-known parlour game of musical chairs. In this particular version of the game, our ego (our notion of self) must vacate his (or her) throne in our mind so that the Divine may in turn occupy the chair. When occupied by the ego, the mind is a flux of desire and thought, but when the Divine occupies the "chair" the mind is pure and quiet.

According to Sai, when the mind is transmuted from thought and desire to Divinity, our speech and action become the direct unhindered expression of the divine will. All actions then originate from the consciousness of God rather than from the individual mind. To illustrate this, Sai tells the story of King Janaka's surrender of his mind, speech, and action to the Divine in the form of the youthful sage, Astavakra. King Janaka asked the sage for that which would bestow liberation. Astavakra replied that in return he would require something of supreme value. King Janaka declared that he was an honorable man, that his word was his seal, and that without even a moment's hesitation he would give whatever was asked. Sage Astavakra then said, "O King, give me your mind, your speech, and your action." The King replied, "Lord, I give you my mind, speech, and action," and fell silent. Astavakra instructed the king, "Sit here on the ground." Then he walked away into the forest. The king's courtiers, unable to get any response when they spoke to the king, brought the queens from their palaces, but not even they could elicit one word from the seated king. The courtiers, now fully alarmed, spread out through the surrounding forest until Astavakra was found. "O Sage," they protested, "You have cast a spell upon our king!" "Not so," replied Astavakra, "Let us return." King Janaka was still seated on the ground, surrounded by the distraught queens. Astavakra said to him, "Arise." When Janaka had done so, Astavakra said, "Speak to the ladies who are now here with you." King Janaka did so. He and his attendants then returned to his city, and for many years thereafter, Janaka, bereft of any sense of self, ruled his kingdom; the Divine Consciousness being expressed through him.

Thus, Sai tells us that a pure mind is a mind that is surrendered to God and bereft of all notions of self. The transformation necessary to acquire a pure mind is no less than "Die man! Be now God!" This transformation from a busy agitated human mind to the purity of a divine mind is said by Sai to represent a quantum jump, not an incremental progress.

Sri Sathya Sai's information is wonderful indeed, but we are inquiring about ourselves as we now find ourselves, and we need more than thrilling and enlightening words. We very much need direct personal experience in this field of the pure mind, so that we may shift our awareness from a theoretical base to a vital and alive experiential base. If this could be accomplished, it would seem that our vitality could be gathered into intense, one-pointed attention to the subjective depths of ourselves. Into that poised alertness there might flash the realization of ourselves as the divine, pure, silent mind. "Purity is Enlightenment" declares Sai.

It would be good to, once again, turn to Sai and ask how we might gain a direct, initial experience in this field of the pure mind. To the writer, at least, it is evident that Sri Sathya Sai has already pointed a way whereby we may gain an initial experience which will, in turn, make the field of the pure mind real to us. The way was revealed by Sai when he said, "Who are you? Sorrows will never cease until you know the answer to this question." Sai placed within our hands a light which we may use without depending on anyone whosoever in this world or in its heavens, a light which can quickly reveal the fact of a pure, silent, mind which *knows* directly without the movement of thought, or notions of self. We need only turn to the feeling of self, of which we are ever aware, concentrate our full vigilant attention there, not in a hard way, but softly. Most surely there will follow that initial experience which we need, and thereafter our life will never again be the same.

Surrender to the Lord

Baba tells his devotees that he is the actual resident of each heart, and if called upon, he is quite willing to guide our life to its glorious fulfillment. A glorious fulfillment of life is certainly what each person wants. We want, and Baba is willing. Why then does not everything immediately fit together?

If the matter were as simple as it seems to be at first glance, we would be in a happy state. That it is not so easy to grasp, is demonstrated by the endless discussions and questions about the topic of surrender to the Divine which arise whenever devotees get together at Sai Retreats and round table discussions. If Baba is to take over responsibility for the course of our lives, we obviously need to surrender our lives to him and let him be the charioteer. About this, the God-Realized saint, Sri Ramakrishna said, "For a devotee, there is no path safer and smoother than that of the 'Power of Attorney.' This means resigning the self to the will of the Almighty, to have no consciousness that anything is 'mine.' If one acquires the conviction that everything is done by God's Will, then one becomes an instrument in the hands of the Lord, and one is free even in this life. He who can resign himself to the will of the Almighty with simple faith and guileless love realizes God very quickly."

117

The question then is, *how* can we surrender our life to Baba, and what actually is surrender, what does it mean?

Baba himself asks, "You say you surrender to me. How will you surrender that which is not yours and which you cannot even control?"

In various ways of saying it, in various conversations, Baba points out that the body and its senses do not obey us, that emotions surge up and down despite us, that we cannot even keep the mind still for it jumps here and there like a monkey. We command memory and intelligence to be sharp and acute but even they fail us quite often. These faculties which we normally regard as "I," do not seem to be "I," so the term, "I" surrender "myself" cannot be applied to them. By this, Baba does not say that we are unable to surrender our lives to the Divine, he is saying that we need to go beyond our initial impulse and earnestly enquire about "self" and about "surrender." The meaning of the words "surrender to the Divine" is given by the God-Realized saint, Sri Ramana Maharshi who speaks from direct knowledge. "Surrender is the same as self-control. The ego submits only when it recognizes the higher power. Such recognition is surrender. Let us not pose as the doers, but resign ourselves to the guiding power." Sri Ramana Maharshi is saying there is nothing to be surrendered: "recognition of the higher power" constitutes surrender to the Lord. But recognition of the higher power is not an idea which can be woven into a plan of action. We can only know what is meant when that "recognition" actually occurs.

In our resolve to surrender our life to the guidance of the Lord, we learn that we are unable to give up those faculties which we thought to be major aspects of ourselves, and we are told by Sri Ramana Maharshi that "surrender" occurs only upon "recognition of the higher power." Everything seems to be pushed away from us into the future, into the future when we are wiser and have better understanding. These are some of the considerations which puzzle Sai devotees and which lead to much discussion when devotees meet together.

All the more or less routine doubts mentioned above, plus the many other doubts which may arise, can be quickly and permanently resolved. We can be brought back from concepts of future accomplishment to present action if we will only give earnest study to the divine teachings of the divine Baba. He tells us that only through love can we surrender to the Lord, and that is now — not in the future. At this very moment, without further thought about it, we can begin the surrender of our lives to the guidance of the Divine. There is no force, external to ourselves, to prevent our surrender to God. This very moment we can start our surrender to God by giving up our attachment to whatever is not us, and we can also give up our attachment to our own actions. At the actual moment of action, we can offer every action to God. We are free to, who is there to prevent us? Baba has said that he, that is, the Omnipresent Divine Wisdom and Divine Energy, will accept our actions and take their consequences upon himself. And, the many things we say "my" to — my anger, my envy, my unhappiness — the very moment such thoughts and impulses arise, we are free to turn to God, the Beloved of our heart, and say, "Take them O Lord, they are unwelcome, they are not mine, they do not belong to me, I am no longer attached to them." Baba once told the writer, "That is exactly right. Give them to me."

Then, there is the most vital element of all: that which *is* our true self can surrender to the Divine, and there is no one to say "nay." What is our true self? Our true self is love. We are love, itself, and we can offer that love to God. Love is irrevocably us, our nature. Even the most depraved person is love at his core; and to fully transform his life, he need only surrender that love, himself, to the Divine. We can joyfully start our surrender to God this very moment by giving ourselves, by giving love to that Name and Form of God which we find to be most dear to us.

No one and nothing in the universe can stop us from devotion to God, from love for Him, from acknowledging Him as the guiding power, from resigning to the will of the Almighty. That has been proven time and again in the lives and cruel deaths of countless martyrs. In love we can surrender to Baba, and he says that our love is all that he wants. It is enough. Everything else will fall in place, naturally and easily. No need even to worry about that glorious final surrender of the particular to the Universal. In love, it, too, will come naturally and easily in due time. Baba says so, and, in love, we may believe him.

To be sure, our love may not be shining in full glory at this moment. Dark clouds hide the sun in dull weather, but that is not to deny the sun. Before long, a breeze comes into being and sweeps the dark clouds away. In our case, Baba's divine teachings will sweep away the dark clouds of thoughts and concepts and bitter feelings which obscure and seemingly deny the fullness of our love.

So, let us put aside worry, doubt, and protest and begin this day to love God with all our heart. Let us this very day begin full surrender to the wisdom and guidance of the Divine and know that He, not ourselves, is the Doer.

Motherhood is the most precious gift of God. Mothers are the makers of a nation's fortune or misfortune, for they shape the sinews of its soul. Those sinews are toughened by two lessons they should teach: fear of sin, and fondness for virtue. Both these are based on faith in God being the inner motivator of all. If you want to know how advanced a nation is, study the mothers: are they free from fear and anxiety, are they full of Love towards all, are they trained in fortitude and virtue? If you like to imbibe the glory of a culture, watch the mothers, rocking the cradles, feeding, fostering, teaching, and fondling the babies. As the mother, so the progress of the nation; as the mother, so the sweetness of the culture.
                                        — Sathya Sai Baba

Awaken, My Dear, Awaken

When we first encounter writings or talk that the world as we experience it is like a dream, we wonder how this squares with the facts of our experience. We know full well that if we step in front of a fast-moving car we are going to be injured. We know that the persons around us are very real and must be treated with care and caution, and we know that millions of events are taking place around the world even though we do not see them. Yet, we hear Baba say that this waking world is little different from dreaming except that night dreaming is of shorter duration if measured by the time-frame of the waking world. Then to further puzzle us, we see Baba paying the most careful and loving attention to we "dream" individuals, and we see him working tirelessly and mightily in this "dream" world for the benefit of the people in this dream of a world. When asked to explain this, Baba replies that he helps people awaken from their dream.

To most of us, born into a Western culture, talk about the unreality of the world is incomprehensible, alien, and nonsense only. Nevertheless, if and when we give some attention to the topic, we will have to acknowledge that quite a number of people, including great sages and saints who were certainly not bereft of intelligence, for ages past, have held that the world, as experienced, is not independently real. Upon considering this, upon considering that people of deep experience have said this, surely we will be bound to wonder what Baba means when he calls to us, "Awaken! Awaken! Awaken, my dear."

If our life in the world is said to be like a dream, then what is a dream? When we fall asleep, the body is given over to its autonomic life rhythm, life continues, and the involuntary nerve and glandular systems of the body continue to function, even though we have forgotten the body and are no longer aware of it. If we do not go into deep sleep where even our mind is forgotten, we begin to dream. In the dream state, our mind continues to be suffused with energy and instantaneously creates a populated world wherein we identify as "I, Myself" with one out of the many human persons appearing in the dream, all of whom our mind has created. The world of the dream and the events which occur in the dream are wonderful to behold. The objects and events of the dream world are totally real to us, at times painful and at other times happy and delightful, yet we at once declare them all to be a dream, unreal products of our imagination, as soon as we awaken. We realize that the dream world which was so real while dreaming was real only so long as the dreamer continued to dream. The awakened person at once realizes that somehow or other his mind created the dream world, created the objects in that world, experienced an imaginary contact of his senses with the imaginary objects — the entire panorama having no "outside" reality, but all created by the mind, contained within the mind, and all made out of the same mind-stuff.

It is in that same way that sages declare the world of common experience to be delusive and non-real as soon as there is an awakening to Absolute Reality. Such awakened ones realize that the apparent world, its animate and inanimate objects, the cosmic panorama: time, space, birth, death, binding, and Liberation — all are mind-created illusion, all are without independent reality, and nothing really exists except God in the primeval state of the Supreme Undifferentiated Absolute. Such is the extraordinary and to us unbelievable fact declared to be so by Self-Realized sages and saints throughout the ages. The words of sage Astavakra bear repeating, "Till one has actually realized the Self, it is hard to believe that the Self is really what the seers describe it to be, and that the universe is really nothing. Have faith. Faith is precedent for a seeker of truth."

We know that for real knowledge, experience is necessary. Disciplined concepts and ideas are good as far as they go, but there is a difference when we directly know that which is the basis for the concepts and ideas. Until there is direct experience, one's understanding is not really clear. In a recent (1984) conversation, I asked Baba about the world as a creation of the mind. I said, "A source of confusion is about everything being a creation of the mind. A creation of whose mind?"

> SAI: It is the mind.
>
> JH: But Swami, how could that be? Is my mind creating the war and all its horrors? I do not find such actions in myself!
>
> SAI: When you think of the world, it exists for you. When you do not think of it, it does not exist.
>
> JH: When I do not think of the world, it is not in my consciousness! Does the war exist only according to my consciousness of it? But there was a beginning to it. How could that beginning be due only to my mind?
>
> SAI: At your stage, it will not be possible to grasp this. As long as the mind exists, it is not possible to comprehend the mind and its activity clearly. When thoughts cease there will be no mind. Mind is a bundle of thoughts. Do not follow the thought. Then the world will not develop for you. Now your thoughts have gone to America, to problems there. But these are just thoughts. If you now follow these thoughts and go to America, they will bring about the world for you.
>
> JH: Does Swami mean that one should just be a witness to the thoughts going through one's mind and not do anything about them?
>
> SAI: Exactly. When the mind is destroyed (i.e. when there is direct seeing without an intervening thought process), then the coming into being of the world will be clear to you. There is only God, God only. Hold to Him. Hold closely to Him, and the matter of the mind will be resolved.

Baba is saying here that even now, while we are still using thoughts to think about the truth, rather than seeing truth directly, we can begin to appreciate that much of what we consider to be our solid world is, in fact, not substantial for us — and we can let it go. He says that the world is as good as being non-existent so far as we are concerned *if we do not follow our thoughts and do not thereby become involved with a world which has been cognized only as a thought process.*

To understand what is meant by the phrase, "as good as," a simile is used, even though all similes are useful only up to a point. Suppose a field is covered by a growth of very sharp thorns. If we walk across that field with our feet enclosed in leather shoes, for us that field is as good as it would be were it paved with leather instead of being covered with thorns. That is, for us, the thorns are as good as non-existent. Our feet know only leather, and the thorns are as good as non-existent for us. In the same way, we may ask, where is the need to bring a world into existence for us when we are at liberty to not follow our thoughts to areas which we need not experience? Such areas of the world need not be our world — they are as good as non-existent for us unless we wish and decide to make them existent by following our thoughts and becoming involved.

If we are interested in finding out the truth of the matter, and if we choose to listen to Baba, we can know what he means by "Awakening." If we give earnest attention to Baba, and with interest and intensity do the spiritual practice and discipline he recommends, we can awaken from the world dream — the apparent world, which is sustained for us by our belief in its independent reality and by our non-inquiry as to its reality, or the nature of its apparent reality. We can awaken to the real presence of our infinitely charming, ever-happy Lord, and then realize with the greatest of wonder, "We are not two. I am He. I am the shining Reality. There is no ignorance. Time is not. There is neither birth nor death."

This is our awakening from the idea and the conviction that the world is being correctly perceived by us and understood correctly by us. This is our awakening from the idea and the conviction that the world is an infinite extension of self-existent objects ranging from our faculty of mind and intelligence, to our body, to the neutron, to still undiscovered suns, and that the correct field for our existence is an infinite range of experiences stemming from contact with objects.

In time we will hear the whisper, "Awaken, my dear, awaken!" And to us, still asleep, the thought will occur, "I hear this whisper, but I am already awake. My own experience and this world are real, how am I to find the meaning that I should awaken?" It is that very question which Baba is answering. He is telling us how we may awaken. We may awaken through the great power of the spiritual discipline — the Sadhana — set out for us by Baba. So great is its power that very soon dispassion is born in us, and we begin to lose our all-consuming fascination with the world. Soon we begin to question the validity and necessity of our habitual reactions to our experiences. We ask ourselves, "Is hate necessary? Is envy necessary? Is it necessary to be miserable and unhappy when experience is painful and unsatisfactory? If this world and its experiences are, like a dream, not independently real, and therefore need not be regarded as being independently real, and if my true nature is bliss and joy, as is said by Baba, then why not right now be happy and refuse the idea that I be miserable?" And this is indeed what Baba says, "Be happy. Be happy!"

That the world is said to be unreal even though apparently real may worry us at first, but if we will put aside our emotional response for the time being and calmly consider the new viewpoint, it will not seem to be so unreasonable after all. It is not that the world is "really" unreal. God is its reality. We do not see clearly because the world is presented to our minds, by our senses, as a medley of names and forms and experiences. Baba explains, "Eyes and mind are products of the world. They must say that their material cause really exists. Body, senses, and mind are products of food eaten by us. They must say their original matter (the world) is real and cannot deny the existence of their original matter." Thus, Baba explains that we cannot expect eyes and mind to deny the reality of their own material cause. Understanding must transcend sensory impressions.

From time to time Baba will briefly mention the topic of the world's ultimate reality, and a selection of his comments follows:

The senses and the intellect can discern only the

external nature of existence — they cannot discern the ultimate reality. The intellect considers all things in terms of ideas or concepts; it searches for reasons, similarities, and differences; it speculates, compares, and arrives at conclusions; and it deals in pairs of opposites — all in terms of ideas. For its ideas are its symbols for things.

The mind experiences the world by flowing along the sense-channels, which are five in number. The world of our experience consists of the objects of these sense organs. The structure of the world is correlative to the constitution of the senses. If there is a further world, we have no way of knowing, we cannot say. The organs do not understand; they merely convey their respective objects to the mind.

Actually, men see the shadow and take it to be the substance. They see length, breadth, height, and thickness and they jump to the conclusion that they have an object before them. They experience a series of sensations and memories, and adding them all up, they infer there are some objects producing them.

Because we have the conviction that things seen by us exist, there must be an element of reality in the world appearance. The Infinite Consciousness is the underlying reality.

Before one's birth, one has no relationship with the world and its material objects. After death, they and all kith and kin disappear. This sojourn is just a game played in the interval. Getting fascinated with this 3-day fair is foolish.

One must be unattached to the whirling worldliness of the world, but he should not detach himself or deviate from the discharge of his duties to the world as a component thereof.

As long as one is in the world, he must do what is ordained.

Baba points out that we experience the world according to impressions relayed to our minds by our senses, and on the basis of these sense-impressions, we form concepts and reach conclusions. But in no way does he suggest that when we see this we should stop action and retire to forest or cave. He tells us:

> Swami is saying one should only 'control' the senses. It is not that one should not have senses. One uses brakes only when there is some danger. If it is within limits and properly done, nothing will be harmful. Sense organs have to be brought under control and used for the welfare of the 'Resident' of the body.
>
> In this same context, Baba quotes Sri Krishna, 'Therefore, Arjuna, control your mind and senses and recognize the defects which are inherent in objects; then you can live in the world.' Use all the senses in a proper and ethical way, according to the time and circumstances.

The "defect" of an object is that we see in it the promise of happiness, whereas, in truth, we find only temporary pleasure.

Baba declares that the world, as experienced by us, is the mind. The world is created by the mind and is then externalized and experienced as being "outside." The process of externalization is familiar.

Each night we see it happen. A dream is a series of thoughts and ideas and feelings which are externalized and then experienced by us as the dream world. A normal intelligence, upon awakening from a dream, at once understands this, and understands there is no independent objective continuing dream world.

Baba informs us that when we are awake, our mind constructs ideas appropriate to our sensory impressions and then we externalize those ideas as the waking world. That externalized world becomes our tangible experience because we do not just witness thoughts, but allow the thoughts to move us into actions. That action with its reaction comprises our tangible world.

We are told that while we perceive the world correctly according to our sensory impressions, we fail to correctly understand what we see. We complain that we cannot see God even though we are looking at Him at that very moment. The simile is given that when we are at the seashore and observe waves and foam and bubbles, we do indeed see them, but we clearly understand that the waves, foam, and bubbles are not separate in identity from the sea, despite the forms they have and the names we bestow upon them. Because these forms rise and dissolve even while we are looking at them, we easily understand that they are real only in a relative sense, that their separate identity is transient and not permanent. We are told that, in like fashion, we do indeed see the world as presented to us through our sensory impressions, but do not realize we are looking at God Himself. We do not realize that the world of forms we see and the names they carry are real only in a relative sense, that their reality is transient and not permanent, and that all these forms will eventually decline and merge back into their substratum, which is the Eternal Supreme Absolute. The many names and forms exist as such for a period of time only and are real only relative to each other during that time period. Only the Absolute Divinity is timelessly real.

Here we are given a warning: Respect relative reality when we are experiencing relative reality. The world is duality; without duality there can be no action, and as name and form, we ourselves live as action. As name and form, we are separate from each other, even though we are One in timeless Reality. Baba warns: keep forms separate and hearts as One. In Baba's life we can observe this principle. He loves all creation as One, as Himself only, but demands strict discipline from everyone associated with him.

Granted that we have faintly heard Baba's whisper, "Awaken, my dear," and granted that we are still lightly dreaming and not yet really awake. What can we do? Baba tells us how to start. We can start by strengthening our faith in his teachings. He clearly states that all is God. Right now we can begin to correct our misunderstanding of what we see. From this moment, we can tell the mind that what we are seeing is God. Throughout the day we may continue to correct our understanding and tell the mind that we and that other person, that tree, that rock — all are really God, that His blissful Divine Presence is wherever we look. If we adopt this spiritual discipline with energy and determination, we will experience a feeling of happiness arising in the heart.

As long as we accept that the world, as it appears to be, is real and true and desirable, we will see it so, and we will continue with attachment to that which we believe in. But if we look outside of the particular shelter of happiness and safety which we may be enjoying for the time being, then we will be forced to ask, "Is the world as desirable and delightful as we now believe it to be?"

Certainly Nature is more than a glorious sunset, more than the divine peace of the distant mountains in the early morning. There is something else too. In the air, on the earth, and beneath the surface of the sea, creatures are busy killing each other for food, or destroying each other because of savagery or meanness; while at the same time, in the world, there are other actions which are selfless and deeply kind and protective. Will this mixed and seriously flawed external world which we are now experiencing provide us with ever-constant peace beyond the limits of time and space? We may be quite old and experienced, but we cannot bring forward even one worldly person who lives in that bliss which is said to be our reality and which nothing in this world can modify. Baba declares, "From the highest planet in the material world down to the lowest, all are places of misery where repeated birth and death take place. But one who attains to my abode never takes birth again."

It is good that some doubt should arise about our dedication to the world as we experience it. It is good to ask ourselves if what seers and sages say about the world is true. It is good that the pain and misery which we observe in the world and in ourselves prompts us to ask questions. It is good to consider that even from a painful dream we may in due course awaken — or now be awakened. Conceiving that the world of our daily life may not be the reality which it appears to be is a very strange idea indeed. But once the possibility is admitted to serious consideration, we will be required by our own intelligence to dig deeply into the matter. Baba's divine teaching reveals to us how to make this inquiry.

He Who Knows

Sri Sathya Sai Baba calls our attention to a familiar aspect of human nature: we long for happiness and try to avoid misery. He informs us that we long for happiness because bliss is our true nature and misery comes into our life because we ignore our own truth. He says that if we apply his teaching to daily life we will realize our truth, and thereupon happiness will be ours forever. In general, people do not or cannot accept this. Many feel that if first of all they could have an experience of that divine ecstasy of which Baba speaks, then they would have faith in his teachings. But, however unpalatable it might be to our worldly wisdom, the fact is that in spiritual life faith comes before experience. First comes confidence and faith. Experience then follows. In the ancient scriptures, the analogy is given: Suppose a man, deathly sick, were to call a doctor. The doctor, out of his knowledge and long experience, prepares a medicine to cure the man. But the man says, "Doctor, I cannot take this pill unless you first prove that it will cure me." The doctor would have no choice but to leave the man to his fate.

The dilemma that faces us is: Baba cannot prove that happiness may be ours in all its gracious fullness if we, on our part, at once reject his wisdom and refuse to take action. But if we "take the pill" and practice spiritual life under Baba's guidance, he assures us the final irrevocable experience of ever-present happiness will follow. We will be cured, once and forever, of the disease of unhappiness, misery, and despair.

If we find ourselves willing to accept Baba's advice and act upon it, now is the right time even though we might be less than pleased with our present state of readiness. For how can even a very skeptical person argue against a minimum amount of faith? Do we not have faith in many things before we have proof? Seeking to drive to a certain address, for example, we ask a stranger for directions, and, in faith, we follow those directions. We are willing to give faith to what a stranger says — cannot we give as much faith in the beginning to what Baba says?

Baba acts for our benefit and he speaks and acts from love. His happiness, the happiness he will guide us to is related to love — not to objects. Love is the eternal timeless reality, and it is from love that Baba teaches. He says, "To give love and to receive love. This is my business. There is no limit to my Ananda (i.e. Bliss). I am always immersed in bliss. This is because my bliss is associated with love and not with material objects. If you follow this path, you will realize peace of every kind."

One might say about Baba that he is the embodiment of an irresistible energy which could be likened to a mighty river, or an ocean tide, or a gentle wind at dawn in that no obstacle can stay that flow of energy. He is a supreme person, yet his favorite role appears to be that of a benefactor to his devotees. His entire life seems to be spent in that role. He is never seen taking time to do anything for himself or to acquire anything for himself. But it would be folly to think we can observe him and in that way really know him. The fact is that even ardent devotees who have been by his side for thirty years or more confess they are unable to define boundaries to his nature.

About himself, Sri Sathya Sai Baba says, "My truth is inexplicable, unfathomable. I am beyond the reach of the most intensive inquiry, the most meticulous measurement. There is nothing I do not see, nowhere I do not know the way, no problem I cannot solve. My sufficiency is unconditional. I am the Totality — all of it."

Such considerations bring us to the heart of Baba's teachings. The heart of his teaching is the astonishing declaration that he is

God, that we also are God, and that the only difference between him and ourselves is that he is ever aware of, and lives fully in his truth, whereas we are unaware of our truth. He says that our unawareness persists mainly because we are not intensely interested. Our attention is divided, and nobody in whom we have strong faith has ever told us that in spite of all appearances to the contrary, we are essentially divine and may come to know our essential divinity if we are intense and earnest about it.

Baba's teaching is a direct statement of his life. He is like a man who holds a pearl in the palm of his hand in a good light and directly weighs what is there. What Baba teaches us is fully self-evident to him; no prior learning is needed. He knows without learning.

Those who teach about Nature and its laws, matter and its properties, forces and their pulls, teach to bind, not to liberate. It is a burden, not bliss. It provides a stone boat for you to cross the sea with waves of grief and crests of joy. It cannot float you along; it is certain to sink. What you need to cross the sea is the bark of bhakthi*, of assurance of Grace, of surrender to His will. Throw off all burdens, become light, and you can trip across with one step on one crest and another on the next. God will take you through. You have no need to bother at all. For, when He does everything, who is concerned about what?
                                        — Sathya Sai Baba

* — Devotion, dedication, the path of love to God.

Silence

The mind can be surrendered to noise and find peace for a while. Noise can be a temporary escape from one's thoughts. It is the distraction preferred by many people, and a vast commercial empire exists to provide pleasant noises. The mind is also able to surrender to silence. Saints and sages throughout the ages have recommended that one's mind be surrendered to silence. It is said that the peace of silence is joyful and can transcend time — that is, it can be forever. Like space, which exists even between atoms, silence is universal. If one observes carefully, it will be noted that silence exists along with noise. It can be noted that each noise is surrounded by silence.

In addition to the possibility of a heart, ardent with love for God, spontaneously awakening to Silence in an instant, Baba tells of two spiritual disciplines which quickly lead to a realization of that divine and indescribable Silence which cannot be conveyed in words, but which one can directly "taste," or experience. These are the spiritual disciplines of the Witness and Ekaantha Bhakthi.

"Witness" is taken in its ordinary dictionary meaning: "A witness is one who personally sees or perceives a thing." Witnessing is already familiar to us because we are always experiencing that role. We witness the passage of the seasons, night and day,

133

war and peace, birth and death, and the events which arise in the lives of strangers, friends, and family. Often, although we see, we remain silent and detached. And, even if we join the action, there still remains an aloof center or aspect of ourselves which is the observer of the whole drama including our own actions, feelings, and thoughts. It is that silent center of ourselves which is called "The Witness." The spiritual practice of The Witness is to never become identified with anything whatsoever which is observed, including any personification of The Witness, even though the mind which is rational and dualistic identifies itself as The Witness. The practice is to remain in that aloof or detached state of witnessing despite mental and emotional turbulence and/or physical involvement.

This state of witnessing is the common experience of everyone. When we are reminded of it, we can see at once that we already know it. We need only stay at the point of witnessing. That is the spiritual practice, to stay at the point of witnessing. It is something like sitting silently at an upper-story window of one's house and witnessing events in the street. With the spiritual practice of The Witness, the mind is not supported in its turbulence. Sooner or later there will be moments when the mind is totally silent. The mind will spring into activity again and again. But once there is that direct conscious experience of witnessing, of silence and peace as one's basis, ignorance can never thereafter be in full command of our life.

The spiritual practice of Ekaantha Bhakthi, as recommended by Baba, has to do with breathing. Explanations of how breath and mind are linked may vary from culture to culture, but there is a general perception that such a link does exist. It is common experience that when our mind is agitated, breath is short and fast and that when we are calm, breath slows down. Baba does not advise us to adopt the practice of any system of Pranayama, the science of breath, except under the supervision of an expert teacher. In fact, he warns us not to adopt practices which include control of the in-breath, retention of the breath, and control of the out-breath. He says that such practices are highly dangerous and that today there are no teachers fully competent to supervise the various modes of Pranayama.

What Baba advises in the practice of Ekaatha Bhakthi is just sitting quietly, breathing evenly, and allowing the breaths to become longer in duration rather than fast and short as is the case when we are agitated.

The spiritual practice of sitting quietly and allowing one's breathing to become slow and even is named "Ekaantha Bhakthi." Baba describes the practice as follows:

> Ekaantha Bhakthi is a subtle thing achieved by effective control of the mind and experiencing one's Self. It is not correct to think that control of the mind means holding it steady without wandering around. To be able to cleanse the mind of impure thoughts is the correct meaning of Ekaantha. This is to be practiced in a quiet place free from noise or disturbance. The best time for practice is during the hours 3 a.m. to 5 a.m. Select a particular time in this period, close the door, sit quietly, and adjust the breath so that the rate of inhaling and exhaling is the same. This is important. And, further, by gradual practice, the number of breathings per minute must be reduced from eight or ten a minute to two or one a minute. You have to take your own time, proceeding gradually in the process of reduction of the number of times of inhaling and exhaling. To control the breath in this manner, there is a very effective discipline that should be followed: the tip of the tongue must be made gently to touch the rear of the teeth. When it is kept in this specific position, the thoughts in the mind become less, you detach yourself from thoughts of the body and things around you and you come to the stage of Ekaantha Bhakthi. Ekaatha Bhakthi is that state of mind without thoughts and desires when it is concentrated on God.

Our Discontent

Is it not true of ourselves that most of us spend our lives seeking to calm and satisfy our discontent? We cannot take whatever comes and be perfectly happy with it. If we are left solitary and lonely without any distraction, we become discontented and in time we seek experience. If our experience does not fully satisfy us, we strive to bring about a change. But full and complete satisfaction is not ours even with radical change.

Why is it that discontent has such a vitality that it continues to arise no matter what we do? There must be some situation which is very general and very much alive for discontent to be so general and so alive. But, everybody experiences discontent, and therefore everyone, if he chooses to look, may see the fundamental causes of discontent. For example: Is there not in everyone the thought that he is going to die? His philosophy may prepare him for death, but not at this very second, please! Our discontent when life is threatened is universally known.

Also, is our thirst for knowledge ever satisfied? From the housewife who inquires about the affairs of her friends and her family, to the businessman seeking to know his industry, to the saint thirsting after God, we strive to know more and more; and until we have perfect knowledge, our discontent will not be eased.

We are even discontented at our poor memory of what we have learned, and we try to make permanent records.

Further, suppose we are in a state of wonderful happiness. Our surroundings are blissful, our companions perfect, and all is peace. Suddenly a small ant takes a bite from our leg, and the pain makes us jump and shout. We cannot rest until the ant is brushed off and the pain subsides. Our peace and happiness was so vast — cannot we be satisfied that we are happy and not worry about one small imperfection? NO! We are discontented at even the slightest modification of perfect, endless happiness.

Putting aside abnormal psychological states, all the activity of we human beings, if analyzed, is aimed at achieving one or all of three goals: to exist always, to know all things always, and to be perfectly happy always and under all conditions. Anything less than perfect realization of these objectives gives rise to discontent.

In short, we have the irrepressible craving to be Divine; for perfect Being, perfect Knowledge, and perfect Bliss is said to be the eternal nature of God. This extraordinary craving to be like God which we cherish at all levels of our being — is this state of Sat-Chit-Ananda really possible, or is it just a myth, something imagined?

Here I state, and a large company of other people support the statement — that full and perfect Being-Knowledge-Bliss is an actual present reality and such an existence may be observed in the daily life of the divine Avathar, Sri Sathya Sai Baba.

Baba tells us that our craving for Divinity arises within us because Divinity is our essential nature, and that only our manifold and changeable impurities prevent us from fully realizing that we are God, that Baba is ourselves, and that we are not different from, nor separate from him.

The sadhana, the spiritual discipline leading to the realization of our essential Divinity is graciously explained to us by Baba in his divine teachings.

Creation

Very likely every person, at some time or other, looks at the universe and at himself or herself and wonders, "How did all this come about, and why?"

The various religions put forward explanations about creation, and so do scientists and philosophers. At times, educational authorities adopt one theory of creation and make its teaching mandatory in the schools of the nation.

Perhaps the mind can truly understand creation, and perhaps it cannot. In any event, what Baba has to say about creation may be of interest. Baba declares, "See in me, yourself, for, I see myself in you. You are my life, my breath, my soul. You are all my forms. When I love you I love myself; when you love yourself, you love me. I separated myself by myself so that I may be myself. I separated myself from myself and became all this so that I may be myself. I wanted to be myself, that is, Anandaswarupa, Premaswarupa. That is what I am and I wanted to be that. How can I be Anandaswarupa and Premaswarupa? And give Ananda and give Prema? And to whom am I to give Ananda and to whom am I to give Prema? So I did this. I separated myself from myself and became all this."[1]

1. "Prema" is the limitless Divine Love. "Ananda" is the limitless Divine Bliss. "Premaswarupa" and "Anandaswarupa" are the embodiment of the Divine Love and Divine Bliss.

Carefree and Happy

The ancient scriptures say that only God *is* and that all else is illusion superimposed on the reality of God. The power which projects people and the universe and invests them with independent empirical reality, whereas in truth God is their reality, is called Ignorance, or Maya. It owes its continued existence to lack of inquiry. This Ignorance comes into existence as Mind, and within the mind illusions are born and dance about as the world and its contents. Baba tells us, "All the names and forms that fill up this universe and constitute its nature are but creations of mind. Therefore the mind has to be calmed in order to see the truth. The ever-flickering waves of the lake have to be stilled so that you can see the bottom clearly."

It is said that this Ignorance, or Maya, is inscrutable because it cannot be explained, yet it exists. The scriptures then go on to say the wise know that Ignorance is not inscrutable because it does not exist at all and that upon inquiry as to the truth of oneself, Ignorance will disappear; in fact, there is God only, and for this reason man should be carefree and happy regardless of all else.

Scriptures are written. The men who related them are long dead. Who can know what errors may have arisen from word to ear and from thought to the written word. For this reason, for lack of deep faith in the truth of the scriptures, men read and hear them but

139

do not put them into practice. But now we must awaken and realize that Baba, the Lord incarnate, who is living today, says from his own reality, "It is my experience that I am in every heart." He tells us the eternal truth of man, nature, and God directly and not from hearsay or books. We can go to him and, with our own faculty of hearing, listen to him declare from his own universality that only God exists, that all else is appearance. We can know this for ourselves and we can, starting from this instant, be carefree and happy. Moreover, out of his love for us, Baba spends every moment in loving service to us and is teaching the truth so that we may be free of ignorance and be happy. Grant us the good sense to have at least provisional faith in what the living Avathar, the living embodiment of divine wisdom, is saying to us.

Acknowledging that many wise people may indeed be doing exactly as Baba says, why is it that even the least of us are not at once carefree and happy as soon as we hear the truth from Baba? Baba tells his devotees that the lack of a heart overflowing with divine love and happiness is due to the confusion which accompanies desire.

Through habit, perhaps ages-long habit, we look upon the objects, situations, and experiences of the world as being real in themselves. The mind will always attend to that which it takes to be real. Happiness and misery are experiences which the mind takes to be very real, and these experiences arise from contact with the world. Desire for more is aroused by the experience of happiness, the desire to avoid misery is aroused by the experience of misery. Sri Sathya Sai points out to us that neither the happiness nor the misery which follow in the wake of desire are lasting, and thereby neither are real. When asked how to kill desire, his response is that it is not possible; that desire is an expression of the universal energy by which we move and have our being. But the confusion which now accompanies desire can be eliminated by turning every desire away from worldly objects and directing it to God. Desire to have God Himself from whom all blessings and all prosperity flows. Why scramble in the dust for coins when we can have the Treasury itself?

Baba teaches us that as soon as a desire arises, turn it to God, then confusion will end, and we can be carefree and happy. When desire is allowed to turn away from God and to fasten itself upon objects, ideas, conditions, or experiences, it becomes attached and reluctant to let go. To illustrate this unhappy attachment, we are referred to the way monkeys are captured. Food is placed in a container which has a narrow neck, into which the monkey thrusts its paw groping for the food. The monkey closes its paw around the food at the bottom of the vessel, but the narrow neck of the vessel will not allow the monkey to pull out its closed fist which is grasping the food. Thereby, the monkey is caught by its attachment to the object of its desire. Were the monkey to abandon its attachment to the food, its fist would open and it would regain its freedom. In our human way, we are suffering the same fate. Whenever there are unhappy or anxious moments, if we can separate ourself from our feelings long enough to take a close look at the situation, we will see that invariably some attachment is involved. Once identified, the attachment can be abandoned by the power of our intelligence and our will, and that particular source of discontent will no longer trail after us.

Be carefree and happy! That is the divine advice. Baba assures us that without doubt it is possible to live in the world, fulfilling all our duties and, at the same time, remain happy and unaffected by events. This illustration is given. Suppose that an actress, taking the role of a poor person, is in fact a wealthy lady with a happy family and vast estates. She plays her role and suffers with such deep feeling that members of the audience find themselves in tears. Despite her wonderful art in portraying suffering and misery, has she ever even for a moment truly forgotten that she is a wealthy, happy person? She plays her role to the full, but always knows deep in her mind that she is wealthy and happy and that when the play is over, she will remove her costume and make-up and will rejoin her family. Baba again and again likens us to actors in a play. He says that the individual self is the role; the reality is God.

If we are unhappy now, if we believe our role and forget that we are the majesty of Divinity, it is of our own choosing; no outside power is forcing us to be inwardly unhappy. Try it now — at this moment be happy and carefree. Happiness will be felt, even if briefly. But that moment of happiness is the proof of itself. Baba says that happiness is one of the essential factors of enlightenment. Take happiness as a spiritual practice. Feel happy and continue to feel happy regardless of conditions and events. Happiness, joy — they are other words for love. Be happy, be joyful, be loving at all times; that is the way to God, declares Baba.

The Will, Free or Not?

A topic which is always sure to spark divergent opinions is that of free will. On the one hand, it is said that not even a leaf falls except by the will of God. This implies there is no individual free will, that the Divine moves us to action and the responsibility is His, not ours. On the reverse side, we have the saying that God helps those who help themselves. This implies that we have free will and therefore the obligation to act according to our perception of what is correct action, and that we are responsible for the result of our action. Then there is the burning debate of freedom itself. Are we free or are we bound? Is the direction and course of our life just the net effect of the multitude of diverse influences bearing upon it? Or, are we free souls, freely choosing our role in life and able to modify and change our role according to our liking? Further, are we able to choose inaction vs. action according to our resolve? Or, is the condition one of mixed freedom and non-freedom? Is it that at certain moments we are free to decide and act in freedom, and at other moments we are slaves to influences imposed upon us by the net effect of our circumstances?

Despite today's lack of agreement about free will, there is some light on the topic which is fully available to us. A most interesting clue is found in the sayings of seers and sages of ancient times. In books about ancient times, occasionally one will note a phrase included in a conversation between a guru and his disciple to the effect that certain answers to questions are intended for the satisfaction of the ignorant, not the wise. The implication is that an individual will not benefit by hearing that which he or she is unable to comprehend, and that what is said reveals varying depths of truth according to the varying capacities of individual minds. If we understand that even great sages, who are speakers of truth, must use discrimination in what they say, then we have a clue to what is said and written about free will, and we can ourselves begin to discriminate in respect to what we hear and read about free will.

Baba has said that not a leaf falls except by the will of God. He has also said that truth-seekers must work very hard; they must use every effort to work their way upstream to the source. And, further, he has said that truth in its entirety can be realized in an instant — three statements in apparent contradiction. He has said that he looks after and arranges every aspect of a devotee's life, which certainly implies there can be a basis for our life other than that of our individual free will. And then, in almost the next breath, Baba has said that a person is free to go his own way and do as he or she wishes. Upon being asked to explain the apparent contradiction, Baba agreed that the statements do seem to be different and do appear to clash, but that each statement was made in respect to a particular situation. Where a person is fully surrendered to God, Baba acts in the mode of Divine Mother, caring for and guarding that devotee, doing more for the devotee than the devotee could ever imagine to ask for. But, if a person chooses to follow ego desire, then such a person is left to work out his or her destiny.

Here Baba is saying that if we surrender to God's will, happiness will be gained and nothing lost, but if our interest and our desire are turned to worldly life, we are then using individual free will and must live by it and accept the responsibility.

The questions then arise, how is free will exercised and when is a particular action a free will action? Free will cannot be for the body, because we manipulate the body as an instrument or vehicle which is used by us. Ourselves as emotion, mind, and intelligence appear to exercise some free will, but we can observe that these faculties are modified by an infinite variety of influences ranging from the powerful rays of the sun and distant planets to inner tend-

encies and predilections as well as to the demands of work and
family. It is difficult to see how we could isolate ourselves from all
external and internal influences and act according to pure free will;
for "free will" subject to influence cannot be "free." Nevertheless,
free will is a fact at some level of our consciousness, for Baba has
quite clearly said so and has further pointed out that, if there were
no free will, we could not gain release from the endless turning of
the wheel of deed and consequence. To solve the puzzle of which
level or aspect of consciousness enjoys free will, it appears that we
will need to put aside every aspect of ourselves which could be
moved by any influence or duress either from our own faculties
and tendencies or from the world outside our skin. It appears that
inquiry about free will brings us back to the fundamental question
facing us at every turn, which is, "Who am 'I'?"

Until we realize that which we truly are, we can never be certain
as to the freedom or slavery of any particular action. We may wonder beforehand about free will and we may speculate afterwards
about it, but the fact is that we decide and then act, or we act spontaneously, or in one way or another are forced to act. Somehow or
other the action takes place. If we are content with the action and
what seems to be its consequence, we don't worry about it. But if we
are not content, the question of free will arises. Free will may or
may not have prevailed. The myriad conflicting influences bearing
upon us may have been at a point of balance for an instant and free
will may have been the final determinant at that point of balance.
At our present stage of limited awareness, we can only speculate.

In an April, 1977, message to American Sai devotees, Baba said:

Nothing is wrong with you — 'Where there is a will
there is a way' is eminently true. At first the will is your
own which has to be strengthened by the thought of
GOD until you convert it into the almighty will of GOD.
You seem to be playing a particular game which you do
not really desire to throw up. You can change the game
if you will. You are not weak and helpless. Every
strength and power is within you. GOD-Vision is yours
that very instant when you will it with concentration.
Why don't you? Simply because you do not choose to.
Sai is not mocking. He is perfectly earnest and is giving

expression from the truths gathered from the depths of his experience. Trust in and submission to the supreme will in all circumstances means the vision of truth, vision of the root principle of all creation. 'If GOD wills' means only if you assert your own all-powerful will. The solution is therefore to awaken the inherent power and splendor of your soul. Do it. You are verily the immortal Truth; the great, deathless and changeless Reality. Be victory ever yours.

With Blessings,

Baba

In the above quoted message, Baba says, "You can change the game if you will." And he continues, "'If God wills' means only if you assert your own all-powerful will." This certainly implies the absence of two separate wills. What is the "game" which Baba refers to? What could the "game" be but the game of apparent separateness?

When we are engaged in the game of separateness we say "will" is "ours." When we realize that the "game," while jolly at times, should not continue for ever and ever, we recollect our Truth, that only Divine Will exists.

In a recent conversation with Baba (1984), I said, "One has the free will to choose to turn to God or to be fully involved with the world. But on the other hand, when Baba looks at a person, at one glance he sees the past, present, and future of that person, so how could there be free will?"

Baba replied, "From that viewpoint, from the Divine, there is no free will, for all is God. But from the ego viewpoint of the individual there is free will. There is general law, and then the individual and society. The individual acts in society according to his free will, but all conform to the general law. The individual must act, and his action is a function of his mind. There are thoughts. Thoughts are seeds. They sprout and become actions. The actions then appear to be free will to the concerned individual. Everyone has been given skills and talents such as intelligence, reason, energy, and they must be put into life action."

One could wish that Baba had continued his explanation, and I will try to continue the topic with Baba at the next opportunity.

But from what was said, it seems fairly clear that "general law" (God's Will) is always the underlying fact, the roots of the tree of life, so to speak, the seed which sprouts and grows. And it seems fairly clear also, that as the individual acts, he feels and thinks he is using his individual will. He thus takes the attitude that he is the doer of the action, and later on he experiences the consequence of his action — all of which would need to be in conformity to general law (God's Will). From what Baba says, action is inevitable and accompanying the action can be either the thought that the action is prompted by one's separate individual will or the thought that one is surrendered to God and there is only His Will. It must also be that a shift away from the self-idea is in keeping with general law and occurs when one is "ripe" for it, just as a fruit will naturally ripen or fail to ripen according to the balance of nature. Similes are limited in their validity and in this simile of the unripe fruit, very happily for us, Baba has said, that while man may fall again and again, there is no such thing as failure, and Divinity will inevitably be realized.

It is not contrary to "God's Law" (God's Will) that a particular individual may suddenly have clear vision and see things "as they are." Baba has said this is always possible. To see with clarity, that everything we are doing is being prompted by God, is suddenly to be free from all worry and anxiety. Then there is no sorrow, no disappointment, no fear of any kind, for then all is God. He is playing every role and whatever happens can be accepted as His Will, as the way that He, the consummate Actor, is developing the destiny of the character being portrayed. Baba advises, "Let God work through you and there will be no more duty. Let God shine forth. Let God show Himself. Eat God, drink God, breathe God, realize the truth and the other things will take care of themselves."

And, why not at once step down from our ego-throne, continue to act with the full force of our intelligence and energy, but attribute everything to God? Where will be the loss? Action will continue — no doubt of it. The only loss will be the happy loss of worry, fear, anxiety, and sorrow. All is God. Our human role is a role played by God, just as the Avathar is another role. Why not shake loose from the entire burden of our life-long ideas and offer the whole bundle of ideas and concepts to God — retire for awhile, make a trial acknowledgement that God is the Actor. There is no cost to us if we do this, and the benefit may be great indeed. The poet devotee of Ramana Maharshi, Sri Muruganar, sang: (translated)

> The substance and power of full
> Surrender is but this state of 'mouna,'
> Where by inquiring who this 'I' is
> Who this ego false, one dies
> And merges in the Being true
> Of God impersonal, the Self.

> The Lord controls the doer till
> The fruits of former action are
> Exhausted; until then no effort
> Can change the course of things
>   ordained,
> 'Tis wisdom then to rest in 'mouna.'

> None can oppose what is ordained
> by God omnipotent. 'Tis wisdom
> Then for the false, weak, villainous
>   mind
> To cast off every care and rest
> In 'mouna' at His feet.

In the midst of all the varying concepts about free will, Baba offers his devotees some firm advice. He says that love cannot be disregarded. That above all concepts there is the reality of love, and that love is the royal highway to Self-Realization. He says that we will find it to be best if we do not take on the burden of intellectual argumentation, but instead do service for less fortunate people, live in devotion to God and be sure that thought, word, and action are in harmony.

God Himself will prompt our action. He is then the doer of the action, we are no longer the doer and the question of free will does not arise. This is a principal teaching of Baba's. If we love God and dedicate every action to Him, He will accept the consequence of the action and the devotee need have no concern about free will or no free will.

His Life Is His Message

Baba says that loving service to those who are in need is the form of devotion most pleasing to the Divine. He asks, "What meaning is there in love for a distant God? Such love is only a construction of words and thoughts."

Baba teaches that if, in truth, we love God, then He is directly before us as the inner reality of our fellow human beings; that God is the Reality, the ground upon which all names and forms have their arising and their passing away. By stipulating that loving service to those in distress is the excellent expression of devotion to God, and by actually requiring such service from those who choose to call themselves devotees of God, Baba is teaching us how to make room in our daily lives for love. He is guiding us in small steps that we can presently manage, so that in due course love may expand in our lives until we are consumed by love and become love and in love merge as one with God who is love itself.

Baba's life is his message. He himself is a flame of love and every moment of his life is devoted to loving service to people who call upon him, no matter where they may be. He may rest late at night, but he never sleeps, for how could the primeval consciousness be unconscious? Indeed, Baba has said that he never sleeps. Day and night, he is intent only on reestablishing righteousness as the mode of human life, on turning the attention of people from the false to the true, and in giving joy and delight to his devotees.

In service to school children, Sri Sathya Sai Baba has brought the government of India to adopt his program of moral and spiritual education. It is now a part of the educational process throughout the nation. From all parts of India, teachers are sent to Baba's university in Puttaparthi for training in how to inculcate moral and spiritual values into the education of school children. This program is now spreading beyond the borders of India under the name of Education in Human Values.

Baba's service to the people of India includes the establishment of trade schools so that poor people may learn how to earn a living in India's changing society. He also builds wedding pandals so that the sons and daughters of the poor may be married there, cost-free, without the families going into life-long debt. Throughout India, in city and country, Baba's devotees, those who are physicians, surgeons, and eye specialists hold free clinics for the poor, for those who are never able to pay doctors' fees. To serve people in the rural villages, there are literally thousands of Baba's service organizations throughout India whose devotee members work strenuously to improve the circumstances and the lives of the village people, and who quickly move into heroic and selfless action wherever people become victims of such disasters as famine, tidal waves, earthquakes, tornadoes, and floods.

Space need not be taken to enumerate all the far-reaching programs of Baba's service activities. Suffice it to say that he, himself, provides the perfect example when he stipulates that service to those in need is a basic requirement for spiritual life in this world.

While he stipulates loving service to the unfortunate, yet he firmly tells us that God is quite able to look after His world and that really, our service is to ourselves.

Service to others is to ourselves because it opens the way for love in our lives and because it directly makes our lives joyful. Further, if even this is not enough to persuade us of the importance of service to the unfortunate as a necessary step in spiritual life, Baba points out that for Self-Realization, our ego must bow in humility at the feet of the inner Divinity and surrender to Him its present dominant role in our life. For this, to deflate the ego, nothing equals humble service to the weaker members of society, to whom we tend to feel superior in the ordinary course of events.

An objection might be raised that such actions of service as have been described are fit for young and mobile bodies, but what about those old, sick, and handicapped people who are also devotees of Baba? There is no need for any doubt. Baba says that if we cannot actively help, we can certainly refrain from working harm upon anyone. He says that the very foundation for help to others is the ground of never doing harm to others. Do not underestimate this declaration. Is it not true that day by day, the world over, screams of anguish rise to the heavens from people who are being mistreated, abused, tortured, and killed by other human beings? Just suppose that now, this very hour, there were a total cessation of people working harm upon other people. Would that not be the greatest, the most extraordinary, the most glorious day of man in the history of our troubled world?

Devotees of able body can engage in service to the unfortunate, and those not able-bodied can totally desist from working harm upon others. Who is to say which is better than the other? Both consist of service to God, to humanity, and to oneself.

Make your heart soft, then success is quick in Sadhana (spiritual practice). Talk softly, talk sweetly, talk only of God — that is the process of softening the subsoil. Develop compassion, sympathy; engage in service, understand the agony of poverty and disease, distress and despair; share both tears and cheers with others. That is the way to soften the heart and help Sadhana to succeed.

— Sathya Sai Baba

Our Experience with Happiness

Individuals occasionally say they are already happy and have no need of Baba's teachings. Happiness is indeed experienced by almost everyone for varying lengths of time. Baba says that were it not for a current of happiness from our Self finding its way into our worldly life, life would be quite intolerable and we could not bear it.

Baba further points out that a present happiness which is due to happy circumstances may change to sorrow because of sorrowful circumstances. He informs us, "No object that is accessible to the senses can give man undiluted, permanent bliss. The charm of an individual person is not exempt from this rule. The ever-beautiful Lord alone can award the ever-available bliss, the eternal Truth of God. The eternal source of joy is also God."

There is a simile which Baba uses in this context. A dog finds a dry bone, bites it and chews it and finds it enjoyable. The rough bone has cut the tender inner surface of the dog's mouth and some bleeding results. What the dog is tasting and enjoying is its own blood, not the dry bone. The dog believes that happiness is in the bone, and will continue to chew dry bones wherever they are found. The dog is not able to pierce the illusion that dry old bones have a wonderful taste, and the dog can never know the truth of the matter. But we humans, according to Baba, can pierce illusion

151

and can know the truth of the matter. He warns that we should not make the same mistake as the dog.

Baba has pointed out that we seem to believe that happiness is in possessions. If this belief were to be correct and if happiness were really in objects, then more happiness could be ours with more things and less with fewer things. With one part of our mind we believe this so strongly that we constantly strive to add to our possessions. Yet at one and the same time our intelligence observes that people who have acquired the most are not the happiest and that people who must do with very little can nevertheless be happy. Baba explains the puzzle in this way. When our desire is satisfied by gaining what is desired, the mind becomes peaceful for the time being, and the bliss of the ever-blissful Self is reflected in the object or circumstance which is being experienced. Before long, however, new desires arise, the mind becomes agitated and the bliss of the Self is clouded over.

A doubt may be expressed, how could the eternally present and real bliss of the Self be hidden by an agitation of the mind? The answer is, we commonly experience that something insubstantial can distort or totally hide the truth — transient clouds can hide the blazing sun; a lie can convince people of untruth, etc., etc.

As long as we continue to feel happiness by incessantly securing new things and new experiences, we survive and live from day to day without too much bother. But if we are able to appreciate the extraordinary danger of this way of living, we will surely step aside for a moment and consider what we are doing and the result. What we are doing is to ensure rebirth, and the result is a limitation and a continuing misery and anxiety which is always ready to take over our life. If we are not actually experiencing limitation, misery, and anxiety at the moment, we can observe the lives of others. Depending upon pleasant sensations for happiness, they become attached to that which gives rise to pleasant sensations. Attachment brings fear and anxiety, and deprivation brings misery. They would be indeed wise to step away from the vicious circle of attachment, pleasure, and misery. There is a way to break out and be free, blissful, and peaceful. In his divine teachings, our divine Baba shows us the way.

Baba has pointed out to us, "All our pleasures and pains arise from the contact of the senses with pleasure-giving or pain-producing objects, thus causing us to desire one and hate the other. But if we feel neither attraction nor repulsion for sense objects, and allow them to come as a matter of course, they cannot produce pleasant or painful sensations."

Consider for the moment the wisdom of the illumined sage, Astavakra, the guru of King Janaka, "He who realizes that it is care for objects — and nothing else — that breeds misery in this world becomes free from it and is happy, peaceful, and everywhere rid of desires. It is desire that binds us to the world and makes us think it real, and this subjects us to the rounds of birth and rebirths. The moment we are free of desire, the reality of the world will vanish and there will be no further reincarnation. It is not sense objects themselves that cause misery, it is one's identification with them and attachment to them. Once free from identification and attachment, one need not shun the world."

The divine Baba, in his love for us, his children, tells us that he has come to awaken us to our inner joy, to our blissful immortal Reality which is not dependent upon anything or upon any circumstance. He declares, "I have come to give you the key to the treasure of bliss, to tell you how to tap that spring, for you have forgotten the way of blessedness. Very few of you desire to get from me the thing I have come to give you, namely Liberation itself. I am the embodiment of bliss. Come, take bliss from me, dwell in that bliss and be peaceful."

The Avathar is without illusion and speaks the eternal verities. Spiritual truth is that which always was and always will be, unchanged and unchangeable. Baba has come to show us where true happiness lies. He tells us that we should be cautious in seeking happiness in the promised treasures of the material world, and we should listen attentively when he tells us that happiness — divine bliss — is found in our divine inner nature, not in the outward things of the world.

Ceiling on Desires

In a recent discourse, Baba once again mentioned that if we aim to live a spiritual life, it is essential to limit desires and to help humanity by serving people who are in need. Baba said in part, "Selfless activity is the hallmark of a person who has equanimity of purpose. Therefore, today, the primary injunction being given to you is to love all living forms and beings in order to secure the grace of God in your daily work. Therefore, we have this four-fold ceiling on desires. We should not waste food; eat what you really need, thereby, you are doing service. Do not waste the faculties given to you. In order that we might save some money, try to curb your expenditures. There are many wealthy people who, on occasions of marriage and so on, spend thousands of rupees. In this process, what do they do? They give to those who are already wealthy. You should give to those who do not have any money. Misuse of money is evil. Therefore, do not waste food, time, money, or energy. When you are no longer wasteful, you will be able to do any amount of service."

Does the above statement by Baba represent the totality of what he means by a Ceiling on Desires? Baba says further, "As a fish is very fond of living in water, just so is man fond of living on the basis of satisfying desires. In the circumstances, a great effort is needed to give up the old habits of living by satisfying desires."

This further statement by Baba has a clear significance for the writer, although another Sai devotee may take a different meaning. We live in a particular body, in a particular environment, in a particular society on Planet Earth, in a Universe which is part of a Cosmos, and these, in total, powerfully affect us. These influences are common to us and thus, by and large, we perceive and experience a common world and can talk to each other about it. However, this common world is not the only world experienced by us, nor is it the most important world to us. We know from experience and observation that each of us lives in a private world of his own which can be a literal hell for a particular person, or a more or less pleasant experience for another person. We may become aware of the private world of another person, but it does not thereby become our world. We are aware, for instance, that Baba's world is pure Being-Consciousness-Bliss, but we do not thereby share his world — we remain in ours.

Our private world is created by what we think and do and feel in response to events and circumstances which become known to us through physical impact or mental awareness. That is, we react to whatever in either subtle or gross form, comes to our knowledge by some means or other. Typically, our reaction is to desire, or at least tolerate, that which is agreeable to us and to resist that which we find to be painful or disagreeable. Both desire and resistance lead to action, and action brings about further reaction, which in turn contributes to our experience. In this way, each of us creates a private world which is joyful, indifferent, or miserable according to our response to knowledge and experience and to the inevitable reactions or consequences which follow.

Our private world, which is the world of our happiness or our misery, is clearly described by Baba in his statement as above quoted. He tells us that we are fond of living on the basis of satisfying desires. That is, most of us are living, moment by moment, in a world which we have built around us by the action of satisfying desires. We have a desire — a desire to resist or a desire to gain, and this desire is the "lumber" with which we build our dwelling, with which we build a private world in which we live out our life. Baba points out that for a period of time, briefly or longer, we are happy in the satisfaction of desires, but sooner or later our desires, which are egotistic, come into conflict with the movement of life, and this conflict inevitably brings about frustration and misery. We then tend to compare our private world of misery with another person's private world which appears to be better, and this adds to our misery, discontent, and rebellion.

Baba is telling us a great secret of life, about a possibility for happiness which few of us will have considered prior to this time. He is telling us that we created our private world and that we have the power and the ability to discontinue the maintenance of our private world by destroying its cause and source, and thereby we can know and live in the world of divine bliss which totally surrounds us, which totally surrounds our isolated private world. He tells us that our private world is created and maintained by choosing to live in a world of desire-satisfaction.

Baba's statement has an extraordinary meaning and, if carefully considered, is bound to have a major impact on us. Here, in our life, day by day, year upon year, we are creating a special world for ourselves which arises from and is based upon the satisfaction of desires. But Baba tells us there is a life-mode, a world of experience, an art of living entirely different from and apart from the sensual world which we create for ourselves and sustain for ourselves by living on the basis of the satisfaction of desires. Baba is inviting us to step out of that sensual life-frame, that desire world, into an entirely different world whose sign or mark is the renunciation of craving and whose reality is a state of freedom from the misery and bondage which follow us as long as we cling to a life of desire and the satisfaction of desire. To the writer, at least, this is the meaning of Baba's *Ceiling on Desires* program.

Astavakra, the God-Realized guru of King Janaka, explained, "Our past actions have not given us any lasting happiness. Why should we then continue these worldly actions (i.e. actions to satisfy desires) which spring from ignorance and cause bondage and misery?"

Sage Astavakra of ancient days and Sri Sathya Sai Baba, the embodiment of the Indivisible Supreme Absolute, tell us the same truth. There is no contradiction when speaking of the eternal ever-constant Truth.

To step out of the peculiar or particular life-frame which we ourselves are creating and sustaining, whose mark is action to satisfy desires, into an entirely different life, whose mark will be renunciation of craving is to face the unknown. We are bound to wonder what our life will be like if we resolve to make this change and do make this change. Baba provides a hint. He says, "The mind will set itself right as soon as you give up all concern with the past and future and live entirely in the now."

This statement by Baba clearly implies that living *entirely in the now*, replaces entirely living in the future. Hence, in the new way of life suggested by Baba there is no looking towards the future for desire satisfaction. If we gather the strength of our will and resolutely refuse to follow a desire-thought to create a circumstance embodying desire satisfaction, we will most certainly find out the truth of the matter for ourselves. Baba further encourages us to gather our strength and make this decision. He says, "Self-negation or self-denial through self-control creates resistances for the creative energy of the body, mind, and intellect to exercise against, to grow in strength and glory so as to know and help Brahma, the Universal Creative Energy, in fulfilling the Divine Purpose."

Here Baba is telling us that to change our life by the renunciation of craving has a glory far beyond its personal benefit, that by ceasing to base our life on the satisfaction of desires we help Brahma (Baba) in His mission as the Divine Avathar.

We do have our life as it is now, but everyone has the desire to continue to be happy or know a deeper happiness. Even a person who loves misery, or even a criminal believe they are choosing ways which will bring happiness to them. Were we to be told that by opening a door and stepping into another room we would find bliss, an ever-constant, ever-new, ever-fresh delight moment to moment, forever and ever, many of us, perhaps most of us, would like to know the whereabouts of the room and how to open the door. Baba tells us where the room is and how to open the door. The "room" is not located either within our skin or outside our skin. It is located in the subtle levels of our being. It is sometimes called "the inside" or "the heart." To locate it, we need to reduce our fascination with the phenomenal world by noticing the defects in the objects of our desires, and by a willingness to admit, that when we secure an object of desire, our happiness is neither perfect nor permanent. This is called "detachment." Having located the room, the door must be opened. Baba tells us that the door will of itself open for us if we realize that only God can bestow perfect happiness, and thus the wise move would be to possess Him. This can be done by desiring Him only, by turning every desire-thought to God instead. That is, desire God only, think God, see God, hear God, taste God, feel God, desire only God. Baba assures us that in this way the door to bliss will open quite easily.

If we have a mind to do as Baba suggests, we can start immediately by loving God, the ever-new source of happiness and bliss, and by interrupting the pattern of our desire-thoughts by refusing to maintain our private desire-world. Like everything new to us, it takes practice to gain control, but we have the power and the ability, and if we think we do not, God will provide us with His power if we but call on Him. When a desire-thought arises in our consciousness, we observe it — "Yes, there is this desire, now it is here and known to me." That is all. We observe the desire-thought, but we do not follow it into action. That is Baba's advice. Do not follow the desire into action. Instead, turn the desire to God and know that He is the happiness we really want.

If we are really intent on realizing the Truth of our own life, we must seriously consider what Baba says, dive deep into its meaning and then use every ounce of strength and energy to apply Baba's teachings to our daily lives.

In a subtle move such as the resolve to end the private world we have known up to this moment, a delicate touch is needed. We will need to fully use our God-given faculties of intelligence and discrimination. We wish to discontinue the private world we have created by the satisfaction of desires, but there is another aspect of desire which we will need to understand. For example, a desire to help another person will arise. And we need food, clothes, shelter, and health — these needs will be expressed as desires. Baba has given us a guideline. He says to examine a desire-thought before following it into action. If intelligence, discrimination, and conscience advise that the desire is neither harmful to oneself nor to another person, then go ahead. Obviously, intelligence and discrimination must be both acute and honest, otherwise we will deceive ourselves and continue to maintain the limitations of a private world constructed out of the satisfaction of desires. This is the meaning of the title, "A Ceiling on Desires," as contrasted to "a suppression of all desires."

Pandora's Box

Pandora's Box, once opened, brings forth a multitude of unexpected troubles. A simple and almost universal human trait could be likened to the cover of Pandora's Box. It is a trait which Baba speaks of continually, for beneath it lurks a very great danger which can result in the destruction of one's chance to have a meaningful and liberating life.

The human trait mentioned is the wide-spread tendency to find fault with others. Other people are often faulty indeed, and our indignation at their misdeeds is almost irresistible in its urge to be expressed in words, if not in action. By itself, on the surface, finding fault with others is damaging enough. It poisons relationships, scuttles the self-confidence of the victims, and brings about a set of circumstances which most assuredly do not contribute to our own happiness. But these are the least of the evils which spring forth when Pandora's Box is opened.

Baba points out that when we yield to the tendency to find, talk about, and dwell on the faults of other people two serious misfortunes are visited upon us: (a) the coarse flow of fault-finding disrupts the subtle flow of self-inquiry and, (b) one's attention is directed outward to the faults of other people and with this mindset one is unable to realize one's Divinity.

159

Self-inquiry, the spiritual discipline which realizes that temporary and partial satisfaction plus much suffering is the fruit gathered in a life dedicated to experiencing the outer world and, having seen this, turns inward instead to find the basis of oneself and the world, is cancelled out when one turns away from self-observation to enjoy the deceptive pleasures of finding fault with others. The practice of finding fault with others, no matter the provocation and the self-righteous satisfaction temporarily experienced, is a heavy price to pay for the loss of sincere, dedicated, and continuous self-inquiry. Baba tells us that it is a desperate blow to Liberation, Self-Realization, God-Realization, (all have the same meaning) if we exchange a commitment to Self-Inquiry for the dubious satisfaction of finding fault with others. Let us learn through our own observation of our own mistakes, and let others learn likewise through their own faults. Neither of the two learnings are aided by the practice of finding fault with others. Survival of ourselves as spiritual aspirants demands that we find a way of living in society which is not based on the practice of finding fault with others.

The second vital spring of life which is cut off by finding fault with others is the confident assertion of one's own true identity as the Divine. Sages of ancient times have declared to their students that as one thinks, so one is; that where one's thoughts are, there consciousness resides. The Avathar of the Age, our beloved Baba has told us this truth of life in even stronger terms. He tells us to never believe that we are human beings who must rise to Godhead, for, in fact, we are God playing temporary roles as human beings, and eventually we will merge again into the Divine, our Source and our Reality. Baba tells us to keep always in mind that we are Divine, and during a discourse delivered at a recent Birthday celebration held by his devotees in Prasanthi Nilayam, Baba gave five statements of fact which he advised we never forget and always keep repeating in our minds. They are quoted in other pages of this book, and they center around the declaration that "I am not different from God; I am the Indivisible Supreme Absolute — I am Sath-Chith-Ananda (Being, Consciousness, Bliss)."

Baba tells us to act in Divinity, in noble ways and not in mean, petty ways. He warns us that in following the practice of finding fault with others we are not acting in accordance with our

Divine heritage. Thus, finding fault with others has the terrible effect of blocking our consciousness from its potential of abiding at the level of Divinity.

It is for these reasons that Baba teaches that we should keep Pandora's Box closed upon this extremely damaging practice.

Baba says to his devotees, "What I want you to resolve from today is: do not find fault in others. Do not scandalize anyone. Do not feel envious or be malicious. Be always sweet in temperament and in your talk. Fill your conversation with devotion and humility."

The foundation for real peace is, according to the Vedas, the quality of My Three. My Three means amicability, compassion, kindness. It can also be taken to mean "my three," that is to say, my word, deed, and thought shall be in accordance with thy word, thought, and deed. That is to say, we shall speak, think and act together, without friction or faction, in the atmosphere of love and understanding. That is what is wanted in the world today, My Three.

— Sathya Sai Baba

The Priceless Secret

Many of us, perhaps most people, are puzzled about the differences in the lives of individuals, puzzled about the lack of equity or fairness in life's distribution of fortune and misfortune. Not only are we born with unequal bodies, intelligences, and talents, but persons of wicked behavior often seem to thrive, whereas people of good heart and behavior are not free of injury, suffering, and misery. It was this very puzzle which impelled Gautama, the Buddha, to extraordinary austerities and to his eventual insight into the existence of misery; its cause, its ending, and the way to its cessation. He saw that each thing comes into existence because of the prior existence of something else, and that with the cessation of one link in the chain of existence, the entire chain would fall apart. The Buddha found that craving was the key link in the chain which binds us to the misery which is inevitably associated with the revolving wheel of birth, death, and rebirth. He held that it was best to become a monk in order to devote one's full attention to the destruction of the binding power of craving and, by this, gain release in this very lifetime; thus realizing Nirvana, the deathless state.

Now, in the span of our life today, the blessed Avathar, Sri Sathya Sai Baba, appears to us as a beloved form and voice to restate the unchanging truth that misery is the eternal companion of

162

craving and ignorance and that we have the innate power to know our truth and thus be free of misery now and forever. Baba tells us that today, in the blessed lifetime of the Avathar, we need not adopt the life-style of a recluse, that release from misery and the realization of innate bliss may come about in all its fullness even while living a family life in the midst of society.

Baba tells us there are differences in the lives of individuals because of two reasons. The first reason is that each person is unique and unlike any other person, even though he or she may be in ignorance of it, may copy others, and may fail to express that uniqueness. The second reason why one person's life is unlike that of another person is because of action and reaction. Baba says that every action is followed by a reaction and that the consequence of action is the dominant cause of an individual's own unique life experience. It is the present consequences of past actions which account for that apparent unfairness in life about which we tend to protest. We learn from Baba, as well as from the sages of ancient times, that the consequence of a present action may be immediate, but that major events which occur in our lives have their roots in the distant past. Events are likened to the fruit of a tree; a seed takes time to sprout, grow, mature, and distribute its fruit. It is this aspect of the universal energy which brings about the birth, life, and death of an individual. So long as this process of nature continues — so long will we be bound to the world of diverse experiences with its alternating modes of happiness and misery. Many people are content with the way of nature, but not every one of us is content. When we observe what is happening, questions occur to us, "Is it inevitable? Are we forever bound to the consequences of our actions? Can one be free of all bindings?" Then the search is on, and if it is our good fortune, we encounter the divine teachings of the divine Baba. He says, in effect, "Yes, the consequences of your action do indeed bind you; even breathing has a result. But there is a way to be free."

Because of his love and compassion for us, Baba reveals the priceless secret upon which our birth, life, and death are hinged. He reveals to us the divine secret of how to be with life yet not be bound by the consequences of action. Were the existence of this secret known, but the secret not revealed, the entire sum of the world's gold and precious gems would fall short of being an adequate price to pay for this knowledge.

Consider that even breathing, without which our life would not continue, is an action and that reaction must follow. And for us to be free, to act with unmodified spontaneous delight each and every new instant, our action must cease to be limited and constrained by prior action. Action and reaction, cause and its result, desire and its consequence create the web which is our own unique world of alternating satisfaction and dissatisfaction. So long as action and reaction weave their web, we are prisoners with no way of escape. Now comes the divine Baba to show us a secret way. He tells us that we, his devotees, may be free to think, talk, and act in purity every moment, not contaminated by the past; that the way of purity for mind and heart can now be our way, and that free from the consequences of action we may be of pure love and know ourselves to be one with the Lord, who is himself love only.

The infinitely valuable secret which Baba now reveals to us is, "The fruit of action belongs to the actor, therefore renounce the fruit! Act, but renounce the fruit of action; dedicate every action to God and renounce all desire for its fruit; call upon God to be the doer of action, and totally and fully, without recourse, renounce every vestige of attachment to the fruit of action!"

To eyes not refined by knowledge and practice, a diamond may appear to be one stone among others. Unless we are vitally interested, the infinitely precious secret of how to escape from all bindings may appear to be just a few words strung together in phrases and sentences. But if we are alert and concerned, from the day we learn of this secret from our divine Baba, our lives will never again be the same. He, the infinite depth of the Absolute, having taken form so that our eyes and minds may be aware, tells us that he, as the infinite power and energy of the manifest Absolute, will take upon himself the fruit of our action if we dedicate all action to him, and that we may thus escape from the binding web of action and consequence and know freedom. An illustration of this, perhaps of minor significance, yet from actual daily life, is the Bombay devotee whose life was in torment because of alcoholism. His business was failing, his family was breaking apart, and his health was weakening. He approached Baba, clasped Baba's feet, and prayed for Baba to save him. He explained his plight and confessed, that despite the desperate circumstances, he was totally unable to resist his craving for liquor. Baba's reply was to this effect, "Do not worry. You need not stop drinking. I ask only that you do one thing. As you take each drink, dedicate it to me." As may be surmised, in this divine circumstance, the devotee's craving for liquor diminished and before long he was free of it. He had dedicated his action to Baba. Baba was then the actor and, so to speak, chewed up the consequence of the action.

How do we dedicate our actions to Baba? Or to that particular name and form of the Divine which is most dear to us? What we are about to do is subjective — not in the ordinary course of objective experience. Faith is a prerequisite, but faith in Baba we already have, for otherwise we would pay no attention. In the light of faith now comes practice. Each morning we speak to Baba (or our own dearest form of the Divine) and ask him to accept the result of our action this day. Each separate action we dedicate to Baba. For example, the man arrives at his work and, within his mind, he addresses Baba, "Lord, my destiny is to be active and I will do my duty now, but it is you, the divine consciousness within, who is the real doer. Please take the fruit of my action." For the woman in the house, she, for example, could say to Baba, "Lord, I am sweeping the floor of this home to make it sweet and clean for you who are my constant companion and who stands beside me as I go about this work."

To dedicate the fruit of action to God, who may be intangible to our eyes and touch, is new to us, but this new way will not be impossible for us since we are already experienced in giving up the fruit of action; we know how to do it. I doubt if there is even one of us who has not acted for the benefit of another, who has not dedicated the fruit of his action to someone other than himself. For example, the endless actions in which mother engages, not for her benefit, but for the benefit of her family. And men have done much for the benefit of true friends, even to giving up life itself. And, since his devotees love Baba very much indeed, it will not be difficult, in love for him, to dedicate all actions to him.

Baba assures us that if we look to the Divine, to Him fully manifest in the Sai form and truly resident in our hearts, He will accept our actions and their consequences and that from this moment onward we may be carefree and happy. This is the priceless secret of human life revealed to us now by the divine Baba.

Our Body

Baba tells us, "To realize his nature, which is Divine, man has to by-pass the human body which is the base for his 'I' personality."

For ages past, individuals have attempted to transcend the limitation of their bodies. Some have regarded the body as an almost literal prison and have tried to escape by austerities, denial of food and sleep, and by using the hammer blows of weather extremes, icy streams, and unnatural postures. But Baba advises, "The body has to be carefully and tenderly fostered. It is a precious gift, a very complicated but well-coordinated machine, given for achieving a laudable task." Baba himself is the example. He is freedom itself, yet we may note that his care for his body is easy and natural. Even the Buddha, whose austerities were the wonder of yogis throughout the India of his day, realized the futility of abusing his body and, thereafter, gave conventional care to his body. He gained Liberation after choosing the middle way between austerity and sensory indulgence.

Baba tells us that, in fact, body is solidified mind, and then goes on to say, "To think that somehow we got this human body more as an accident than for a purpose and to think we should feed it with all the pleasures and then let it wither away and die is a great mistake. It is not proper to spend our life in such a thoughtless manner."

Baba points out that the body itself is not a prison and he carefully explains this. He tells us that it is we, ourselves, who make the body into a prison, and this comes about because we have accepted that our body is our very self. The people in one's life automatically accept that one's body is oneself, and, we, also, accept it automatically. Every pain felt and every pleasure felt confirms that the body is "me." Yet, Baba, and the great sages of all ages tell us it is not so. Baba comments, "When you say this is my body, my mind, my intelligence, and so on, it implies that you are different from the body, the mind, the intelligence, etc. You are in the body, in the mind and elsewhere, but they are not in you. They belong to you, but they are not the same as you. They are you, but you are not they."

This puzzle, the puzzle that we know the body as our own very self (yet sages declare the body to be non-self) requires some careful consideration. About this, the sage Sri Nisargadatta Maharaj said to a devotee, "Is it not important to you to know whether you are a mere body or something else? Or maybe nothing at all? Don't you see that all your problems — food, clothing, shelter, family, friends, name, fame, security, survival — all these lose their meaning the moment you realize that you may not be a mere body?"

The great saint, Ramana Maharshi, explained the error of body-identify to Paul Brunton, the English writer:

How does the desire for eternal life arise? Because the present state is unbearable. Why? Because it is not your real nature. Had it been your real nature, there would be no desire to agitate you . . . Consider what happens when a stone is thrown up. It leaves its source, is projected up, tries to come down and is always in motion until it regains its source where it is at rest . . . Where there is a sense of separateness from the source, there is agitation and movement until the sense of separateness is lost. So it is with yourself. Now that you identify yourself with the body, you think that you are separate . . . To identify oneself with the body and yet to seek happiness, is like attempting to ford a river on the back of an alligator . . . To continue in that state will only kept one in an endless tangle and there will be no peace . . . The Self remains ever, even after the

body perishes. The discontent is due to the wrong identity
of the Eternal Self with the perishable body.

Surely we can "see" some distinction between body and ourselves. For instance, an eye or a leg may be lost in an accident. Yet
"we" do not become partial thereby. Even a one-time insight is
enough to undo the illusion that body and self are one and the same
at all times. About identification with the body, Baba has this to
say, "What is your shadow? Is it not something separate from you?
Does its length or clarity or career affect you in any way? Understand that the same is the relationship between the body and
yourself."

What Baba says is clear. From the viewpoint of "I," the Self-
Reality; one is body, mind, intelligence, and everything else as well,
including the void of everything. But to believe that the body is one's
Self-Reality is an error, for one's body will change, deteriorate, and
eventually perish, whereas the Self-Reality never changes. If we are
unable to appreciate this distinction, we are bound to make many
painful mistakes, all founded on the erroneous concept that our
body is our very self. Baba asks, "Why does man worry? Body identity. How did he acquire the body? By past activites. What caused
them? By the twin pulls of love and hate. How did they originate?
They were born out of entanglement in the opposites. Why did man
get snared in the opposites? By ignoring the Truth, the One."

Let us feel our way into it. We notice so many changes in ourselves as body. But is there not one thing which is always present,
even during changes? If we are watchful, will we not notice that all
these changes are observed by "me" and are known to "me"? Just
"see" it, that is all. We will then know directly that there is some
point in us which is apart from the changing body and able to
observe the changing body. That insight is irrevocable. Now the
spiritual journey is really begun, and although we may fall away
for a time, we will never be the same again.

In this way, by watching — compassionately and quietly, we
may continue to live in the world and yet achieve that goal for
which anchorites and yogis labor so strenuously and often pain-
fully. Now we will have broken the bondage of wrong body-idea.
Now we are free to explore to infinity the divine teachings of our
divine Baba and be with him always, all the way.

Seva

Baba teaches that service to others is esential to spiritual life.
He gives two clear directives. The first and basic service is to arrange our lives so that we are not engaged in working harm upon
anyone, including ourselves. The wisdom of this is self-evident and
everyone from the young to the aged has it in his or her power to
adopt this first principle of service.

Baba's second teaching about service is to serve God in
oneself and in others. He points out that while a formless God is
not an object to Whom we can render service; yet God is the ever-
present Resident in each and every heart, and we may joyfully
worship and serve Him there. He tells us, "Everyone wants love,
happiness, ananda from me. So, each one must offer unto my
Immanence — manifest as my creatures — the same love, happiness, and ananda that he or she seeks from me."

Because we are under social pressure to engage in service, we
may tend to do service as a social or cultural responsibility. This
can lead to the error of doing what someone else tells us to do
without thinking it through for ourselves. Baba reminds us, "Compassion without wisdom is as disastrous as wisdom without compassion." Prior to engaging in service actions, it is good to look inward to conscience and test the proposed service action in the light

169

of Baba's two principles of seva as described in the first two paragraphs. Baba has said many times that one's inner conscience is the voice of God within us.

Baba has taken form as a blessing to all beings on this planet Earth — and perhaps beyond. He, himself, is a pure flame of selfless service — everything is done for others, and he does nothing for himself. He tells us, "He who selflessly renders seva, sweetened with prema, to my creatures, he who sees me in everyone and in everything, he who remembers me at every moment is the yogee nearest to me."

About himself, Baba tells us, "The totality of Divine Energy has come as Sathya Sai unto humanity to wake up the slumbering Divinity of every human being. I will not forsake you. I have come to help, to accompany, and to carry you. I can never forsake you. I will never fail in my duty to my children; but I shall be very grateful to each child of mine who helps in my task." In selfless seva to others, not only are we able to worship the Divine and serve Him directly, but, wonder of wonders, the Lord will be grateful to His devotee who helps in His task.

A doubt may arise that on the spiritual path the world will lose its dominance in our life; yet through seva we are urged to be in contact with the world even more intimately than ever. Baba comments on this, "One must be unattached to the whirling worldliness of the world, but he should not detach himself or deviate from the discharge of his duties to the world as a component thereof."

In the above quotation, Baba warns us to take care that selfishness does not masquerade as yogic solitude. He expands his warning, "Selfishness is the greatest negative tendency in human beings. Selfishness distracts the mind, disturbs the equilibrium, distracts perception and endangers progressive evolution. The six essential weaknesses — lust, anger, avarice, attachment, pride, and jealousy are only consequences of selfishness."

As we continue our study of the divine teachings of the divine Baba, we cannot but note and be impressed with the tremendous value given to service to others. This is clear in the following statement from Baba, "When a devotee seeks with humility and purity to give seva and prema to my creatures who are in need of such selfless service and sublime love; when he considers all creatures as my children, as his beloved brothers and sisters, as the blessed manifestations of my Immanence, then in fulfillment of my role as Sathya Sai, I descend to help, accompany, and carry that yogee. I am always near such a yogee to guide him and to shower my love on his life."

We are warned most emphatically of the deadly danger of selfishness. Yet, of itself, service to others is of deep and far-reaching benefit to ourselves. It has a profound influence on one's destiny. About this, Baba says, "Only human beings are blessed with the abilities to acquire the powers of supra-human beings, and even to surpass them, to attain Divinity earlier through selfless service and dedication to the divine purpose, and through surrender and dependence on the Divine Will."

Service in all its forms, all the world over, is primarily spiritual discipline — mental clean-up! Without the inspiration given by that attitude, the urge is bound to ebb and grow dry, or, it may meander into pride and pomp. Just think for a moment: Are you serving God? Or, is God serving you? . . . When you offer milk to a hungry child, or a blanket to a shivering brother on the pavement, you are but placing a gift of God into the hands of another gift of God! You are reposing the gift of God in a repository of the Divine Principle! God serves; He allows you to claim that you have served! Without His Will, no single blade of grass can quiver in the breeze. Fill every moment with gratitude to the Giver and the Recipient of all gifts.
— Sathya Sai Baba

Divine Vision

A spiritual practice, so ancient that its beginning cannot be known, carries the name of Divine Vision, or Equal Vision. This spiritual practice gets high praise from Baba. It is in the category of day-long meditation as contrasted to brief, sitting meditation. It is not hard to do, it is joyful in the beginning, joyful in the middle, and its joy does not end.

Baba tells us that it is his experience that he, the omnipresent Divinity is in each heart, and we have faith that this is so. We are prepared to accept that the Divine is the constant reality and that names and forms come and go. The practice of Divine Vision is like this: A person comes into our field of vision. It may be a complete stranger, or it may be someone close to us. We accept that God is the inner Reality of that person. If we accept that Jesus or Krishna or Jehovah or Baba or God — by whatever name is the Reality of the person upon whom our eyes fall, we greet and acknowledge Him, saying quietly in our mind some salutation such as, "Dearest Lord, I love Thee." That name and form of God which is most dear to us will naturally come to mind.

When the Lord is acknowledged and greeted, we will experience a flash of happiness, as would be only natural when we meet the beloved of our heart. If we have adopted the spiritual practice

172

of being happy always, then Divine Vision will intensify that happiness each time we acknowledge the Lord and tell Him that we love Him. Baba has said, "Love God without reserve. To love God destroys all the barriers to love. The faulty personalities so difficult to love are by-passed and transcended."

The practice of Divine Vision is secret to ourselves and no other person can observe us or know of our practice. The individual in whose heart we salute the ever-loving divine Lord, is unknowing of our action, and we in no way interfere with him or her. If the person is a sister, we treat her as is our custom. If the person is a cultured diplomat, a beggar on the street, a taxi driver, or an employee, we continue to treat that person conventionally according to their status and actions. Divine vision is between God and ourselves and is not the business of any person, beloved family member, or stranger. It is a secret of our hearts and let it remain so.

Upon first hearing of the practice of Divine Vision, one may exclaim, "But some people are so vicious and horrible, or so obnoxious and irritating that I cannot bear to even look at them much less say, 'I love you.'" The point of the practice is to look right through the obnoxious personality, or deformed body or mind, and pay no attention to it. We are looking only at the constant divine Reality which is the essence of every person. Baba explains the situation by this simile: Two houses are opposite to each other on the same street and are occupied by two families who are enemies. It so happens that above the door of each house there is fastened a picture of Sri Sathya Sai. The two families may hurl insults or even rocks at each other, in anger and hatred of each other, but neither family is angry at Baba, even though his picture is fastened above the door of the enemy's house. In like fashion, we may be unable to control a negative emotion which may arise when we see a particular personality, but that is no reason to be angry at the Lord who is the constant Reality behind that personality.

The spiritual practice of Divine Vision is a blessing to the personality whose inner Divinity we worship, for God responds from the heart of that personality when we, His devotee, call upon Him; and the practice of Divine Vision will purify our minds and hearts and thus make us ready for illumination. Divine Vision can start the moment we know of it. It will give joy ever after if we continue with that spiritual practice.

Holding to Truth

Baba often puzzles people by telling them they are divine, whereas they know very well from a lifetime of mistakes and other experiences that they are only too human. Such statements by Baba introduce the spiritual practice of Holding to Truth. Baba declares, "Do not think that you are human and that you have to reach the state of the Divine. Think rather that you are God, and that from that state you have become a human being. If you think this way, all the attributes of God will manifest in you. Know that you have descended from God as human beings and that eventually you will go back to your source."

If our minds hold to the idea that a certain faulty human person is oneself then that is where our consciousness will be, and it is that concept which will guide our life. Whereas, if our mind holds to the idea that the Divine is us and we are the Divine, that is where our consciousness will reside. Long ago, the sage Annamacharya said, "How much you think you are, so much, not more are you." And, centuries ago, the Self-Realized sage, the 14 year-old Asta-vakra, guru of King Janaka, said to him, "In our present condition, we are not in our own Self. We are conscious only of the body and the mind and all the various things of the world. Wherever our consciousness is, there we are." Today, the Avathar of the Age,

174

Sri Sathya Sai Baba tells us, "He who considers himself free is free indeed, and he who considers himself bound remains bound. Think yourself to be free, the eternal unlimited Consciousness-Bliss and you will be free and happy. Constantly think of yourself as the eternally free Self. Realize! You are ever free."

Why do we not accept this as soon as we are told this marvelous and extraordinary truth about ourselves? Baba says, "Do not be discouraged that you do not have the ability. As you feel, so you become. Feel you are Divine, feel that nothing is impossible for you. Feel that you are Divine, that you are good and Godly."

Who tells us that we are a limited human personality and that we need to adjust to the human state? We are told so by family, schools, T.V., friends — in fact everyone with whom we are usually in contact so tells us. And who tells us to not accept that we are merely a variant from the common denominator of the average man? We are told so by our Baba; he who knows the truth because he *is* the truth. About himself, Sri Sathya Sai says, "Divine energy has come as Sai to wake up the Divinity in everyone."

To devotees who ask, Baba advises, "Wake up my children! Wake up to the dawn of knowledge, wake up to your Divine Duties, wake up to your Divine Rights, and wake up to your Divine Reality."

One small match, if struck, contains the fire which can burn down imprisoning walls. Just one of Baba's teachings can be that match in one's life. Consider deeply — what if the truth is as Baba says it? To young children, he declares, "Listen, all ye children of immortality! You, children of the eternal. You are not lumps of flesh. You are embodiments of the eternal. You are repositories of Bliss. Your hearts are shrines of the Divine. The whole of nature is your playground; all the things in it are your playthings. Regard yourselves as masters of the universe and not its bond-slaves."

We adults did not have Baba to guide us when we were children. We have been taught incorrect ideas from childhood, and are still holding to them. Why not discard all such ideas? Consider! Maybe Baba is telling us the greatest truth! What a tragedy if we refuse to let go of our past conditioning, and thus remain caught in a false life. The wonderful opportunity of this moment when Baba tells the truth to us may never be ours again. What can we lose by doing as Baba teaches? And everything may be lost if we do not!

This is the spiritual practice of Holding to Truth, which Baba says will bring us to realize that we are the Divine. Do not equate his teaching with "Mesmerism" or "Positive Thinking." What Baba teaches is no modern fad. Centuries ago, in the ecstasy of Self-Realization, King Janaka declared to his guru, "I am pure consciousness. Through ignorance I have imposed limitations upon myself. Constantly reflecting in this way, I am abiding in the Absolute."

In an almighty revelation, cutting away the very ground of ignorance where until now we have taken our stand, Baba gave the spiritual practice of Holding to Truth as part of his Birthday Discourse, November 23, 1983. He said,

> If your yearning to experience Brahmananda, the Sath-Chith-Ananda, is sincere and pure, from this day, keep ever in your memory what I am about to tell you:[1]
>
> (1) "I am God; I am not different from God." Be conscious of this always. Keep it ever in mind. "I am God; I am God, I am not different from God." Be reminding yourself of this. Pray that you may not fail in this spiritual exercise.
>
> (2) "I am the Indivisible Supreme Absolute." This is the second Truth to be established in the consciousness by unremitting repetition and prayer.
>
> (3) "I am Sath-Chith-Ananda." (i.e. Being, Awareness, Bliss).
>
> (4) "Grief and anxiety can never affect me." Develop this faith and convince yourselves of this Truth by repeated assurance and prayer.
>
> (5) "I am ever content; fear can never enter me." Feel thus for ever. Pray that this conviction grows stronger and stronger.
>
> As the physical body is maintained healthy and strong by the five vital airs (prana), these five prayers will endow you with the 'awareness of Brahman' which is the same as 'the status of Brahman Itself!

1. Brahmananda and Sath-Chith-Ananda mean the supreme Being, Consciousness, and Bliss of Divinity

Blessings to American Members of the Sai Family

. . . Love is vital. Love is Divine. To render an act fit to be offered to God and pure enough to win His Grace, it has to be a manifestation of Love. The brighter the manifestation, the nearer you are to God. Prema (Divine Love) is not affected or modified by considerations of caste, or creed, or religion; it cannot be tarnished by envy, malice or hate . . . Fill every word of yours with Love, fill every act of yours with Love. The word that emerges from your tongue shall not stab like the knife, nor wound like the arrow, nor hit like the hammer. It has to be a fountain of sweet nectar, a counsel of consoling vedantic wisdom, a soft path of blossoms. It must shower peace and joy . . . Love knows no fear. Love shuns falsehood. Fear drags man into falsehood, injustice, and wrong. Love does not crave for praise; that is its strength. Only those who have no Love in them itch for reward and reputation. The reward for Love is Love itself.

When you are eager to place offerings before the Lord, instead of transitory materials, let your offering be Love. Love is the very Light of Life; it is the only comprehensive Code of Conduct . . . Let it flow clear from the heart, as a stream of Truth, a river of wisdom. Let it not emanate from the head, nor from the tongue. Let it emerge, full and free, from the heart. This is the highest duty, the noblest Godliness.

Start the day with Love. Live the day with Love. Fill the day with Love. Spend the day with Love. End the day with Love. This is the way to God.

(Excerpts from a letter to devotees dated July 18, 1969).

Bhagawan Sri Sathya Sai Baba

TELE No. 33
BRINDAVAN
WHITEFIELD

TELE No. 30
PRASANTHINILAYAM. P O
ANANTHAPUR DT.

My Dears! what is primarily needed for one who wants to ultimately surrender himself entirely to The Lord is a consciousness of perfect security under The protecting grace of the supreme Lord. This consciousness can never leave us if we constantly practise the remembrance of Him. Verily, remembrance itself is Darishan. The repetition of GOD's name must lead to dedication of all your actions to Him. This remembrance will be yours even when you are intellectually and physically active in all the walk of life when you consider that those activities are performed in the name and for the sake of The Lord. During your off-moments do not fail to keep your thoughts engaged in the contemplation of GOD an at the same time meditate upon the truth that all your physical and mental powers have their source and inspiration from the Cosmic energy of the Divine

With Blessings
Baba

BHAGAWAN SRI SATHYA SAI BABA

PRASANTHINILAYAM P.O.
ANANTHAPUR DT.
TELEPHONE No. 30.

BRINDAVAN
WHITEFIELD
TELEPHONE No. 33.

Date :

Message

you as body, mind or soul are a dream.
but what you really are is EXISTENCE, Knowledge,
Bliss. You are the GOD of This universe. you are
creating The whole universe and drawing it in.
To gain The infinite universal individuality The
miserable little prison individuality must go.
Bhakti is no crying or any negative condition.
it is seeing of all in all we see.
it is the heart That reaches the goal. follow the heart.
A pure heart seeks beyond the intellect. it gets
inspired.
whatever we do reacts upon us. if we do good,
we shall have happiness and if evil, unhappiness
within you is the real happiness, within you is the
mighty ocean of nectar divine. Seek it within you,
feel it, feel it; it is here, the self. it is not the body,
The mind, The intellect, The brain. it is not the desire of
The desiring. it is not the object of desire. Above all
These, you are. All These are simply manifestations.
you appear as the smiling flower, as The twinkling
stars. what is There in The world which can make
you desire anything?

With Blessings and
Love
Sri Sathya Sai Baba

Baba Talks to the Indian Air Force
Dec. 5, 1982
(written down after the talk)

"Man's natural state is happiness, and he cannot be blamed for craving that which is his own. But man is making a serious mistake. He believes that the happiness for which he craves comes from objects which he can experience. The truth of the matter is that he does not experience these objects. On the contrary, the objects experience the man, and in this process the man is further weakened. The man comes home from his work feeling tired and frustrated. In order to seek relaxation and a renewal of a feeling of happiness, the man goes to a cimema and gets his mind filled with faulty life values portrayed by the glamorous actors and actresses. Or, the man goes off to his club. There he engages in conversation about the world, perhaps plays cards, and perhaps takes liquor. This is all a waste of time; and waste of time is waste of life. Instead of renewing the man's strength, it further weakens him.

"What is the remedy? The remedy is to consider the truth which represents this ancient and sacred land of Bharat. The eternal truth is that there is only one ever-lasting, never-failing happiness, and that is God. You are God, and to drink deeply of that ever-flowing spring of happiness, you must turn to yourself, to the Divine Atma which, however obscured, is always the resident of your heart, the subtle truth of your being.

180

"The Atma, the Lord, the Divine Happiness is not our ever-constant experience, for it is obscured by such activities of the mind as doubt, depression, hatred, jealousy, envy, craving, attachments to objects and persons, and ignorance about oneself, about God, and about the world.

"In order to expel these dangerous and harmful tendencies from one's life, one needs to engage in Sadhana. The objective of all types of Sadhana is purification of mind and heart. For this reason it is said that one should do good, see good, and be good.

"Love is the vital and essential reality of spiritual life. In human life, love takes a number of different aspects — love for wife and children, for various habits and indulgences, for various objects, for certain ideas, and for God. God *is* love, and He is there in each aspect of love. It is as when pure clear water is poured into bottles of different colors. In each differently-colored bottle, the water appears to be differently-colored. Yet, truly, the water remains pure and clear. Although love, which is God, appears to be modified and even distorted in man, yet, truly, that Divine Love remains pure and perfect. That love in man, which is pure and perfect, is his love for God. Only love for God is perfect. Gather your love from all aspects of your life and let it flow as one strong, deep river of love to God. Nothing else is needed. No other Sadhana is necessary. Happiness and peace will be yours."

The sage, Paramananda, had ten disciples, each a notorious example of sloth and stupidity! On their travels, they came across a river, which they waded through, to the other bank. The water came up to their necks in some places, and so, when they struggled onto land, they decided to find out whether all had arrived safely. They feared that some of them must have been swept away by the swift current. Fear and the consequent confusion heightened their native stupidity. At last, they discovered that one of them had been washed away, for, whenever each of the ten counted the others standing in a line before him, he left himself out and found only nine men before him. All ten confirmed the conclusion that one of them had disappeared in the flood! And, the ten wailed for the lost man and were so plunged in sorrow that the hullabaloo they raised brought a farmer to their side. He asked them why and got the answer that of the ten who waded across, one was drowned! The farmer saw that there were ten men before him! They challenged his verdict and demonstrated how they counted and verified that one had really been lost. The farmer then told them that each one had omitted to count himself. The outward vision was wrong; the inward vision alone can reveal the truth, he advised them.

We are trying to discover God, searching for Him throughout the Universe. But we omit to investigate His existence within ourselves as the very core and keystone of our Being. When you discover yourself — your Self — all wailing ceases and you attain supreme happiness. This is real self-knowledge.

— Sathya Sai Baba

CONVERSATIONS
WITH BABA

January, 1978

JH: Devotees in New York would like to have a guideline for personal life, similar to the administrative Guidelines for Centers.

SAI: The principal thing is that the life and the work should be dedicated to God.

JH: Swami, they would like a series of do's and don'ts to guide them through the day.

SAI: There are so many different vocations and professions that each has its appropriate code of behavior. One vital principle for everyone is to do no harm to others. We should do everything in our power to help others.

JH: A big problem that faces these young people is that of drugs. It is the general belief that marijuana is not harmful.

SAI: At first, a drug may make the person feel strong and confident. But all drugs are unnatural in their effect on the mind, and they do positive harm to the brain and to the spiritual capacity. The spiritual aspirant, the devotee of God should not make use of drugs.

JH: Most young people, not only in New York, have the desire to, or feel pressure to engage in intensive social life. What is the correct attitude for Sai devotees?

SAI: Social Service, yes. Idle social life is not good.

185

JH: Swami, the devotee arises in the morning, and then what for the day?

SAI: The awakening each morning should be a new birth. After awakening, be quiet for a few minutes. Pray to God for strength to live the day in dedication to Him, and for the strength to help others. At night time, there is a new death. Recollect the day — but not in detail, and offer it to the Almighty. In the morning, the day was dedicated to God. At night, the day's work and its fruit is laid as an offering at His Lotus Feet.

October 25, 1978

JH: Swami, new Centers, with maybe only three people, want to have some other people come to their meetings, but months pass and nobody comes. Could they do something like posting a notice of their meeting at places like health food stores?

SAI: No. Swami prefers that additional people come only through observing the virtuous lives of the Center members, and by word of mouth. Notices and such might start small, but in time they will get out-of-hand. Even such small things as notices will be taken as an advertising of Swami. Other Swamis have to advertise and even provide transport, but Sai does no advertising, yet thousands come. Sai even tells the people here to go home, but they stay. There is this difference.

JH: Then the small Centers will need to just patiently wait for membership increases?

SAI: Yes.

JH: Swami, some questions arise in the American Centers for which I do not have an answer. Many people of Jewish faith do not understand why the symbol of the Jewish faith is not included in the Sai symbol of all religions, since the Jewish people exceed in numbers some of the religions represented in the Sai symbol.

SAI: It is not through any intention that the Jewish symbol is excluded. In India, there is not a general awareness that the Jewish symbol is substantially different. Does the Cross fail to symbolize the Jewish faith to a substantial degree?

MG: Yes, Swami. There is a substantial difference.

SAI: Then let the Jewish people make a proposal to us and we will give consideration to it.

JH: Swami says that there is the duty of self-preservation. People wonder how far this goes. To save one's own life, should one kill the person who is attacking?

SAI: To preserve one's body is an important duty. One may take whatever means are necessary for self-preservation. About the other part of your question: to kill the person attacking — the answer is "yes," if that is the only way to preserve one's own life. But keep in mind that many alternate actions might be taken to avoid being killed. Only if every possibility is exhausted may one take the extreme measure of killing the attacker.

JH: Swami's discourse about people going to the Moon Loka and the Sun Loka created much confusion.

SAI: Sai has explained it before, and perhaps the people asking the question did not read. People may think there is a journey over a distance to the realm of Indra, the Moon, and the Sun. All such changes are within the person. If a person develops his life so that he has great physical force and strength, he is said to have centered his life in the Indra Loka. If he has developed his mind to such an extent that it is beyond the comprehension of an ordinary person, his life is said to be in the Moon Loka. And, if a man had developed intelligence to a maximum extent, his life is said to be in the Sun Loka.

JH: Another question that arises has to do with Swami's statement that, by virtuous actions in the past, a human birth is gained. In this context there must have been virtuous animal actions, but how can this be when the animal acts by instinct?

SAI: A good action is good whether accomplished by instinct or reason. Is not the shelter provided by a tree good for both animal and man? When a cow denies milk to its calf because the milk is taken by the herdsman, the result is beneficial for the human persons who drink the milk, and the benefit enjoyed is no less because the cow did not think, but is only being itself. And the dog in the house, does he not guard and care for the master, and love him too? A human guard must be paid, but the dog gives love and loyalty without concept of payment. There are endless examples throughout nature of good and virtuous action being fully effective, even though, by instinct, the animal or plant is only being true to its own nature.

Human life is not being depleted even though millions die and, in addition, there is a constant transition from humanity to the Divine. Instead of depletion, the human population is growing, and this new supply comes from the rock, the insect, the animal. Even science testifies that the rock decomposes and becomes the tree; the vegetation is eaten and becomes the animal; and the animal in its various aspects is consumed and becomes the human. It is a constant process of passing from one grade to another. The human birth is the final birth and, dependent on the virtue of the life, it ends in the Divine, or is reborn again.

JH: Is degrading possible? Is there a rebirth back to the animal?

SAI: The possibility is not denied, but it is only rarely that such a thing happens. The degrading of human life due to lack of virtue will normally result in rebirth as a lower grade human. The total process is always present. Table and wood are equally present. If attention is given to wood, table is not seen. If attention is given to table, wood is not seen. This cushion is not without thread, nor is the thread without cotton. How it is viewed is a matter of emphasis. Here I am now drawing three circles, the smaller within the larger. This middle one represents the Jiva (the individual "soul"); the smaller circle, the body; and the largest, the Atma (the ultimate Self).

The smaller circle is what you think you are, the next one what others think you are, and the third is what you really are: the Atma. The smaller circle may expand and expand until it merges with the larger, the Atma.

JH: Swamiji, that is the present list of questions that have come up for which I did not have the answers.

SAI: It is good. It is important that the questions be asked. They are the questions that are presented to the many gurus, but Sai can give the correct answers.

December, 1978

SAI: Crime has become very bad in India. There is no safety.

JH: Swami, this is not particular to India. The same is true all over the world. How will it all end?

SAI: To the good. In a few years, all will be peaceful.

JH: But Swami, it is getting worse, and it is the Kali Yuga (a world period of diminishing virtue).

SAI: No. It is not as bad now as it was. It is like in the ocean. There is a time of high waves, and there may be some peak waves that crash heavily on the shore, but this is followed by a calm and peaceful sea.

JH: Many people are saying that, very shortly, we will enter a period of great catastrophe.

SAI: There may be some peak waves, as I mentioned, but the world will be happy, peaceful, and prosperous.

GUEST: No world war?

SAI: No. No world war.

JH: We are fortunate to be alive so that we may see this peaceful world.

SAI: You will all see it. Even old men will live to see it.

GUEST: Then Prema Sai will not have much work to do! Swami will have made the world peaceful.

SAI: That is some 40 years away. At that time the world will be peaceful. That is the Name: Prema Sai. All will be love — love, love, love everywhere.

GUEST: It would be good to be reborn in the time of Prema Sai!

SAI: It is best to merge with God. No rebirth.

November 7, 1980

SAI: In all countries there is a rapid deterioration of the human quality.

JH: When will it change for the better?

SAI: Soon there will be a change.

JH: When is soon, Swami? Twenty years? Ten years?

SAI: No. Now. Already there is some slight improvement in India. One cause of the general deterioration in the world is rapid communication. This allows advertising and publicity to have a strong influence on people. Your American election is an illustration of how the leaders are television actors.

JH: Swami, there is no evidence of a change for the better.

SAI: If there is a change, it will be a universal change. Not local. It will occur everyplace.

JH: This rapid world-wide communication also results in common knowledge of how to build an atom bomb. Is there not a great danger of some small nation using the bomb?

SAI: The danger is not of someone using the bomb. People are no longer afraid of death from the bomb. So long as they can pursue their objective of getting money, they are willing to risk death and to die. It is not the bomb that is the danger, it is the mind that is the danger. The bomb exists only as an instrument of the mind. The need is for a change of mind.

JH: But Swami, people do not care to learn about that. They have no interest in Swami or in listening to him.

SAI: Minds can and do change. For example, the life style of people can be so bad that they become ashamed and change. The hippies' life style is so low and so dishonest and immoral that groups of hippies, observing their own life reflected in another group, become ashamed and of themselves they change.

JH: Well, at least Swami's devotees know about changing the mind and can do so.

SAI: Were it not for the mind change of Sai devotees the world would already have fallen into complete chaos. The deterioration of mind and man has been very rapid and abrupt, even precipitous during the last fifteen years. That the world is not in total destruction is due to the change in mind of Sai devotees and to Sai's Grace. You are not aware of it, just as you are not aware of your eyes until they are lost. In the same way, the world is not aware of Sai's Grace.

December 1, 1980
An Interview at Prasanthi Nilayam
with Jewish devotees

A request was made to Baba that he deliver a discourse directly to the Jewish people; a unique, ancient and powerful minority in the society of the world. The occasion for a major discourse was not at hand, but Baba graciously called all the Jewish devotees presently in the ashram for an interview, and included a few additional persons, of whom I was one, fortunately indeed for me. Unhappily, I was unable to keep up with the rapid exchange of questions and answers and could not remember afterwards, largely, I think, because of my unfamiliarity with the subject matter. I did manage to take a few notes and believe it worthwhile to make them a part of the book.

Prior to the questions and answers, Baba made a few comments:

"The great scriptures of mankind came into being through sound, the word of God. This is fully true of the ancient Jewish religion. It was the word of God. Over the centuries, however, man has made changes in the Bible, and present misunderstandings are due to these man-made changes. In the early days there were differences between the Jews and the Christians, but they are not appropriate today. Today the standard should be the brotherhood of man, based on the divine love of God for all mankind. Each religion should follow that which is its own and not follow a path which belongs to others, but which is not its own. Follow your own tradition, but do not hate others. Be broad-minded, as are the followers of Sai.

"The Bible, the Koran, the Vedas, the Granth — all represent the same creation. All were following the voice of God. All arose from the whisper of God which, in the pure minds of the hearers, flowered into eight sounds, eight letters, and from this, all words evolved. The eight sounds were the vowels and consonants of language. The foundation of the Jewish religion is precisely the same as that of the Vedas. The breath of God, cognized by the pure attention of the ancient seers, was heard as eight sounds, and these sounds have been given names. (Baba here pronounced each of these eight primeval sounds, but I could not catch them with my pencil.)

"The Sai symbol of five religions represents the five major religions found in India. For the West, the Jewish Star may be added as a sixth representation on the Sai symbol."

Q: Was Jesus the Messiah of the Jews?

SAI: No. He did not represent the ancient Jewish tradition. He represented the factor of change.

Q: In the Bible it says that the Jews are God's chosen people.

SAI: All peoples were created by God. Thus all are His chosen people.

Q: What is the significance of Hitler?

SAI: Hitler's actions were activated by ego and power.

Q: For what reason have the Jews been persecuted?

SAI: For every event there is a cause. There is no reason. Sai acts only for love, for the benefit of others. He has no desires. He has no selfish interest.

Q: God appeared to the Jews as a burning bush.

SAI: God appears in any form. It is according to His wish, not because of any necessity or limitation. It is His choice. God is formless. He is Sound. He can take any form according to His wish.

Q: Is Sai the Messiah of the Jews?

SAI: That is not for Sai to say. That must be determined by you. The real Messiah is the totality of good. Sai is not any particular thing. He is everything.

December 2, 1980

In the car with Swami at Brindavan:

Sai to devotee driver: "To the Gokulum."

SAI: This area is now very busy. The College is here, and now there are the fields to the left. There are 60 acres, and there is the land on the college side also.

JH: Are the lands irrigated?

SAI: All is under irrigation.

JH: Where does the water come from?

SAI: We have dug wells. They produce a large volume of water.

JH: Is the water good? Is is fit to drink?

SAI: It is good, sweet water.

JH: How deep are the wells?

SAI: Fifteen to twenty feet deep.

JH: But Swami, that is very shallow. Usually wells need to go beneath the surface water table in order to be sweet.

SAI: But Swami located where to dig.

JH: Well, that is different!

SAI: The Government experts came to locate wells, but even though they went down 100 feet no water was found.

JH: Swamiji! I cannot understand how the Government does not come to Swami, touch his feet and ask him to run the country!

SAI: It is not that the Government is unaware of what Swami is doing. They do not think it would be good for Swami to be involved in politics. Nor does Swami wish that. His interest is with his devotees and with what he is now doing. If the Government should really know Swami's Reality and his power, they would declare him to be a ward of the Government, surround him with security and he would be unable to continue to see the devotees. It is not Swami's wish. With a move of his hand, Swami could have the entire world acknowledge him — but to what end? It would be spectacular only and would accomplish nothing of value.

MG: When will the whole world know about Swami?

SAI: Even now Sai is known in many countries of the world. This is entirely without precedent. Never before have so many known of the Avathar. In the time of Rama, he was known only in the city-state where he lived. And he was naturally venerated there because he was the ruler. Knowledge about Krishna was also very limited. In his earlier days, Krishna was known only in two small villages.

JH: Is the difference due to changes in communication, or to the will of the Avathar?

SAI: Rapid communication and transportation are largely responsible. In olden days to move from Puttaparthi to Whitefield (i.e. about 120 miles) would be like a trip to a foreign continent. Now, Americans come here from the other side of the world in just a few hours time.

MG: Will the University be here?

SAI: No. In Puttaparthi only. This college and others will remain as colleges.

JH: Swami, may Mr. Kasturi publish Swami's talk to the Jews?

SAI: Why? I said words which were just heart-to-heart.

JH: Is there enough milk from the Gokulum to provide the college?

SAI: Oh, yes. Enough also for the canteens and the residents in the compound. Some of the cows provide as much as 32 liters of milk a day.

JH: How about the two cows at Prasanthi Nilayam? Are they still good?

SAI: Yes. The two from you and Mrs. Hislop still give more than 30 liters of milk a day. Now they have had five calves each. Very good cows.

MG: Will the new university use computers?

SAI: No. No computers. The National Exams were put on computers. It was a disaster. The many errors caused severe distress. Some students committed suicide. Afterwards, when the parents were told that the deceased students had really made high passing grades, much suffering resulted. The growing tendency to rely on computers and calculators to provide answers to problems is bringing about a rapid deterioration of intellect. In times past, people had to use their brains to think long and hard on problems. Now, the mental work is handed over to a computer and the mental faculties deteriorate through disuse.

MG: But is it not possible to use computers in a constructive and beneficial way?

SAI: Yes, this is going on. There is the intention to use them in ways that are beneficial and constructive. The immediate results appear to be very good. But in the long run the use of computers and calculators will result in a severe deterioration of human intellectual power.

JH: Swamiji, a personal question, please. Is December 9 the correct day for our departure, or would another date be better?

SAI: December 9 is the correct day. It is a good day.

JH: Dr. S. wants to publish Swami's Christmas day talks.

SAI: Go ahead. He may do that.

JH: The translations are those that Mr. Kasturi once showed to Swami. I carefully read every word.

SAI: It is all right.

MG: Swami, on Wednesday the Jewish festival of lights starts and continues for 8 days. Could the Jewish devotees have the lights burning here at Brindavan?

SAI: Oh, yes. They may do so.

MG: Where, Swami?

SAI: Under the central tree in the compound.

MG: Would Swami light the first lamp in the evening?

SAI: Yes, yes, I will do that.

December 9, 1980

JH: I have asked important persons around Sai if Sai is all knowing at all times, or only when he so chooses. They give different answers.

SAI: Sai knows everything. That people are in doubt is due to the Maya of the Avathar. You know that Sai is in your heart, yet you think, "Is Sai upstairs in his room, or is he elsewhere?" It is the human element. The body has the name of "Hislop," but you are not the body. You are the Atma. There is no desire in Sai. There is total purity only. This entire body is Amrith. Where is there space for desire in Sai? Everything is already mine. Sai does not think. My will is immediately realized. Whatever it may be, it instantly appears. An envelope, gold, everything. Where is there room for desire? I have no thought. If I think, it is for you, it is not for me. Sai requires no food. If I eat, it is for the benefit of everyone. If I give Darshan, it is not for me, it is for others. I am talking to you now — it is for you, not for me. A point does not appear in Sai. First a point, then disappoint! I am always the same. I am love, always love. If there are angry words, that is action. Inwardly, I remain the same. I have the same tender love for that person.

JH: Swami, some tragedy happens to a person, and they try to find a reason for it in the actions of this lifetime.

SAI: Yes, that can be.

JH: But I thought that all that happens in this life is the result of our behavior in past existences.

SAI: Not always. Something could happen with its cause in this life.

January 29, 1981

JH: Swami, please restate or redefine the goal, the objective of the American Sathya Sai Organization.

SAI: It is not just the American, it is the objective for worldwide Sathya Sai Organizations.

People, the world over, do not know they are Divine. They do not even realize what it is to be human. They have ego, anger, greed, envy, lust, hatred. These are not human qualities; they are animal qualities.

Unless Sai devotees are, at the very least, human persons free of animal qualities or characteristics, how can such devotees suggest spiritual life to others? Such suggestions will have no impact.

If devotees in general are not yet free of animal characteristics, there should be in each Sathya Sai Baba Center two or three members who live a life as true human beings.

The individual does not progress alone. He is not separate from Society, and he must do his bit to uplift the society. Therefore, the individual's work to free himself from animal characteristics and to live a spiritual life is not done for himself, but is done for all of God's creatures. The work of freeing the individual's nature from animal qualities is done, in love, for God, and done in His Name and with His help. Each member of the Sathya Sai Baba Center should work very hard to purify the quality of his life, and the goal should be to lead a perfect life, an ideal life; to be an ideal exemplar of the divine teachings of Bhagavan Sri Sathya Sai Baba.

The world will respond to the ideal life of a Sai devotee. The world is yearning for the ideal life and will, of its own accord, adopt such a life if it comes into view. They will respond, and they will follow such a life.

JH: Swami, does that mean that our Centers should now move beyond the task of working with Center members and tackle the world?

SAI: The Center members must carefully work to become truly human before they venture to instruct the world.

November 21, 1981

SAI: How do you like the pictures? (i.e. Portrait photographs for the college building to be dedicated on the 23rd).

RB: We were afraid they were too large.

SAI: They are not too large. Swami's picture will be the same size. Do you like the pictures?

JH: Bozzani looks like a movie star!

SAI: No, no. He is smiling, whereas Mrs. Bozzani is more serious. Come. Sit down.

SAI: At the center everything is liquid.

RB: Does Swami mean the world?

SAI: Yes, everything is melted. No temperature.

RB: No heat, Swami?

SAI: No temperature. Everything is liquid. Like water. Gold, iron, silver, gems, all are liquid. Next there is solid. Then trees.

JH: Trees, Swami? Trees like we see around us?

SAI: Yes, trees. Then human beings and animals. At the very center is the Divine. It is the support of everything. First is liquid, chemistry. Then solid, physics. Then trees, botany. Then man, the pinnacle of life. But at the center, supporting all, is the Divine. Without the Divine, where is chemistry, physics, botany? Like this will be the teaching of all courses at the University. The students will understand the full picture.

JH: In this picture, Swami, where do the devas and demigods and other creatures of the cosmos fit in?

SAI: They are above the senses. Man is below the senses. Those others are above the senses.

JH: But all must come to be humans in order to merge with God, is it not so?

SAI: Not totally so. There is love.

JH: Then, can man take a further step and go into the world above the senses.

SAI: That is possible.

JH: But is it not possible to realize the Self, or merge with God, while in the human state?

SAI: Oh, yes. That can be done.

JH: Does Swami mean that both possibilities exist, that man could go one way or the other?

SAI: Yes, one way or the other.

JH: Then what makes the difference? What is the difference in man that he would make one choice or the other?

RB: That is what I want to know, too.

SAI: Love is the dominant reason. Compassionate love is pure love, unselfish. In the animal there is love, but it is mixed with lust. But compassion is pure love. Only man has compassion. Through love he may realize the oneness of life, and in this way, by love, he will be one with God.

JH: Then, Swami, man can definitely realize God while in the human birth?

SAI: Yes.

JH: But suppose he fails in that, and thus eventually finds himself as a being above the sensory level, what then?

SAI: The same holds true. God is love and wherever there is pure love and love only, that is God. Love is everything, but people do not understand love. Their understanding is confused. For example: There is a child. Mother and father love the child with pure love. The child is kissed and fondled and showered with affection. This is the action of pure love. In this action there is no lust; there is no lust in that love. Another example: A father is 40 years old. There is the wife and the daughter who is 18 years of age. The love of the father for his family leads him to kiss his daughter. In this action of love, there is no lust. It is pure love, compassion. The husband also kisses his wife, and in this kiss there is some mixture of lust. In both cases, the kiss was the action of love, but the love was different.

JH: Swami, that is a wonderful explanation. The difference is very clear, and very important to understand.

SAI: Pure love, Divine love is everything.

RB: How do human beings realize and become that divine, pure compassionate love?

SAI: It will come with sadhana. There is a big mistake in the consideration of meditation as the principal sadhana. What is meditation? Meditation controls the mind. It is mental. The genuine sadhana is that pure love which is not different from the Divine.

November 30, 1981
(In the Car with Baba)

JH: In America, when they hear of Sai, some people declare that he is the Anti-Christ.

SAI: Some individual ideas of some people. Goldstein has individual ideas. Hislop has individual ideas. I know what is not good, and I know what is good. All my ideas and actions are based on what is good for the world. I am pure, I have no worries, I have no anxieties, I am happy always, I have no anger. I want nothing, take nothing, do nothing for myself. All I think, all I do at all times is for the good of the world.

JH: We could also have the same ideas by doing as Swami does.

SAI: Yes, to follow Swami is the important thing. To follow this example is best.

RB: I am trying to follow Swami's instructions.

SAI: Trying? Trying is no good. Do it! Do it!

JH: We can ask Swami for strength!

SAI: I will give strength! Sometimes there is wavering of faith in Sai. Thoughts arise, "Why does Sai do this? Why does he do that?" Peter was near and dear to Christ. But he denied Christ.

JH: Did he deny Christ because of fear for the safety of his body? Because of feeling that he was the body?

SAI: Yes. It was because of body identification. Judas was also near and dear. He was a good devotee. Jesus did not divide the disciples into good and bad.

JH: I pray that my faith in Sai will not waver.

SAI: The important thing is to do good and be good. Do not see the bad. See only the good.

December 14, 1981
(In the Car with Baba)

SAI: This land (on our left beside the University) was bought today.

JH: Today! How far does it go?

SAI: All of it, 28 acres. Cost is a lakh of rupees per acre (i.e. about $9,000 U.S.).

JH: That *is* expensive. The new buildings have raised the price.

SAI: Some owners are asking 3 lakhs per acre. Some years ago, the land was 100 rupees per acre. (i.e. about $8 U.S. per acre).

JH: Will more buildings go up on this new land?

SAI: Yes. More buildings. Laboratory, library, and housing for instructors and their families.

JH: This year, with the new University and the teachers' training plan for instruction in human values throughout the entire school system of India, I can see that Sai is getting hold of India.

SAI: Amongst the spiritual leaders of India there is some jealousy.

JH: But they do not have public works. Only Swami is doing that.

SAI: Sai Baba is working for the public twenty-four hours a day. Even the interviews are public work. Twenty-four hours per day, 365 days per year. Not even one holiday.

JH: But that is beyond man. It is possible only for the Divine.

SAI: Yes. Only for the Divine. I need no holiday. I am always happy, always in bliss.

December 30, 1981
(In the Car with Baba)

AC: What to do with a devotee who is making friction in a Center?

SAI: Out. Put them out.

JH: Our discipline is very strict in the American Centers.

SAI: That is correct. Sai's English has improved?

JH: Yes, Swami. It is greatly improved.

SAI: All is love. All is love. The Russians are rationalists. Faith is of the greatest importance. Words, words, words; reason will not do. Faith is from the heart, the language of the heart.

JH: But faith is a gift from God. Man can only have it if God wills.

SAI: Yes, God blesses. Purity helps. Swami is soft as butter, but hard as a diamond. Butter soft, diamond hard. Some small freedom I allow. Not very much. The end of wisdom is freedom. That is the true freedom. Discipline is important. Swami demands strict discipline. Many foreigners are outside in the village. There man can sit beside woman. And they can smoke. Inside the Ashram, Swami does not allow that.

JH: A good small pamphlet explaining the rules of the Ashram should be given to everyone. The people do not know.

Germans in the round building play loud tape recorders because they do not know better.

SAI: In a room next to Admissions, someone should repeat the rules to each newcomer.

JH: An important statement of Swami's is that we should ignore the faults of others. But how does one put this into practice? If one is dealing with a person, the fault must be taken into account; the fault may ruin the situation.

SAI: Inside himself, the person is not like that. He knows he is wrong. If the fault is being expressed, move away from the person, keep a distance. Then the person will see he is wrong and will approach you in penance.

November, 1982

SAI: What counts is faith. Faith is of great importance. God should be installed in every thought and act. There may be a person who is the owner of a house. A tenant may be taken into the house, and year after year the tenant may pay the rent. At last, after many years of paying the rent, the tenant owns the house.

JH: Why would that be?

SAI: The owner might say, "The house is mine." But the tenant will reply, "No. The house is now mine." That is the law.

JH: Is that the law in this situation?

SAI: Yes. It is the same with the Lord. He is the "renter." Your body and mind is the "house." Once you have brought Him into the house and installed Him there, in due course, He is the "owner." The house no longer belongs to "you." It is now the dwelling of God. It is fully "owned" by Him.

JH: Swami! That is wonderful! That is the way to come to the point of "Surrender to the Lord." By keeping Baba in heart and mind, gradually and naturally, there is full surrender.

SAI: Yes, it comes to be quite naturally. But not everyone is able to do it. Devotion and faith need be very strong.

JH: But cannot everyone make a start?

SAI: Yes, certainly, a start can be made.

JH: May I tell this to our Sai Centers in America?

SAI: You may tell.

December 2, 1982
(In the Car with Baba)

JH: Swami gives three stages of evolution beyond the human: Superhuman, Cosmic, Absolute. What does superhuman mean?

SAI: Superhuman is the stage of complete detachment from Body and World. Something may be said or done at this stage to benefit humanity and the world, but the Superhuman is no longer a part of the world of men nor involved in the interests of men.

JH: Are there such people now?

SAI: Oh, yes.

JH: Are they those people in the Himalayan Mountains who can be invisible and do the extraordinary things we hear about?

SAI: No. Those individuals are still seeking liberation. But it is temporary.

JH: Temporary, Swami! That is awful! To get liberation and then lose it!

SAI: There are three kinds of liberation. It is experienced in one type of Samadhi. Then, a person who is engaged in Sadhana can suddenly — like a flash of lightening — have a clear vision of the Truth, but it fades and ordinary life resumes. Liberation cannot be permanent without total surrender.

JH: Then, if not the people in the Himalayas, who are the Superhumans?

SAI: (Naming half a dozen or so of the ancient sages) These people were totally above human and worldly life, although for the benefit of others, they would give certain advice and engage in certain actions.

JH: But that was long ago. Are there Superhumans in this day and age?

SAI: Oh, yes. There are. But today, outwardly, they live in Society and outwardly cannot be recognized.

JH: What is the Cosmic stage?

SAI: No body, no mind. Both have disappeared. Body, feelings, mind, intelligence are no longer there. Just love, just spirituality.

JH: Are there entities, individuals, in the Cosmic stage?

SAI: No. No individuals. More similar to currents of spiritual power.

JH: Well, the Absolute is Swami. That is understood. When Swami says He will confer liberation at death, what does that mean?

SAI: It means that birth is finished with, there is no more birth again.

JH: But Swami, there is this temporary liberation that was mentioned. Maybe it is that kind?

SAI: No, it is not like that. Sai gives total, final, liberation.

JH: Could there be the ending of individuality, too?

SAI: There could be.

JH: Individuality is a nuisance.

SAI: Yes, individuality is a nuisance.

JH: Devotees often ask what happens after death. All that I am able to reply is that I understand from Swami that the after-death experience is not uniform, that it is not the same for every person.

SAI: That is the correct answer. In each case there is a corpse. That is similar. But beyond that, it is not similar.

JH: Well, Swami, one has to die. Is there some skill in dying? That is, is there a correct road through death which one can hold to and not get lost in the process?

SAI: That is not up to you at the time. You are influenced at that time by the net effect of your life.

JH: Swami says that God acts to save the devotee from perdition. What is meant by perdition?

SAI: What do you understand from the word?

JH: It seems to me that it means Hell.

SAI: That is just mental.

JH: But the Buddha speaks of Hell as a place.

SAI: It is a place. A place of the mind. A mental state in which there is much worry and suffering. It is an after-death state. Sai is here to guide His devotees so they do not fall into that state.

JH: One of Swami's statements is not understood. Swami has said that man is born with a dual gift from God — Discrimination and Conscience. And, that because of conscience, everyone knows right from wrong; for if he were to do wrong, his conscience would trouble him.

SAI: Yes, that is the case.

JH: But people point out, Swami, that people of one religion kill people of another religion, and they do it because their conscience tells them it is right to do it.

SAI: It is not that way. When such things occur, it is because the individual has surrendered his judgment to someone else, or to an idea propagated by someone. If the person were to reject ideas and rely upon himself, his conscience, even though deeply buried, would be there to prompt the person; for Conscience is God, Resident in the person.

JH: Throughout the world, crime is growing rapidly. But in America, there is doubt about how to deal with criminals. How should criminals be dealt with?

SAI: There must be punishment. In areas of the Middle East, for example, if a person commits the crime of theft, the hand is cut off. When a person commits a crime, punishment must follow.

JH: Swami, people are thinking that after His 60th Birthday, Bhagavan Baba will step away from contact with the world and that His devotees will no longer have access to Him.

SAI: No, not at all. Sai is not separating from the world, nor will He separate from His devotees. The course of an Avathar goes invariably through the same stages. It is the same for every Avathar at all times. The first 16 years are characterized by constant Leelas. Then Leelas and teachings up to age 45. From age 45 to age 60, the emphasis is almost wholly on teaching. At age 60, there is a very big change.

JH: How, Swami? (Sai listed some things I should not repeat, but then . . .)

SAI: After age 60, Sai will directly give added strength to the minds of those persons who are actively working with Him. Now is starting a time of change. It is just as when a strong wind comes up and blows away the husks, leaving only the sound kernels. In these times, many devotees will fall away from Sai, leaving only those devotees whose faith is sound and solid. Have not you yourself noted a change? In the early years Sai came to your room to talk with you. Now, you come to the veranda each day and Sai does not even stop and speak with you. Such changes occur in the different stages of the Avathar.

JH: Swami has said that the entire world will know of his presence. At this time only a relatively few people know of Sai. As of now only local individuals represent him, and they do not draw the attention of people of substance and importance throughout the world.

SAI: Sai does not look at status and worldly importance. He looks at the heart.

JH: Yes, Swami, but it is the leaders in society who tend to arouse the attention and interest of the general population.

SAI: Sai does not force such things. He will be in body for many more years. What you refer to will develop naturally. Devotees of world stature, able to speak of Sai, will be present when the time is correct for them.

JH: What were the mistakes, if any, in the teachings of the Buddha?

SAI: There were no mistakes in his teachings. One mistake he made was to allow women to come close to him in the Sangha. It was a woman who gave him the meat, the poisoned meat which killed him.

JH: It was his custom to accept whatever was given into the begging bowl, even if it was meat.

SAI: That was a second mistake. Here he failed to put his teaching into practice – his teaching was Ahimsa – total non-violence to all creatures.

JH: The Buddha taught that Nibbana (Nirvana) was the ultimate goal. Is that different from the Liberation of which Swami speaks?

SAI: It is the same. Nirvana, Liberation, Realization are just different words.

(**NOTE:** On the road to Anantapur, we came upon a woman beggar who was blind. Baba gave her money and she responded with "Sai Ram, Swami." It had been two years since he had been to Anantapur, but without Baba even speaking, she recognized him.)

JH: The woman seems to be happy.

SAI: She was born blind but is always happy. She has no worries.

JH: How could that be? Look at her life. It must be a life of misery.

SAI: Why? She has no desires and is content. She does not know the life of the person who has eyes. She does not think that others are different from her. Her family is worried about her condition, but she has no worries.

206 MY BABA AND I

JH: How could she not want a life different from that of a beggar?

SAI: Desires arise from the tendency of the mind to compare. It is chiefly the eyes, the vision, which presents to the mind opportunities for comparison. She is blind, her mind is not busy with comparison, so desires do not arise.

JH: If she continues happy and content, will she be finished with life and death and be free at the time she dies?

SAI: No. That requires spirituality.

JH: It is very important to know what Swami said, that the ground from which desires arise is the mind making comparisons.

Before I had the good fortune to meet Swamiji, my wife and I went to Burma every year for the practice of Vipassana meditation. It starts with Anapana.

SAI: I know, the watchman at the point where nose and lip meet.

JH: After the mind got concentrated enough to sit there, the Meditation Master directed the concentration to the top of the head.

SAI: Then there was a sensation like ants crawling on the scalp.

JH: Yes, Swami. Wherever I placed my attention, there was intense burning. That fire is said to be the direct perception of the arising and immediate disintegration of the smallest particles of matter which comprise the body. The conscious perception of the fire burns up all impurities. Was the Meditation Master correct in what he said?

SAI: It does not matter if the Meditation Master knew correctly or not. You did the work and you got the result. This is illustrated by a story. There was a guru and he had a woman disciple. The guru worshipped Krishna, and he had a lingam which required daily puja. Each day at the time for puja, the disciple would bring the required milk. However, guru and disciple lived on opposite sides of the river. Heavy rains came, and the river rose to flood stage. The disciple had to wait for a boat, and this made her late with the milk for the guru. He became angry that the puja could not be performed at the proper time and told the disciple, "You are late because of lack of faith in the sacred Name of Krishna. With faith in Him and reciting His sacred Name, you could walk across the surface of the river and not have to wait for a boat."

The next day, the disciple, accepting the word of her guru as the word of God Himself, walked across the surface of the river and delivered the milk on time. After two or three days of this, the guru became curious and asked the disciple how she had arrived on time even though the river was still in flood.

The disciple replied that she did as instructed by the guru and walked across the river, constantly chanting the sacred Name of Krishna.

The guru could not accept this story and secretly followed her as she departed. To his astonishment, the woman never hesitated, but walked directly across the river.

Instantly resolving to try it himself, he pulled up his dhoti above his knees and ventured to step on the water. The water failed to sustain him and he was instantly immersed.

This story illustrates the vital role of faith. The woman enjoyed full faith, and it never occurred to her to even lift the hem of her sari for fear of the water; whereas faith was lacking in the guru.

JH: Swami, conflict between people appears to be inevitable. What to do?

SAI: Conflicts do come about, but they should be limited to that point, to the fact of conflict and should not be allowed to spread into additional words and feelings. If the conflict is allowed to expand, anger will deepen, bitter feelings will arise, and strong hatred will develop. On the other hand, love also starts as a point, and if allowed to do so, will expand until it fills one's entire life. This is spiritual truth. If there is conflict and disharmony between two people, and if they will leave it at that and not allow it to move further, then before long both parties will soften and harmony can again come into the relationship. At the worst, the conflict will remain dormant and will not grow to involve other people.

The practice of limiting disharmony and allowing love to freely expand will bring an organization to a harmonious unity. That harmony will attract public admiration and make possible great accomplishments in the large, wealthy country of America.

Each member of the organization would do well to do each and every action for Sai. If every action is done for Sai, then Sai will be added to every action and will bring success with that action. If every action is with Sai, then the actor is with Sai. The actor will then not be different from Sai. He will be Sai. He who becomes like Brahma is Brahma. Sai divided into Jiva becomes Jiva. Sai divided into infinity becomes infinity. Jiva divided into Sai becomes infinity.

In spiritual life, the first point of attack for any problem is to observe the situation in respect to oneself, and first improve that situation. If, after that, the other person continues to offend, he may be warned once, twice, or three times. If there is still no improvement, the person may be removed from organization office. Then, the person should be forgiven. This act of forgiving will bring about a change in the person, and also in the one who forgives. Suppose, for example, someone does something which brings severe pain into Swami's heart. What is the medicine which will cure the pain — cure and totally remove the pain? The medicine is forgiveness. Forgiving is the medicine which will totally remove the pain from Swami's heart.

People who have developed a big intellect use it to entertain many ideas, and in this soil doubts grow. The humble, ordinary person knows much truth directly and does not cultivate as many doubts. Best of all is to have faith like a mountain of ice or a mountain of fire which does not provide soil for even a single doubt to germinate and grow. Where energy has been stored as intellect, that energy must be channeled into constructive activity.

JH: In the America Sai Organization, we presently require all Officers to pay for all the expenses of their office (i.e. there is no expense reimbursement).

SAI: That is correct. Additional expenses must come from the American Sai Organization.

JH: There could be 50,000 or more people in the U.S.A. who are Sai devotees, but less than 1,000 who are in the Centers. The Organization seems to be of minor importance. Why bother with it? Even the United Nations has dozens of non-organizational Sai devotees.

SAI: The Organization gives a chance to people. In America and other countries, there are large numbers of people who know about Sai, have faith in Him, talk about Him, His leelas, and His teachings, but who do not join the Organization. The Organization imposes some discipline and requirements which these people do not wish to take on.

The Sai Organization may be limited in size now, but as time goes on, it will attract so many people that the general public will not be able to be accommodated in the Sai gatherings. All available spaces will be assigned to the people within the Sai Organization. Thus, the Sai Organization membership affords a chance.

For example, you are Chairman of the American Sai Organization, and Bozzani is the Officer of the Foundation (i.e. Sathya Sai Society of America). Because of this, you are in the car with Swami, having some nine hours of interview instead of half an hour in the interview room.

December 11, 1982
Group Interview with Baba

SAI: Faith is like a fire mountain. It is like an ice mountain. There is nothing else. There is no doubt.

JH: What is doubt?

SAI: Doubt is confusion. When reading books, one writer says one thing and another writer says another thing. Take one idea and follow it. Rama had one will, one arrow, one mind. The arrow is intelligence.

JH: Where, then, does discrimination play its part?

SAI: Discrimination is to look to conscience.

JH: In choosing a path to follow, one should not decide amongst ideas by the use of logic?

SAI: No. Not by ideas. By conscience, by Self-confidence. Do not follow another. Follow yourself. To follow another is to be a slave. Who are you? "I am not body, not mind, not even Atma." For, "I am Atma" is two — "I" and "Atma." Neti, neti, neti — not this, not this, not this — that is the way of the Vedas. Swami is in your heart. Think of Him there.

JH: What is God's Light, Swami — what is the light of God?

SAI: When Truth is joined with Love. That is the light of God. It is not outside light, like the electric light bulb. It is inner light.

JH: Swami, how to be in that Light? Everyone here would like to be in that Light and stay all day in that Light.

SAI: When in a dark room and you are looking with a torch, everything can be seen except one thing. Yourself, you do not see. With your eyes you are seeing, but if the torch is turned on you, the objects of the room are not seen. As long as your attention is on the light which lights the world, you will not be enjoying God's Light.

JH: To be in God's Light, the union of truth and love, how is that to be approached?

SAI: Meditation. Meditation is looking inward. It is light. (**NOTE:** The implication seems to be that as long as our attention is centered on our worldly life, we will be seeing the world and not seeing God).

SAI: I see good only. Everyone is God. There are some bad actions only.

JH: That is very hard to understand, Swami.

SAI: No. Not hard. Easy.

SAI (to Malaysian group): All of you are God. There is only He.

SAI (to Barbara): Who are you?

BB: Barbara.

SAI: No! That is only body name. Body is not you. Body has relatives, but soul has no relatives. There is only one Soul, and that is God.

January 10, 1983
In the Car with Baba, Srinivas, and Radhakrishna

We had gone to the Sai school at the foot of Nandi Hill. A beautiful and peaceful setting, with a hundred-acre campus including orchards, dairy, and farm crops. There was a grand reception for Baba by the boys and the faculty. Two students spoke at the meeting after the reception and Baba gave a discourse. One of the speakers broke down in tears. During his discourse, Baba would stop for a moment and question some of the small boys to see if they were paying attention to what he had been saying.

SAI: What did you think of the first speaker? (The boy spoke in English).

JH: He tried and was doing fine, but then dissolved in tears.

SAI: It was his first talk in front of Swami. He won a Lion's Club award for speaking. But that little boy who Swami asked — how fast he replied — even before Swami finished asking! What attention and concentration on what Swami was saying!

JH: All the little boys were totally silent and absorbed. I was watching them. They were not even restless.

SAI: The parents of these boys, although needing the help of these children, tell the sons, "No, stay in school. It is fortunate for you." Often there is only the mother living, and even in such cases the mother insists on the son staying in the school. Where the mother has nothing but the son, Swami takes care of the mother. These mothers stay at the girls' school near Mangalore and work in the kitchens and dormitories. There are 300 acres there and the boys' school is on the same land. The boys' school has 80 instructors and this school here has 60 instructors. Now, it is vacation time with the high school and junior college students away. All the teachers are unmarried, and no teacher takes any salary.

JH: Swami! 140 teachers and all work without salary? It is unheard of. They sacrifice marriage so they can do seva for Swami without need of salary! This is the most extraordinary situation. Why is it not known?

SAI: Swami thinks it best to carry on such activities without fanfare.

JH: Swami, this is a big puzzle. In discourses, Swami says that he is looking for a true devotee, but does not find that devotee. How could that be? What wonderful devotees are these teachers. How is it that Swami can say he has not found a devotee?

SAI (He laughs and says): That is a different category. The true devotee is the same inside and outside.

JH: Then it seems that the status of that sought-for devotee cannot be reached!

SAI: Oh, yes. It can be reached.

JH: Swami, Rama and Krishna must also have been searching for a true devotee in those times.

SAI: Yes, every Avathar is searching for a true devotee. Rama was not regarded as God. Would they have sent Him to the forest, as God? He was looked upon as a King. He acted so. Only a very few sages knew His Divinity. Krishna also was a king. As God, would He have been put to work as the driver of a chariot?

JH: But in the Bhagavad Gita, Arjuna calls Krishna "Divine."

SAI: But still there was the body view of comrade, friend, relative. Only after Krishna left the body did Arjuna realize that Krishna was God. Even in their status as kings, only the residents of their respective cities gave Rama and Krishna homage and worship. The Sai Avathar is the only such where his Divinity is known to all peoples of all religions. Never has there been that before. With Krishna, only the gopis were aware of him as God — but they were rishis.

JH: They were rishis, Swami? As rishis they took birth as ignorant villagers?

SAI: Yes, Great rishis they were before taking that birth. When Krishna died, the gopis stopped taking food, and they discarded their bodies in that way.

JH: Swami, the matter of a true devotee in this Avathara is still a big puzzle. Swami has said that in this very lifetime there are men fully liberated from delusion. Would not even they meet the test for a true devotee?

SAI: A life fully liberated would meet the tests of a true devotee as set by Swami.

JH: Then for those who would seek that status?

SRINIVAS: They should do perfect Sadhana.

SAI: Sadhana! No! That is physical. It is a matter of love. Confidence comes first. Where there is love, there is peace. Where there is peace, there is truth. Where there is truth, there is bliss. Where there is bliss, there is God.

(**NOTE:** Swami's words were translated only when he was talking with me. The rest of the time he was talking in Telugu to Radhakrishna (who was driving) and to Srinivas.)

JH: Swami, in this matter I am not clear. Swami says that money should not be a part of spiritual matters, that money should not be paid. I accept this and have been strict about it to the extreme in the American Sai Organization. But I do not understand the principle. It seems to me, and it does to most Americans, that almost no value is given to that which is free. Whereas, when money has to be paid, care is given, attention is given, and what costs money is valued.

SAI: Yes, at first that is the case. But it does not last. The value given is sudden and, like fireworks, it rises fast. But, like fireworks, the fall is also fast. With the payment of money there is no love or appreciation. You go to the shop and pay for what you want. Why thank the seller, or have any appreciation? You paid in full and that is the end of it.

A guru will start a philosophy, a method of sadhana. Money will be charged and paid, interest will rapidly expand, and people will think they must join and take part. Then, in a few years, where is it all? A recent example is the young person, (name deleted), was that his name? The world over, people gave money to receive instruction. Where is he now? There is no word of him.

Swami does not do like that. He builds slowly, but it is firm and sound and it continues. You remember Prasanthi Nilayam fourteen years ago, and now you see the slow but solid growth of Swami's work.

Spiritual matters must occur only in a context of love. When advice and instruction and help is given in compassion, in love — and not for money paid, there will be some feeling of appreciation; and in the context of appreciation and confidence there will be some spiritual benefit. Moreover, when the actions are done in love and not as part of money raising, money comes anyway.

An example: Here is a coconut palm tree. (Baba raised his arm in an upright position). And up here (touching his wrist) are the coconuts. This tree has a shadow which extends for a distance on the ground. Now, a man who wishes to secure the coconuts climbs up the coconut tree. At the very time he is climbing the tree, his shadow may be seen climbing the shadow tree. And, when he plucks the coconuts, his shadow may be seen plucking the shadow coconuts. The man who climbs the real tree secures the real coconuts and, at the same time, his shadow self climbs the shadow tree and plucks the shadow coconuts. But if the man does not relish the task of climbing the real tree, and instead limits his action to the climbing of the shadow tree, he will not get satisfaction from the shadow coconuts.

The shadow tree represents the world, and the shadow coconuts represent worldly prosperity. The real tree represents spiritual life, and the real coconuts represent the fulfillment of life. Thus, the person who devotes his life and energy to spiritual values will automatically get worldly benefits.

JH & SRINIVAS: Swami! What a wonderful example! What a wonderful way to convey Swami's teaching that one should do his work in the context of love and not for money! Automatically, the worldly needs are cared for.

SAI: It is a good example?

JH & SRINIVAS: Swami, it is a perfect example!

JH: Swami, a puzzle in daily life is this: Daily life is a continuous sequence of small choices, and we select the option which gives the best pleasure or comfort. In this way, our entire life is directed to comfort and pleasure, and such a life cannot take us to "Liberation." What to do?

SAI: The principle which Swami teaches is to like that which we have to do instead of doing that which we like.

Every action should be done for Swami, every action dedicated to Swami. Then, duty, discipline, and devotion are the guides for action. So long as you take the body to be yourself, action will be for comfort and pleasure. Realize that you are not the body, and be free of the need for pleasure and comfort.

JH: This question will sound silly to Swami, but it is serious to me.

SAI: What?

JH: I write many letters to Swami about activities, problems, and accomplishments in the American Sai Organization. But often I think it is silly to describe problems and events, since I know from my own direct experience that Swami is omnipresent and knows all about the events.

SAI: There is much nonsense about Swami being omnipresent and ominpotent! People start to think they need do nothing, that Swami will do everything! Then they do not bother to do even their daily duty.

In spiritual life, the relationship between you and Swami is heart to heart. But in worldly life, Swami has given you work to do. This requires work in the world, activity in the world. You are required to do your duty to the very limit of the task. So far as writing is concerned, the writing of letters to Swami is for your satisfaction.

JH: For my satisfaction, Swami?

SAI: Yes, for your satisfaction. You write to Swami, and your mind is then free of the matter. It is not that Swami does not know. Suppose you withhold some troublesome point, you then have a guilty feeling. But you tell Swami, and there is no guilty feeling. Do your duty fully and completely in the work which Swami has given to you.

January 14, 1983

JH: Swami, two questions important for our work in daily life, and in preparation for the Symposium in Rome:

In his Discourses, Swami says that God should be recognized as the Doer of all actions and that we should not take it upon ourselves to be the doer. Further, Swami also says that instead of depending on limited human strength, we should call upon the strength of God. Since Swami says these two things in his Discourses, then the instructions must be intended for everybody?

SAI: Take the viewpoint that God is working through you.

JH: What does that mean, Swami? How does that apply in the actual actions taking place each day?

SAI: You think you are engaging in the action, but it is your body doing so, or your mind, or your intelligence. But God is working through them. It is only the Atma in you which is the source of action. The Atma is God.

JH: Then, instead of considering that it is myself acting, I should tell myself — and appreciate — that "I" am just a word, and that all these actions and movements going on are not coming from "Hislop" but are actually God Himself acting?

SAI: God is using your intelligence, mind, and body as His instruments for doing that particular work. You write with a pen, or cut paper with scissors — but it is not those instruments that are doing the work — it is you who are using the instruments for the purpose of doing the work. Likewise, the instruments you call "yourself" — intelligence, mind, and body — are used by God for His purpose.

JH: Is that a practical thing to do, hour in and hour out? Tell myself that my mind and body, at any and every moment, are at that moment being used by God as His instrument? Is that a practical way to live and move through the day?

SAI: Yes. That is the fact, and it is practical.

AC: But Swami! Then it is God doing evil!

SAI: At first, maybe (i.e. apparently), but then not. It is not God who does evil. Evil is from the ego.

AC: When I die . . .

SAI: (interrupting) Who are you? You do not die! The body is like clothes — off and on.

AC: Then after the body dies, I take another? Why? Why?

SAI: Balance of desires. Desires are like seeds — they sprout. These desires cause rebirth. Finish with desires — no more birth. Mind is a desire bundle.

AC: But this creation — world, body, and mind — is it a projection of the Atma? Mind, body, intelligence are creations, projections of the Atma?

SAI: Creation is from the Atma. The Atma, God, is the positive. Body is the negative. They join and action results. Otherwise, nothing.

AC: There is the Atma, and then creation as the projection from the Atma . . .

SAI: No! That is where the mistake is made! Creation is not a projection from the Atma. The Atma, God, is permeating every fibre of the creation. The form is just appearance . . . It is energy, God, the Divine Energy which causes the form and which is the actuality of the form. (Following this exchange there was some personal conversation with C, which is omitted.)

JH: To do all these tasks, Swami, takes a lot of energy. Human energy is low, and Swami says to call on the Divine Energy. How?

SAI: Yes, human energy is low and the Divine Energy is without limit! You are God!

JH: Does Swami mean that when the human energy limit is felt, that I should reject it as false, and instead identify myself as God, as He Who is limitless energy?

SAI: Yes. Reject it! Look at your shadow — you are sitting and your shadow is there. When you stand up, your shadow also grows. Your shadow is the human energy. You are the Divine Energy. When you rise, and also do the Divine work, your energy grows.

January 15, 1983

JH: Swami, the Divine Energy versus limited human energy . . .

SAI: There is only Divine Energy.

JH: But what seems to me to be my human energy does not seem to be sufficient; for example, the trip to Central America.

SAI: All is God. Know that it is He who is Energy. Then all is well.

JH: Oh! When the human energy slows, leave it and know that the truth is Divine Energy! Like when some years ago on long drives, Baba would look a little tired; and then, instantly, he would be fresh like a flower.

SAI: Do not equate this body with human bodies. It is only the appearance of a form for the sake of the devotees. There is nothing of Swami except for his devotees. There are no desires. This body is just an appearance of form . . . There is matter. There is human. There is Divine. Matter is selfishness; human is selfishness plus help (i.e. help to others); God is no selfishness, just total love. As the base, selfishness is essential for health and prosperity. Without health, what can be done? Work for these must be done? Work for these must be done; then help others; then God only.

JH: But Swami, even in that worldly work of necessary "selfishness," where is "I"? Surely it is only God who is doing that work?

SAI: That is better. That is the best way. You are only an instrument for Swami, an instrument which Swami is using for his purpose — U.S. Chairman, speaking of Swami's teachings and so on.

November 7, 1983

The interview of November 7 was very brief in terms of the group. Almost all of the time was devoted to individual interviews with Baba in the inner interview room. Families were taken together, but single persons were interviewed individually.

SAI: What is Being?

Q: It is "Sat."

SAI: That is just a Sanskrit word. Being means immortality, always.

Q: How to feel that Divine Love in the heart?

SAI: Your love, my love, they are the same. There is only One and He is God.

Q: Do You mean we should affirm that, that we should always say it?

SAI: Here is humanity (pointing to a line in the wall denoting a layer of bricks). Below is the world, above is God. Aim up, not down. You are God. There is only One. For so many lives you have been declaring that you are human, with limitations, "I am faulty . . . I am . . . so and so . . ." That is wrong. Now say, "I am God." Never feel or say that you are other than God. You will show Godly qualities. You will have Godly powers. You will be God. Thoughts. If there are no thoughts, there are no actions. How is your health, Hislop?

H: It is very good, Swami.

(During the group portion of this interview, a lady with a dull-colored bracelet on her arm, shoved her wrist in front of Baba and asked him to change the bracelet into something pretty. It seemed to me that Baba was not pleased with the demand, but nevertheless he removed the bracelet, held it with two fingers, blew his breath upon it, and it became a new shining gold bracelet of an entirely different pattern and configuration.

At this point, the group portion of the interview ended and Swami began the series of private conversations in the inner interview room.)

November 14, 1983
A Group Interview with Baba at Prasanthi Nilayam

Baba first created some gifts, a ring for a lady — a green diamond in the center flanked by two white diamonds, all gems showing large flat facets. Then, for a lady who had a large Jappmala of seeds, Baba created a Jappmala of matched pearls, and showed her how to use it: The thumb, standing separate, may be taken to represent God. The first finger, representing the individual person, is joined to the thumb, to the Divine. The three remaining fingers represent the three gunas — the three modes of temperament, thought, and action observable in all people — the middle finger being the Sathwic guna (calm, pure, balanced nature). The Jappmala is then drawn across the Sathwic finger by the thumb and the forefinger movement.

SAI: (Demonstrating the use of the Jappmala) Like this, Swami holds all of creation in His hand.

(A man from Nigeria was in the group, and Baba next turned to him.)

SAI: What religion? What is your religion?

ANSWER: Christian.

SAI: Do You like Jesus?

ANSWER: Yes.

Moving his hand, Baba creates a ring, the center stone of which carries a very fine portrait of Jesus. First, he shows the ring to those of us sitting near his chair, and then to the Nigerian, saying, "Do you like Jesus? Which do you want, Jesus or Sai?" The Nigerian replied, "I would be pleased with either." Baba holds the ring between thumb and forefinger about six inches from his lips and blows his breath upon it. Then he shows it to those close to his chair. The portrait on the center stone has changed from that of Jesus to a portrait of Sai. To the Nigerian, Baba then says, "Now you have both. Come here." The man moves forward and Baba places the ring on his finger. Baba says, "See, a perfect fit."

Later on it was the Nigerian's turn to go into the inner interview room for a brief, private conversation, and when he came out we could see that the ring had changed yet once again. Baba had again recreated the ring and it was now a single large diamond in an appropriate setting. As Sai followed the man into the main room, he said, "He didn't like a large ring!" This remark caused considerable merriment. In fact, the entire interview was joyful in the extreme and Baba was in a great mood, constantly cracking jokes. Hearing such happy laughter coming from the group, the people outside were wondering what on earth was happening.

SAI: Any questions? Spiritual topics?

Q: How to live with worldly desires which rise endlessly?

SAI: Turn all wishes and desires to God, then all will be well. Mind is like a key to the door of a prison. Turn it to the left, the door opens and the person is free to turn towards God and spiritual life. Turn the key to the right, and the person is locked into worldly life. Turn every wish and every desire into desire to be with God, and be happy.

Q: Swami, what is the truth of the mind. How to use thought and the mind?

SAI: There is no mind. Just as cloth is seen as thread, then as cotton only, there is only God. God is like a perfect mirror; your desires, thoughts, and actions are perfectly reflected in that perfect mirror, which is God. When your desires, thoughts, and actions are reflected back to you, you may think God sent them, but they are really your own.

Q: But what to do about bad thoughts and desires?

SAI: Human thoughts and desires. If you think, "I am human," then such human aspects as anger and jealousy will be reflected and will return to you. But you are not human. You are Divine. You are God. Think and feel, "I am Divine." Then you will think and feel only love, for God is Love. Everyplace, everything is Love, Love only.

Q: I have a desire which I cannot put away.

SAI: What?

Q: Privacy. I must have privacy.

SAI: Physical privacy is first, then mental privacy.

Q: And I make mistakes. The same mistakes. Can I give my mistakes to Baba?

SAI: Oh, yes. I am always ready. Give your life to me. Be my instrument. I act through you.

Q: Then even bad thoughts and acts are by you?

SAI: Human thoughts and acts. God is love only. You are Divine. Be Love. Act in Love.

Q: But, Swami, the mistakes I make. Even though I know better, I make the same mistakes. Can I give you my repeated mistakes?

SAI: Once, or twice, or three times perhaps the same mistake, but repeating and repeating is not mistake. It is habit!

JH: Swami says that if one is so fortunate as to have God's Love, then no spiritual practice, no sadhana is necessary?

SAI: Yes. If you have God loving you, then no sadhana, no meditation, no inquiry, nothing more is needed, for then everything is God, thoughts are of God, only God is seen, the whole day is God only.

Q: What is soul?

SAI: Soul is the Atma. It does not die. You are Atma, not body.

Q: But Swami, there is something else. Something has results.

SAI: Yes, result is from desire. It is like this golden watch band you are wearing. You wish for a ring; the gold is taken from the bracelet and it becomes a ring. Then you are no longer pleased with a ring, but instead long for a golden necklace. The gold is taken and it becomes a necklace. All are different forms, but the gold is the same.

JH: Swami informs us that this life in the world is a dream only.

SAI: Yes, a dream.

JH: But Swami works endlessly in the dream. Why?

SAI: If the dream is realized as such, then the world is done with. Swami helps those caught in the dream.

JH: But it is still a dream, without purpose or end. Why bother with it?

SAI: A big scientist may know that a child's world is a dream and has no reality which is lasting. But this does not prevent him from sitting down with the child at the child's level. Again, Sai could be likened to an aircraft which briefly touches down in order to take passengers up from the ground.

JH: Swami! There is room for only a limited number!

SAI: Limited, yes! Always there is room for a limited number only.

JH: Swami! How to get a booking?

SAI: By Grace. Booking is through Grace.

JH: The limitation is severe.

SAI: Yes. It is true that reservations have been made. But on the plane, the Government has some seats reserved. Swami can say, "Hislop is given one of those reservations."

JH: What is the difference between Swami's Grace and Swami's Blessings?

SAI: They are the same. Swami's Blessings, his Grace, his Love — all mean the same.

Q: How to get Swami's Grace?

SAI: Swami's Grace is always here. Swami is always here. He is here for all; for everyone. I am always calling, but they do not listen, they do not come. What can I do?

(Now Swami calls people in turn to the inner interview room for a brief, private conversation. As he moves to the doorway, he says, "I am always happy. My bliss is ever full and never disturbed.")

JH: Because Swami knows that this world of experience is only a dream. (Sai makes no reply.)

October 22, 1984
Interview with Baba

JH: Ten years ago when Swami formed the American Sai Organization, he gave what he said was the single most important rule for American Sathya Sai Baba Centers. For the next ten years, what is the single most important rule for our Centers?

SAI: What is your idea?

JH: Swami's first rule — have as little as possible to do with money — it seems to me it must continue.

SAI: Yes, that is correct. The rule cannot be changed. It must continue unchanged through the next ten years.

JH: Then what shall be the particular emphasis for American devotees for the next ten years?

SAI: The emphasis must be on the Sadhana of Purity and Sacrifice. Purity is Divinity. Through sacrifice there is purity of mind and heart. By purity, Divinity is realized. Sacrifice is an offering, a giving up to the Lord, a dedication to the Lord. What is to be sacrificed to the Lord is the sense of ego, of "mine." Once all sense of ego is sacrificed to the Lord, given up to the Lord, heart and mind are purified of ego attributes and Divinity can then be realized.

JH: During the course of the next ten years is the American Sai Organization to remain a Spiritual Organization or is it to change its mode of life so as to become primarily a Seva Organization?

SAI: The Organization is to continue to be a Spiritual

Organization with some changes, but not major changes. Devotion to God: the purifying of mind and heart, by sacrificing to God all ego tendencies, is to be the purpose and the practice of the Sai devotees in the American Sai Organization.

JH: Swami, for the past several years my neck has been painful and doctors can do nothing. What should I do for it?

SAI: (rubbing the neck with his hand) Don't do anything. Swami will take care of it.

JH: I have some questions I do not know how to answer. About living in the moment, what is meant?

SAI: Those are general questions. Ask Kasturi to be here tomorrow morning and I will answer those questions.

October 23, 1984
Interview with Baba, Mr. Kasturi Translating

JH: Baba, may I make a donation to the Whitefield Hospital?

SAI: Why?

JH: Well, my operation was there.

SAI: No. Not necessary. It is our hospital, all is ours. No.

JH: Swami, as I travel the nation, I am asked questions. I do not know the answers to some of them. One question which always comes up is free will. One has the free will to choose God or the world. But on the other hand, Baba in one glance sees past, present, and future. So how can there be free will?

SAI: From that viewpoint, from the Divine, there is no free will, for all is God. But from the ego viewpoint of the individual, there is free will. There is general law, and then the individual and society. The individual acts in society according to his free will, but all conform to the general law. The individual must act, and his action is a function of his mind. There are thoughts. Thoughts are seeds. They sprout and become actions. The actions then appear to be free will to the concerned individual. Everyone has been given skills and talents such as intelligence, reason, energy; and they must be put to use in life action. (After discussing the interview with Mr. Kasturi the next day, it seems to me that for the individual person it boils down to this: The individual acts according to his talents and capacity at any particular moment. If he is ignorant of Vedanta and has never listened to Baba, the individual feels he or she is acting freely according to his inclinations and his will. On the contrary, if the individual has reached a conviction that everything is absent except God, the individual then feels that everything he is doing is being prompted by God and thus the question of free will does not bother him).

JH: Swami, perhaps I will be able to understand it and explain it. Swami said that the mind would fix itself, if one would live in the moment. What does Swami mean by living in the moment? How does one live in the moment?

SAI: Past is gone, future is not here, there is only the moment. Live fully now without worry about the future.

JH: But, Swami, one has to look forward to judge the consequences of the action.

SAI: Why? Live now. Act according to your best feelings and thoughts and do not worry.

JH: But Swami said that Krishna chose Arjuna because Arjuna had foresight and looked ahead to the consequences.

SAI: Don't think about Arjuna. He was worried about his relatives.

JH: But Swami, when I make some move in respect to the American Council, I have to consider what the consequences will be before I go ahead. That does not square with living in the moment.

SAI: But that is duty. In duty you must look into the future and weigh the consequences.

JH: Oh! That is what is meant. Now I understand it. Another question which arises is: do actions come about because of Baba, or by Baba? That is, action takes place because of the sunlight, but the Sun is not regarded as the doer, whereas it is said that Swami is the doer in respect to our actions.

SAI: The Sun gives light — but the Sun also does work. It makes changes in plant life, for example.

JH: Does that mean that Swami is the actor, the actual doer in our lives?

SAI: Consider that you are an instrument and Sai acts by using you as his instrument for action.

JH: That implies that it is foolish to think that we act, for the fact is that the action is the result of a prompting by God?

SAI: Yes. The action is prompted by God.

JH: But Swami, it is not clear in practice. I forgot to bring the check I wanted to donate to the hospital. Then, after reaching the veranda here, I remembered it and felt I should go back to the room and get it. That action of returning to our room had to be a prompting by Baba. But then, after Baba prompted me to get the check, Baba refused to accept the check! The principle in practice is not clear.

SAI: Only in that way was there an occasion to teach you how Swami regards such matters. Had you given the check from love, perhaps Swami could have accepted. But you were giving in return for the operation. But you are family and there is no payment in family. For work outside the family, there may be some employment and some payment.

JH: But it was Swami prompting me that sent me for the check?

SAI: Yes. It was Swami prompting you.

JH: Swami, the lesson of the check is learned. It is a very clear case of payment for services instead of the family feeling! Now I take it to be the case that whatever is done by me is being prompted by Baba.

SAI: That is the correct attitude. That is the correct way.

JH: But could not a person then say that he had no volition and therefore would sit and do nothing unless Swami moved him? Can a man choose to be lazy?

SAI: Yes, he could be lazy.

JH: By the prompting of Sai?

SAI: Yes.

JH: Is it the waking 'I' who dreams, or does the dream state create its own 'I'?

SAI: It is one 'I' only in waking, dream, and deep sleep states.

JH: For life in this world, Swami, the goal is reunion with God. What is the purpose of life in the rest of this vast universe?

SAI: All life may flow toward God. Even frogs in a pond and insects.

JH: But Swami, that is life in this world. I mean life elsewhere in the universe.

SAI: In this world, there is duality and therefore striving. But, even here, insects and small creatures may live in a pond feeling everything is all right and feeling happiness. The question about life in the universe arises because you project your own particular circumstances. You feel that other ways of life would be intolerable because such ways would be intolerable for you. In the hot, blazing Sun, for instance, beings are living. This life exists in circumstances considered to be intolerable by you. Elsewhere in the universe, life feels it is Divinity, is one with Divinity, and is quite happy, and feeling all is right.

JH: Then this world is a very peculiar place!

SAI: Yes, this small planet Earth is very special. It is unique in the universe. This is a very important topic. It is of very great significance. One who can understand the mystery of the Earth is great indeed. He is infinite.

JH: Is the Earth mystery unveiled in Baba's divine teachings?

SAI: Swami can reveal this mystery. (In talking with Mr. Kasturi next day, he believes the mystery of planet Earth, which Swami refers to, is the extraordinary configurations of the five elements (Space, Air, Fire, Water, Earth) which makes the Earth unique throughtout the vast cosmos. Next time in India, I will try for a chance to ask Swami to elaborate on what he means by the mystery of planet Earth).

JH: Everybody is self-conscious; conscious that he is, conscious of his being. Is this consciousness the base, or is there something prior to this?

SAI: That consciousness is second. First is God-consciousness. God-consciousness is the base.

JH: A source of confusion is about everything being a creation of the mind. Creation of whose mind?

SAI: Yes, it is the mind.

JH: But Swami, how could that be? Is my mind creating war and all its horrors? I do not find such actions in myself.

SAI: When you think of the world, it exists for you. When you do not think of it, for you it does not exist.

JH: When I do not think of the world it is not in my consciousness! Does the war exist only according to my consciousness of it? But there was a beginning to the war. How could that beginning be due only to my mind?

SAI: At your stage it will not be possible for you to grasp this. As long as the mind exists, it is not possible to comprehend the mind and its activity clearly. When thought ceases, there will be no mind. Mind is a bundle of thoughts. Do not follow the thoughts. Then the world will not develop for you. Now your thoughts have gone to America, to problems there. But these are just thoughts. If you now follow these thoughts and go to America, they will bring about the world for you.

JH: Does Swami mean that one should just be a witness to the thoughts going through one's mind and not do anything about them?

SAI: Exactly. When the mind is destroyed, then the coming into being of the world will be clear to you. There is only God, God only. Hold to Him. Hold closely to Him and the matter of the mind will be resolved.

JH: Swami! I do hold to God! My thought is always on Swami. I am always regarding Swami as being in my heart, not someplace else. But my mind is not destroyed.

SAI: It will come. To have that strong confidence is important.

JH: I have no trouble seeing that my mind creates my personal world — that is, Mr. Kasturi and Swami are known to me only because of the senses relaying messages to the mind, which then forms concepts and externalizes Mr. Kasturi and Swami. But the creation of something big outside, like the war, I cannot comprehend.

SAI: When the mind is destroyed and the world goes, God also has no existence.

(Now the evening Bhajans start and the interview is over, with many questions still unasked. Hopefully, Swami will grant some time again at the next visit).

Examine this question, for example: Is man enslaved by external objects and the attraction they exercise over him? Or, is it some inner impulse that urges him forward to shackle himself to sorrow? I shall give an example: There are professional monkey-catchers in the villages who employ a crude device for the purpose. They place in the orchards or gardens infested by the marauders a number of narrow-necked earthen pots, with a handful of peanuts inside each. The monkey approaches the pot, knows that it has the delicious nuts inside, puts its long hand in and collects the nuts in its fist. Now, it finds it cannot take its arm out; the neck is too narrow for the nut-full fist! So, it sits helpless and forlorn and is easily caught and transported! It thinks that there is someone inside who is holding back its arm, when it tries to take it out! If only it had loosened the grip and got rid of the attachment to the nuts, it could have escaped! So, too, you are the victims of desire and the attachments that the desire entails. You are bound by the shackles you have yourselves fastened around you! Liberation, too, is in your hands. Contemplate the unchanging Glory of God; then desire for the transient baubles of the earth will fade and you can be free.

— Sathya Sai Baba

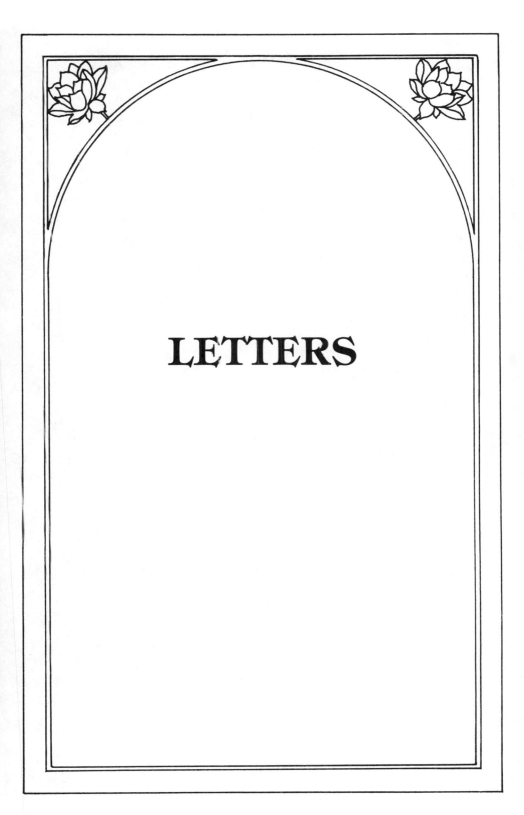

LETTERS

Letters

In the biography of a person whose life rises high above the norm of his era and which is like a powerful magnet attracting the thoughts, feelings, and aspirations of mankind over thousands of years, every small aspect of that life is of consuming interest. How precious, for instance, would be letters written by Jesus, Sri Krishna, Muhammad, Sri Rama, and the Buddha. How fortunate it is that in ages to come students of Baba's teachings will have a number of his letters, some in his handwriting. Sri Sathya Sai Baba is a towering personage in the world today. His stature in the eyes of men will grow to a supreme height before death removes him into the realm of history. A thousand years from now, five thousand years from now Baba's correspondence will be a treasure for historians as well as for people of that age whose hearts are pulled to him as they read of his glorious life. Baba's letters are intimately addressed to particular devotees and have a warmth and candor beyond that found in other writings. And, further, letters written to Baba by his devotees throw a soft yet true light on the feeling and tone of his relationship with his devotees — something which, if not caught at that moment, could never be known later on.

It was with the above mentioned considerations in mind that I approached Baba and asked permission to select a portion of our

231

correspondence to be part of this book. He gave his consent. Usually Baba writes by hand on letterhead stationary, although at times he will have someone type his letters. In this section, letters in his handwriting are reduced in size so as to fit the pages of the book. My letters to Baba are all typewritten and appear on these pages without a letterhead.

I write to him about anything and everything that comes to mind. His letters to me guide my spiritual discipline. The reader will notice that at times I mention an illness when writing to Baba. Whenever illness comes, my wife and I mentally hand it over to Baba and never worry about it. The first paragraph of one letter mentions a prayer which Baba wrote out for us; a photocopy of the prayer follows the letter.

Bhagavan
Sri Sathya Sai Baba

Camp. "Brindavan"
Near white field station
Bangalor Dl.

PRASANTHINILAYAM
PHONE NO. 30, PENUKONDA
ANANTHAPUR DT.

DATE: 24-3-71

My dear Hislop! i am very happy
I received your lovely letter yesterday, now How
is your health? don't worry about that; your Lovely
GOD is always with you, in you, around you.
Hislop! from some days your sister-in-law is with
me (at Brindavan) she is very happy dayly doing
Bhajan and Dhyanam jani also with her.
My dear! all are our fellow passengers, our travell-
ers— all life, plants, animals, not only my Bhakth
but our brother brute, our brother plant, not only our
brother the good, but our brother the evil, our brother
the spiritual and our brother the wicked. they are
all going to the same goal. all are in the same
stream, each is hurrying towards that infinite freedom
Hislop! the moments of realisation are those when
all thoughts of worldly relations, worldly connec-
tions, worldly ties, worldly property, worldly desires,
worldly needs, are all melted into GOD, into truth.
My dear one! every being that is in the universe has
the potentiality of transcending the senses. even the
little worm will one day transcend the senses and
reach GOD. No life will be a failure.

There is no such thing as failure in the universe.
a hundred times man will hurt himself, a
thousand times he will trumble, but in the end he
will realise that he is GOD.
my Boy! you and I are both outlets of the same
cannel and that is GOD. as such your nature is
GOD and so is mine. you are of the nature of GOD
by your birth right, the pure heart is the best
mirror for the reflection of truth so all these
disciplines are for the perification of the heart
and as soon as it is pure all the truths flash upon
it in a minute all truth in the universe will
mani fest in your heart if you are sufficiently
pure.
Hislop! the harder the circumstances, the more
treying the environ ments the stronger are the men
who come out of those circumstances, se welcome
all these out side troubles and anxieties.
when the bubble bursts, it finds itself the whole ocean
you are the whole, the infinite, the all. out of long
churning this milk of the world comes butter and
this butter is...... GOD. men of heart get the
butter, and the butter-milk is fe lift for the
intellectual.
MY Love! tell my Grace and Blenwig to your wife and
Sai Brother's and sisters
                              With Love
                                Baba

PRASANTHI VIDWANMAHASABHA
PRASANTHI NILAYAM

8-9-69

Hislop, accept this shower of Love and Joy. I received all the letters you wrote, and felt happy, reading them. Since I could not get a moment of leisure, due to the various items of work connected with the Whitefield College, and since the hurdle of language had to be crossed — that is to say, since I could not write to you directly in Telugu, and I did not have with me persons who could correctly translate what I write — I had to send you this letter after so much delay. Though letters may be distant, I assure you, Love is not distant. It will not be distant, it can never be distant. I am ever in your heart, as hai (unchanging, unceasing joy) and as Sai — immersed in Bliss and conferring Bliss.

Hislop, though I wanted to come to America, there were some urgent matters in connection with the development of the Colleges here, that I had to attend to. The Colleges have correlations with the Government of India, and so, they have to be equipped accordingly; laboratories, libraries, permanent college buildings, and other facilities for the students and faculties have to be provided. The Committee has the responsibility to see that no rule or regulation is neglected, no deficiency creeps into the institution, and no handicap is imposed on the activity of learning and teaching. Therefore, I had to look into all these matters myself.

On September 18th, Pathak, our Vice-President of India, is laying the Foundation for the Building of the Women's College at Anantapur. The Sathya Sai Educational Trust is allotting Rupees 11 lakhs for the completion of this project; that is to say, we are spending two hundred thousand dollars, for the construction of the College Building.

Both Colleges are progressing nicely and attaining first class standards in the Universities, to which they are affiliated. The

2

training given to the students has to be improved, still more. We are giving instruction in Prayer, Japa, and Dhyana and laying special emphasis on character-building and the practice of discipline. The teaching of arts and science, both secular and spiritual, with emphasis on moral, religious, and spiritual values, is also given. It prepares the students for the courses leading to University Degrees. Since I decided to ameliorate some of these very urgent problems regarding students, I refrained from tours this year.

As the saying goes, "Master the home, then master the world." Commendable traits have first to be developed in this country, isn't it, so that its influence may be felt as an inspiration for those who are in other lands? While what is near is neglected, though dirt-ridden, any attempt to cleanse what is far away will necessarily be ridiculed. For me, the near and the distant are of equal consequence. I am not affected by feelings of "far" and "near." But, ordinary folk are different, isn't it? Therefore, it is highly beneficial to teach Indian students what is essentially good for them, and encourage them to exemplify it in action. When the culture of India is not understood even by Indians, how can others understand it? How can others follow it? The American tour had to be postponed.

My Love is love, for all mankind; my Truth is truth, for all mankind; my Intent is content, for all mankind. However, it is only by evincing these in some Form or other that my nature can declare itself. At the present time, there is an urgent need to transform methods of education. Today, the field of knowledge that man has yet to acquire is much vaster than what he says he has known. What he knows is very little; it is just an atom of the vast unknown. But, man is blinded by the flash of pride, on this petty achievement. In reality, if man can only know the Beginningless and Endless, if he conceives the All-pervasive Immanent Energy, pride can find no place in him.

In fact, many errors are committed in the name of religion. Religion is three-fourths character. Only those who preserve character can be pronounced truly religious. Without that character, of what profit is it, to bluster forth arguments and explanations? As a first step, character has to be fostered in the

3

young children of today; then only will the country achieve progress. The curriculum, methods of teaching and learning, the atmosphere of the institution, the behaviour and attitudes of those in charge of teaching must also be shown as conforming to the ideal. That alone can bring about reform. Or else, men behave like beasts. When scholarship and virtues are considered as of no value, when spiritual effort becomes wordy exercise, when all activity is directed towards the secular and the temporary, real spiritual exertion is insulted. Spiritual yearning ought to be either completely free from attachment to the sensory and objective world, or, it should recognise and visualise God-head, the Lord of the Universe, in the sensory and objective world. That sacred vision and that holy feeling have to be asserted in action. It is only thus that the individual Atma can instantly realise and merge in the Universal Atma, isn't it?

Hislop, I shall certainly come. It may be a little later, but do not feel disappointed. Convey this decision of mine to the Raymer Group, the Cowans, Indra Devi, Charles Penn, and their societies and give joy to all members of the Sai Family. I shall certainly come. After the celebrations of Dasara and Birthday, I shall come and be with you, leisurely for an extra month, showering bliss on you all.

Special Blessings for Mrs. Hislop.

With Blessings
Bah.

BHAGAWAN SRI SATYA SAIBABA
PRASHANTHI NILAYAM

CAMP ___ __ _ . _ _____

DATE__15=1=70_____

Hislop, accept my blessings. The letters you sent have all been received I have read them all . . but, I was not able to send you replies, immediately. Many thousands of devotees had gathered during Dasara, the Birthday, and the All-India Conference of Office Bearers of Sathya Sai Organizations; and so, I could not avail myself of even a moment's leisure. Besides, since the building of the College has started, I have been at Bangalore, for about a month. Kasturi was at Prasanthi Nilayam, and, letters to you had to be translated, and typed. So, the delay lengthened. This is what happened. Therefore, do not imagine that I have forgotten you. I shall never forget you. Wherever you are, you are mine. Wherever I am, I am yours. The bond between these two is Atmic, (Soul and soul) not dependent on time, space, and the vagaries of physical encasements.

Hislop, I am drawing your attention to the happenings in some homes, of which you have written. Spiritual discipline and endeavour are not pomp-oriented; they are practice-oriented. One has to earn the experience of spiritual progress, through practice. Later, that experience is to be revealed only to those nearest to one, those who have earnest and devoted interest in such experiences. I do not like the advertisement of such matters in newspapers, announcing them to all and sundry, as if they are cheap commodities of the market place.

The sweetness of the spirit is not a dish, which can be served over the counter. It cannot be procured from a shop; no firm can supply it to its customers. It is of the nature of Divine illumination; it has to be evoked, from oneself, for oneself. To advertise the experience of this illumination is to indulge in a paltry pastime.

There are some people who engage themselves in Sadhana,

study, and the listening to discourses, for transient mental satisfaction or even entertainment. They feel that, that little is enough effort. But, the task is not over with these . . . Food has to be cooked, it has to be consumed, and, it has to be digested and assimilated. The body can develop strength only when these three steps are accomplished, one after the other. Similarly, what is heard has to be pondered over, what is pondered over has to be put into practice. It is only when all three are accomplished that Atmananda (Atmic Bliss, the Bliss of the Realisation of the Reality) can be attained.

Instead, if what is accomplished is very little, and what is advertised about oneself is much more, one becomes the target of ridicule. He who puts into practice a single item of spiritual discipline derives much more benefit, than he who preaches about a hundred items! A seed embedded in the soil sprouts, grows into a tree, and yields fruit. If, however, it is cast on the surface, it does not sprout. So too, faith implanted deep in the heart will express itself as a tree, that is to say, it will yield fruit — spiritual experience. But, if faith is on the surface only, it will be wafted away in publicity, and in the ridicule it provokes. Only the commodity that has no demand is advertised in plenty. For the pure and the holy, what need is there for advertisement? Advertisement of spiritual experiences is an evil habit, quite contrary to the spiritual attitude.

I do not need name and fame. They are as disgusting as spittle. Do not publicise, without filling the heart with Love. Live and act, in the spirit of full fraternity, with love and regard for all, and demonstrate that you have known the ultimate Truth through the spontaneous manifestation of that genuine experience. Any other method will only foster disbelief, atheism.

Those who seek to acquire steadiness of faith must first acquire the strength to bear grief and pain, insult and injury. They should not slide from a term of self-control (Yoga) into a bout of excess (Bhoga) and end up with a period of illness (Roga). Self-control must persist as self-control, until the very end. The Yogi must continue as Yogi, till the end of life. The succession of joy and grief must help confirm the faith and make it immovable. That alone can evidence true devotion.

When there is no gust of wind, an iron ball and a dry leaf, both lie unmoved, and in similar manner, upon the ground. To conclude that they are therefore of the same nature would be wrong.

Let but the wind blow a little fast, the leaf will rise and fly far; the iron ball is unaffected. Such is the nature of false and true devotees. When there is no pain or grief, both the false and the true are alike; when pain or discord presents itself, false devotion takes to flight. The devotion that seeks publicity is not true steady devotion. Devotion, that is confirmed in and through practice, can alone be the spring of lasting Bliss.

Experiences can be communicated among ourselves or to ourselves, or even to those who evince delight in listening to them and are eager to share; but, if they are announced in public to whomsoever may listen, they may not be seen in true light, they might even be misinterpreted and ridiculed. Those who are hungry will themselves come seeking places where food is available. Those who have no hunger will not be impressed, even when a variety of tasty dishes is placed before them.

Where Divinity is sought after, one ought always to behave in the spirit of Love, devoid of the slightest trace of hate, envy, and anger. Sadhana should first be directed towards the elimination of these traits. When worldly relationships are accepted as the basis of activity, one is inevitably drawn into the mire of separateness and distinction. When one cultivates the inner look, one attains the conviction of the basic equality of all. Observe the trunks of trees (not the branches, twigs, flowers, and leaves), and you will be convinced of the sameness of all trees. Similarly, when one observes only the status and stages, the office and authority; only differences and distinctions will strike the mind. But, in every one, as the very basis of existence, there is the one and only Soul, the Atma. *That* is to be known and realised.

Man derives all the joy and peace that he needs from within himself and not from sources outside himself. So, the best spiritual discipline is: strengthen the inward vision.

My dear Hislop! Do not let yourselves be drawn by other pursuits; carry on Sadhana, unaffected by them. I, Swami, am with you, beside you, before you, behind you, in your home; my love, my compassion, my grace are ever with you, you will never be without them. You will experience the Bliss of the Atma, the Reality, very soon.

Convey my numberless blessings to your grha-lakshmi (the Goddess of the Home, conferring peace and prosperity on the Home), Mrs. Hislop. May both of you be showered with mutual

concord, peace and joy; may you attain the glorious consumma-
tion of your Sadhana – the realisation of the Reality.

Blessings for the Sai Family. Discard malice, hate, envy, and
pomp; develop love and tolerance . . . progress in Sadhana, by
these means. Secure Ananda (spiritual bliss) first, and then, try to
convey it to those who crave for it, among the people. When the
tank is dry, how can the taps give water? Fill the tanks with pure
potable water; only then can the taps give water to the thirsty.

With Blessings
Baba.

PHONE: KOTHA CHERUVU 30
WHITEFIELD 33

ॐ

BHAGAWAN SRI SATHYA SAI BABA

PRASHANTI NILAYAM (A.P.)

Date..................

I   The best method of spreading vedanta Philosophy is to live it; There is no other royal Road.

II   Let God work Through you. and There will be no more duty. ~~to~~ Let God shine forth, Let God show himself, live God. Eat God. Drink God, breathe God. realise the truth and the other things will take, Them ~~self~~ selves

III   True Love expands the self. attachment contracts it.

IV   Heaven is within you. seek happiness ~~of~~ not in the object of senses, realise that happiness is within your self,

V   Ther is no rose without a thorn unmixed happiness is not to be found in this material world, all happiness ~~is~~ is in self supreme.

VI   in the lowest worm as well as in the highest human being the same divine nature is present The worm is the lower form in which the divinity has been more over shadowed by maya.

That is the highest form in which it has been least over shadowed behind every thing the same divinity is existing and out of this comes the basis of morality.

With Blessings
Baba.

BHAGAWAN SRI SATYA SAIBABA
PRASHANTHI NILAYAM

CAMP "Brindavan"
DATE 27. 5. 7L

Hislop! Receive my Blessings

I have received the two letters from you. I have noted what you have written. you have taken a lot of trouble regarding the helicopter and gathered a number of details about it. The number of Satya Sai organisations has grown in this country. I have to travel by car to visit these organisations and such journeys are not very convenient besides taking a lot of time. I therefore propose to dispose of the 3 or 4 cars I have and get a helicopter.

Travel by service planes is also inconvenient. recently the Government have imposed rigid rules and passengers are closely checked. besides crowds gather at every air-port. I feel a helicopter is better in every respect for my journeys. I can visit a large number of Satya Sai organisations, more quickly and with less inconvenience to every one and thus satisfy thousands of devotees.

Hislop! it was first proposed to get the new college building at Anantapur opened by the president of india on the 10th june 1971. But certain difficulties have now arisen. There is a strike of Government officials going on in Andhra. so the date has been changed for the present to the 15th of july. but. the finishing stages of the new building are getting completed briskly. but I wonder if the president can take part; for some time to come, in public engagements.

What will the Bangladesh problem in east-bengal and the non-gazetted officers, strike etc. I do not propose to move out anywhere in july and August.

Hislop! my special Blessings to your wife. may you both continue to enjoy Ananda. good health and mutual understanding and companionship.

Convey my blessings to Cowan and mrs. Cowan, gerry and Mrs gerry, and all sathya sai family

With Love and Grace

Baba.

BHAGAWAN SRI SATYA SAIBABA
PRASHANTHI NILAYAM

CAMP
DATE 24 · 7 · 71

My dear Hislop! I received your letter
I am very happy. How is your health? and practice
Hislop! The secret of perfect health lies in keeping the
mind always cheerful. never worried, never
hurried, never borne down by any fear, thought ~~anxiety~~
or anxiety.

have all your attachments severed from every
object and concentrate yourself on one thing. the
one fact; one truth, your divinity, immediately
on the spot you gain realisation

nothing is done in a day. religion can not be
swallowed in the form of a pill. it requires hard
and constant practice. The mind can be conquired
only by slow and steady practice.

Hislop! moderation in temper is virtue
moderation in principle is a vice. impurity is a mere
superimposition under which the real nature of
man has been hidden.

my dear! you are the embodiment of GOD. fill yourselves
with the thought of your almightiness, your majesty and
your glory. open the gates of wisdom. Enter the abode
bliss. Rest in peace forever

Hislop. How is your Mrs. give my Blessings to her and all
family. I am always, in you. with you   with
                                          Love Baba

To _Hislop_ with Blessings (1.01.1971)

My Dear! you will find it deep within yourself.
Think it many times. ponder it; it tells you about
your true na-ture. it gives you hope, it gives you
now life. it points the way. it proves to you that GoD
is within you. and you are not man, man is GoD
it shows you that it is possible for you to realize
GoD (Swamiji) but you and you alone must ponder
this work deeply. you will find that you will begin to
know what is meant by the statement: "the Self"
cannot be explained, the mind knows of its existence,
"the Self-GOD" is within man man, you are that Self,
all else is illusion of the mind's creation, the mind that
creates, preserves, and destroys

My Love! the great joy, the subtlety of the bliss, that
you will feel. as you come closer and closer to your
Real Self. if you strive to find your self. by by using
your mind, you will strive and strive in vain, Because
the mind, cannot give the you the truth; A lie cannot
give you the truth; A lie can only entangle you in a web
of deceit. but if you sensitize yourself. awaken your
true, fine, beautiful beautiful qualities

above you - nothing Below you - nothing, to the right of you -
or to the left of you - nothing; and dissolve yourself
into that nothingness. that would be the best way
you could explain the realization of the Self.
and yet that nothingness would not be the
absence of something like the nothingness.
that nothingness is the fullness of everything, the power,
of the existence of that appears to be everything. - Baba -

(Note from Sai Baba hand-delivered by messenger to Jack Hislop
at the ashram.)

To Hislap.   12·11·71.
                         at 9·A·M.

To try to meditate, to try to become quiet
To try to relax. Keep trying. Every positive effort
That you make, is not in vain. Every Single
brick added to a temple made of brick
brings that temple closer to completion.
So keep trying and one day All of a sudden
you will pierce the lower realms of your
mind and enter into Contemplation
and you will be able to say: "yes, I know,
I have Seen, Now I know fully the path that
I am on" Keep trying. you have to start
somewhere. The self you can cannot speak of,
you can at only try to think about it,
if you care to, in one way: feel your mind
body and emotions, and know.

                  With Blessings
                     Baba

(Note from Sai Baba hand-delivered by messenger to Jack Hislop
at the ashram.)

Aug. 8, 1972

Beloved Swamiji:

On Thursday, Baba's Day, July 27, second day of the full moon, we packed our furniture in a truck and moved to the new house in Mexico. The move was finished the next day, third full moon day. The combination of days and dates should be auspicious?

We are *camping* in the house for the time being, since there are no cabinets, only a rough floor, only partial plumbing, etc. However, the site is beautiful, and so is the house (Swami's North American residence). In mind's eye, we can see Swami moving lightly, with his graceful walk, through the white-columned arches of the house center.

Indeed, Swami *is* here. Victoria was washing the floor of the salon and there, clearly visible on the damp cement, were Swami's footprints. *She* had footwear on . . . so, there can be no mistake that it was Swamiji's footprint! By the time she called me in from outside, the prints had almost faded . . . but I could still see a portion of one footprint. It was a great thrill to us to realize that by virtue of Swami's Grace, He is here with us; so much so that we can even see the physical print of His Lotus Feet.

Then 3 days ago, Swami again showered His Grace in great abundance. While at the market Victoria lost her balance on the waxed floor and fell hard, striking the left breast on a corner of a wooden step near floor level. The blow was so severe that blood came through the pores of the skin. Such a rough hard blow to the breast has the reputation of quickly inducing cancer. We rushed home and she applied Swami's Vibhuti. The miracle at once followed. Pain ceased and the breast regained its normal color; whereas a lesser blow on the leg from the same accident has produced an area fully black and blue!

God is surely omnipresent; and God is Swamiji and Swamiji is God! To any person with open eyes, mind, and intelligence, Divinity is surely visible throughout Swami's daily action. But, for ourselves (man), God may be us — indeed must be us . . . but it is certainly difficult to see the obverse side of the coin . . that we are

God. I suppose it is only through practice that we can be still and allow God to be seen through our action. Swami advises that we declare a strike against the mind. Just as we are silent and non-active in relation to a person who is harmful but with whom we do not wish any controversy, we should be likewise in relation to the mind until it decides to stop its aggressive empire-building. Such brave words are easy for one to say, but one's practice is not so easy!

Victoria and I send all our love.

Hislop

August 24, 1973

Beloved Swamiji:

One is tossed here and there by circumstances, health, emotions, mind, and even unstable intelligence. The tendency is to
become subject to despair at one time and to temporary elation at
other times. One turns to Swamiji as the only reality — that is,
Swamiji within, and I hold to him as the nail cleaves to the timber,
as the sea creature is anchored to its rock. Even though one falters
and fails, yet only if every act is dedicated to worship of the
Divine, is there any sense at all to life.

Dearest Baba, enclosed are photo prints. Walter Wolfe, a
devotee of Swamiji, from the Cowan Center, took the pictures of the
crucifix using excellent equipment. He will send a full set of the
photos to Swami. He will also ask if Swami places any particular
restriction on the uses of the pictures. The photos of the crucifix were
shown at the Santa Ana Center last month, and everyone wants
some.

The figure of Christ as created by Swami is the most outstand-
ing work of art any of us have ever seen. Only by enlarging the
small crucifix can the amazing detail be seen. One realizes at once
that Jesus must have looked just like that after days on the cross.
How different the reality is as compared to the conceptions of
mundane artists! The blood, the agony, the spittle caked with
dust, the upturned eyes, all create a most penetrating feeling for
those people with a Christian background. If it would please him,
perhaps Swamiji could send a note to Mrs. Cowan giving a release
on the pictures, or noting the restrictions on their use.

For myself and Victoria, I am at work again, as per my letters
to Swamiji, and Victoria is staying at the Mexican house. This
afternoon I will drive home; I was there last weekend also.

With all love,

Jan. 26. 1975

Dearest Swamiji:

Now we are quite happy, for in two weeks we are going to see Swami — no reason to look further for the occasion of the happiness!

Regardless of the fact that anticipation is a bad fault, I feel more and more thrilled that soon we will see Swami. One can sympathize with the Gopis wherein they knew that Krishna was in the heart of each one of them, yet their life became very sweet only when their eyes were seeing Krishna's person and their ears were hearing Krishna's voice.

Unless there is a last minute change of schedule, we should arrive in Bangalore on February 12.

On February 2, we will attend Mrs. Cowan's first Sri Sathya Sai Baba meeting of the new year. Every few weeks we drive to Santa Ana and stay with Mrs. Cowan for a day or so. She is remarkably well with strong energy, and her will of iron is quite unbent by the years.

Victoria and I send all our love to our beloved Sri Baba,

With all love,

P.S. If we would have Swamiji's approval, we plan to stay a couple of months and then return again in November.

Bhagawan Sri Sathya Sai Baba

TELE NO. 30
BRINDAVAN
WHITEFIELD-560 067
TELE NO. 35
PRASANTHINILAYAM P. O.
ANANTAPUF DT 515134

My dear Hislop,

Accept my blessings. Your letter and the circular sent for the direction of devotees reached me. I am very happy that things are progressing well. I am glad you are healthy and active.

Hislop! It is not advisable to publicise defects by mentioning them specifically. These are subjects that can be dealt with indirectly, rather than directly. We must encourage people to correct themselves by highlighting the good points; for the very goodness will shame the others into giving up their vices. When others develop their faith in the right path, those who are in the wrong will also try to fall in line. When we write about a certain defect in character and draw attention to it, undue importance is thereby given to the individuals. We are also likely to be misunderstood and maligned as prejudiced. Let us lay stress more on positive virtues and positive ideas among devotees in our Organisation — like love, service, brotherhood. Let these be the distinctive marks of our Organisation, making it distinct from the rest. Let us keep away from the undesirable and ignore it, steadily and silently. Discussing it and publicly condemning it will only soil us. Maintain the atmosphere of purity and divinity; there, evil cannot sprout or thrive.

I am happy that even at this old age you are so earnest and active in serving the Organisation. The Organisation in America is your responsibility. Sai devotees have to give support to each other and share the labour. They must infuse into their groups love, courage, confidence, and a sense of sacrifice so that the Message can transform more and more into seekers and sadhaks of the Truth.

Dear Hislop! I bless that you carry on your programme of directing and developing the Organisation with success. I am highly satisfied with what you have done and are doing in this respect. Of course, such success always attracts obstacles, opposition and even vilification. But, do not pay them any attention. The diamond becomes brighter with the cutting of more facets. One's duty is to continue along one's chosen path and fulfil the task, with undiminished enthusiasm. Truth cannot fail to be valued and appreciated, one day or other. Be as happy as ever, whatever happens.

My blessings to your wife. Convey my love and blessings to Goldstein, Krystal, Sandweiss and others. Also to the Centres.

With love and Blessings
Sri Sathya Sai Baba
(Baba)

Oct. 7, '78

Beloved Sai:

It is only by the Grace of Swamiji that the lives of Victoria and myself are not caught up in the general disaster of people. Thus we are not expectant of anything beyond the ordinary routine when in Bhagavan's sacred Presence, and it is with much hesitation that I presume to ask more.

But, of His own volition, Swamiji said that He would satisfy my doubts. And it is from this that I gather the courage to ask for one or two interviews (with able translator present).

I have one very large doubt of my own. Also, my wife has run into a sort of barrier in her inner life and has a very strongly felt need to ask Swami.

In addition to the above, as I visit Sathya Sai Centres, questions are asked — some of which I cannot answer, and I need to ask Swamiji about these questions from devotees.

With all love
Hislop

Bhagawan Sri Satya Sai Baba
Prasanthi Nilayam P.O.
Anantpur Dt.
A.P. 515134

Dear Hislop,

Accept my Blessings to you and Mrs. Hislop. I received your letter, conveying your reaction to recent happenings. I am pained to find they have upset you so much. Every one is eager to serve Swami, and carry out the duties assigned to him. No one is high or low, no one is a competitor to another. In order to facilitate the projects that are planned by the devotees, people have been assigned tasks, but that does not mean they are in sole or superior charge. Every one should join hands in loving service.

When the tasks which the Organisation takes up increase in number and size, naturally, new Committees have to be formed and entrusted with the new duties.

Mutual adjustment and constant consultation are necessary if a programme of spiritual service is to succeed. Over-enthusiasm may make some people commit blunders or do incorrect things. These have to be overlooked in a generous spirit. Love and brotherhood must be expressed as both understanding and sympathy.

Dear Hislop, do not lose your peace of mind, when such things occur. Give your best to the cause and let love flow from your heart to all. Appreciate the devotion that moves thousands in America and help in every way to deepen it. I will not allow you to give up the role I have blessed you with. Know that I am always with you, in you, beside you, before you.

With Blessings and Love

Baba

PHONE NO. 30
PRASANTHI NILAYAM P.O. ANANTPUR DISTRICT. ANDHRA PRADESH 5′5 ′:4

May 20, 1982

Dear Hislop,

Blessings to you and your wife.

I received your letter and the enclosed newspaper cutting. The world has all sorts of people with all sorts of notions. This is its nature, Hislop. We should not pay attention to such people and their activities. Devotees must concentrate on Sadhana for their own advancement, instead of worrying about happenings outside their sphere.

I saw in the American Newsletter, a contribution sent by you to share with readers. It deals with trivial topics. We must discriminate between what is worthwhile and what is not. Seek always to help readers and members to progress in Spiritual Sadhana and to understand and practise Swami's teachings.

There are so many constructive and positive directions for spiritual success that Swami has given. Stress these while writing and speaking. Meditation transcends the senses. With the mind made serene by such meditation, one can bravely enter the activities of life.

Convey my blessings to Mr. and Mrs. Goldstein, Mr. and Mrs. Bozzani, Mr. and Mrs. Krystal, and all other devotees there.

With love and.
Blessings
Sri Sathya Sai

Sept. 23, 1982

Dearest Lord:

We (Victoria and myself) are scheduled to arrive in Bangalore on Thursday, November 4, and to depart Bangalore on Tuesday, December 28. It will be marvelous for us to be again in the divine presence of Swamiji.

Dearest Swamiji, it would be good if Swami could give a grand discourse on the World. Right now the world is especially painful and impossible for limited minds to comprehend without divine help.

The horror of the slaughter of men, women, and children without distinction or mercy which now goes on in Lebanon, Central America, and parts of Africa strikes the people here like a rod of blazing iron plunged into the heart. And yet we are so helpless to intervene. People hold protest parades, contribute to relief, write and phone their representatives in the Government, but no one can do anything.

Swamiji! What is the meaning of these hellish eruptions of world events?

What is the world?

The world seems to be me; for I do not know the world as a thing in itself, but know it only as a picture drawn by sensations arising in body and mind. Yet, how can these evil and demonic actions be me? I do not find these hellish passions and deeds in myself.

What is the world to an individual?

If the overwhelming impact of the world on my mind and feelings is due to ignorance, delusion, and to the lack of having someone who knows how to point out the truth of it, then may the divine Swami point out the truth of the matter.

One presumes that since Swami has adopted body and mind that he will also receive the common sensory and mental impressions. But Baba is without ignorance and delusion, and therefore will see a thing in itself — if there be such. How does Swami see the evil events which are now rising up to a peak in the world?

How are these events perceived by Swami?

And, how is the world perceived by Swami?

Dearest Swamiji! In His mercy, let Baba enlighten us in respect to the puzzles mentioned.

With all love,

Sept.22, 1983

Dearest Swami:

Victoria and I cannot even attempt to express in words our appreciation to Swami for his grace showered so lovingly on us during our visit. The beautiful prayer that Baba wrote for us is our guide throughout the day. We remember Baba all day long and feel his presence beside us wherever we go.

Swami's teaching to live God, eat God, drink God, breathe God is surely the greatest of inspirational statements, and we feel a genuine intensity to bring our whole lives into tune with God's Will. To awaken with love, talk with love, act with love, and end the day with love is the ideal Baba has given, and although we fall short, it is our strong desire to live like that.

We remember with deep gratitude Baba's divine teaching to meet each experience with "Yes, Yes, Yes," convinced that every experience carries God's love and is for our good. His teaching that there is only one "I" in essential reality and that we are in fact each living creature that we see, despite "good and bad" actions, is called to mind each day, and with the eye of reason we try to see each creature as not different from ourselves. Swami's extraordinary and amazing explanation of real "surrender to God" is constantly in mind, and we understand there is no genuine surrender to God until the eye of wisdom sees everything, even the impermanent world, as God only.

Every time I go to India, the body gets back home with a severe cold, but the present cold is tapering off and will soon be gone. Also, the constant headache that has been a nuisance for a year is lessening and is strongly felt now only when the brain is jarred by coughing. Victoria is also recovering her strength which was depleted by the flu, caught while she was in India. Why she had to be in bed with the flu, while there, instead of spending each day with Baba as close to him as possible is a great puzzle to her!

Victoria and I both send our love,

ॐ

PHONE: KOTHA CHERUVU 30
WHITEFIELD 33

BHAGAWAN SRI SATHYA SAI BABA

PRASHANTI NILAYAM (A.P.)

Date...............................

PRAYER

Oh ! Lord ! Take my love and let it flow in fuller
    "   Take my hands and let or devotion to thee
             them work
                    incessantly for thee
    "   Take my soul and let it be merged in one
                         with thee
    "   Take my mind and thoughts and let them
             be in ~~tone~~ tune with thee
    "   Take my everything and let me be an
                    instrument to work.

With Love and Grace
    Baba.

Bhagavan Sri Sathya Sai Baba
PRASANTHI NILAYAM P.O
ANANTPUR DT. (A P.)
PHONE NO : 30.

My Dear's! The time will come when
the whole of this dream will vanish. To
everyone of us there must come a time
when the whole universe will be found
to have been a mere dream, when we
shall find that the soul is infinitely
better then its surroundings. In this struggle
through what we call environments,
there will come a time when we shall
find that these environments were almost
zero in comparison with the power of the
soul. It is only a question of time, and
time is nothing in the Infinite. It is a drop
in the ocean. we can afford to wait
and be calm.

With Blessings

(Baba)   Sri Sathy: Sai Bah

EPILOGUE

On Directly Experiencing
the Presence of God
(A Talk to a Gathering of Sai Devotees)

Baba, in conversation this year, said something which is a great secret, for I have never heard him say it before. He told me that that which happens physically, on the outside, in terms of actions and so on, is not of major importance — that what is important is that which comes from the inside. It is the inside that changes the outside and not the outside that brings about the change inside. For example, Baba went on to say, "Take a car: it is driven from the inside." It seems from that statement, that what we must do now is to look inward and then bring it to the outside.

What is this inside activity that is going to change the outside? It is love. Love is the most powerful force in creation! Baba says that it is because of love that the universe was created, and the whole Cosmos is just a dance of love. So, we should be thinking of God all the time, praying to Baba, talking to him, keeping our mind with him. In this manner, when we affirm, or rather cease to deny that love, which is our true nature, and which can be brought to the forefront and expressed by loving God, then that love, that inside purity will come out and will change the outside circumstances.

Now, how are we going to practice this, to uncover this inner love for God which is there and of which we may not be aware?

Baba advises various ways in which it can be done. First of all, there has to be an intensity! One cannot just sit back and say, "God is everything, so He can fix everything! I do not need to take any action whatsoever!" Baba warns against such an attitude. In India there are groups that think that way, and this attitude is the great fault of these groups. Baba says that until we are fully realized, fully God-Realized, we must work and work hard. Man is born into this world in order to work. But work is not fully effective unless it is done with intensity. In fact, Baba told me that the real reason we do not fully realize the love that is within us, is because we do not have that intensity. And how are we going to get that intensity? We are going to get it by fully appreciating the situation in which we find ourselves.

For example, if we were in a dark room with a poisonous snake, with what intensity we would be listening to every little noise, with what intensity we would be gauging every littlest movement that we made! Or, in another way: when we sit in the darshan line and Baba is approaching us, with what intensity our gaze and our attention is fixed on him — maybe he will stop and say something to us; maybe he will tell us to come into the interview room — at that moment our intensity is full and we are really alert!

Now, what is there about our present situation that will bring about such intensity in our life? Where does danger lurk?

We are born in this body, in this society. We are subject to all sorts of influences — our parents, our schoolteachers, our government, our sex, our age, our size, our health, the influences from the stars . . . everything is moving and twisting us here and there . . . we are not free . . . and think of the hurricane of past karma that looms high and menacing behind the next embodiment! Where will it blow the frail vessel of body and mind if we miss this once in a million opportunity that we have now, to be alive during the time of the Avathar and listen to the truth that he proclaims! Now our luck has changed, the turn of the tide is with us! If we don't take this opportunity, when will it come again? Isn't that danger enough to bring some intensity to mind and heart?

Given that intensity, how do we now apply it in order to realize the inner world which must be projected onto the outside?

There are a number of sadhanas, spiritual practices, as Baba has told us; a number of ways to look at that situation. There is no time at this brief meeting to deal with the entire range, the whole situation, although it would be very interesting to do so. Let me just briefly talk about one aspect alone: how to make room for the love of God, how to cultivate it, how to have the love of God always alive in us, to be thinking of God, loving God all the time.

It can be done, first of all, by Divine Vision — that is seeing through the transient personality, the transient characteristics of the person with whom you are dealing. I look here at these ladies and these gentlemen — everyone appears to be different, everyone has his or her own characteristics, his own history, his own quirks and so on. So, the thing to do is to realize that this is just the appearance, just as on the movie screen when there is a battle going on, people are running, shooting, buildings are burning, and bombs are exploding. All this seems very real to us; our kids are afraid, some ladies even cry because of what is happening to the hero, and yet — when it is all over — the screen has not been touched, it has not been burned, there are no bullet holes in it! The whole thing has just been a show, a play! We have to realize that this is true in terms of people also; that this play is going on with all the various personalities and differences. Behind all, there is one reality which is permanent and unchanging — Baba tells us that the unchanging Reality is God, that God is the resident of every heart, that God is the permanent, unchanging, One Reality.

So when we see people day by day, throughout our workday, our day at home, when we look at a person, let us look through that personality and with our intelligence, with our discrimination, let us appreciate the fact that God is the reality of that person, even though he or she may be so obnoxious that we wouldn't want them to come within ten feet of us. Nevertheless, we can look through that and appreciate the fact that God is in the very heart of that person. and we can say, looking at God in his or her heart, "Dearest Lord, I love Thee, I love You, Baba." Silently, in our mind and heart, we say it.

To the person, we pay no attention. Let him go by, let him go his own way, live his own life, don't interfere with him or her. But look through the changeable personality, start to appreciate, that in essence, all is one, that God is every place. Greet God, tell Him that you love Him, tell Baba you love him, tell him every time you look at anybody.

If you will do this, you will feel a flash of happiness course through your being. A thousand times you do it, a thousand times you will feel that flash of love and happiness. In that way, all the time you are looking at people, even though you are behaving in a perfectly commonsense and logical way, at the same time you are feeling that love, the Love of God which is within you.

Now, extend that love in another direction — the practice of the constant presence of God, which is a discipline we know very well in the Christian religion. As you know, a sculptor, a creative artist, can take a block of stone, a block of granite, and as far as he is concerned, every possible form, every possible face is implicit within that block of stone. Here is that block of granite: does the artist have to chisel a deer or a face upon the stone? No! Every possible form already exists within that block of granite, and all it requires is a creative artist in order to bring out that face or that form which he wants to bring out from the latent to the patent.

Precisely the same is true in respect to God. He is omnipresent; omnipresent means present at all times in all places. Baba has told us explicitly again and again, that he, Baba, is omnipresent. I daresay that almost every person in this room has experienced the fact that Baba is omnipresent. Has Baba not come into your life at one time or another, in a very plain fashion, even though his body is far away in India? I dare say that almost everyone in this room has experienced Baba's omnipresence.

In any block of space — this block of space in front of me now, the block of space beside your bed when you waken in the morning — God is fully there, completely there. All we need do is to bring Him out of that block of space, with the spiritual artistry of a devotee of God, from the latent to the patent. With energy, with resolve, with your strength of being, bring God's form out of that block of space directly beside you every morning when you awaken. Visualize God, conceive Him in the form of the Divine most dear to you . . . it may be the form of Jesus Christ, of Krishna, of the Divine Mother, or it may be the form of Baba whom many of us love most dearly as a form, alive today, fully charged with the glory of the Divine, as the infinite Divine appearing as form to give us joy. See God, visualize His form, pray to Him, bring Him out of that block of space, then take His hand and hold His hand every moment of the day from waking until you go to sleep at night, committing yourself to His care. When conscious, be with Him consciously, holding tightly to His hand; when consciousness fades at sleep, pray to Him to hold and protect you, and He will be with you the night through. Day and night you can be with Him. It can be done; it is always done by God's devotees. It is an old, old practice. It works, because Name and Form are not separate. We also can do it; we can take God's hand and hold onto Him from now to the last moment of our existence in this transient body.

Now, if we were walking with our beloved Baba all day wherever we went, would we not feel love in our heart for him? Would it not be almost impossible for us to have thoughts of hatred or jealousy or anger while holding Baba by his hand? Almost impossible! All bad traits, all these dark flowers of the night; they grow in darkness, they thrive in darkness. How can they be there, how can they persist when you are holding Baba's hand throughout the whole day?

So if we just take these two practices, that of Divine Vision — seeing God as the Reality wherever you look, and holding His hand throughout the day, committing yourself to His care when asleep; then that love which is your reality will grow and expand and will fully realize itself. And then that love will come from the inside to the outside and that will change your whole life.

That is the way to approach the uncovering of the inner love for God, that inside beauty and purity and energy which is going to change the outside. That is the way to start, it is a perfectly practical way. In that way we can implement Baba's teachings. There is no reason we cannot do it — nobody sees us do it. When we approach somebody and we pass that person — saluting God who is the reality of that person — they do not know it. They can't point a finger at us saying, "Look at that crazy person." Or, when we are walking in the street or sitting in the office, holding God's hand — nobody can see us doing this — they can't say, "Hey, this person cannot work for us, he is not all there!" It is all inside, all in your heart. Therefore there is no reason for anyone to say, "It cannot be done!" It can be done!!

Every person here has freedom, God-Realization, within his or her grasp. Every person here has immortality next door to him, by his side, within him, above him . . . We should never lose sight of this fact. Of all the millions, all the billions of people in the world, how many know Sri Sathya Sai Baba? How many go to India to see Sai? How many read his books and consider his teachings? How many look for him in their hearts and feel love for him, devotion to him, feel his love for them? Of all the millions in the world, it is just a handful.

To let that great chance go because of lack of thought, because of lack of consideration, is really and truly a crime.

So many times we are born, so much suffering we have gone through, so much desperation we have felt. The chance is here for us to be free of the quicksand, to reach the firm bank, to realize the divinity which Baba says is our true nature, to feel and be that which never changes, which is always the same, that bliss that passes all understanding, that peace that passes all understanding . . . That is within the grasp of everyone of us!

Any day, any moment we forget, it is a day lost, a moment lost! How quickly our life passes away, how rapidly the years go by! In no time at all it's all over, we're too old to pay attention, and the opportunity is lost, when and where to come again? Every life is taken on to work out a certain load of Karma — the next life, who knows what karma will come into play? Who knows what our circumstances will be, where we will be? This opportunity, so tangible, so precious — once lost may be gone for so long — aeons of time!

Every day we should remind ourselves of our heritage, of our opportunity, of the meaning of our life right now, and pray to Baba, pray to the Lord to help us realize that!

To Sum It Up

Baba has told us that as long as the ego-mind is the charioteer of our lives, we will never be able to know the changeless Truth; and that until we know the truth of ourselves we will continue with birth, death, rebirth, temporary joys, and inevitable suffering. Mind, ego, concepts, reactions, and tendencies must be perceived and acknowledged as that which is experienced but which is not oneself. In order to know the full and real truth about oneself, one will need to make this inquiry the dominant interest of one's life.

Not that we must make such a decision until we choose to do so. An eternity of what we are experiencing now and have experienced in the past is ours, if such be our choice. Baba has clearly told us that birth, death, and rebirth is a game of our own choosing. But if we have enjoyed our game enough and now yearn for realization of "that peace which passeth all understanding," then Baba offers to help us "awaken."

We are told by Baba that a divine incarnation is an extraordinary circumstance beyond the possibility of verbal description. He tells us that the time is ripe for us to realize the absolute goal of all life — reunion with Godhead, and that it will be a major tragedy for us if we waste this unique lifetime in the pursuit of worldly desires, worldly ambitions, and sensory enjoyments. This challenge may awaken us from our ordinary daily life and we may resolve, "I will search for my Truth." Here we need to be alert and understand what "I search for my Truth" means in this context. The everyday meaning will be that "I" am an individual person positioned in time and space, that "Truth" can be found and recognized and is "mine," yet somehow "my Truth" is apart from me and thus requires search.

Baba assures us that what "I search for my Truth" really means is that "my Truth" is myself and not something separate from me. That "search" is to *clearly* see wrong notions and discard them, and that "I" is the Undifferentiated Supreme Absolute Divinity, which only appears to be limited to individuality in somewhat the same context as bubbles on the leading edge of an ocean wave appear to be separate, but in fact are neither separate from the ocean nor different from the ocean. In terms of daily life, this means that the finality of everything is one and the same Divinity — that we appear to be apart from the Divine but are not actually so.

Saints and sages, from the most ancient of times, have told us that the path to the realization of our Divine Reality is that of detachment from the objects and affairs which we are presently attached to because of desire and craving and misconceptions; and Baba teaches us that this detachment will come about when we examine objects and affairs closely so as to clearly perceive their deficiencies.

We have experiences such as joy, boredom, or agony as a result of contact with worldly objects. But relationships between ourselves and objects are changeable, temporary, and not reliable. Experiences of boredom and agony are temporary and that is all to the good, no doubt. But conversely, we cling tenaciously to the experience of joy, and we easily become attached to objects which provide a range of pleasant experiences. However, all objects, even one's beloved spouse or child, come into existence, stay for a while, change much or little, and then are no more. The promise of bliss which we perceived in the object is aborted by its inherent seeds of decay and one's hope of lasting joy in these relationships is betrayed time and time again. This happens to everyone, and this is the principal deficiency of an object, yet we ignore repeated lessons and continue to seek worldly objects hoping to experience happiness thereby.

Baba teaches that a search to find happiness in something perceived outside ourselves is bound to fail. He tells us that only when one realizes oneself is there happiness. Limitless unqualified bliss is our natural self, our reality. Being-consciousness-bliss is our name, but that name is good only for communication; our true reality is beyond words. Baba teaches that our reality is perfect love, divine love, and that bliss *is* love. He tells us that our task as pilgrims on the spiritual path is to purify mind and heart; for only a pure mind and heart can reflect the immaculate truth which is beyond the opposites. Baba informs us that all truth will instantly flash into a purified heart.

Since the omnipresent consciousness, the Divine Principle, is the reality of both mind and heart, it cannot be difficult to realize the inherent purity of mind and heart. Baba tells us that in this time and age, wherein we encounter imperfection wherever we turn, the most effective means to get rid of the impurities which now crowd mind and heart is to directly call upon the ever-perfect Divine Principle: one's innermost reality. The way is simple and immediately available to every person. The way is to fill the mind with that particular name of Divinity which is dear to one's heart and fill the heart with devotion to the Divine. It is the experience of people that, in the presence of the Divine Name, one's manifold impurities weaken and fall away without struggle and without the application of any other type of discipline.

Sri Sathya Sai Baba declares that consciousness is omnipresent. "Omnipresent" means everywhere at every moment. Omnipresence of consciousness means that one's consciousness is the consciousness of everything in creation. It means that consciousness is present in everything in creation regardless of how the object or the expression of life might be classified on our scale of values. The same omnipresent consciousness is in God, in the most distant universe, in the block of granite, in you, and in me. Apparent differences are those of name, form, and function, and of the density of the cloud of ignorance which obscures the brilliant light of consciousness. Here, the word "ignorance" is used to indicate an uncritical acceptance of separateness, of duality. We can easily understand how ignorance hides the omnipresence of consciousness by noticing how we ourselves feel that we are separate, and how we do not seem to demonstrate the love and the glory of our essential reality — Divinity. Baba declares that consciousness is the Lord and, in reality, God alone exists.

Baba likens consciousness to an electric current, a phenomenon within the knowledge of almost everyone. The diverse expressions of electricity multiply year by year as technology ad-
vances, but it is all one aspect of energy — electricity. The ignorance of which Baba speaks arises because in life we see the
diversity, the duality, but fail to appreciate the unity. With simple
instruction and simple experiments, our ignorance about electricity is easily lifted and done away with. But it is not so easy for us to
see that a person of ugly behavior, the worm found in freshly turned earth, our beloved Baba, and the countless thousands or
millions of universes in space are all part of the one omnipresent
consciousness. And it is, perhaps, even more difficult to see that
we must be helped in order to be free of ignorance, even though no
one but oneself is responsible for continued ignorance.

To understand how we may be helped to free ourselves of ignorance, it is best to take a simple, but true, example. A simple example, evident to all of us, is the ocean and the shore. Ocean is
commonly understood as the vast body of water which surrounds
the continents. The ocean is one vast ocean. The names, Atlantic
Ocean and Pacific Ocean, do not alter the fact that it is one vast
ocean. This we know. We learn it in school and later on directly
experience the fact as we travel about the world. Yet, at the shore
we see separate waves and so name them. We see separate foam
and bubbles, and so name them, when the wave rises to a crest and
breaks upon the shore. We actually see these phenomena, and the
phenomena are real and tangible when we venture into the waves,
foam, and bubbles. We know that waves, foam, and bubbles are
just ocean, but we see and experience wave, foam, and bubbles
and we respond to the experience in that context. A child, fascinated with the bubbles may capture some in his hand and may say
to his father, "I will take them home." Father smiles and explains
that bubbles are transitory forms of ocean water which appear to
be real but quickly die away. This perfectly obvious fact had never
occurred to the child, but it was at once understood when pointed
out by his father, who had a correct understanding of both the apparent duality and the underlying unity. In this case, father was
the guru. That which calls our attention to truth is the guru. Unless
something occurs to remind us of ignored truth, we would remain
as we are; we would continue to engage in actions arising from

false notions and suffer the painful consequences again and again, ad infinitum. That this unhappy situation can exist is widely understood. The common statement is, "He who fails to understand history is bound to repeat it." Blessed is he who has been found by a true guru. To a devotee, the teachings of Baba is the enlightenment lovingly offered by a true guru.

We perceive duality at the seashore. However, that perception of difference, of duality, is harmless because the phenomenon of duality arises and subsides so rapidly that our basic understanding of the ocean is not affected. But the great body of our experience is not so simple and direct. At the shore, the appearance of duality, — waves, foam, and bubbles — quickly and plainly subsides into the ever-present underlying unity of ocean; but in more complex experiences, the appearance of duality persists, and we do not see or understand the omnipresent unity of the omnipresent consciousness. Thus we disregard the unity, focus on the appearance as something unique and real in itself, and thus fall victim to wrong notions.

The experience of physical, emotional, and mental phenomena is indeed real in relation to the senses. But such phenomena is unreal; for that which appears and then disappears, dependent upon this or that, which neither lasts nor can be relied on, is as good as unreal. For this reason, the world is said to be neither real nor unreal. In the simple experience of the ocean and the shore, we clearly understand the duality of appearance, and we also understand the underlying unity of the ocean. The ocean *is* its waves and its bubbles, and the waves are not the ocean; for the ocean remains as the ocean even when bubbles and waves have lost their separate forms and no longer exist. But in the more complex experiences of our life, we do not clearly understand the duality of the world of appearances and of ourselves, nor clearly understand the unity of the underlying omnipresent consciousness, the Divine Principle. That Divine Principle — the omnipresent underlying consciousness — *is* oneself and is also everything else that can be imagined or perceived, just as the ocean is its visible waves and bubbles and also its invisible variations in temperature and currents. But neither the world nor oneself, this apparent duality, limits the Divine Principle, for the omnipresent consciousness remains as omnipresent consciousness even when I (as a person) have lost my separate form and no longer exist. In like fashion, we are told that if the entire creation were to subside, the Divine Principle would remain, without modification.

In the illustration of the ocean and the shore, the child understood that he could not take ocean bubbles home. He gained correct understanding when his father pointed to the truth of the situation. If the child willfully decided to ignore correct understanding and tried to carry the ocean bubbles home, no harm was done. But to apply such willfulness to more serious matters is to invite disaster. If, even though we have been fortunate to have been found by a true guru, we willfully disregard correct understanding; our actions will be based on wrong understanding, and we will continue to invite the misery and suffering which follows serious errors of judgment.

Sri Sathya Sai Baba tells us again and again in his discourses, writings, and conversations that God alone exists, and that He and we are not different. Baba points out in the clearest of terms that the duality of oneself and the world is an illusion; that duality is transitory appearance only, and that the entire creation of an infinite number of universes and an infinite number of beings of manifold types and forms resolve into the one Reality, God, the Omnipresent Consciousness, the Divine Principle. Baba has pointed out this truth to those whom he has found, which means — those who will listen. Having listened and having reasoned out this truth in simple situations which we can easily comprehend, we are bound by our intelligence to no longer be unknowingly subject to illusion in respect to duality. The understanding of duality and unity means that no matter what we perceive, no matter how tangible or intangible it might appear to be, we penetrate it with our understanding and know that whatever we perceive is Divinity at its core, and that we ourselves are not truly different from what we perceive, from each other, from the world or from the Divine. The understanding of duality and unity will transform our lives *if we do not allow a host of predetermined concepts to hold us as prisoners*. From the day of our understanding we can surely know and feel the joyful presence of the Lord as the one reality everywhere, and be happy. Baba says to us always, "Be happy, be happy." He says that in ourselves the stream of happiness should be as constant as the stream of consciousness.

Realization of unity, realization that nothing is apart from omnipresent consciousness requires us to face a practical problem. This problem could be named "The problem of identity," or, "The problem of sanctuary."

Ordinarily, regardless of what one's intellectual or philosophical understanding may be, one considers his body to be himself. But when one's intelligence has come to understand and appreciate the omnipresent nature of consciousness, the burning question arises, "Who and/or what am I?" In consciousness I am unity, but as an embodiment engaged in action, I am duality. Therefore one asks, "As long as I am in action and therefore subject to the swings of the opposites, where can I position my sense of being, of existing?"

One's native intelligence, once it is applied to the question, can quickly see that while "I" am everything, yet everything is not myself, for "I" continue unmodified regardless of what happens. For example, "I" am my body, which is the sum of its parts, but if an arm and a leg are destroyed, "I" continues undiminished even though my body is diminished by the loss of some parts. The alert intelligence can at once pursue this clue and quickly realize that one can take one's stand as a witness to all that happens at any level of consciousness and remain unaffected by all happenings.

At this level of purity, a guru will certainly appear. The guru may point out that if one wishes to realize the essence of his being and take his stand there, then the idea that the "witness state" is oneself is not substantially different from the idea that the "embodied state" is oneself even though having taken one's stand in the "witness state" there is no longer identification with the miseries and pleasures which afflict the body. The guru may point out that all ideas can be relinquished, even the idea of self, and that in reality, one's essence is pure consciousness not limited by a center or a periphery or ideas of any sort whatsoever. If, when listening to the guru, all ideas give up the ghost, so to speak, and are destroyed, then the mind is totally void of movement, and "Liberation" is said to be "achieved." The pilgrim is said to be no more. Long, long ago the pilgrim became the idea, "I am a spiritual aspirant and I will take to the spiritual path." Now all ideas are extinguished and the pilgrim has ceased to be. Consciousness is merged in consciousness, and being-awareness-bliss-love is timeless, ever-fresh, ever-fragrant Reality.

In this way, understanding cannot but begin to deepen somewhat when one takes that first step advised by Baba, "See the deficiencies of objects." Now, when one has realized that unity and duality are coincident in the experience of one's embodiment as a human person, one is required by his native intelligence to engage in a constant self-effort of self-inquiry.

The teachings of Baba as briefly described in the second section of this book are all to be found in his discourses, essays and conversations. The writer has simply reported on his study of Baba for the past seventeen years. The writer views Baba as a flame of love and bliss dancing in ecstasy against the background of the apparent world and making himself accessible to all devotees who yearn for enlightenment. Baba is viewed as incarnate wisdom, as a particular embodiment of the omnipresent consciousness without the shadow of particularity — fully aware of himself as you, as me, and as the total of creation. The writer's viewpoint reflects his experiences with Baba over the years, and he fully acknowledges his human capacity to misinterpret experience. The foregoing is the bias of mind which the writer spoke of in the chapter "From Age 16" and which the reader is entitled to know as he or she works through the pages of this book. The writer has implicit faith in Baba and in his motives and, in the company of thousand of fellow devotees, he applies Baba's teachings to daily life as best he can.

Almost every teaching of Baba's can be found, couched in different words and phrases, in the course of a diligent study of the several great spiritual and religious traditions of mankind. Such studies have been published and are available in libraries and from publishers. What is unique about the Avathar, Sri Sathya Sai Baba, is that Baba is alive, vigorous, able to be seen and listened to and competent to put into words the truth about man, God, and the world — all of which he directly observes as he speaks. We attend the Avathar not for more information, but for an actual experience of our essential truth. Undistorted truth is Baba's nature: he is that truth — that is, the Divine. The significance of this for us is beyond and superior to all calculations, for it brings into our life an infinitely powerful potential. That potential is the removal of the illusion of our separateness from the Divine by experiencing our direct connection with the Divinity of the sentient, alive-in-this-world Sri Sathya Sai Baba. He tells us that Salvation, abidance in the actuality of our Divine Reality, is here, as close to us as self is to Self. He tells us that the Avathar is with us, incarnate, for the very purpose of our Salvation, our Liberation, our Enlightenment. How different is this from the books we consult and the lectures we hear; how different from these is the love of the incarnate Divinity for His children.

The Avathar, Sri Sathya Sai Baba, whose actual beingness is Truth Absolute, tells us that the direct pathway to God-Realization, to the realization of our Self, is love; that He is love and that love unites us with Him. He tells us to let love come first, and the direct realization of our Truth will inevitably follow.

How to open one's mind and heart to love for God, to devotion to Him, to the liberating truth of Divinity now, in this very lifetime, is set forth in Baba's teachings to be followed up by practice and by visiting Prasanthi Nilayam so as to place oneself in the direct physical presence of the Avathar. For most of us, Baba as our Divine Charioteer becomes meaningful when we have had the joyful experience of his physical presence.

For me, a pilgrim on the spiritual path who yearns to break free from illusion and delusion, Baba is the key to freedom. I have total confidence that what he says is the truth. What Baba teaches I put into daily preactice, and what he says does happen. For instance, while I still remain a standard, "general issue" western man, yet my dominant aggressive and hostile tendencies have fallen away without my struggling to change them. Baba informs us that bad characteristics cannot survive in the presence of the sacred name of that embodiment of Divinity dearest to one's heart. He tells us that when the sacred name is said with devotion to the supreme value, Divinity, even the powerful ego of voracious individuality will retreat from its throne as the ruler of one's life. Often, as I go about the day, I feel that the Hislop person, to whom I refer as "me," is like the insubstantial shadow which accompanies the real body as one walks on a sunny day. In his teachings, Baba declares it will work out best for us if we feel that God is the Reality and that one is but an instrument used by God to carry out His design. Our reason can accept this, for there is no way it can be challenged by the limited mind with which we have day-to-day familiarity. If the position strikes us as being reasonable,

it will do away with mountains of anxiety and will add much enthusiasm to the way we carry out action. For myself, my mind, by
now, constantly recites the sacred name — for me it is "Om Sai
Ram" — and when things happen as they do, I say and feel, "Thy
Will, Lord." I act with my maximum energy and according to my
duty, as duty becomes apparent, and say and feel, "Thy Will,
Lord." And I accept the consequence of action without worry —
feeling and saying, "Thy Will, Lord." If I happen to forget this
base, this viewpoint, I recollect and again take this position.

Glossary

ASTAVAKRA: A famous Sage who was King Janaka's guru, his spiritual preceptor.

ATMA: Just as "space" refers to the one space whether considered to be the vastness of the universe or the space inside one's body, Atma is the one infinite consciousness whether manifest as the universe or oneself.

AVATHAR: Divinity apparently born and existing as a human person, but in reality remaining as the limitless Divine.

AVATHARA: The life-period or lifetime of an Avathar.

DASARA: A Hindu festival wherein age-old symbolic sacrifices are performed for the benefit of the entire world.

DRAUPADI: The principal woman in the household of the Pandavas, a clan with which Lord Krishna had a lifetime relationship.

GOKULUM: A shelter or special place where one's herd of cows are fed and cared for.

JANAKA: A famous king in India who continued to live in the world and rule his kingdom even though fully God-Realized.

KARMA: Action and its reaction. Unless dedicated to the Lord, all action reflects on its doer.

LIBERATION, SELF-REALIZATION, GOD-REALIZATION: The state in which an apparent individual realizes his or her oneness with infinite consiousness.

LORD KRISHNA: An Avathar who is said to have lived some 5,000 years ago and whose name and life story are as familiar to Indians as that of Jesus is to Christians.

MANDIR: A temple.

MAYA: A mysterious and subtle aspect of existence which leads us to see and give attention to the unreal and thereby disregard the real.

RAMA: An Avathar, said to have lived thousands of years prior to the lifetime of Lord Krishna. The life story of Rama, his consort, Sita, and his brothers is known in detail to all Indians and is constantly referred to, as is the story of Lord Krishna.

SANATHANA DHARMA: That righteous behavior which corresponds to unchanging truth.

SANKALPA SHAKTI: A term which means one's inherent but seldom realized will power.

SITA: The consort of the Avathar, Rama. In herself, she is said to represent an aspect of Divinity. Her story is part of the cultural heritage of India.

VIBHUTI: Ash is referred to as vibhuti when it is used to represent the impermanence of all things. When burned in fire, all things even though different relative to each other, resolve into ash. Vibhuti, when touched by Baba, or manifested by him, often seems to be the catalyst or agent which cures disease and wards of severe misfortunes.

WOOD-APPLE: The woody-textured fruit of a large tree found in wooded areas.

INFORMATION CENTER

Centers for the study and practice of the teachings of Sathya Sai Baba have been established worldwide. More than a hundred Sathya Sai Baba Centers are located in the United States. Many are listed in local telephone directories under the title Sathya Sai Baba Center of (name of city or town). For further information about the location of a Center in your area, write:

Sathya Sai Baba Information Center
c/o Sathya Sai Baba Book Center of America
305 West First Street
Tustin, California 92780

NOTES

NOTES

NOTES

NOTES

NOTES

101
Strength
Training
Workouts
& Strategies

Acknowledgments

This publication is based on articles written by Chris Aceto, Jose Antonio, PhD, David Barr, CSCS, Josh Bryant, CSCS, Rob Fitzgerald, Shelby Starnes, Jim Stoppani, PhD, Mark Thorpe, Eric Velazquez and Joe Wuebben

Cover photography by Frank W. Ockenfels III

Photography and illustrations by: Art Brewer, Blake Little, Ian Logan, Marc Royce, Ian Spanier and Pavel Ythjall

Project editor is Joe Wuebben

Project creative director is Brian Kahn

Project managing editor is Jared Evans

Project copy editor is Kim Thomson

Project photo coordinator is Erica Schultz

Project art assistant is Brandi Centeno

Founding chairman is Joe Weider. Chairman and CEO of American Media, Inc., is David Pecker

This book is available in quantity at special discounts for your group or organization. For further information, contact:

Triumph Books LLC
542 S. Dearborn St., Ste. 750
Chicago, IL 60605
(312) 939-3330
fax (312) 663-3557
triumphbooks.com

ISBN: 978-1-60078-586-3

Printed in USA.

MUSCLE &FITNESS® PRESENTS

101
Strength
Training
Workouts
& Strategies

TRIUMPH
B O O K S

TRIUMPHBOOKS**.COM**

Contents

Chapter 1

Warm Up to a New Idea

Touching your toes has gone the way of parachute pants in the weight room. This is your new preworkout mandate: **"Don't stretch. Move"**

When you get to the gym,

there are two paths you can take. You could use the first 15 minutes of your session to prime your body for peak performance, or you can risk being weaker and more prone to injury. It's your call. Once you begin to understand the principles behind a sound dynamic warm-up, we think we know how you'll decide.

Your days of strolling into your gym, tossing out a few arm swings and diving right into your workout have come to an end. It's time to start treating your body with the same care a world-class athlete does, and one thing elite athletes and coaches have figured out is that static stretching and an inadequate warm-up don't cut it when you want to perform your best. Your body needs to prepare for the work it's about to undertake, and warming up dynamically is the best way to get the job done.

Don't Stretch. Move

When you're about to train with weights — or run, jump or do anything athletic — the idea is to thoroughly warm up your body and get more blood flowing to your muscles using movement vs. standing or sitting in one place and stretching. This idea of warming up your muscles rather than elongating them is a major advancement beyond the traditional static stretching you did in gym class. Starting your workouts with an intelligent movement progression is the ideal way to construct an optimal foundation for success in the gym.

"A comprehensive dynamic warm-up will accomplish everything you need to bring to your workouts," says Nate Winkler, co-owner of Juggernaut Training Systems in Laguna Hills, California, and a former collegiate track athlete. "When you put the right moves together and finish your warm-up sweating, everything's going to be ready to go."

10 SECOND TIP

Try to swing your knee and leg across your body as quickly as possible

High-Knees Crossover Run

START: Stand with your feet shoulder-width apart, knees bent, lower back arched and elbows bent approximately 90 degrees with your hands in front of you.
EXECUTION: Run sideways by raising the knee of your back leg as high as you can and stepping across your body. Go for 20 yards, then reverse direction.

3-Way Jumping Jacks

START: Perform this series of movements the same way you'd do traditional jumping jacks from the waist down. With your feet together and your weight on the balls of your feet, jump from this position and land with your feet wider than your shoulders, then bounce back to the start.

EXECUTION: For the first 10 reps, swing your arms so they cross in front of you with your hands at your midsection. For the next 10 reps, swing your arms at chest level. Perform the final 10 reps in traditional fashion.

10 SECOND TIP

Don't stop after finishing each variation. Think of this as one continuous set of 30 reps

Our dynamic warm-up progression is simply a series of movements designed to raise your core temperature, increase joint mobility and activate the central nervous system (CNS) before putting your body through a strenuous workout. Accomplishing these three objectives is vital to your progress when you want to add mass and get stronger: When you add poundage to your lifts each week, you should give yourself every possible competitive advantage while bulletproofing yourself against injury.

If you're still using an antiquated static stretching warm-up — or not taking the time to warm up at all — you're courting disaster. Static stretching won't appreciably raise your core temperature, which is a must for motor-unit recruitment and coordinated muscular contraction. Stretching also lengthens your tissues and leaves you susceptible to injury by promoting muscle, joint and ligament laxity. When you lift heavy weights, you want your muscles warm, coiled and ready to explode as opposed to loose, cold and vulnerable to the forces you're applying to them.

"To perform your best athletically, you need your CNS firing on all cylinders," Winkler says. "Static stretching puts your central nervous system to sleep. Warming up dynamically activates your CNS. In my experience, it's best to save your serious static stretching for after your workouts."

Total-Body Readiness

Our dynamic warm-up is a general sampling of movements that'll warm up your body from head to toe as opposed to stretch individual muscles. By the time you're finished, the core temperature of every major muscle group will be raised and you'll be prepared to begin your warm-up sets with the first exercises in your workout. We guarantee you'll feel the difference

Prisoner Squat

START: Stand erect with your feet shoulder-width apart and your fingers interlocked behind your head, your weight over your heels.
EXECUTION: Descend into a thighs-parallel squat, then return to standing.

Side Lunge

START: Stand erect with your feet together and your arms at your sides.

EXECUTION: Step directly to the side with one leg and descend into a lunge. Keep your anchor leg extended — you should feel a stretch in your groin — and the knee of your working leg directly over that foot. Return to standing and repeat for reps, then switch sides.

Bird Dog

START: Kneel on all fours on the floor, hands shoulder-width apart and arms straight under your shoulders.

EXECUTION: Simultaneously extend your left arm directly in front of you and your right leg straight behind you so they're parallel to the floor and in line with your torso. Return to the start and repeat with the opposite arm and leg.

Iron Cross

START: Lie faceup on the floor with your arms forming a "T" perpendicular to your torso with your palms down. Keep your feet and knees together, and bend your knees and hips 90 degrees so your thighs are perpendicular to the floor and your shins are parallel to it.

EXECUTION: Keeping your hands on the floor and squeezing your knees together, twist your hips and touch the outside of one knee to the floor, then reverse the motion and repeat on the opposite side.

Low Pogo Jump

START: Stand erect with your feet hip-width apart, knees slightly bent and elbows bent approximately 90 degrees with your hands in front of you.

EXECUTION: Bounce up and down in a low jump as quickly as you can for five seconds. Envision jumping rope without a rope.

Leg Swing

START: Grasp the vertical post of a power rack or other stationary anchor with one hand, or place one hand against a wall.

EXECUTION: Keeping your outside leg as straight as possible, kick it as high as you can in front of you, then swing it as far behind you as you can. Repeat for reps, then switch sides.

Supine
Kick

START: Lie faceup on the floor with your legs straight, feet together and arms forming a "T" perpendicular to your torso with your palms down. Anchor one leg to the floor.
EXECUTION: Maintaining minimal flexion in the opposite knee, kick that leg as close to your head as possible until you feel a stretch in your hamstring. Lower your heel to the floor and repeat for reps, then switch sides.

Crossover
Leg Swing

START: Turn and face a stationary anchor or the wall and use both hands, keeping your body erect but in a slight forward lean.
EXECUTION: Keeping one leg straight, kick it out to the side as high as possible, leading with the outside of your foot, then swing it down and across the front of your body until your hips are slightly turned. Repeat for reps, then switch sides.

Side
Shuffle *(not shown)*

START: Stand with your feet shoulder-width apart, knees bent, lower back arched and elbows bent about 90 degrees with your hands in front of you. Your weight should be primarily on the balls of your feet.
EXECUTION: At a comfortable pace and without letting your feet cross over each other or touch, shuffle laterally for 20 yards, then reverse direction. Keep your head and chest aligned and at consistent levels.

Broomstick
Stretch *(not shown)*

START: Grasp a broomstick, dowel or piece of PVC pipe in a snatch grip with your hands well outside shoulder width.
EXECUTION: With your arms extended, raise the broomstick overhead and behind you as far as you can until you feel a stretch in your shoulders. Reverse direction and lower the stick to your thighs.

10 SECOND TIP

To help yourself nail the proper form on backpedaling, think "nose over toes"

Backpedal

START: Stand with your knees bent, lower back arched and elbows bent about 90 degrees with your hands in front of you.
EXECUTION: Staying low, push off backward with one foot so you jog in reverse with your head directly over the foot that's propelling you. Backpedal for 20 yards, then turn around and repeat. When you push off, drive your opposite elbow back toward your destination.

immediately in both strength levels and range of motion.

"You want to progress from the general to the specific," Winkler says. "Start out with an easy movement such as jogging or jumping jacks, then gradually make it more specific. Most people I train start out with such stiff hips that they can't get to parallel when they squat. Consistently performing a good dynamic warm-up will solve that problem and many others."

To perform these movements, you may have to retreat to your gym's aerobics room or take things outside to the parking lot or sidewalk. If you're easily embarrassed, you might feel silly jumping around before your session, especially when you're the only one in the gym doing it. Look at it this way: Instead of being "just another gym guy," you're preparing yourself to train the same way professional and Olympic athletes do. Better yet, you'll experience marked performance improvement across the board — gains that'll eventually offset any potential embarrassment when you try this for the first time.

Hip Circles

START: Kneel on all fours on the floor, hands shoulder-width apart and arms straight.

EXECUTION: Keeping one knee bent 90 degrees, raise it out to the side and draw wide forward and backward circles at approximately waist height. Keep your arms fully extended with your elbows locked. Repeat for reps, then switch sides.

Hip-Flexor Stretch

START: From a standing position, step forward with one leg as far as you can into a lunge. The knee of your back leg should touch the floor.

EXECUTION: Put your hands on your hips and lean back until you feel a stretch in the hip flexor of your back leg. Hold for a 10-count, then stretch the same-side arm overhead and behind you before switching sides.

10 SECOND TIP

Execute a full hip turn. Don't just try to reach by stretching your quadriceps

Prone Scorpion

START: Lie facedown on the floor with your arms forming a "T" perpendicular to your torso with your palms down.

EXECUTION: Keeping one leg anchored to the floor, turn your hips, bend your top knee and try to touch that heel to the opposite hand. Return to the start position and repeat for reps, then switch sides.

• WARM-UP PROGRESSION

EXERCISE	SETS	REPS/TIME/DISTANCE
3-WAY JUMPING JACKS	3	10
PRISONER SQUAT	1	10
SIDE LUNGE	1	10 EACH SIDE
LOW POGO JUMP	2	5 SEC.
LEG SWING	1	10 EACH SIDE
CROSSOVER LEG SWING	1	10 EACH SIDE
SUPINE KICK	1	10 EACH SIDE
IRON CROSS	1	10 EACH SIDE
PRONE SCORPION	1	10 EACH SIDE
BIRD DOG	1	10 EACH SIDE
FORWARD HIP CIRCLES	1	10 EACH SIDE
BACKWARD HIP CIRCLES	1	10 EACH SIDE
HIP-FLEXOR STRETCH	1	10 SEC. EACH SIDE
SIDE SHUFFLE	2	20 YARDS
BACKPEDAL	2	20 YARDS
HIGH-KNEES CROSSOVER RUN	2	20 YARDS
BROOMSTICK STRETCH	1	10

Chapter 2

Stronger in Two Months

Boost your strength across the board — by about 25% for each bodypart — with this eight-week progressive program

Barbell Overhead Press

Getting stronger and pressing more weight means bigger, wider shoulders. Use a wide grip to maximize delt involvement and minimize triceps work.

BODYMASTERS

Being massively strong isn't useful for only powerlifters, home run-hitters and that guy at the gym whose only training goal is to bench-press four plates for reps. Take a look at any successful athlete or otherwise impressive human specimen and you'll see a guy with a high level of overall strength. Lance Armstrong, LeBron James, all those ripped guys in the movie *300* — none of them are renowned for breaking lifting records, but all of them are mighty strong in their own right.

But since gaining strength by way of pedaling up the Alps (like Lance) or having most of it attributable to natural selection (like LeBron) is probably out of the question, you'll have to attain it more like the *300* crew did: with iron, in the gym. The subsequent eight-week program promises to make you 25% stronger in all major lifts, from presses to rows to squats. Follow it to a T, and if it doesn't leave you with a yellow jersey or NBA scoring title, at least you'll be a more impressive human specimen for it.

Strength Factors

You don't have to train like a powerlifter to get stronger. Quite the contrary. This program is designed to increase your overall strength by 25% on each of nine exercises, one for each major bodypart: bench press (chest), barbell bent-over row (back), barbell overhead press (shoulders), squat (legs), barbell shrug (traps), barbell curl (biceps), close-grip bench press (triceps), leg-press calf raise (calves) and barbell wrist curl (forearms). With your newfound strength, you can go back to higher-rep training — the typical 8–12 reps — for size and overload each muscle group with even heavier weight for further growth.

Barbell Shrug

Even though the movement is short — just a few inches — your traps are seriously strong. Use straps as the weight becomes too heavy for your grip. Don't roll your shoulders; use a smooth and powerful up-and-down motion.

HERE'S A RUNDOWN OF THE PROGRAM'S THREE MAJOR ASPECTS.

1) 5RM Testing:

You'll test your strength three times in this program — at the start, after the fourth week and at the end, after week 8. But there's no need to suit up like a powerlifter and have three or four spotters on hand, nor will you have to perform an actual 1RM set. Research shows that using a five-rep max (5RM) to determine your 1RM is about 99% accurate for upperbody exercises and 97% accurate for lowerbody exercises. That's close enough.

To calculate your 1RM for each of the nine exercises, perform 2–3 warm-up sets using progressively heavier weight, then find a weight that permits you to get five and only five reps; you shouldn't be able to get a sixth rep on your own. If the weight is too heavy or too light to hit five reps, terminate the set and rest 4–5 minutes, then select a new weight to attempt for a 5RM. For example, if after two reps you can already tell the weight is too light, end the set immediately and increase weight for your next attempt. Point being, don't expend too much of your strength on failed 5RM attempts.

Take each 5RM weight and use one of these two equations to determine your 1RM for the particular exercise.

For upper-body exercises:

(5RM weight x 1.1307) + 0.6998 = 1RM

Example: If you bench 300 pounds for five reps, your 1RM would be:

(300 x 1.1307) + 0.6998 = 340 pounds

For lower-body exercises:

(5RM weight x 1.09703) + 14.2546 = 1RM

Example: If you squat 400 pounds for five reps, your 1RM would be:

(400 x 1.09703) + 14.2546 = 453 pounds, or 455 pounds (rounded up)

Barbell Curl

Nothing adds thickness to your biceps like the barbell curl. Keep the emphasis on your bi's by avoiding backward sway and keeping your elbows pinned to your sides.

WEEKS 0 + 4 + 8

FRIDAY

MUSCLE GROUP	EXERCISE	SETS/REPS[1]	REST
CHEST	Bench Press	1/5	4–5 min.
LEGS	Squat	1/5	4–5 min.
BICEPS	Barbell Curl	1/5	4–5 min.
TRICEPS	Close-Grip Bench Press	1/5	4–5 min.
FOREARMS	Barbell Wrist Curl	1/5	4–5 min.

SATURDAY

MUSCLE GROUP	EXERCISE	SETS/REPS[1]	REST
SHOULDERS	Barbell Overhead Press	1/5	4–5 min.
BACK	Barbell Bent-Over Row	1/5	4–5 min.
CALVES	Leg-Press Calf Raise	1/5	4–5 min.
TRAPS	Barbell Shrug	1/5	4–5 min.

[1] Does not include warm-up sets and failed 5RM attempts.

2) Heavy Days:

The foundation of any good strength program is heavy lifting. But how you lift to get stronger is different than for sheer muscle-building: You don't want your body to be as fatigued, so the volume will be slightly less than you may be used to. You'll also need to rest longer between sets on core lifts (up to three minutes) to ensure adequate recovery. It's important that you're as strong as you can possibly be for each and every set, and short rest periods won't allow for this. Another difference between strength training and bodybuilding is frequency. You'll train each muscle group twice a week, whereas many bodybuilders train each bodypart just once a week.

Sets of between three and 10 reps that get progressively heavier from week to week will comprise the

majority of your training in our eight-week program. For the nine core lifts, the weight used will be a percentage of your 1RM based off your 5RM testing. For all other exercises, no rep-max testing is necessary; simply select a weight that'll cause you to fail at the target number of reps. The first three sets listed for each core exercise (50%–70% 1RM) are warm-up sets and the last set listed is a burnout set.

3) Explosive-Rep Training:

During Weeks 1–3 and 5–7 (all nontesting weeks) you'll perform explosive-rep training on Fridays and Saturdays (see "Explosive-Rep Workouts" on page 25). You'll do only the core exercises in these workouts for a total of three sets, in addition to one warm-

Squat

Gain strength in the squat and every other bodypart will grow as well. Vary your foot position (narrow or wide) as well as bar placement (low bar/high bar) to match your body's needs.

HEAVY Training Days
WEEKS 1–2 + 5–6

MONDAY

CHEST >	WEIGHT	SETS/REPS	REST
BENCH PRESS	50% 1RM	1/10	1–2 min.
	60% 1RM	1/5	1–2 min.
	70% 1RM	1/3	2 min.
	(Weeks 1–2) ~80% 1RM[1]	4/8–9	2–3 min.
	(Weeks 5–6) ~90% 1RM[1]	4/4–5	2–3 min.
	60% 1RM	1/to failure	2 min.
DUMBBELL	(Weeks 1–2) 10RM	3/10	2 min.
INCLINE PRESS	(Weeks 5–6) 6RM	3/6	2 min.
DUMBBELL FLYE	(Weeks 1–2) 10RM	3/10	2 min.
	(Weeks 5–6) 6RM	3/6	2 min.

BICEPS >	WEIGHT	SETS/REPS	REST
BARBELL CURL	50% 1RM	1/10	1–2 min.
	60% 1RM	1/5	1–2 min.
	70% 1RM	1/3	2 min.
	(Weeks 1–2) ~80% 1RM[1]	4/8–9	2–3 min.
	(Weeks 5–6) ~90% 1RM[1]	4/4–5	2–3 min.
	60% 1RM	1/to failure	2 min.
DUMBBELL	(Weeks 1–2) 10RM	3/10	2 min.
INCLINE CURL	(Weeks 5–6) 6RM	3/6	2 min.
ROPE HAMMER	(Weeks 1–2) 10RM	3/10	2 min.
CURL	(Weeks 5–6) 6RM	3/6	2 min.

FOREARMS >	WEIGHT	SETS/REPS	REST
BARBELL	50% 1RM	1/10	1–2 min.
WRIST CURL	60% 1RM	1/5	1–2 min.
	70% 1RM	1/3	2 min.
	(Weeks 1–2) ~80% 1RM[1]	4/8–9	2–3 min.
	(Weeks 5–6) ~90% 1RM[1]	4/4–5	2–3 min.
	60% 1RM	1/to failure	2 min.

TUESDAY

LEGS >	WEIGHT	SETS/REPS	REST
SQUAT	50% 1RM	1/10	1–2 min.
	60% 1RM	1/5	1–2 min.
	70% 1RM	1/3	2 min.
	(Weeks 1–2) ~80% 1RM[1]	4/8–9	2–3 min.
	(Weeks 5–6) ~90% 1RM[1]	4/4–5	2–3 min.
	60% 1RM	1/to failure	2 min.
FRONT SQUAT	(Weeks 1–2) 10RM	3/10	2 min.
	(Weeks 5–6) 6RM	3/6	2 min.
LEG EXTENSION	(Weeks 1–2) 10RM	3/10	2 min.
	(Weeks 5–6) 6RM	3/6	2 min.
LEG CURL	(Weeks 1–2) 10RM	3/10	2 min.
	(Weeks 5–6) 6RM	3/6	2 min.

CALVES >	WEIGHT	SETS/REPS	REST
LEG-PRESS	50% 1RM	1/10	1–2 min.
CALF RAISE	60% 1RM	1/5	1–2 min.
	70% 1RM	1/3	2 min.
	(Weeks 1–2) ~80% 1RM[1]	4/8–9	2–3 min.
	(Weeks 5–6) ~90% 1RM[1]	4/4–5	2–3 min.
	60% 1RM	1/to failure	2 min.

TRICEPS >	WEIGHT	SETS/REPS	REST
CLOSE-GRIP	50% 1RM	1/10	1–2 min.
BENCH PRESS	60% 1RM	1/5	1–2 min.
	70% 1RM	1/3	2 min.
	(Weeks 1–2) ~80% 1RM[1]	4/8–9	2–3 min.
	(Weeks 5–6) ~90% 1RM[1]	4/4–5	2–3 min.
	60% 1RM	1/to failure	2 min.
PUSHDOWN	(Weeks 1–2) 10RM	3/10	2 min.
	(Weeks 5–6) 6RM	3/6	2 min.
OVERHEAD TRICEPS	(Weeks 1–2) 10RM	3/10	2 min.
EXTENSION	(Weeks 5–6) 6RM	3/6	2 min.

WEDNESDAY

SHOULDERS >	WEIGHT	SETS/REPS	REST
BARBELL OVER-	50% 1RM	1/10	1–2 min.
HEAD PRESS	60% 1RM	1/5	1–2 min.
	70% 1RM	1/3	2 min.
	(Weeks 1–2) ~80% 1RM[1]	4/8–9	2–3 min.
	(Weeks 5–6) ~90% 1RM[1]	4/4–5	2–3 min.
	60% 1RM	1/to failure	2 min.
DUMBBELL OVER-	(Weeks 1–2) 10RM	3/10	2 min.
HEAD PRESS	(Weeks 5–6) 6RM	3/6	2 min.
LATERAL RAISE	(Weeks 1–2) 10RM	3/10	2 min.
	(Weeks 5–6) 6RM	3/6	2 min.

BACK >	WEIGHT	SETS/REPS	REST
BARBELL BENT-	50% 1RM	1/10	1–2 min.
OVER ROW	60% 1RM	1/5	1–2 min.
	70% 1RM	1/3	2 min.
	(Weeks 1–2) ~80% 1RM[1]	4/8–9	2–3 min.
	(Weeks 5–6) ~90% 1RM[1]	4/4–5	2–3 min.
	60% 1RM	1/to failure	2 min.
LAT PULLDOWN	(Weeks 1–2) 10RM	3/10	2 min.
	(Weeks 5–6) 6RM	3/6	2 min.
DUMBBELL	(Weeks 1–2) 10RM	3/10	2 min.
BENT-OVER ROW	(Weeks 5–6) 6RM	3/6	2 min.

TRAPS >	WEIGHT	SETS/REPS	REST
BARBELL SHRUG	50% 1RM	1/10	1–2 min.
	60% 1RM	1/5	1–2 min.
	70% 1RM	1/3	2 min.
	(Weeks 1–2) ~80% 1RM[1]	4/8–9	2–3 min.
	(Weeks 5–6) ~90% 1RM[1]	4/4–5	2–3 min.
	60% 1RM	1/to failure	2 min.

[1] Use the percentages from the previous 5RM test (performed before Week 1 or at the end of Week 4). The suggested percentages are just estimates of the amount of weight you should be using. Adjust the weight accordingly to perform the prescribed number of reps.

Chapter 2

10 SECOND TIP

—

When training for muscle power, the weight should be light (somewhere around 50% 1RM), the reps should be low (3–5 in this program) and the rest periods sufficient (around two minutes).

Barbell Wrist Curl

Keeping your thumbs under the bar is the best way to get the most out of this great forearm exercise. Allow the bar to roll as far out onto your fingertips as possible before curling the weight back up.

Close-Grip Bench Press

One of the few compound exercises for triceps, the close-grip bench helps overload the tri's with serious weight.

HEAVY Training Days

WEEKS 3-4 + 7-8

MONDAY

CHEST >

	WEIGHT	SETS/REPS	REST
BENCH PRESS	50% 1RM	1/10	1–2 min.
	60% 1RM	1/5	1–2 min.
	70% 1RM	1/3	2 min.
	(Weeks 3–4) ~85% 1RM[1]	4/6–7	2–3 min.
	(Weeks 7–8) ~95% 1RM[1]	4/2–3	2–3 min.
	70% 1RM	1/to failure	2 min.
INCLINE	(Weeks 3–4) 8RM	3/8	2 min.
BENCH PRESS	(Weeks 7–8) 4RM	3/4	2 min.
CABLE	(Weeks 3–4) 8RM	3/8	2 min.
CROSSOVER	(Weeks 7–8) 4RM	3/4	2 min.

BICEPS >

	WEIGHT	SETS/REPS	REST
BARBELL CURL	50% 1RM	1/10	1–2 min.
	60% 1RM	1/5	1–2 min.
	70% 1RM	1/3	2 min.
	(Weeks 3–4) ~85% 1RM[1]	4/6–7	2–3 min.
	(Weeks 7–8) ~95% 1RM[1]	4/2–3	2–3 min.
	70% 1RM	1/to failure	2 min.
PREACHER CURL	(Weeks 3–4) 8RM	3/8	2 min.
	(Weeks 7–8) 4RM	3/4	2 min.
HAMMER CURL	(Weeks 3–4) 8RM	3/8	2 min.
	(Weeks 7–8) 4RM	3/4	2 min.

FOREARMS >

	WEIGHT	SETS/REPS	REST
BARBELL	50% 1RM	1/10	1–2 min.
WRIST CURL	60% 1RM	1/5	1–2 min.
	70% 1RM	1/3	2 min.
	(Weeks 3–4) ~85% 1RM[1]	4/6–7	2–3 min.
	(Weeks 7–8) ~95% 1RM[1]	4/2–3	2–3 min.
	70% 1RM	1/to failure	2 min.

TUESDAY

LEGS >

	WEIGHT	SETS/REPS	REST
SQUAT	50% 1RM	1/10	1–2 min.
	60% 1RM	1/5	1–2 min.
	70% 1RM	1/3	2 min.
	(Weeks 3–4) ~85% 1RM[1]	4/6–7	2–3 min.
	(Weeks 7–8) ~95% 1RM[1]	4/2–3	2–3 min.
	70% 1RM	1/to failure	2 min.
LEG PRESS	(Weeks 3–4) 8RM	3/8	2 min.
	(Weeks 7–8) 4RM	3/4	2 min.
LEG EXTENSION	(Weeks 3–4) 8RM	3/8	2 min.
	(Weeks 7–8) 4RM	3/4	2 min.
ROMANIAN	(Weeks 3–4) 8RM	3/8	2 min.
DEADLIFT	(Weeks 7–8) 4RM	3/4	2 min.

CALVES >

	WEIGHT	SETS/REPS	REST
LEG-PRESS	50% 1RM	1/10	1–2 min.
CALF RAISE	60% 1RM	1/5	1–2 min.
	70% 1RM	1/3	2 min.
	(Weeks 3–4) ~85% 1RM[1]	4/6–7	2–3 min.
	(Weeks 7–8) ~95% 1RM[1]	4/2–3	2–3 min.
	70% 1RM	1/to failure	2 min.

TRICEPS >

	WEIGHT	SETS/REPS	REST
CLOSE-GRIP	50% 1RM	1/10	1–2 min.
BENCH PRESS	60% 1RM	1/5	1–2 min.
	70% 1RM	1/3	2 min.
	(Weeks 3–4) ~85% 1RM[1]	4/6–7	2–3 min.
	(Weeks 7–8) ~95% 1RM[1]	4/2–3	2–3 min.
	70% 1RM	1/to failure	2 min.
LYING TRICEPS	(Weeks 3–4) 8RM	3/8	2 min.
EXTENSION	(Weeks 7–8) 4RM	3/4	2 min.
PUSHDOWN	(Weeks 3–4) 8RM	3/8	2 min.
	(Weeks 7–8) 4RM	3/4	2 min.

WEDNESDAY

SHOULDERS >

	WEIGHT	SETS/REPS	REST
BARBELL OVER-	50% 1RM	1/10	1–2 min.
HEAD PRESS	60% 1RM	1/5	1–2 min.
	70% 1RM	1/3	2 min.
	(Weeks 3–4) ~85% 1RM[1]	4/6–7	2–3 min.
	(Weeks 7–8) ~95% 1RM[1]	4/2–3	2–3 min.
	70% 1RM	1/to failure	2 min.
BARBELL	(Weeks 3–4) 8RM	3/8	2 min.
UPRIGHT ROW	(Weeks 7–8) 4RM	3/4	2 min.
LATERAL RAISE	(Weeks 3–4) 8RM	3/8	2 min.
	(Weeks 7–8) 4RM	3/4	2 min.

BACK >

	WEIGHT	SETS/REPS	REST
BARBELL BENT-	50% 1RM	1/10	1–2 min.
OVER ROW	60% 1RM	1/5	1–2 min.
	70% 1RM	1/3	2 min.
	(Weeks 3–4) ~85% 1RM[1]	4/6–7	2–3 min.
	(Weeks 7–8) ~95% 1RM[1]	4/2–3	2–3 min.
	70% 1RM	1/to failure	2 min.
REVERSE-GRIP	(Weeks 3–4) 8RM	3/8	2 min.
LAT PULLDOWN	(Weeks 7–8) 4RM	3/4	2 min.
SEATED	(Weeks 3–4) 8RM	3/8	2 min.
CABLE ROW	(Weeks 7–8) 4RM	3/4	2 min.

TRAPS >

	WEIGHT	SETS/REPS	REST
BARBELL SHRUG	50% 1RM	1/10	1–2 min.
	60% 1RM	1/5	1–2 min.
	70% 1RM	1/3	2 min.
	(Weeks 3–4) ~85% 1RM[1]	4/6–7	2–3 min.
	(Weeks 7–8) ~95% 1RM[1]	4/2–3	2–3 min.
	70% 1RM	1/to failure	2 min.

[1] Use the percentages from the previous 5RM test (performed before Week 1 or at the end of Week 4). The suggested percentages are just estimates of the amount of weight you should be using. Adjust the weight accordingly to perform the prescribed number of reps.

Bench Press

We have to say it: How much do you bench? Well, this program will have your bench strength on the rise along with the size of your pecs. Bring the bar to your lower chest and press up in an arc over your face for best results.

up set. By improving your explosive power, you improve how fast you can apply force to the bar. The faster you can apply force, the faster you can get the bar moving, which relates to the ability to move more weight.

On explosive-rep training days, you won't use a lot of weight. In fact, it may seem too light for you. The key here is to move the weight through the positive portion of the lift as quickly as possible. For the eccentric or negative phase of the rep, lower the bar under control as you would normally. When you get the target number of reps for each set, you'll feel like you can still do more — but resist the urge to keep going. Training for power isn't about reaching muscle failure. When your muscles fatigue, the speed of movement slows down, which defeats the purpose of explosive training.

At the end of eight weeks you should be roughly 25% stronger on each core exercise, at which point you should return to more of a mass-gaining program. We recommend coming back to this or another strength-focused routine every six months or so to keep your power levels on the rise, because the stronger you are, the better you'll perform in all other areas of the gym.

Barbell Bent-Over Row

Unparalleled in its ability to add strength and mass to your back, the bent-over row is a must. Change your grip from overhand to underhand as well as wide to narrow for balanced development.

Leg-Press
Calf Raise

It's easy to overload your calves using the leg press, and you don't even have to undo the safeties. Just get in position and blast your calves.

EXPLOSIVE-REP Workouts

Perform the following workouts on Friday and Saturday of Weeks 1–3 and 5–7 (Friday and Saturday of Weeks 4 and 8 are reserved for 5RM testing). After one warm-up set of 10 explosive reps with no weight on the bar, perform three sets of explosive reps, starting with five reps the first set, four reps the second set and three on the final set. Rest two minutes between exercises. Perform the concentric (positive) portion of each rep as explosively as possible. The eccentric (negative) portion should be more controlled.

WEEKS 1-3 + 5-7

FRIDAY

CHEST >	WEIGHT	SETS/REPS	REST
BENCH PRESS	empty bar	1/10	1–2 min.
	(Weeks 1–3) 50% 1RM	3/5,4,3	2 min.
	(Weeks 5–7) 60% 1RM	3/5,4,3	2 min.

LEGS >	WEIGHT	SETS/REPS	REST
SQUAT	empty bar	1/10	1–2 min.
	(Weeks 1–3) 50% 1RM	3/5,4,3	2 min.
	(Weeks 5–7) 60% 1RM	3/5,4,3	2 min.

BICEPS >	WEIGHT	SETS/REPS	REST
BARBELL CURL	empty bar	1/10	1–2 min.
	(Weeks 1–3) 50% 1RM	3/5,4,3	2 min.
	(Weeks 5–7) 60% 1RM	3/5,4,3	2 min.

TRICEPS >	WEIGHT	SETS/REPS	REST
CLOSE-GRIP BENCH PRESS	empty bar	1/10	1–2 min.
	(Weeks 1–3) 50% 1RM	3/5,4,3	2 min.
	(Weeks 5–7) 60% 1RM	3/5,4,3	2 min.

FOREARMS >	WEIGHT	SETS/REPS	REST
BARBELL WRIST CURL	empty bar	1/10	1–2 min.
	(Weeks 1–3) 50% 1RM	3/5,4,3	2 min.
	(Weeks 5–7) 60% 1RM	3/5,4,3	2 min.

SATURDAY

SHOULDERS >	WEIGHT	SETS/REPS	REST
BARBELL OVER-HEAD PRESS	empty bar	1/10	1–2 min.
	(Weeks 1–3) 50% 1RM	3/5,4,3	2 min.
	(Weeks 5–7) 60% 1RM	3/5,4,3	2 min.

BACK >	WEIGHT	SETS/REPS	REST
BARBELL BENT-OVER ROW	empty bar	1/10	1–2 min.
	(Weeks 1–3) 50% 1RM	3/5,4,3	2 min.
	(Weeks 5–7) 60% 1RM	3/5,4,3	2 min.

CALVES >	WEIGHT	SETS/REPS	REST
LEG-PRESS CALF RAISE	no plates added	1/10	1–2 min.
	(Weeks 1–3) 50% 1RM	3/5,4,3	2 min.
	(Weeks 5–7) 60% 1RM	3/5,4,3	2 min.

TRAPS >	WEIGHT	SETS/REPS	REST
BARBELL SHRUG	empty bar	1/10	1–2 min.
	(Weeks 1–3) 50% 1RM	3/5,4,3	2 min.
	(Weeks 5–7) 60% 1RM	3/5,4,3	2 min.

The 5/3/1 Phenomenon

Personalize your workouts like
a pro with one of the Internet's
most popular programs

We all have a training arsenal at our disposal. It consists of our equipment, capabilities, ideas and knowledge. When we know what we want, we break out our weaponry and take dead aim at whatever athletic target we're looking to hit. The idea is to strive for better accuracy, which means knowing what you need to get the job done. You want to use what you've got in an organized, coherent way so you make progress week after week.

Enter Jim Wendler's 5/3/1 program. The longtime director of strength and development at Elite Fitness Systems in London, Ohio, and former starting fullback at the University of Arizona (Tucson), Wendler is uniquely qualified to create a program that's adaptable across the entire spectrum of strength disciplines. As an elite powerlifter with a 1,000-pound squat to his credit, he knows a thing or two about getting strong. Ten years of consulting with strength coaches, athletes and gym owners from all over the world has helped him form some definitive conclusions on what lifters need in terms of programming, exercise selection and equipment.

According to Wendler, 5/3/1 is more than a program, template and set-and-rep scheme: It's a new way to think about your arsenal. It's a way to break out your weapons with confidence and know exactly how to apply what you've got. It takes what we already know — exercises with which we're already familiar — and teaches us a better way to put everything together.

"This program is all about training economy," Wendler explains. "Everything you do supports your four main lifts: bench press, squat, deadlift and military press, or whatever else you choose to do. Building your program around these lifts instead of doing endless sets per bodypart gets you in and out of the gym in less than an hour with better results."

5/3/1 gives you a set of parameters so you can design your own program and emphasize what's important to you. "When you're training for strength and size, squats, bench presses and deadlifts are essential. But with 5/3/1 you choose exercises that work the muscles that support these movements," says Matt McGorry, a trainer at New York City's Peak Performance. "That's why this program is ideal for anyone looking to add overall size or strengthen lagging muscle groups."

5/3/1 SAMPLE REP-MAX PROGRESSION

WEEK 1

EXERCISE	1RM	WORKING MAX (90% 1RM)
BENCH PRESS	200 POUNDS	180 POUNDS
SQUAT	300 POUNDS	270 POUNDS
DEADLIFT	325 POUNDS	292.5 POUNDS

WEEK 5

EXERCISE	ORIGINAL WORKING MAX	NEW WORKING MAX (90% 1RM)
BENCH PRESS	180 POUNDS	185 POUNDS
SQUAT	270 POUNDS	280 POUNDS
DEADLIFT	292.5 POUNDS	302.5 POUNDS

Rep-Max Calculator: Weight x Reps x .0333 + Weight = Estimated 1RM

Everything starts with big multijoint moves. You can choose whichever compound movements you like, but the program recommends constructing your weekly workouts around the bench press, squat, deadlift and military press — none of which require specialized equipment or fancy machines. "These are the most efficient exercises for building size and strength," Wendler says. "This isn't a secret, but everyone acts like it is."

Next, you begin and work almost exclusively with weights that are 60%–85% of your one-rep max. Using submaximal loads has several advantages: You won't kill yourself in the gym every day, which will help you recover faster, and you'll eliminate the anxiety of handling heavy weights every session. "When I ask somone how much he can bench, the answer is always more than he realistically can,"

Chapter 3

Bench Press

Wendler points out. "When you take a step back like this, you know you're working with weights you can actually handle."

Everything you do in the weight room has a cumulative effect. Using lighter weights on your main lifts vs. working up to one big set accumulates tonnage, which is the aggregate total of everything you move in the gym. The more tonnage you accrue over time, the bigger and stronger you get.

"You need enough stimulus to get stronger, but you don't want to go overboard," Wendler notes. "Your body is like a car. If you press the accelerator to the floor all day, every day, the engine is going to burn out. That's exactly what most people do in the weight room."

The third major 5/3/1 principle is the notion of slow, steady progress. Instead of ramping things up quickly and trying to blast through your sticking points, 5/3/1 increases training volume a little at a time, making improvements manageable and consistent. Your body

adapts to weight increases over a four-week period, allowing you to progress slowly and surely before you move on. These month-to-month increases may not seem like much until you've added 50–60 pounds to all your main lifts in a year's time.

"[The typical method of switching] programs every few weeks guarantees you won't learn enough about your body to optimally design a routine for yourself," McGorry says. "However, with this program, you will be provided with a solid line of improvement that will give you the proper feedback and let you know exactly where you stand."

Finally, you're encouraged to compete against yourself and break personal records every time you're in the gym. On your last set of every main exercise, perform as many reps as you can at a given percentage. Then plug the weight and number of reps into a rep-max calculator and compare your results to what you did in previous weeks. This gives you a definitive goal for each workout.

5/3/1 is a precise percentage-based system, so you'll need to know your one-rep maxes for your 3–4 main lifts before you begin. If you train alone and don't feel safe attempting a one-rep max, do as many reps as you can with a weight you can lift for 8–10 reps. Then plug your results into the rep-max calculator: Weight x Reps x .0333 + Weight = Estimated 1RM

Once you establish your numbers, multiply each 1RM by 90%. This is your working max, and you'll use it to derive the percentages of weight you'll train with in your daily workouts. (See "5/3/1 Sample Rep-Max Progression.") For your 5/3/1 working sets, you'll use 65%–95% of your working max, or 60%–85% of your 1RM, progressively increasing the weight on each of your three sets. You do five reps per set in Week 1 and three in Week 2, then pyramid down from five reps to three reps to one rep in Week 3. (See "5/3/1 Sample Training Split.") Wendler suggests starting with an empty bar, then repping out using 30%–40% of your working max until you're comfortable.

Remember, these numbers are percentages of your working max, not your 1RM. If a percentage of your working max yields an odd number, round up or down depending on how you feel. Week 4 is a deload week, when you reduce the intensity and give yourself a break after three weeks of climbing the percentage ladder.

There's a final caveat, and it's what makes 5/3/1 special. For the last main set each week — using 85%, 90% and 95% of your working max, respectively — the split lists corresponding sets of five reps, three reps and one rep. These, however, are only the minimum requirements. Do as many reps as you can, then plug the weight you used and the number of reps you performed into the rep-max calculator.

"You're forced to be objective about your training because you record your sessions and chart

5/3/1 SAMPLE TRAINING SPLIT

MONDAY

EXERCISE	SETS	REPS	REST
BACK SQUAT	5/3/1	5/3/1	2 MIN.
BARBELL LUNGE	3	6	1 MIN.
INCLINE SIT-UP	3	20	1 MIN.

WEDNESDAY

EXERCISE	SETS	REPS	REST
BENCH PRESS	5/3/1	5/3/1	2 MIN.
DUMBBELL INCLINE BENCH PRESS	5	10	1 MIN.
DUMBBELL ROW	5	10	1 MIN.
SHRUG	5	10	1 MIN.

FRIDAY

EXERCISE	SETS	REPS	REST
DEADLIFT	5/3/1	5/3/1	2 MIN.
GOOD MORNING	5	10	1 MIN.
HANGING LEG RAISE	3	15	1 MIN.

SUNDAY

EXERCISE	SETS	REPS	REST
MILITARY PRESS	5/3/1	5/3/1	2 MIN.
CHIN	5	10	1 MIN.
DIP	1	100[1]	1 MIN.
BARBELL CURL	5	10	1 MIN.

Note: For all 5/3/1 exercises, use percentages of your working max (90% 1RM): In Week 1, do three sets: 65%x5, 75%x5 and 85%x5 or to failure. In Week 2, do three sets: 70%x3, 80%x3 and 90%x3 or to failure. In Week 3, do three sets: 75%x5, 85%x3 and 95%x1 or to failure. In Week 4 (deload), do three sets: 40%x5, 50%x5 and 60%x 5.
[1] Take as much time as you need to get 100 total reps.

Deadlift

your progress," McGorry says. "After awhile, you'll notice patterns and spot trends in your programming that'll help you break records and move forward."

Once you complete a full four-week cycle, add 10 pounds to your lower-body working maxes and 5 pounds to your upper-body working maxes. Use these new numbers to calculate the next month's percentages. (See "5/3/1 Sample Rep-Max Progression.")

The exercises that follow your main lifts are your assistance work, and this is where 5/3/1 is adaptable to your needs. You can choose assistance moves to strengthen weak points, support your main lifts, build muscle mass or any combination of these. The options are limitless.

Wendler suggests sticking with the basics here, which means doing primarily barbell and dumbbell lifts, and eschewing machines. "You want to do exercises that give you the best transfer to the main lifts," he says. "This will get you in and out of the weight room in less time because when you do movements such as dips and chins, you hit your chest, shoulders, triceps, upper back, grip and biceps in just two exercises. What else do you need to do after that?"

Structure your assistance work according to your needs. If your lower-back strength is a limiting factor in your squat, add good mornings or hyperextensions to your routine. If your goal is to put on mass, do your assistance moves bodybuilder-style: Use higher rep ranges (10-plus) for the bodyparts you think are lagging.

Pay attention to which exercises improve your main lifts and which ones don't. If something's working, keep it in your rotation until you stop making progress, then try something else. You'll need to perform assistance moves for at least two cycles — eight weeks — before judging their efficacy, but it's important to constantly reevaluate the ones you select.

"But don't make assistance work too important in your template," Wendler warns. "Caring more about that than your main lifts is wrong. That minutiae ends up detracting from the greater good. Just choose well-rounded exercises and work your whole body through a full range of motion, and the rest will take care of itself. You won't have any weak points."

Squat

Chapter 4

Cluster Flux

Trigger new growth and break through plateaus with this high-intensity technique

Regurgitating your last bite of chicken breast on training day is only one barometer of bringing your A game to the weight room. But it's an important measure, one that removes all doubt of whether you showed up that day to permanently alter your DNA or just go through the motions.

To be fair, we know you can't achieve that level of intensity every time you lift. Still, it's easy to spend weeks mired in a lacka-daisical slump or stuck on a superplateau that seems to resist your best efforts. In the circle of gym life, there are training deaths and rebirths, near-crippling experiences and maintenance days, and times when just getting through the door was harder than what followed.

This program is the proverbial bucket of cold water, a slap in the face, a shin-kick to the groin. It'll snap you out of that malaise and remind you what it takes to keep your gains growing. To take full advantage of this program you should have already been training with heavy weight — no leg warmers allowed. But in four weeks you'll be bigger, stronger and making the physical changes that used to always seem just a few reps away.

What the Flux?

Cluster training is a progressive program that uses heavy weight, low reps and long rest periods. This is a four-week test of your resolve, but consider taking the fifth week off to recuperate. You'll start with 80% of your one-rep max (1RM) and move up 5% each week until you're lifting what was 95% of your 1RM at the beginning of the program. In Weeks 3–4, you'll drop a rep from each set.

You'll also try to achieve maximum acceleration with each rep. In other words, you'll push or pull the weight with as much force as you can muster. On every exercise you'll

WHAT NOT TO DO

Don't just press the bar up. Visualize pressing your body away from it. Also, don't flare your elbows out to your sides.

Bench Press Cluster

START: Set the safety bars of the power rack to the level of the bottom of your bench press. Lie faceup on the bench with your feet flat on the floor and the bar at your lower chest.

EXECUTION: Use an overhand grip, hands slightly wider than shoulder-width apart. Keep your elbows at a 45-degree outward angle to your torso and your forearms vertical, and press up explosively as you drive your body into the bench. Stop just short of elbow lockout.

CLUSTER TRAINING: THE PROGRAM

Since cluster training is so intense, begin each session with a five-minute dynamic warm-up followed by one set of eight reps at 25% 1RM, one set of eight reps at 50% 1RM and one set of five reps at 75% 1RM for each of the six cluster exercises. When you begin training, perform the positive portion of each cluster move at maximal speed followed by a two-second negative.

CLUSTER EXERCISES

WEEK	LOAD	SETS	REPS	REST PERIODS FOR ALL WEEKS
1	80% 1RM	4	5	3–5 MIN. BETWEEN SETS,
2	85% 1RM	4	5	10–15 SEC. BETWEEN REPS
3	90% 1RM	3	4	
4	95% 1RM	3	3	

NONCLUSTER EXERCISES

SETS	REPS	REST PERIODS FOR ALL WEEKS
4	8	1–2 MIN. BETWEEN SETS

Squat
Cluster

START: Set the safety bars of the power rack to the level of the bottom of your squat. This is your starting position.
EXECUTION: With the bar across your upper traps, feet about shoulder-width apart and toes turned out slightly, keep your head neutral and core tight as you forcefully drive through your heels, and extend your hips and knees to reach the standing position.

Deadlift Cluster

START: With your feet flat on the floor under the bar, squat down and grasp it with a slightly wider than shoulder-width, mixed grip. Allow the bar to rest against your shins.

EXECUTION: With your chest up and back flat, drive the bar up by extending your hips and knees. Be sure to keep your arms straight as you drag the bar up your legs until you reach the standing position.

start the move from the positive position, then focus on a controlled negative. The effort you put in on each rep is a key component of your success.

A cluster involves 1–2 specific moves per workout with noncluster exercises filling out each session. You'll be in the gym four days a week, but count on being sore for seven. See why we suggest that recuperation week?

Some Nerve

The sheer intensity involved here means you'll stress your body in a way that requires an all-hands-on-deck physical response. By pushing maximum loads with as much force as you can generate, you engage your nervous system — the information highway that starts in your brain, travels down your spine and con-

DAY 1

SQUAT CLUSTER[1]
ROMANIAN DEADLIFT
DOUBLE CRUNCH
SIDE PLANK (HOLD FOR 45 SEC.)

DAY 2

BENCH PRESS CLUSTER[1,2]
LAT PULLDOWN CLUSTER
PEC-DECK FLYE
ROPE PUSHDOWN
DUMBBELL INCLINE CURL

DAY 4

DEADLIFT CLUSTER
LEG PRESS
WEIGHTED ROMAN-CHAIR SIT-UP
FRONT PLANK (HOLD FOR 45 SEC.)

DAY 5

SEATED OVERHEAD PRESS CLUSTER[1,2]
SEATED ROW CLUSTER
DUMBBELL INCLINE FLYE
NEUTRAL-GRIP LYING TRICEPS EXTENSION
BARBELL PREACHER CURL

[1] Start at the bottom of the move, preferably in a power rack.
[2] Do one cluster set, take a 1-2-minute break, then do a cluster set of the following exercise. Repeat until you complete three sets of each.

Lat Pulldown
Cluster

START: Sit at a lat pull-down station with the bar directly overhead or slightly in front of your body and adjust the pads so they fit snugly over your thighs.

EXECUTION: Grasp the bar with a wide, overhand grip. Keep your abs tight, back slightly arched and feet flat on the floor. Squeeze your shoulder blades together and drive your elbows down, pulling the bar to your upper chest.

nects with your muscles — more completely than if you did 10–12 reps with a much lighter weight. This intensive nervous-system recruitment means you stimulate more muscle contractions and likely generate more strength.

"I've done Cluster Training on and off for many years," says Mike Mahler, a Las Vegas-based fitness information provider and author of *The Aggressive Strength Solution for Size and Strength* e-book. "It generally has to be restricted to 4–6 weeks because it's so intense; burnout will follow if you do it too long."

Rest Between Reps

With all the carrying on about intensity, you may be slightly bemused by the 15-second breaks between reps and five-minute breaks between sets. Trust us, you'll cling to every second. "The main benefit of cluster training is the increased intensity it allows on every rep," Mahler says. "Because you're sufficiently rested before each lift, you can recruit the most muscle possible in every set."

Since fatigue doesn't limit your strength or speed, each rep will be of optimal quality. You'll lift with max-

WHAT NOT TO DO

Don't overarch your lower back to cheat the weight up.

Seated Overhead Press Cluster

START: Set the safety bars of the power rack so the bar is at upper-chest level. Sit erect against the back-pad, and keep your low back slightly arched and feet flat on the floor.

EXECUTION: Grasp the bar just outside shoulder width with a palms-forward grip, elbows pointing down and out. In one explosive motion, press the bar straight up to just short of elbow lockout.

Seated Row Cluster

START: Attach a close-grip handle and sit erect on the bench facing the weight stack. Place your feet on the platform, bend your knees slightly, and reach forward to grasp the handle while keeping your back flat and chest up.
EXECUTION: Pull back until your torso is erect and your arms are fully extended. Retract your shoulder blades and drive your elbows back, pulling the handle toward your midsection.

imum effort and generate maximum force. Plus, the heavier-than-normal load places more overall stress on the muscle, helping stimulate growth.

Explode Slowly

Conventional strength-training wisdom calls for explosiveness and speed from the bottom of each lift. With 90% of your max on the bar, however, speed becomes something of a relative term because the bar won't move very fast with that much weight on it. Bar speed is still an important consideration, though, and it's something you should strive for throughout this program. If you can move 315 pounds faster than your training partner, odds are you're a good bit stronger than he is.

How do you recruit the fast-twitch muscle fibers necessary to generate maximal bar speed? By allowing yourself almost full recovery times between sets and reps. This takes fatigue almost completely out of play, allowing you an unfettered rehearsal of what really matters when it comes to heavy lifting: an all-out, full-power assault on a singular point of impact.

Fast-twitch fibers are more resistant to growth than the slow-twitch variety but have greater capacity for size. "When you use the 5x5 cluster style in this program and focus on the proven mass-makers such as squats, deadlifts, and overhead and bench presses, you not only enhance strength but build size as well," Mahler says.

Total-Body Blitz

Let an old-school training style — the whole-body workout — light a match under your current routine for significant physique gains

Chapter 5

The split system, as Joe Weider termed it decades ago and defined simply as training different parts of the body in separate workouts, is sort of like indoor plumbing: You take it for granted and can't imagine it ever not existing. But as the original source of training information, early issues of M&F (then titled *Your Physique*) discussed whole-body routines exclusively; in fact, the three-day routine was addressed in the very first issue back in 1940. Like the master bath that comes right off your master bedroom, not too long ago that chest-and-tri's, back-and-bi's and leg day split was yet to be realized.

As time passed, split routines came along and never left because of the endless variety they offer. But this doesn't make whole-body training obsolete. Quite the opposite: Hitting every bodypart in every workout is an untapped method that can be used to breathe new life into your training. If you've used splits exclusively, it's time to break out of your comfort zone for better results. No matter how burned out you are with your current program, something as dramatic as whole-body training can make hitting the gym feel as shiny and new as your first Weider barbell set.

Temporal Awesomeness

"Often the best program for muscle growth is the one you aren't doing," says Mark Young, CK (clinical kinesiologist), a Canadian exercise and nutrition consultant and owner of Mark Young Training Systems. "Changing from a bodypart split to a whole-body training routine can provide an incredible stimulus for new size and strength."

Initial impressions can be a problem, which is why "too taxing" is the most common excuse people give for not wanting to use whole-body routines. Though it may seem like training every muscle group in a single workout is more demanding, it actually takes no more recovery time than most split routines. Here's why: Each time you train you activate your nervous system, even using a split routine. That means that in spite of the prolonged recovery each muscle group enjoys, the rest of the nervous system is activated.

But this discrepancy between muscle and nervous system recovery explains why you need complete breaks from training every so often: Even if your muscles are fully recovered, the rest of your body may not be. Whole-body training makes use of this phenomenon by keeping the overall stress low in each session so it can be repeated more frequently. As a result, you activate both muscle and the nervous system in a more cohesive manner.

In the whole-body workouts in this program, you'll notice that you do two sets per exercise, which may not seem like a lot of volume, especially if you're accustomed to split routines. But this fear has kept far too many people from experiencing the benefits of whole-body training. Remember, you hit most bodyparts every two days, and this increased frequency makes up for the lower inter-set volume so your total weekly volume is about the same as if you used a split routine.

This type of loading can, in fact, be advantageous. "Whole-body training repeated throughout the week provides an opportunity to use heavier loads than doing numerous sets of the same exercise in one workout," Young says. "And more intensity equals more mass."

Training causes a stress to which the body must adapt — in this case, by making the muscle bigger and stronger. Of course, this doesn't last forever, and you need another training insult to trigger further adaptations. If you wait too long before another session, the muscle will regress back to its original size and strength. Ideally, you want to train at the very peak of the adaptation so you build on the improvements, and continually grow bigger and stronger.

Research from McMaster University (Canada) shows that training stimulates protein synthesis for 48

201
—
The percent increase in **blood flow to working muscles** during resistance training

Hanging Leg Raise
Workout A

TOTAL-BODY BLITZ PROGRAM

Sets/Reps: 2/10-12 per exercise • **Rest Periods:** 60-90 seconds between sets • **Frequency:** 3 days per week (Monday, Wednesday, Friday)
Weeks 1 + 3: Workout A on Monday + Friday; Workout B on Wednesday • **Weeks 2 + 4:** Workout B on Monday + Friday; Workout A on Wednesday

WORKOUT A

BODYPART	EXERCISE
LEGS	WALKING LUNGE
CHEST	DUMBBELL BENCH PRESS
BACK	BENT-OVER ROW
ABS	HANGING LEG RAISE
TRICEPS	PUSHDOWN
SHOULDERS	LATERAL RAISE

WORKOUT B

BODYPART(S)	EXERCISE
FULL BODY/LEGS	DEADLIFT
SHOULDERS	DUMBBELL OVERHEAD PRESS
TRICEPS	DIP
BACK	PULL-UP
CORE/OBLIQUES	WOODCHOPPER
BICEPS	DUMBBELL CURL

hours, so by training every two days you trigger it again just as it comes down. Numerous adaptations respond in this wavelike manner. If you use a split routine, you may miss some of this activation because the muscle has already returned to its pretrained state. But by hitting the muscle every two days, you build on what was already constructed before it has the chance to wane.

Another reason people are returning to whole-body routines is the time factor. Even though you move a lot of weight each session, it doesn't have to take you all day to do it. In fact, if you hustle, two sets each of six exercises can take less than 30 minutes. Limited time is probably the biggest excuse for not training at all, and now that it's destroyed, there's every reason to add a whole-body training cycle to your program.

Upsides Abound

You may know that the muscles trained first in any session get hit with the most aggression, since this is when you're freshest and able to apply the greatest intensity. This leads to a potential downside that afflicts many whole-body routines: The body adapts to the stagnation and some bodyparts flourish better than those that are trained later.

Fortunately, there's a simple remedy: To prevent any imbalances, be sure to mix up the order of your exercises each session. For example, in one workout you might begin with walking lunges, while the next you'd start with the bench press and the one after that with bent-over rows, and so on. For maximum benefit, also rotate the order of single-joint exercises. This technique ensures that you won't place an inappropriate emphasis on any single muscle group by training it first each time. Mixing up the routine also helps keep you mentally fresh.

Another benefit of whole-body training deals with blood flow. The pump is an awesome feeling — Arnold Schwarzenegger likened it to an orgasm in the famed documentary Pumping Iron — and you can just imagine the ecstasy of a head-to-toe pump with this

10 SECOND TIP
—
To further boost your fat-burning efforts, keep your rest periods short and your heart rate up

Walking Lunge
Workout A

DON'T
BE THAT GUY
—
Whole-body training doesn't mean you do four sets of five exercises per bodypart. Those marathon sessions are counterproductive and went out in the '70s. Stick with low volume and high frequency for best results.

Dip
Workout B

training method. These massive increases in blood flow have to come from somewhere, and since your body doesn't manufacture blood that quickly, that means your heart's getting a workout, too. It has to distribute much more blood to more areas of the body than during typical exercise, a concept called peripheral heart action that was developed in the early 1960s by innovator Bob Gajda. Make no mistake, we're not talking about circuit training here; this is still a typical resistance-training program that just so happens to offer additional benefits like cardiovascular improvements that may not come with split programs.

Arguably the biggest upside of whole-body training is the hormonal response you get. Due to the huge amount of muscle mass recruited, your anabolic hormone levels will go through the roof, which is good for not only building muscle but also burning fat. The prescribed exercises, rep ranges and rest periods are specifically designed to ensure maximal hormonal response. In fact, part of the reason whole-body routines are popular for fat loss is because the combination of growth-hormone response and enormous mass recruitment is perfect for calorie-burning. "Including whole-body exercise that influences all the large muscle groups increases calorie expenditure," Young says. "This can definitely help accelerate fat loss."

We're offering whole-body training as an alternative to traditional split routines, but we're not suggesting that's the only way to train. Whole-body training has a dedicated, often fanatical, fan base, but unlike these extremists we support the notion that there's no single best way to train. Give this program a try for four weeks, then feel free to return to the split system of your choice. Variety is the spice of life and looking good doesn't hurt, either.

Lateral Raise
Workout A

Deadlift
Workout B

WORLD SPORTS CENTER

48
—

The number of hours that resistance training stimulates muscle-protein synthesis. By training every two days, you keep this growth process triggered

Pull-Up
Workout B

Epic Fail

These six techniques will help you pass the point of training failure and enter a new dimension of incredible muscle gains

Before we tell you exactly how to build more muscle by manipulating muscle failure in your workout, allow us to break it down scientifically.

Muscle failure is defined as the point in a set when you can't perform another rep with proper form. And while there's much debate over whether training to failure boosts strength, it's absolutely crucial for inducing growth. Going to failure (and beyond) signals the body to produce more critical anabolic hormones and growth factors such as growth hormone (GH), testosterone and insulinlike growth factor-1. The further you can take a set past failure, the higher you can increase levels of these natural muscle-building hormones and the further you can push muscle growth.

Taking a set to failure is pretty straightforward: Go until you can't go anymore, then stop. But training past failure can be done a number of ways. The following six techniques are proven to be the most effective, so get acquainted with these intensity-boosters and push your hypertrophy to new heights.

M&F TIP

Drop sets work best with dumbbells or selectorized weight machines. They allow you to reduce the weight in minimal time, which keeps intensity high.

Drop Sets

As the name implies, drop sets involve decreasing the amount of weight you're using after you reach muscle failure. It's a fairly simple premise, but you want to make sure you lighten the load by the proper amount. A study conducted by the Weider Research Group found that when trained subjects reduced their weights by 20%-30%, they could complete roughly the same number of reps (nine reps for a 20% drop and 11 reps for a 30% drop) as they did before reaching failure (10 reps).

The number of reps you complete on each drop set is important for triggering adequate GH production and mechanical stimulus to incite muscle growth. Too few reps may not boost GH levels high enough, while too many may mean the resistance isn't heavy enough to overload the muscle and produce growth. So be sure to drop the weight by 20%-30% to stay within your rep range and maximize results.

PRESCRIPTION: Add 1-2 drop sets to the last 1-2 sets of each exercise.

DROP-SETS SHOULDER WORKOUT		
EXERCISE	SETS[1]/REPS	REST
Dumbbell Overhead Press	4/8-10	2-3 min.
Dumbbell Lateral Raise	4/10-12	2 min.
Machine Overhead Press	3/12-15	2 min.
Reverse Pec-Deck Flye	3/12-15	1-2 min.

[1] Perform two drop sets on your last two sets.

EXTENDED-SETS CHEST WORKOUT

EXERCISE	SETS/REPS	REST
EXTENDED SET:		
Dumbbell Incline Press	3/10–12	—
Dumbbell Flat-Bench Press	3/to failure	—
Dumbbell Decline Press	3/to failure	2–3 min.
EXTENDED SET:		
Dumbbell Incline Flye	3/12–15	—
Dumbbell Flat-Bench Flye	3/to failure	—
Dumbbell Decline Flye	3/to failure	2–3 min.

Extended Sets

Extended-sets training involves doing increasingly easier variations of an exercise as you fatigue to allow you to continue past failure. Each successive alteration places your body in a stronger biomechanical position than the previous one so you can use the same weight throughout the set. Here's how to apply it to dumbbell incline presses: After you reach failure, adjust the bench to flat and continue pressing. Once you fail on flat presses, immediately move to a decline bench and go to failure again. On presses, you're stronger on a flat bench than you are on an incline, and you're strongest on a decline bench. So even after you reach failure on incline presses, you can continue pressing the same weight on a flat and decline bench. Extended sets can also be done on barbell or Smith machine presses and dumbbell flyes.

PRESCRIPTION: Do 1–2 extended-set complexes per workout for 3–4 sets each.

M&F TIP

Don't decrease weight within an extended set, even if your reps drop with each variation. Just go to failure and keep moving.

Forced Reps

It's easier to train past failure using forced reps than it is with drop sets and extended sets. Just rep out to failure, then have a spotter help you complete 2–4 more reps. Research from Finland shows that forced reps work because they boost GH levels higher and recruit more fast-twitch muscle fibers than when you stop at muscle failure, which results in greater hypertrophy over time.

The key to forced-reps training is the amount of help the spotter provides after you reach failure. If he supplies too little assistance, you won't be able to complete the number of forced reps needed to stimulate muscle growth; if he provides too much assistance, the reps will be too easy and your muscles won't be sufficiently overloaded. The spotter should contribute just enough help to get you past the sticking point of each rep so you're still doing the majority of the work.

PRESCRIPTION: Perform 2–4 forced reps on the last 1–2 sets of most exercises.

FORCED-REPS BICEPS WORKOUT

EXERCISE	SETS/REPS	REST
Barbell Curl	4[1]/8–10	2 min.
Dumbbell Incline Curl	3/8–10	1–2 min.
EZ-Bar Preacher Curl	3[1]/10–12	1–2 min.
Dumbbell Concentration Curl	3[1]/12–15	1–2 min.

[1] Perform 2–4 forced reps on your last two sets.

Negative Reps

Negative-reps training is another method with which it's critical to have an experienced spotter. Go to failure, then have your spotter lift the weight through the positive part of the rep. Continue by performing the negative part of the rep very slowly — 3–5 seconds — then have your partner again lift the weight for you. Repeat for a total of 2–3 negative reps.

Although you need a spotter when doing negative reps on most exercises, you can perform them when training alone by doing unilateral moves (similar to forced reps), using your nonworking arm or leg to assist through the positive rep. Negative reps work best at the end of sets of 10 or fewer reps. Lighter-weight, high-rep sets not only make the negatives too easy but also don't offer sufficient mechanical stimulus to promote muscle growth.

PRESCRIPTION: Perform 2–3 negative reps on the last 1–2 sets of 2–3 exercises per workout.

NEGATIVE-REPS CHEST WORKOUT

EXERCISE	SETS/REPS	REST
Barbell Bench Press	4¹/6–8	2–3 min.
Barbell Incline Press	4¹/8–10	2–3 min.
Dumbbell Incline Flye	4/12–15	1–2 min.
Pec-Deck or Machine Flye	4¹/8–10	1–2 min.

¹ Perform 2–3 negative reps on your last two sets.

USE IT, DON'T ABUSE IT

There's one caveat regarding these techniques: You should have at least six months of consistent training under your belt before using them in your routine. Without adequate lifting experience, these high-intensity tactics can be counterproductive. Those with gym experience have a couple of options for incorporating these tools. The first is to rotate them continuously within your workouts. For example, use drop sets in one routine, negative reps in the next, partial reps in the workout after that and so on. The second way is to stick with one technique for 3-4 weeks, then swap it out for another for the next 3-4 weeks. Don't bombard your program with multiple techniques every workout or you'll be asking to suffer overtraining.

M&F TIP

If you use partial reps on exercises such as bench presses or squats, have a spotter on hand — not to assist you but to make sure you can rack the bar.

Partial Reps

When you reach failure on the last rep of an exercise, it's because you can't move the weight past your sticking point. Your sticking point is usually only a small portion of your range of motion (ROM), and chances are the muscles you use in the rest of the ROM aren't fatigued. So to continue past failure, shorten your ROM to avoid your sticking point and proceed with partial reps.

On lat pulldowns, for example, you're weakest when the bar is close to your chest. So when you can no longer touch the bar to your upper pecs, simply pull the bar as far down as you can. Your ROM will get shorter on each rep until eventually you can't move the bar more than a few inches. That's when you've reached total muscle failure.

PRESCRIPTION: Use partial reps on the last 1-2 sets of most exercises.

PARTIAL-REPS BACK WORKOUT		
EXERCISE	SETS/REPS	REST
Pull-Up	3[1]/to failure	2-3 min.
One-Arm Dumbbell Row	3[1]/8-10	1-2 min.
Lat Pulldown	3[1]/10-12	1-2 min.
Straight-Arm Pulldown	3/12-15	1-2 min.
Seated Cable Row	3[1]/12-15	1-2 min.

[1] Perform partial reps on your last 1-2 sets after reaching failure on full-ROM reps.

Rest-Pause

For rest-pauses simply go to failure, rest briefly, then continue the set. Your muscles fatigue because they can no longer produce the energy to contract. A short rest of just 15 seconds will allow your muscles to replenish enough energy to eke out a few more reps without having to decrease the weight.

Using squats as an example, perform a set to failure. Rack the bar and rest 15 seconds, then rep out to failure again. Do this 2–3 times per rest-pause set — any more than that and you won't be able to recover enough in 15 seconds to squeeze out even one more rep. Much like partial reps, you can do rest-pauses on any exercise. With moves such as bench presses and squats, however, you should have a spotter and engage the safety bars in case you underestimate your fatigue and need help reracking the bar.

PRESCRIPTION: Do 2–3 rest-pauses on the last 1–2 sets of each exercise.

M&F TIP

Don't rest too long within a rest-pause set. If you rest 30 seconds or more, you're essentially doing straight sets.

REST-PAUSE LEG WORKOUT

EXERCISE	SETS[1]/REPS	REST
Barbell Squat	4/8–10	2–3 min.
Leg Press	4/10–12	2–3 min.
Leg Extension	4/12–15	1–2 min.
Romanian Deadlift	4/8–10	2–3 min.
Leg Curl	4/12–15	1–2 min.

[1] Perform 2–3 rest-pauses on your last two sets.

Bookend Training

Double-dipping on multijoint moves in the same workout builds size and strength, and incinerates fat

Enduring a squat workout can be as emotionally taxing as it is physically exhausting. Afterward you feel a confused mix of relief and something like shock, trying to walk on shaking legs as though you'd just been in a car accident. But there's a reason you punish yourself so thoroughly: Squats build size and strength.

Now imagine starting a session with squats but putting the workout to bed with three more sets of this body- and soul-breaker. Sounds masochistic, but that's the principle behind bookend training: performing an effective mass-builder such as incline presses, overhead presses, curls and, of course, squats at the beginning and end of the same workout.

With the exception of barbell curls, and exercises for calves and abs, our "Bookend Training Program" features all multijoint moves that allow you to lift more weight, and thus stimulate greater gains in strength and size. You'll also burn more calories than when doing single-joint or isolation moves, helping ensure the mass you gain is lean and hard (see "The Big Fat Burn" sidebar).

Barbell Shrug

Shrug

❯ Stand holding a barbell with an overhand grip in front of your thighs. Both your hands and your feet should be spaced shoulder-width apart. Lift your shoulders toward your ears as high as possible while keeping your arms straight. Hold the contraction for a second before lowering the bar back to the start.

Hanging
Leg Raise

10
SECOND TIP
—

On the last two sets of the last exercise for each muscle group, perform the first five reps as fast and explosively as possible. This will target the fast-twitch muscle fibers, which not only grow the biggest and strongest but also burn the most calories and boost fat-burning.

SPLIT BOOKENDS

Although you can do these four workouts any days of the week, this is the optimal split. Follow the routine for four weeks to experience the best possible results.

DAY	WORKOUT
MONDAY	CHEST, BICEPS, ABS
TUESDAY	LEGS, CALVES
WEDNESDAY	OFF
THURSDAY	SHOULDERS, TRAPS, ABS
FRIDAY	BACK, TRICEPS
SATURDAY	OFF
SUNDAY	OFF

❯ NOTE: Monday and Friday pair opposing muscle groups — chest and biceps, and back and triceps. Follow this order. Training triceps after chest or biceps after back would fatigue the smaller bodyparts so they couldn't be trained as hard later, which would diminish results.

Barbell Overhead Press

Use your legs to help you squeeze out a few more reps.

Squat

BOOKEND TRAINING PROGRAM

MONDAY: CHEST, BICEPS, ABS

EXERCISE	SETS/REPS	REST
CHEST		
INCLINE PRESS	3/6–8	2–3 min.
DUMBBELL BENCH PRESS	3/8–10	2 min.
DUMBBELL INCLINE FLYE	3/10–12	1–2 min.
CABLE CROSSOVER	2/12–15	1–2 min.
INCLINE PRESS	1/to failure[1]	1 min.
	2/12–15	1 min.
BICEPS		
BARBELL CURL	3/6–8	2–3 min.
DUMBBELL INCLINE CURL	3/8–10	2 min.
CABLE CONCENTRATION CURL	3/10–12	1 min.
BARBELL CURL	1/to failure[1]	1 min.
	2/12–15	1 min.
ABS		
HANGING LEG RAISE[2]	2/6–8	1–2 min.
CRUNCH	3/to failure	1 min.
HANGING LEG RAISE	1/to failure	1 min.
	2/to failure[3]	1 min.

1 Use the same weight as the first time you did this exercise.
2 Hold a dumbbell or medicine ball between your feet.
3 Use your bodyweight.

TUESDAY: LEGS, CALVES

EXERCISE	SETS/REPS	REST
LEGS		
SQUAT	3/6–8	2–3 min.
LEG PRESS	3/8–10	2 min.
DUMBBELL REVERSE LUNGE	3/10–12	1–2 min.
LEG EXTENSION	3/12–15	1 min.
LYING LEG CURL	3/12–15	1 min.
SQUAT	1/to failure[1]	1 min.
	2/12–15	1 min.
CALVES		
STANDING CALF RAISE	3/6–8	1–2 min.
SEATED CALF RAISE	3/15–20	1 min.
STANDING CALF RAISE	1/to failure[1]	1 min.
	2/12–15	1 min.

1 Use the same weight as the first time you did this exercise.

First & Last Blast

Doing a multijoint move at the beginning of a workout when you're strongest helps maximize the mechanical overload on your muscles. In this routine you'll use heavy weight and low reps (6–8 per set), which is ideal for building strength and mass, and stimulating the production of testosterone. When you revisit the move at the end of your workout, you're already fatigued. Such muscle exhaustion is critical to hypertrophy because the biomechanical waste products produced in muscle cells boost levels of anabolic hormones. (See "Go Hormonal" sidebar.) The final three sets are designed to max out your muscles and promote even more growth.

In the first of your final three sets, use the weight with which you started the workout. You'll be able to get only a few reps, but each one will provide an impetus for increased mass. For the final two sets, reduce the weight so you can get 12–15 reps. This higher rep range coupled with one-minute rest periods will take your muscles to the outer limits of fatigue. Consider using a partner for these sets lest you find yourself pinned to the bench.

Despite its name, there's nothing particularly bookish about this kind of training — unless you consider it the kind of thing you'd read about in the book of Job or the book of Revelation. The revelation being that bookend training is painful...but it works.

BOOKEND TRAINING PROGRAM CONT.

THURSDAY: SHOULDERS, TRAPS, ABS

EXERCISE	SETS/REPS	REST
SHOULDERS		
BARBELL OVERHEAD PRESS	3/6–8	2–3 min.
DUMBBELL UPRIGHT ROW	2/8–10	2 min.
CABLE LATERAL RAISE	3/10–12	1–2 min.
BENT-OVER LATERAL RAISE	3/12–15	1 min.
BARBELL OVERHEAD PRESS	1/to failure[1]	1 min.
	2/12–15	1 min.
TRAPS		
BARBELL SHRUG	3/6–8	2–3 min.
BEHIND-THE-BACK SHRUG	2/10–12	1–2 min.
BARBELL SHRUG	1/to failure[1]	1 min.
	2/12–15	1 min.
ABS		
CABLE CRUNCH	2/6–8	1–2 min.
REVERSE CRUNCH	3/to failure	1 min.
CABLE CRUNCH	1/to failure[1]	1 min.
	2/12–15	1 min.

[1] Use the same weight as the first time you did this exercise.

FRIDAY: BACK, TRICEPS

EXERCISE	SETS/REPS	REST
BACK		
BENT-OVER BARBELL ROW	3/6–8	2–3 min.
PULL-UP	3/to failure	2 min.
SEATED CABLE ROW	3/10–12	1–2 min.
ONE-ARM STRAIGHT-ARM PULLDOWN	3/12–15	1 min.
BENT-OVER BARBELL ROW	1/to failure[1]	1 min.
	2/12–15	1 min.
TRICEPS		
CLOSE-GRIP BENCH PRESS	3/6–8	2–3 min.
PUSHDOWN	3/8–10	2 min.
CABLE OVERHEAD TRICEPS EXTENSION	3/10–12	1 min.
CLOSE-GRIP BENCH PRESS	1/to failure[1]	1 min.
	2/12–15	1 min.

[1] Use the same weight as the first time you did this exercise.

The Big Fat Burn

❯ Multijoint exercises enhance fat-burning by recruiting more muscle fibers during the workout. Incorporating high reps with short rest periods boosts calorie- and fat-burning potential during your training session. And doing heavy weight for fewer reps keeps you in fat-burning mode long after the workout is over. Norwegian University of Sport and Physical Education (Norway) researchers found that training with heavy weight and low reps (about six per set) raised subjects' resting metabolic rates (calorie burn) higher and for longer (up to 48 hours) than training with lighter weight and high reps. This is why high-intensity interval training beats steady-state cardio for fat loss.

Bent-Over Barbell Row

Cable Crunch

Go Hormonal

❯ The biochemical waste products produced in muscle cells during a workout signal increases in anabolic hormones and growth factors such as growth hormone and insulinlike growth factor-I. Such anabolic factors, along with testosterone, promote growth of new muscle fibers that replace damaged ones and enhance muscle-protein synthesis, which builds up all muscle fibers by providing them with more protein.

Chapter 8

10-Ton Workout

Lift beyond your limits to ramp up gains in size and strength

Your Imagination, like your knees, gets stiffer with age. As a kid, leaping over tall buildings in a single bound was an everyday occurrence. But being a grown-up has a way of stifling the belief that you can do heroic things, and the monotonous drone of self-preservation often drowns out the primal call to challenge yourself.

We have the Superman antidote for your Clark Kent malaise. We can't help you fly faster than a speeding bullet or develop X-ray vision, but we can help you lift a *whopping 10 tons.* That's right: 10 tons. That's 20,000 pounds.

The 10-Ton Workout is your remedy for stagnation and self-abnegation. It's the phone booth that'll transform you from a bumbling milksop into a man of steel. Without making a concerted effort to find new ways to keep the whole endeavor fresh, it's easy to find yourself floundering, lifting the same weights month after month. This is your chance to overhaul your physique.

How It Works

You're going to get stronger in 30 days. Bigger, too. In fact, every time you train using this program, you'll set a new personal record. Better yet, you're not going to just perform the workout each day, you're going to do it better each day.

"You're going beyond sets and reps," says Nick Tumminello, a strength and conditioning coach in Baltimore who works with bodybuilders, NFL players and professional fighters. "You're focusing on total amount of weight moved, and the more weight you move, the stronger you are. Period."

The program is simple yet punishing. Seven main lifts are split into three training days: bench presses and shrugs; squats and romanian deadlifts; and push-presses, bent-over rows and close-grip benches. During each workout, you'll lift 10 tons using our sets-reps-weight formula with the primary exercises. For example, in week 1, day 1, you'll do five sets of eight reps using 185 pounds on the bench, then six sets of nine reps using 225 pounds on shrugs to equal roughly 10 tons. Accessory exercises are then performed but don't contribute to the total tonnage.

Your goal is to start as close to 10 tons as you can in the first workout and then improve on it in each subsequent gym session (we include 12- and 15-ton workout options, as well). By the time you complete the program, you'll have increased your total weekly load by yet another 10 tons (or 12 or 15).

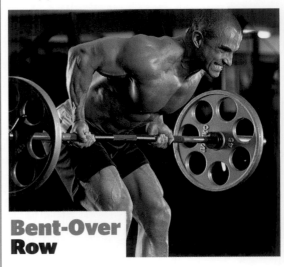

Bent-Over Row

Woodchopper

Push Press

Romanian Deadlift

QUICK TIP
—

Descend to mid-shin level on Romanian Deadlifts. Then fully lock out at the top of the movement

Why It Works

The main effects — hypertrophy and strength — come from minor changes each week. When you start with our week 1 bench press, you're moving a total of 7,400 pounds in that one exercise (sets x reps x weight). The next week, after your muscles have grown slightly bigger and stronger, you'll add just one rep per set.

While this may seem insignificant, it isn't to your muscles because it adds another 800 pounds of growth-inducing stimulus. Adding a rep in each subsequent week means more muscle stress and thereby growth. By the end of the four-week program, you'll be benching nearly 8,000 pounds more than you did in week 1. That's a lot of payoff for small but consistent improvement.

A key motivator built into this routine is its progressive nature. "This program gives you a specific performance goal for each workout," Tumminello says. "Nothing ensures you eat, sleep and train properly like walking into the gym and knowing you must set a new personal record."

If you can't hit the 10-ton mark, don't worry; the progressive overload in each session is what really matters. Just plug a weight you can handle into our sets-and-reps formula and follow the program from there.

Mediocrity or Mass?

"There's working out and then there's training," Tumminello points out. "Training is when you have a progressive plan with measurable goals and continual challenges. Working out is anything that makes you sweaty and tired but not necessarily bigger or stronger because it lacks consistency, direction and specificity. The 10-Ton Workout is for those who want to train using a progressive program that ensures success." Are you in?

Weighted Decline Sit-Up

Face Pull

THE 10-TON PROGRAM

The first number under "weight" corresponds to the 10-Ton Workout, and the next two are for the more challenging 12- and 15-Ton workouts. Find the one that's right for you and stick with it for four weeks, then work up to the next highest weight. The total tonnage for the first week comes in at just less than 10 tons per workout. From there, the weight increases slightly each week. By week 4, you'll lift upward of 10 tons per workout and 10 tons more than in week 1.

WEEK 1

EXERCISE	WEIGHTS (LBS)	SETS/REPS	TONNAGE (LBS)
DAY 1	10/12/15 TON		10/12/15 TON
BENCH PRESS	185/225/275	5/8	7,400/9,000/11,000
BARBELL SHRUG	225/275/335	6/9	12,150/14,850/18,090
SEATED DUMBBELL CURL	30/35/45	4/8	—
FACE PULL	50/60/75	4/8	—
DAY 2			
SQUAT	225/275/335	5/10	11,250/13,750/16,750
ROMANIAN DEADLIFT	165/195/245	5/10	8,250/9,750/12,250
WEIGHTED DECLINE SIT-UP	15/25/35	4/10	—
DAY 3			
PUSH PRESS	135/165/205	6/9	7,290/8,910/11,070
BENT-OVER ROW	95/115/145	5/9	4,275/5,175/6,525
CLOSE-GRIP BENCH PRESS	165/195/245	5/10	8,250/9,750/12,250
WOODCHOPPER	50/60/75	4/10 EACH SIDE	—

WEEK 2

EXERCISE	WEIGHTS (LBS)	SETS/REPS	TONNAGE (LBS)
DAY 1			
BENCH PRESS	185/225/275	5/9	8,325/10,125/12,375
BARBELL SHRUG	225/275/335	6/10	13,500/16,500/20,100
SEATED DUMBBELL CURL	30/35/45	4/9	—
FACE PULL	50/60/75	4/9	—
DAY 2			
SQUAT	225/275/335	5/11	12,375/15,125/18,425
ROMANIAN DEADLIFT	165/195/245	5/11	9,075/10,725/13,475
WEIGHTED DECLINE SIT-UP	15/25/35	4/11	—
DAY 3			
PUSH PRESS	135/165/205	6/10	8,100/9,900/12,300
BENT-OVER ROW	95/115/145	5/10	4,750/5,750/7,250
CLOSE-GRIP BENCH PRESS	165/195/245	5/11	9,075/10,725/13,475
WOODCHOPPER	50/60/75	4/11 EACH SIDE	—

WEEK 3

EXERCISE	WEIGHTS (LBS)	SETS/REPS	TONNAGE (LBS)
DAY 1			
BENCH PRESS	185/225/275	5/10	9,250/11,250/13,750
BARBELL SHRUG	225/275/335	6/11	14,850/18,150/22,110
SEATED DUMBBELL CURL	30/35/45	4/10	—
FACE PULL	50/60/75	4/10	—
DAY 2			
SQUAT	225/275/335	5/12	13,500/16,500/20,100
ROMANIAN DEADLIFT	165/195/245	5/12	9,900/11,700/14,700
WEIGHTED DECLINE SIT-UP	15/25/35	4/12	—
DAY 3			
PUSH PRESS	135/165/205	6/11	8,910/10,890/13,530
BENT-OVER ROW	95/115/145	5/11	5,225/6,325/7,975
CLOSE-GRIP BENCH PRESS	165/195/245	5/12	9,900/11,700/14,700
WOODCHOPPER	50/60/75	4/12 EACH SIDE	—

WEEK 4

EXERCISE	WEIGHTS (LBS)	SETS/REPS	TONNAGE (LBS)
DAY 1			
BENCH PRESS	185/225/275	5/11	10,175/12,375/15,125
BARBELL SHRUG	225/275/335	6/12	16,200/19,800/24,120
SEATED DUMBBELL CURL	30/35/45	4/11	—
FACE PULL	50/60/75	4/11	—
DAY 2			
SQUAT	225/275/335	5/13	14,625/17,875/21,775
ROMANIAN DEADLIFT	165/195/245	5/13	10,725/12,675/15,925
WEIGHTED DECLINE SIT-UP	15/25/35	4/13	—
DAY 3			
PUSH PRESS	135/165/205	6/12	9,720/11,880/14,760
BENT-OVER ROW	95/115/145	5/12	5,700/6,900/8,700
CLOSE-GRIP BENCH PRESS	165/195/245	5/13	10,725/12,675/15,925
WOODCHOPPER	50/60/75	4/13 EACH SIDE	—

NOTE: Accessory exercises don't contribute to tonnage totals.

Chain Reaction

Bodybuilders are just catching on to what powerlifters and elite athletes have known for years — that bands and chains can help you build strength and heaps of dense, quality muscle

Weight belts, chalk, straps and truckloads of iron. For decades, these items have served as the base equipment for building not only mounds of muscle but also raw, bar-bending strength. Over the years, these primitive implements have helped push the limits of the human physique, making it possible to win the battle against gravity day in and day out. But their most important contribution may be to one of the most basic mandates of weightlifting: progressive overload.

The principle of progressive overload simply states that an increase in volume and intensity is required to achieve a targeted goal. Weight begets weight, and each workout is a step toward your objective. Bench-pressing 405 pounds one time, for example, requires a lifter to work his way up from his starting one-rep max with incrementally heavier loads until he reaches that 405-pound benchmark. How long it takes to reach a given goal is, of course, unique to each lifter. It could conceivably take one person years to hit that standard, while another may land in the coveted four-plates-per-side promised land after only months of training.

What about achieving progressive overload with each rep? Imagine the benefits you could reap from repetitions that get harder and heavier with each inch the weight is moved — challenging reps that offer no rest for muscles accustomed to recovering during lockouts or benefiting from elasticity. Weight belts, chalk, straps and truckloads of iron — they build muscle, all right. But to these things we now add chains and bands.

The Future Of Strength?

The secret to both chains and bands is that they provide what's known as linear variable resistance. Linear variable resistance training (LVRT) refers to progressively increasing the resistance with the range of motion. Using the bench press as an example, the resistance gets progressively heavier

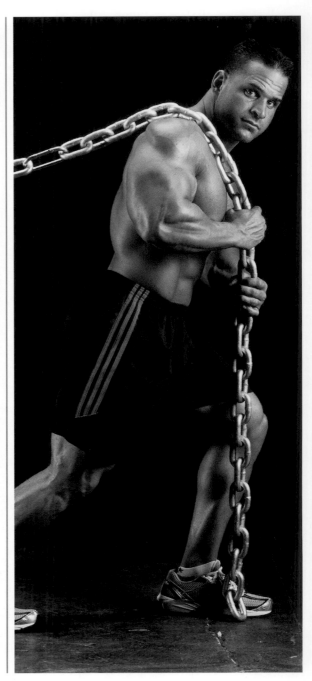

Banded & Chained

You can perform many exercises with bands and chains, but the bench press and squat best capitalize on their vertical resistance

Use heavy dumbbells to anchor your bands.

Bands

How you set up bands depends on the equipment you have available in your gym. Do your squats in a power rack. You can loop the bands around the bottom of the rack or place the safety bars in the lowest position and loop the bands around them. Wrap the other end around the end of the bar. The bench press may also need to be performed in a power rack with the bands set up as suggested for the squat, or you can loop the bands around very heavy dumbbells. Regardless of how you set up your bands, be sure you do so properly and evenly. If not, one side may have more tension than the other and cause the bar to be uneven. See the photos that follow for examples.

You'll need to know your one-rep max (1RM) to determine the amount of free-weight and band resistance to put on the bar. Do a true 1RM test under partner supervision or estimate it by using our 1RM formula (see "One-Rep Max Calculator" sidebar).

Band
Bench Press

 When bench-pressing with bands, you can use heavy dumbbells to anchor them (see right) or loop them around the base of a power rack. As with squats, be sure to fix collars on the ends of the bar to hold the bands securely in place. As with the squat, aim to generate maximum force on the positive rep.

Banded
Resistance

To determine the resistance supplied by unmarked bands, stand on a scale holding an empty bar in the top position of a squat with the bands set up. Be sure to deduct your bodyweight and the weight of the bar (most Olympic bars are 45 pounds). If you get the band pack from Elite Fitness (elitefts.com), it supplies several different bands with the amounts of resistance specified. Find the one that supplies the amount of resistance needed. In some cases, you may need to use more than one band to obtain the right resistance.

BENCH PRESS BAND PROGRAM

WEEK 1

EXERCISE	WEIGHT	SETS/REPS
BENCH PRESS	BAND = 10% 1RM	3/3–5
	FREE WEIGHT = 20% 1RM	
	TOTAL = 30% 1RM	
BENCH PRESS	FREE WEIGHT = 70% 1RM	3/8–10
INCLINE BENCH PRESS	–	3/10–12
DUMBBELL FLYE	–	3/10–12

WEEK 2

EXERCISE	WEIGHT	SETS/REPS
BENCH PRESS	BAND = 15% 1RM	3/3–5
	FREE WEIGHT = 25% 1RM	
	TOTAL = 40% 1RM	
BENCH PRESS	FREE WEIGHT = 75% 1RM	3/8
INCLINE BENCH PRESS	–	3/10
DUMBBELL FLYE	–	3/10

WEEK 3

EXERCISE	WEIGHT	SETS/REPS
BENCH PRESS	BAND = 15% 1RM	3/3–5
	FREE WEIGHT = 35% 1RM	
	TOTAL = 50% 1RM	
BENCH PRESS	FREE WEIGHT = 80% 1RM	3/6–8
INCLINE BENCH PRESS	–	3/8–10
DUMBBELL FLYE	–	3/8–10

the farther you press the bar toward full arm extension. The increased resistance necessitates the application of more force toward the top of the lift.

So what's the benefit to you? More muscle, that's what. As the range of motion lengthens and the resistance increases, the number of muscle fibers being used in the exercising muscle increases as well. The more muscle fibers being used, the greater the adaptations in muscle strength that can be achieved.

Bands also boost force during the negative part of a rep because they increase its speed. This means you have to apply more force to stop the weight at the bottom of the rep. Again, the more force you have to apply, the greater the sum of muscle fibers that are called into action.

Band Aid

Need more convincing? One study performed at Truman State University (Kirksville, Missouri) found that athletes who included elastic-resistance training in their regimens had a significantly greater increase in bench-press strength and power compared to those who utilized only free-weight resistance.

Another study, performed

WEEK 4		
EXERCISE	**WEIGHT**	**SETS/REPS**
BENCH PRESS	BAND = 20% 1RM	3/3–5
	FREE WEIGHT = 40% 1RM	
	TOTAL = 60% 1RM	
BENCH PRESS	FREE WEIGHT = 85% 1RM	3/4–6
INCLINE BENCH PRESS	–	3/8
DUMBBELL FLYE	–	3/8
WEEK 5		
BENCH PRESS	BAND = 20% 1RM	3/3–5
	FREE WEIGHT = 50% 1RM	
	TOTAL = 70% 1RM	
BENCH PRESS	FREE WEIGHT = 90% 1RM	3/2–4
INCLINE BENCH PRESS	–	3/6–8
DUMBBELL FLYE	–	3/6–8
WEEK 6		
BENCH PRESS	BAND = 20% 1RM	3/3–5
	FREE WEIGHT = 60% 1RM	
	TOTAL = 80% 1RM	
BENCH PRESS	FREE WEIGHT = 95% 1RM	3/1–2
INCLINE BENCH PRESS	–	3/6
DUMBBELL FLYE	–	3/6–8

at the University of Wisconsin, La Crosse, reported in a 2006 issue of *The Journal of Strength and Conditioning Research* that when athletes used elastic-band training in addition to free-weight training, they had significantly more leg power than when they performed only free-weight training.

Research shows that when comparing the same exercise performed with elastic bands vs. free weights, the amount of muscle fibers activated and the amount of force provided by the muscle fibers is similar. Studies also show that programs using elastic tubing, elastic bands and similar devices by themselves increase muscle strength and size and decrease bodyfat in a manner similar to free-weight training.

Chain Gang

As you've probably gathered by now, most of the research done on LVRT has used elastic-band equipment, a rehabilitative device and fitness tool, for almost a century. Chains, on the other hand, are new implements in the weight room, and they provide similar benefits to bands. The major difference is in how they work.

Chains provide resistance through the weight of each link. As they hang off the bar and pool on the floor, the only extra weight they provide is from the links between the bar and the floor. As you lift the bar higher, more links

SQUAT BAND PROGRAM

WEEK 1

EXERCISE	WEIGHT	SETS/REPS
SQUAT	BAND = 10% 1RM	3/3-5
	FREE WEIGHT = 20% 1RM	
	TOTAL = 30% 1RM	
SQUAT	FREE WEIGHT = 70% 1RM	3/8-10
LEG PRESS	-	3/10-12
LEG EXTENSION	-	3/10-12
ROMANIAN DEADLIFT	-	3/10-12

WEEK 2

EXERCISE	WEIGHT	SETS/REPS
SQUAT	BAND = 15% 1RM	3/3-5
	FREE WEIGHT = 25% 1RM	
	TOTAL = 40% 1RM	
SQUAT	FREE WEIGHT = 75% 1RM	3/8
LEG PRESS	-	3/10
LEG EXTENSION	-	3/10
ROMANIAN DEADLIFT	-	3/10

WEEK 3

EXERCISE	WEIGHT	SETS/REPS
SQUAT	BAND = 15% 1RM	3/3-5
	FREE WEIGHT = 35% 1RM	
	TOTAL = 50% 1RM	
SQUAT	FREE WEIGHT = 80% 1RM	3/6-8
LEG PRESS	-	3/8-10
LEG EXTENSION	-	3/8-10
ROMANIAN DEADLIFT	-	3/8-10

WEEK 4

EXERCISE	WEIGHT	SETS/REPS
SQUAT	BAND = 20% 1RM	3/3-5
	FREE WEIGHT = 40% 1RM	
	TOTAL = 60% 1RM	
SQUAT	FREE WEIGHT = 85% 1RM	3/4-6
LEG PRESS	-	3/8
LEG EXTENSION	-	3/8
ROMANIAN DEADLIFT	-	3/8

Band Squat

When performing squats with bands, you can wrap them around the bottom of the rack, as shown, or around low-set safety bars. Set the bands in such a way that taking the bar off the rack doesn't pull you forward or back or make the movement awkward. After a careful descent, explode upward to counter the additional resistance of the bands.

WEEK 5		
EXERCISE	**WEIGHT**	**SETS/REPS**
SQUAT	BAND = 20% 1RM	3/3-5
	FREE WEIGHT = 50% 1RM	
	TOTAL = 70% 1RM	
SQUAT	FREE WEIGHT = 90% 1RM	3/2-4
LEG PRESS	-	3/6-8
LEG EXTENSION	-	3/6-8
ROMANIAN DEADLIFT	-	3/6-8
WEEK 6		
SQUAT	BAND = 20% 1RM	3/3-5
	FREE WEIGHT = 60% 1RM	
	TOTAL = 80% 1RM	
SQUAT	FREE WEIGHT = 95% 1RM	3/1-2
LEG PRESS	-	3/6
LEG EXTENSION	-	3/6-8
ROMANIAN DEADLIFT	-	3/6-8

Chains

Setting up chains is a bit simpler than bands, but carrying the extra weight with you to the gym can be a clangy, awkward mess. But hey, if that's all you have to bear to add some new bulk, so be it. If you order the complete set of chains from elitefts.com, you'll get two ⅜" chains and two ⅝" chains. The ⅜" chain is used to wrap around the end of the bar and hold the ⅝" chain. One ⅜" chain (5 pounds) plus one ⅝" chain (20 pounds) weighs about 25 pounds. You may have to use additional chain weight depending on your strength. When setting up the chains on the bar, it's crucial that the ⅝" chains rest completely on the floor in the bottom position. For the squat, consider setting up the chains so that a few links still rest on the floor in the top position. This will prevent the chains from swinging, especially when you walk the bar out of the rack. For the bench press, only about half of the links will be off the floor in the top position due to the short range of motion. That means if you have one set each of ⅜" chains and ⅝" chains on the bar, you'll be using an additional 30 pounds of chain weight, not 50 pounds.

Chain
Bench Press

Your 1RM on the bench press will determine what your chain weight and starting free weight will be. With each inch you move the bar upward, you pick up additional links, which increases the resistance and recruits more muscle fibers.

For chain weight, see "Off the Chain" to determine how much resistance to use.
Remember, on bench presses you're using only half the weight of each 5⁄8" chain

WEEK 1

EXERCISE	WEIGHT	SETS/REPS
BENCH PRESS	CHAIN = TBD	3/7–8
	FREE WEIGHT = 40% 1RM	
BENCH PRESS	FREE WEIGHT = 60% 1RM	3/12–15
INCLINE DUMBBELL PRESS	–	3/10–12
DUMBBELL FLYE	–	3/10–12

WEEK 2

BENCH PRESS	CHAIN = TBD	3/6–7
	FREE WEIGHT = 50% 1RM	
BENCH PRESS	FREE WEIGHT = 70% 1RM	3/10–12
INCLINE DUMBBELL PRESS	–	3/10
DUMBBELL FLYE	–	3/10

WEEK 3

BENCH PRESS	CHAIN = TBD	3/5–6
	FREE WEIGHT = 55% 1RM	
BENCH PRESS	FREE WEIGHT = 75% 1RM	3/8–10
INCLINE DUMBBELL PRESS	–	3/8–10
DUMBBELL FLYE	–	3/8–10

WEEK 4

BENCH PRESS	CHAIN = TBD	3/4–5
	FREE WEIGHT = 60% 1RM	
BENCH PRESS	FREE WEIGHT = 80% 1RM	3/6–8
INCLINE DUMBBELL PRESS	–	3/8
DUMBBELL FLYE	–	3/8

WEEK 5

BENCH PRESS	CHAIN = TBD	3/3–4
	FREE WEIGHT = 65% 1RM	
BENCH PRESS	FREE WEIGHT = 85% 1RM	3/4–6
INCLINE DUMBBELL PRESS	–	3/5–8
DUMBBELL FLYE	–	3/5–8

WEEK 6

BENCH PRESS	CHAIN = TBD	3/3
	FREE WEIGHT = 70% 1RM	
BENCH PRESS	FREE WEIGHT = 90% 1RM	3/2–4
INCLINE DUMBBELL PRESS	–	3/4–6
DUMBBELL FLYE	–	3/6

One-Rep Max Calculator

No partner to help you test your 1RM? Finding your 5RM is just as good

Just in case you're afraid of getting a bar pinned across your neck on a one-rep max (1RM) test, we've got a pretty reliable alternative. Research shows that using a five-rep max (5RM) to determine your 1RM is about 99% accurate for upper-body exercises and 97% accurate for lower-body exercises. That's close enough. Not to mention, it's more important for bodybuilders to be strong with a weight they can lift for several reps than for just one — you don't get bigger by doing singles. To calculate your 1RM for an exercise, find a weight that permits you to get five, and only five, reps; you shouldn't be able to get a sixth rep on your own. Take each weight and use one of these equations to determine your 1RM for the particular exercise.

FOR UPPER-BODY EXERCISES
(5RM weight x 1.1307) + 0.6998 = 1RM
Example: If you bench 300 pounds for five reps, your 1RM would be (300 x 1.1307) + 0.6998 = 340 pounds.

FOR LOWER-BODY EXERCISES
(5RM weight x 1.09703) + 14.2546 = 1RM
Example: If you squat 400 pounds for five reps, your 1RM would be (400 x 1.09703) + 14.2546 = 453 pounds, or 455 pounds (rounded up).

Off The Chain

1RM BENCH PRESS	SUGGESTED CHAIN WEIGHT	1RM SQUAT	SUGGESTED CHAIN WEIGHT
< 200 pounds	20-30 pounds	< 200 pounds	40-50 pounds
200-400 pounds	40-50 pounds	200-400 pounds	50-60 pounds
400-500 pounds	80-90 pounds	400-500 pounds	60-70 pounds
		500-600 pounds	80-90 pounds

come off the floor and add weight to the bar. Elastic bands, on the other hand, provide resistance by a restoring force, which attempts to move the two ends of each band back to their original resting positions when they're pulled farther apart. The more you pull the bands (such as at the top of the range of motion of a squat), the greater the resistance.

Tools Of The Trade

We're not telling you to use LVRT in place of free weights; we're telling you to consider using chains and bands with free weights. By increasing the amount of force it takes to move a weight from point A to point B, chains and bands can build denser, stronger muscle. And what bodybuilder wouldn't want that?

SQUAT CHAIN PROGRAM

For chain weight, see "Off the Chain" to determine how much resistance to use.

WEEK 1

EXERCISE	WEIGHT	SETS/REPS
SQUAT	CHAIN = TBD	3/7-8
	FREE WEIGHT = 40% 1RM	
SQUAT	FREE WEIGHT = 60% 1RM	3/12-15
SMITH MACHINE FRONT SQUAT	–	3/10-12
LEG EXTENSION	–	3/10-12
LEG CURL	–	3/10-12

WEEK 2

EXERCISE	WEIGHT	SETS/REPS
SQUAT	CHAIN = TBD	3/6-7
	FREE WEIGHT = 50% 1RM	
SQUAT	FREE WEIGHT = 70% 1RM	3/10-12
SMITH MACHINE FRONT SQUAT	–	3/10
LEG EXTENSION	–	3/10
LEG CURL	–	3/10-12

WEEK 3

EXERCISE	WEIGHT	SETS/REPS
SQUAT	CHAIN = TBD	3/5-6
	FREE WEIGHT = 55% 1RM	
SQUAT	FREE WEIGHT = 75% 1RM	3/8-10
SMITH MACHINE FRONT SQUAT	–	3/8-10
LEG EXTENSION	–	3/8-10
LEG CURL	–	3/8-10

WEEK 4

EXERCISE	WEIGHT	SETS/REPS
SQUAT	CHAIN = TBD	3/4-5
	FREE WEIGHT = 60% 1RM	
SQUAT	FREE WEIGHT = 80% 1RM	3/6-8
SMITH MACHINE FRONT SQUAT	–	3/8
LEG EXTENSION	–	3/8
LEG CURL	–	3/8-10

WEEK 5

EXERCISE	WEIGHT	SETS/REPS
SQUAT	CHAIN = TBD	3/3-4
	FREE WEIGHT = 65% 1RM	
SQUAT	FREE WEIGHT = 85% 1RM	3/4-6
SMITH MACHINE FRONT SQUAT	–	3/6-8
LEG EXTENSION	–	3/6-8
LEG CURL	–	3/6-8

WEEK 6

EXERCISE	WEIGHT	SETS/REPS
SQUAT	CHAIN = TBD	3/3
	FREE WEIGHT = 70% 1RM	
SQUAT	FREE WEIGHT = 90% 1RM	3/2-4
SMITH MACHINE FRONT SQUAT	–	3/4-6
LEG EXTENSION	–	3/6
LEG CURL	–	3/6

Chain Squat

As with the bench press, your 1RM squat will dictate what your chain weight and free weight should be. Take advantage of the extra resistance by moving into the bottom position slowly before exploding up and fully extending your hips at the top. As usual, be careful not to lock out your knees.

Hardcore Anywhere

How to keep your training consistent, heavy and intense at big-box gyms and everywhere else

First comes the advice you've heard a thousand times before: train hard and heavy with compound, multijoint lifts like the bench press, squat and deadlift. Then, once we've hammered you with that for months on end, the best fitness clichés in the industry come out with a vengeance. These moves give you the most "bang for your buck," and they're great "tools for your toolbox" because they "recruit more muscle."

We're not about to contradict the instruction we've given you over the years in M&F, much less in the preceding pages of this book, but when it comes to getting the job done in your typical commercial gym — or in unfamiliar circumstances when you're traveling — everything is decidedly not what it seems.

With the proliferation of gyms offering a kinder, gentler fitness experience, it has become a lot harder of late to find places where it's acceptable to do the hardcore kind of work you need. On the following pages, we'll show you how to build mass, get stronger and shred fat, all within the confines of your friendly neighborhood commercial gym.

MORAL MINORITY

Two main exercises in particular, the squat and deadlift, are moves you've been told are definite "must-haves" in any program, whatever your fitness goals may be. This is sound advice, but when you head into your local big-box gym, you won't see many guys, if any, performing either lift. You'll see countless sets and reps being cranked out on the leg press and leg-extension machines — and almost no lower-back work going on at all unless it's by accident — but squat and deadlift sightings are typically few and far between.

There are reasons for this. Go at it too hard in your typical neon-and-chrome joint and you may be shown the door, especially if you scream, grunt or drop your weights on the floor. This doesn't bode well for the prospect of heavy deadlift workouts, because no matter how many times the front desk attendants warn us not to slam our weights on the floor, we still haven't

Hammer Curl

 Hold a dumbbell in both hands at your sides. Maintaining a neutral grip, curl until the top edges of the dumbbells make contact with your front deltoids. Return to start position and repeat for reps.

figured out a way to lower 500-plus pounds to the floor gently.

Fear not, however, because you don't need to compromise as much as you think. Assuming the gyms you're using are reasonably well-equipped, it's entirely possible to train hard and heavy without violating the rules or alienating people who aren't used to your style.

THE LOGIC OF LIFTING

Let's get one thing straight right away: Your goal, when it comes down to it, is to figure out a way to keep your main lifts, or variations thereof, in your program at all costs, despite your potentially less-than-ideal surroundings. The idea, then, is to keep that pesky front desk attendant — the one who doesn't give a damn whether you break a sweat or not—from influencing the quality of your workouts by dictating what exercises you can and can't do.

"Whether you're a bodybuilder, power-lifter, athlete or just a guy who's trying to get in the best shape you can," says Harry Selkow, a strength and conditioning coach in Pleasanton, CA, "you can't think about making permanent substitutions for your main lifts unless you have some kind of debilitating injury that's hampering your quality of life. Using a leg press or a Smith machine full time just isn't going to get it done like one of the big lifts."

Clichés become clichés for a reason — because there's an underlying element of truth behind them—and the aforementioned examples regarding the main lifts are weight-training's gospel. Research has shown, time and again, that you activate and build significantly more muscle with the free-weight bench press, squat, and deadlift than you can with machine equivalents. The same concept applies to keeping things simple with your isolation movements, as well.

Shrug

Squat

With a loaded barbell across your traps, assume a shoulder-width stance. Push your hips back and down, and descend to a slightly below-parallel squat position. Fire your hips, hamstrings, quads and glutes, and return to the start position.

THE PROGRAM

The Commercial Grade program template is a serious, six-week, six-days-per-week cycle that relies heavily on the basics of strength, mass and power development, with a dose of bodybuilding-style assistance work thrown in to bring up your weak points and give you the stability you need to move your numbers northward with your main lifts. With this program, you'll always know exactly what you have to do, and the exercises are simple enough to take to any gym, anywhere.

"Wherever you train, you can't go wrong by tailoring your assistance lifts to the weak points of your primary lifts," Selkow says. "Suppose you start pitching forward and bending over when you squat, and that's where your point of failure is. If you focus on building your lower back and your core, these areas will both function better and look better, and who doesn't want that? Funny how that works."

Each week, three workouts will focus on your main lifts: the bench press, squat, and deadlift. The other three days will feature a mix of an extra body-part day, combined with some intensive conditioning work, utilizing those endless rows of cardio machines found in every big-box gym, which will help you shred excess fat.

For your main lifts, you'll need to know your one-rep maxes, so you can either estimate these or find out what they are the week before you get started. Start with 50% of your 1RM for these lifts for your working sets in Week 1, then increase your intensity by 5% each week. For certain assistance lifts, we're using the total reps method. For this program, when you're able to perform 50 reps of an exercise at a given weight, in as few sets as it takes to hit your number, increase that weight significantly the following week, drop down to 20 total reps, and repeat the process.

"A 5x5 setup like this, using submaximal weights, is a great way to develop a base of general strength and mass you can build from," Selkow says. "After six weeks of this, you can branch out into whatever kind of program you want."

MONDAY

EXERCISE	SETS	REPS/TIME	REST
SQUAT	5	5[1]	90 SEC.
ROMANIAN DEADLIFT		20–50[2]	60 SEC.
45-DEGREE BACK EXTENSION		20–50[2]	45 SEC.
DECLINE SITUP		20–50[2]	60 SEC.
UPHILL TREADMILL WALK[3]		20–30 MIN.	

[1]Begin with 50% of your 1RM in Week 1, then add 5% each week.
[2]Begin with 20 reps in Week 1, and add 5 to 10 total reps each week.
[3]Set treadmill to highest possible grade you can handle.

TUESDAY

EXERCISE	SETS	REPS/TIME	REST
UPHILL TREADMILL SPRINT	10	10–12	30 SEC.
SIDE PLANK	3	15	30 SEC.
CABLE CRUNCH	3	20	30 SEC.
UPHILL TREADMILL WALK		15–20 MIN.	

Dumbbell Row

Stand with a flat bench directly to your side and place your knee and shin on it, holding its edge with your same-side hand. Hold a dumbbell with your other hand in a neutral grip, then pull it to your belly button. Hold for a second, then return to the start position.

45-Degree Back Extention

Place your feet on the foot plate, with your toes and heels straight up and down, and lower the hip pad to its lowest possible setting. Bend at the waist and use your hamstrings and lower back to lower your torso and then raise it back to the start position.

Decline Situp

On a decline bench, hook your feet under the pad provided and lie back until your shoulder blades touch the bench. Bend at the waist and raise your torso as far as you can, then return to the start position with your shoulders touching the bench.

WEDNESDAY

EXERCISE	SETS	REPS/TIME	REST
BENCH PRESS	5	5[1]	90 SEC.
DUMBBELL BENCH PRESS	3	10	60 SEC.
DIP		20–50[2]	60 SEC.
DUMBBELL ROW		20–50[2]	60 SEC.
SEATED CABLE ROW		20–50[2]	60 SEC.
LAT PULLDOWN		20–50[2]	60 SEC.
UPHILL TREADMILL WALK		20–30 MIN.	

[1]Begin with 50% of your 1RM in Week 1, then add 5% each week.

[2]Begin with 20 reps in Week 1, and add 5 to 10 total reps each week.

THURSDAY

EXERCISE	SETS	REPS/TIME	REST
LYING TRICEPS EXTENSION	3–5	10	60 SEC.
ROPE PUSHDOWN	3–5	10	45 SEC.
OVERHEAD ROPE EXTENSION	3–5	10	45 SEC.
BARBELL CURL	3–5	10	60 SEC.
HAMMER CURL	3–5	10	45 SEC.
PREACHER CURL	3–5	10	45 SEC.
UPHILL TREADMILL WALK		20–30 MIN.	

Overhead Rope Extention

Hook a rope attachment onto a high pulley and stand with your back to the weight stack. Hold the rope over your head, take a long step with one leg, and lean forward until you feel resistance. Extend your arms forward, then return to the start position.

Bench Press

Lay a pair of strength bands lengthwise across a flat bench. Most commercial gym benches don't have enough friction to allow you to arch properly, but benching atop bands in this manner will allow you to arch and incorporate leg drive into the movement.

FRIDAY

EXERCISE	SETS	REPS/TIME	REST
PADDED RACK PULL	5	5[1]	90 SEC.
SQUAT	3	10	60 SEC.
45-DEGREE BACK RAISE		20–50[2]	45 SEC.
DECLINE SITUP		20–50[2]	60 SEC.
UPHILL TREADMILL WALK[3]		20–30 MIN.	

[1]Begin with 50% of your 1RM in Week 1, then add 5% each week.
[2]Begin with 20 reps in Week 1, and add 5 to 10 total reps each week.
[3]Set treadmill to highest possible grade you can handle.

SATURDAY

EXERCISE	SETS	REPS/TIME	REST
DUMBBELL BENCH PRESS	5	10	60 SEC.
MILITARY PRESS	3	8	60 SEC.
SHRUG	3–5	10	60 SEC.
REAR/SIDE/FRONT DELT RAISE[1]	3	8 EACH	60 SEC.
UPHILL TREADMILL SPRINT	10	10–12	30 SEC.
UPHILL TREADMILL WALK		15–20 MIN.	

* Tri-set, done consecutively.

Military Press

Stand with your feet approximately shoulder-width apart with a barbell resting on your front deltoids. Grasp the bar in an overhand grip at about shoulder width. Without any influence from your lower body, extend your arms to press the bar into the lockout position over your head and slightly behind it.

Padded Rack Pull

In a power rack, fasten the squat pad that typically goes over the middle of a barbell to the center of each of the spotter bars. Then, place the bars as low as you can set them. Once you're done, simply deadlift the bar from this position. Stand on plates or anything else solid to increase your range of motion.

Chapter 11

Squat 2.0

The definitive **guide to the most important move** in your program

It's the "king of all exercises" for a reason: The back squat is the foundation of any solid weight-training program

Everything they say about squatting is true — and they say plenty. They call the squat the "king of all exercises," and they're justified. When your squat goes up, they'll tell you, everything goes up, and they're right. It's the most effective exercise you can do in the gym.

If you're physically capable of putting a barbell on your back and performing a free squat, you're in the lineage. You're next in a long line of succession from the original strongmen to the most powerful modern strength athletes — all of whom have relied consistently on one exercise as the cornerstone of their physical training: the squat.

To make sure you're doing it right or to start you off correctly if you're a beginner, our mission on the following pages is to show you the same sound technique and programming these legends of the iron game have used through the years to exploit the myriad benefits of the mighty king.

To initiate the squat, push your hips straight backward and sit back, not down

Squatting for Size

When it comes to building overall size — not just leg size — the squat is king. Adding squats to your training program will rapidly grow every muscle group from

THE "GET BIGGER" SQUAT PROGRAM

WEEK 1

EXERCISE	SETS/REPS	REST
SQUAT	4/8–10	2–3 MIN.
LEG PRESS	4/8–10	2–3 MIN.
LEG EXTENSION	4/8–10	2–3 MIN.
ROMANIAN DEADLIFT	4/8–10	2–3 MIN.
LYING LEG CURL	4/8–10	2–3 MIN.

WEEK 2

EXERCISE	SETS/REPS	REST
SQUAT	1/50	2–3 MIN.
SQUAT	3/20–25	1–2 MIN.
DUMBBELL LUNGE	4/20–25	1–2 MIN.
ONE-LEG EXTENSION	4^2/20–25	—
ROMANIAN DEADLIFT	4/20–25	1–2 MIN.
ONE-LEG LYING LEG CURL	4^2/20–25	—

head to toe because squatting involves your entire lower body as well as a significant percentage of upper-body muscle groups that serve to balance the bar on your back.

Squatting overloads not only your quads but also your hamstrings, glutes, adductors and even your calves to some extent. With all these bodyparts working in concert, you can train heavier with the squat than with any other free-weight exercise. Using all of this muscle mass floods your body with anabolic hormones including growth hormone, testosterone and insulinlike growth factor-1. These hormones surge through the bloodstream, reaching all your muscles and encouraging growth.

If your goal is to strip off unwanted fat, look no further than the squat. Anecdotal evidence tells us that squatting shreds fat better than any other lower-body exercise. In fact, one study found that the squat burned 50% more calories than the leg press. No matter what your primary focus is — adding mass or dropping fat — the squat should be a staple in your program.

Now that you know why you need to squat, it's time to learn how to add this movement to your mass-building workouts. Your best bet for maximizing size is to squat at the start of your leg routine because that's when you'll be strongest. The more weight you squat, the more you'll overload the involved muscle groups and the more growth you'll stimulate.

The 8–12 rep range has been shown to be the sweet spot for muscle growth, but the legs respond well to higher reps — very high reps, that is — for hypertrophy. If you can survive the occasional 50-rep set, significant leg growth will follow. To do this, find a weight that allows you to complete at least 30 reps of squats. If you can't hit all 50 reps without stopping, utilize the rest-pause principle by taking quick 15-second breaks to rack the bar and breathe. When you're capable of performing 50 consecutive reps without resting, increase the weight for your next workout.

WEEK 3

EXERCISE	SETS/REPS	REST
SQUAT	3/6–8	2–3 MIN.
FRONT SQUAT	3/6–8	2–3 MIN.
HACK SQUAT	3/6–8	2–3 MIN.
LEG EXTENSION	3/6–8	2–3 MIN.
ROMANIAN DEADLIFT	3/6–8	2–3 MIN.
LEG CURL	3/6–8	2–3 MIN.

WEEK 4

EXERCISE	SETS/REPS	REST
SQUAT	1/50	2–3 MIN.
SQUAT	3/20–25	1–2 MIN.
DUMBBELL STEP-UP — SUPERSET WITH —	4/15–20	—
DUMBBELL ROMANIAN DEADLIFT	4/15–20	1–2 MIN.
LEG EXTENSION — SUPERSET WITH —	4/15–20	—
LYING OR SEATED LEG CURL	4/15–20	1–2 MIN.

WEEK 5

EXERCISE	SETS/REPS	REST
SQUAT	4³/6–8	2–3 MIN.
LEG PRESS	4³/6–8	2–3 MIN.
LEG EXTENSION	4¹/8–10	1–2 MIN.
ROMANIAN DEADLIFT	4³/6–8	2–3 MIN.
LEG CURL	4¹/8–10	1–2 MIN.

WEEK 6

EXERCISE	SETS/REPS	REST
SQUAT	1/50	2–3 MIN.
SQUAT	3³/10–12	1–2 MIN.
SMITH MACHINE REVERSE LUNGE — SUPERSET WITH —	4/10–12	—
SMITH MACHINE ROMANIAN DEADLIFT	4/10–12	1–2 MIN.
LEG EXTENSION — SUPERSET WITH —	4¹/10–12	—
LYING OR SEATED LEG CURL	4¹10–12	1–2 MIN.

[1] Perform two drop sets on the last set by reducing the weight by 20%-30% each time.
[2] Don't rest between legs. Alternate legs until you've done four sets per leg.
[3] Perform two rest-pauses on the last set.

Chapter 11

2

Squat:
From Head To Toe

1. Head
Keep it level at the beginning of the squat, with your eyes focused directly forward. Think "head up" as you come out of the hole.

2. Hands
Squeeze the bar tightly in an overhand grip with your hands far enough apart to control the bar but narrow enough to create the shelf with your traps.

3. Elbows
They should point at the floor directly under the bar.

4. Abs
Push them out by drawing a big breath and flex them as if to brace yourself to take a punch.

5. Feet
They should be wider than shoulder width with your toes pointed slightly outward. Keep your weight primarily on your heels.

6. Knees
Don't let them pass your toes on the descent or turn inward at any point.

7. Hips
Start the movement by pushing your hips directly back as if to sit in a chair.

8. Lower Back
Keep it tight and flat.

9. Shoulders
Squeeze your shoulder blades together to bunch up your traps and create a "shelf" for the bar.

10. Chest
Keep your chest as high as possible throughout the squat. You should be able to read the logo on your shirt in the mirror.

Since you use your leg muscles all day for activities like standing and walking, you'll need to take them out of their comfort zone in training to encourage serious growth. In addition to your 50-rep sets, take your sets past muscle failure with techniques such as rest-pause, drop sets, supersets and forced reps. This daily usage also necessitates a higher volume of training than you'd do with other bodyparts. If you have a year of consistent leg training under your belt, perform at least 16–20 sets for your lower body, including hamstring-focused work.

Squatting for Strength

Developing a strong, powerful back squat will profoundly affect everything you do in the gym. It's the one exercise that's guaranteed to make you stronger across the board. Have you hit a sticking point with your bench press? Start squatting and you'll slam through it in no time. Want to run faster or jump higher? Put a barbell on your back and go to work. Squatting, it would seem, solves everything.

When it comes to strength, the squat is a more technical lift than most people realize, especially given the rather significant risk of injury incurred when you start adding serious weight to the bar. The better your technique, the more you'll squat and the less chance you'll have of getting hurt, so make technical skill a priority.

"When you set up to squat, pull your shoulder blades together and tighten your whole upper body," says Juggernaut Training Systems (Laguna Hills, California) co-owner Chad Smith, who has squatted more than 800 pounds with no assistive gear. "This makes a good shelf for the bar. As you start your descent, take a big breath into your belly, flex your abs like you're about to get punched, then push your hips straight back and drive your weight through your heels to come back up."

The six-week workout cycle provided here focuses on a few characteristics of strength development: You'll learn to strain under a heavy load, you'll get faster from the bottom position of the squat, and you'll add the mass and muscle needed to move more weight. To cover all these bases, you'll squat twice per week, performing a vastly different workout each day.

Keep your head up and shoulder blades squeezed together to create a solid "shelf" for the bar to rest on

Day 1 entails getting accustomed to heavy squatting with sets of five reps or less. On Day 2, the idea is to build supportive mass, so you'll perform sets involving significantly more reps. To develop speed out of the hole (the bottom position), focus on exploding through your entire range of motion as fast and as powerfully as you can. Lastly, a word to the wise: For your Day 1 workouts, make sure you squat in the presence of an experienced spotter.

Proper squat technique entails recruiting muscles other than just your quads and glutes. Your hamstrings, lower back and abs play a huge role, so your assistance exercises — the ones you'll perform after squatting — necessarily focus on these muscle groups. When you sit back on your descent, you add the power of your hamstrings to your quads and glutes. When you stand back up, it's your abs and lower back that hold you in place and keep you from pitching forward. Strengthen these supporting muscles and you'll squat more weight. It's that simple.

"Most missed squat attempts happen because guys either lower the bar too slowly or they roll forward onto the balls of their feet as they come out of the hole," Smith says. "A quick descent, and keeping your head pushed back into your traps and your chest up are what I emphasize. When I stand in front of you, I want to be able to read the logo on your T-shirt the whole time you're squatting."

THE "GET STRONGER" SQUAT PROGRAM

WEEK 1

DAY	EXERCISE	SETS/REPS	REST
1	BACK SQUAT	1/5RM	2 MIN.
	ONE-LEG PRESS	3/10	60 SEC.
	ROMANIAN DEADLIFT	— /50 TOTAL	—
	45-DEGREE BACK RAISE	— /50 TOTAL	—
	DECLINE SIT-UP	3/10	45 SEC.
2	BACK SQUAT (50% 1RM)	— /50 TOTAL	—
	ONE-LEG PRESS	3/10	60 SEC.
	ROMANIAN DEADLIFT	— /50 TOTAL	—
	45-DEGREE BACK RAISE	— /50 TOTAL	—
	HANGING LEG RAISE	3/10	45 SEC.

WEEK 2

DAY	EXERCISE	SETS/REPS	REST
1	BACK SQUAT	1/5RM[1]	2 MIN.
	ONE-LEG PRESS	3/10	60 SEC.
	ROMANIAN DEADLIFT	— /50 TOTAL	—
	45-DEGREE BACK RAISE	— /50 TOTAL	—
	DECLINE SIT-UP	3/10	45 SEC.
2	BACK SQUAT (50% 1RM)	— /50 TOTAL	—
	ONE-LEG PRESS	3/10	60 SEC.
	ROMANIAN DEADLIFT	— /50 TOTAL	—
	45-DEGREE BACK RAISE	— /50 TOTAL	—
	HANGING LEG RAISE	3/10	45 SEC.

WEEK 3

DAY	EXERCISE	SETS/REPS	REST
1	BACK SQUAT	1/3RM[2]	2 MIN.
	ONE-LEG PRESS	3/10	60 SEC.
	ROMANIAN DEADLIFT (INCREASE WEIGHT)	— /40 TOTAL	—
	45-DEGREE BACK RAISE	— /40 TOTAL[3]	—
	DECLINE SIT-UP	3/15	45 SEC.
2	BACK SQUAT (50% 1RM)	— /50 TOTAL	—
	ONE-LEG PRESS	3/10	60 SEC.
	ROMANIAN DEADLIFT (DAY 1 WEIGHT)	— /40 TOTAL	—
	45-DEGREE BACK RAISE	— /40 TOTAL[3]	—
	HANGING LEG RAISE	3/12	45 SEC.

WEEK 4

DAY	EXERCISE	SETS/REPS	REST
1	BACK SQUAT	1/3RM[2]	2 MIN.
	ONE-LEG PRESS	3/10	60 SEC.
	ROMANIAN DEADLIFT (INCREASE WEIGHT)	— /40 TOTAL	—
	45-DEGREE BACK RAISE	— /40 TOTAL[3]	—
	DECLINE SIT-UP	3/15	45 SEC.
2	BACK SQUAT (50% 1RM)	— /50 TOTAL	—
	ONE-LEG PRESS	3/10	60 SEC.
	ROMANIAN DEADLIFT (DAY 1 WEIGHT)	— /40 TOTAL	—
	45-DEGREE BACK RAISE	— /40 TOTAL[3]	—
	HANGING LEG RAISE	3/12	45 SEC.

WEEK 5

DAY	EXERCISE	SETS/REPS	REST
1	BACK SQUAT (50% 1RM)	— /50 TOTAL	—
	ONE-LEG PRESS	3/10	60 SEC.
	ROMANIAN DEADLIFT (INCREASE WEIGHT)	— /30 TOTAL	—
	45-DEGREE BACK RAISE	— /30 TOTAL[3]	—
	DECLINE SIT-UP	3/20	45 SEC.
2	BACK SQUAT (50% 1RM)	— /30 TOTAL	—
	ONE-LEG PRESS	3/10	60 SEC.
	ROMANIAN DEADLIFT (DAY 1 WEIGHT)	— /30 TOTAL	—
	45-DEGREE BACK RAISE	— /30 TOTAL[3]	—
	HANGING LEG RAISE	3/15	45 SEC.

WEEK 6

DAY	EXERCISE	SETS/REPS	REST
MAX	BACK SQUAT	1/1RM[4]	2 MIN.
	ONE-LEG PRESS	3/10	60 SEC.
	ROMANIAN DEADLIFT (WEEK 1 WEIGHT)	— /30 TOTAL	—
	45-DEGREE BACK RAISE (BODYWEIGHT)	— /30 TOTAL	—
	DECLINE SIT-UP	3/15	45 SEC.

[1] Begin with 40% of your perceived one-rep max for a set of five, then work your way up by adding 5%–10% each set until you find your five-rep max. [2] Begin with 40% of your perceived one-rep max for a set of five, then work your way up by adding 5%–10% each set until you find your three-rep max. [3] Hold a 25- or 45-pound plate across your chest. [4] Begin with 40% of your perceived one-rep max for a set of five, then work your way up by adding 5%–10% each set until you find your one-rep max.

Chapter 12

Bench Press 2.0

Everything you need to know about the most popular — and least understood — exercise in the gym

Nobody can say for certain exactly when the first barbell was conceived, but at some point in history someone surmised that sliding weighted discs onto an iron bar was an astonishingly effective means of strengthening the human body. Then, somewhere down the timeline, someone else decided that the ultimate measure of humankind's physical strength was a feat performed lying on one's back.

Therein lies the irony of bench-pressing and the genesis of a question we haven't been able to escape since. Train with weights long enough and you'll be asked the same thing over and over again: "How much do you bench?"

You have an answer for this, of course, but is it one you're proud of? If not, you'll need to learn a few

things. From programming to technique, there's exponentially more to benching than flopping on your back and pushing the bar. On the following pages, we'll get you started the right way.

Benching for Strength

Building massive pressing power won't be easy, but you can take comfort in the fact that the trail to a bigger bench has already been blazed. There are rules to follow, and improving any individual aspect will pay dividends almost immediately. Making a few simple changes to your technique and programming will have you setting personal records on the bench faster than you ever imagined.

When designing bench workouts with strength in mind, you'll first need to perfect your technique. The more weight you load on the bar, the more your technique comes into play in terms of exploiting your body's natural leverages and preventing injury. Refer to the technique and body position on the following pages, and spend some time perfecting them with an empty barbell.

"Focus on digging your shoulder blades and traps into the bench," says Vincent Dizenzo, a world-class powerlifter who has benched more than 800 pounds multiple times in competition. "Arch your back, squeeze your glutes together, push your toes to the front of your shoes, and drive your hips like you're having sex and want to go deeper."

Your workout programming for this cycle will focus on three critical aspects of bench-pressing. You need to learn to handle weights heavier than you're accustomed to, develop and ingrain the concept of bar speed, and start adding the muscular cross-section necessary to support and move bigger loads. To accomplish these three things, you'll bench twice per week but with a completely different set and rep scheme each time.

On Mondays, you'll go heavy for sets of five or fewer reps. Three days later on Thursdays, you'll per-

form tons of reps to build the muscle you need. For each individual rep on both days, lower the bar under control, then train yourself to explode the weight off your chest as fast and as powerfully as you can into a locked-out position at the top.

Once you start practicing and perfecting proper technique, you'll quickly understand that there's much more to bench-pressing than simply relying on your pecs to grind out a rep. Multiple muscle groups are involved, and you'll need to learn how to both use them effectively and strengthen them. That's why your assistance exercises — which strengthen and build muscle in your triceps, delts and lats — are just as important as benching itself. Your lats are the foundation you push from when the bar's on your chest, your shoulders provide stability throughout the lift, and your triceps take over halfway through your stroke and enable you to lock out the weight at the top.

"When you bench correctly, your entire body is involved," Dizenzo says. "You need to learn the feeling of lowering the bar into your lats. Once the bar hits your chest, use your legs to push your hips into your lats, then carry that connected push into your shoulders and triceps to finish the lift. Getting these techniques down is the single most effective way to add pounds to your max bench."

Chapter 12

Bench Press: From Head To Toe

1. Bar Path
Move straight up and down or back toward your head depending on your bodytype.

2. Elbows
On the downstroke, tuck your elbows close to your chest instead of flaring them out. This will prevent shoulder injuries.

3. Feet
Keep them firmly on the floor, with your toes pushing into the front of your shoes.

4. Forearms
At the bottom of the lift your forearms should be perpendicular to the floor, forming a straight line from your elbows to your hands.

5. Glutes
Keep them squeezed together and in place on the bench.

6. Hands
Grip the bar very tightly at shoulder width or slightly wider. Try to "break the bar in half" to better activate your triceps.

7. Head
Keep it flat on the bench or raised slightly.

8. Hips
Develop a feel for driving your hips up and toward your traps without lifting your glutes off the bench.

9. Lower Back
Keep it arched so your weight is on your upper back and traps.

10. Shoulder Blades
Retract them as tightly as you can when you set up.

11. Traps
Set up with the weight of your upper torso mainly on your traps and upper lats. When you push your toes into the front of your shoes, it should put pressure on your traps.

Benching for Size

When it comes to putting on mass, the bench press is undoubtedly the king of all upper-body exercises. It's a compound, multijoint movement that, to be performed correctly, calls on your deltoids, triceps, lats, abs and even legs to assist your chest muscles in moving a loaded barbell to the top of your range of motion.

This team effort allows you to use more weight with a conventional barbell bench press than you can with other chest exercises so you're able to overload your pecs. Pushing heavy weights encourages greater

THE "GET BIGGER" BENCH PROGRAM

WEEK 1

EXERCISE	SETS/REPS	REST
BENCH PRESS	4'/8-10	2–3 MIN.
REVERSE-GRIP BENCH PRESS	3'/8-10	2–3 MIN.
DUMBBELL INCLINE FLYE	3/10-12	1–2 MIN.
CABLE CROSSOVER	3/12-15	1 MIN.

WEEK 2

EXERCISE	SETS/REPS	REST
DUMBBELL FLYE	4/12-15	—
— SUPERSET WITH —		
BENCH PRESS	4/12-15	2–3 MIN.
DUMBBELL INCLINE FLYE	4/12-15	—
— SUPERSET WITH —		
DUMBBELL INCLINE PRESS	4/12-15	2–3 MIN.

muscle growth by boosting your testosterone and growth-hormone (GH) levels during your workouts. Both are critical anabolic hormones for promoting hypertrophy.

Research has shown that the bench press is, in all probability, the best exercise in existence for activating the greatest number of muscle fibers in your chest. One study conducted by the Weider Research Group found that the barbell bench press stimulated significantly more muscle fibers in the pecs than the dumbbell bench press. The more muscle fibers you stimulate, the more overall size you can add to a muscle group.

One common misconception — at least among guys with poorly developed chests — involves underestimating the flat bench press as a means of building muscle in the upper pecs. Research shows that the incline bench press increases muscular activity in the upper pecs by approximately 5% more than the flat bench. In terms of overall chest development, however, this increase is negligible when you consider that the incline bench places more of the total load on the front deltoids, away from your pectoral region.

Now that you know why the bench press is so effective for adding size, it's time to learn how to properly integrate the movement into your chest workouts. Because the bench press is a compound, multijoint exercise, it's best to bench at the beginning of your sessions when

WEEK 3

EXERCISE	SETS/REPS	REST
BENCH PRESS	4[1]/6-7	2-3 MIN.
DUMBBELL INCLINE PRESS	3[1]/8-10	2-3 MIN.
CABLE FLYE	3[1]/10-12	1 MIN.
LOW-PULLEY CABLE CROSSOVER	3[1]/10-12	1 MIN.

WEEK 4

EXERCISE	SETS/REPS	REST
CABLE CROSSOVER	3[2]/15-20	1-2 MIN.
DUMBBELL FLYE	3[2]/15-20	1-2 MIN.
BENCH PRESS	4[2]/15-20	1-2 MIN.
REVERSE-GRIP BENCH PRESS	4[2]/15-20	1-2 MIN.

WEEK 5

EXERCISE	SETS/REPS	REST
BENCH PRESS	4/4,6,8,10[3]	2-3 MIN.
DUMBBELL BENCH PRESS	3[4]/10-12	2-3 MIN.
DUMBBELL INCLINE FLYE	3/12-15	1-2 MIN.
LOW-PULLEY CABLE CROSSOVER	3/15-20	1 MIN.

WEEK 6

EXERCISE	SETS/REPS	REST
TRI-SET:		
DUMBBELL FLYE	4/10-12	—
BENCH PRESS	4/10-12	—
REVERSE-GRIP BENCH PRESS	4/10-12	2-3 MIN.
TRI-SET:		
LOW-PULLEY CABLE CROSSOVER	3/15-20	—
CABLE CROSSOVER	3/15-20	—
PUSH-UP	3/TO FAILURE	2-3 MIN.

[1] Perform two rest-pauses on the last two sets.
[2] Perform two drop sets on the last set.
[3] On the last set, immediately reduce the weight and do 30 reps.
[4] Perform two drop sets on the last two sets.

THE "GET STRONGER" BENCH PROGRAM

WEEK 1 > MONDAY

EXERCISE	SETS	REPS	REST
BENCH PRESS	1	5RM[1]	2 MIN.
DUMBBELL FLOOR PRESS	3	8	45 SEC.
DIP	—	50 TOTAL	45 SEC.
INVERTED ROW	3	12	45 SEC.

THURSDAY

EXERCISE	SETS	REPS	REST
BENCH PRESS (50%)	3	10	45 SEC.
DUMBBELL FLOOR PRESS[2]	3	6	45 SEC.
DIP	—	50 TOTAL	45 SEC.
INVERTED ROW	3	12	45 SEC.

WEEK 2 > MONDAY

EXERCISE	SETS	REPS	REST
BENCH PRESS	1	5RM[1]	2 MIN.
DUMBBELL FLOOR PRESS	3	10	45 SEC.
DIP	—	50 TOTAL	45 SEC.
INVERTED ROW	3	15	45 SEC.

THURSDAY

EXERCISE	SETS	REPS	REST
BENCH PRESS (50%)	4	10	45 SEC.
DUMBBELL FLOOR PRESS[2]	3	6	45 SEC.
DIP	—	50 TOTAL	45 SEC.
INVERTED ROW	3	15	45 SEC.

WEEK 3 > MONDAY

EXERCISE	SETS	REPS	REST
BENCH PRESS	1	3RM[3]	2 MIN.
DUMBBELL FLOOR PRESS	3	10	45 SEC.
DIP	—	60 TOTAL	45 SEC.
INVERTED ROW	3	12	45 SEC.

THURSDAY

EXERCISE	SETS	REPS	REST
BENCH PRESS (50%)	5	10	45 SEC.
"CLAPPER" PUSH-UP	5	5	60 SEC.
DIP	—	60 TOTAL	45 SEC.
INVERTED ROW	3	12	45 SEC.

WEEK 4 > MONDAY

EXERCISE	SETS	REPS	REST
BENCH PRESS	1	3RM[3]	2 MIN.
DUMBBELL FLOOR PRESS	3	12	45 SEC.
DIP	—	60 TOTAL	45 SEC.
INVERTED ROW	3	15	45 SEC.

THURSDAY

EXERCISE	SETS	REPS	REST
BENCH PRESS (50%)	5	10	45 SEC.
"CLAPPER" PUSH-UP	5	5	60 SEC.
DIP	—	60 TOTAL	45 SEC.
INVERTED ROW	3	15	45 SEC.

WEEK 5 > MONDAY

EXERCISE	SETS	REPS	REST
BENCH PRESS (50%)	3	5	60 SEC.
DUMBBELL FLOOR PRESS	3	8	45 SEC.
DIP	—	35 TOTAL	45 SEC.
INVERTED ROW	3	15	45 SEC.

THURSDAY

OFF (TAPER)

WEEK 6 > MONDAY

EXERCISE	SETS	REPS	REST
BENCH PRESS	1	1RM[4]	2 MIN.
DUMBBELL FLOOR PRESS	3	12	45 SEC.
DIP	—	35 TOTAL	45 SEC.
INVERTED ROW	3	15	45 SEC.

[1] Begin with 40% of your max for a set of five, then work your way up, adding 5%-10% each set until you find your five-rep max.
[2] Use a dumbbell that's 10-20 pounds heavier than you used on Monday.
[3] Begin with 40% of your max for a set of three, then work your way up, adding 5%-10% each set until you find your three-rep max.
[4] Begin with 40% of your max for a set of three, then work your way up, adding 5%-10% each set until you can't do triples anymore. Then do single reps until you find your new max.

you're not fatigued and can work with the heaviest weight possible.

Believe it or not, you should also bench-press at the end of your chest workouts. Since benching relies so heavily on your triceps and delts, those muscles tend to fail before your pecs have been adequately fatigued. When this happens, you miss out on an important process for muscle growth. By using pre-exhaust methods — performing an isolation exercise like the dumbbell flye before you bench, for example — you can ensure full muscle fatigue in your pecs.

Although research has established that performing 8–12 reps per set is ideal for stimulating growth, you should vary your intensity and rep schemes to continue progressing and avoid plateaus. For building mass, you can occasionally go as low as four reps or as high as 30. It's also important to encourage muscle fatigue by using techniques such as drop sets, rest-pauses, supersetting and tri-setting to accelerate the process.

Chapter 13

The Deadlift Encyclopedia

Everything you need to know about tugging heavy iron

Deadlift:
From Head To Toe

1. Pull with your hips, not with your arms.

2. Maintain full extention in your elbows throughout your range of motion.

3. Lower the bar in a mirror image of how you raised it.

4. Extend your back. Don't round it.

5. Squeeze your glutes tightly to prevent pulling with your lower back.

6. Push through your heels.

It's safe to assume the deadlift is

the oldest strength training maneuver in existence. There's no real documentation to back this up, but it makes perfect sense when you think about it. Benching and squatting took our forefathers some ingenuity to contrive, but picking something up? Putting it down and picking it up again? *That's instinct.*

A caveman points at a rock. He tells another to pick it up. If the guy can, he gets to eat a raw woolly mammoth steak. If he can't, he's clubbed over the head. Those were the stakes in the world's first powerlifting meet — and not much has changed since then. Deadlift training technique and programming have been refined, but the main objective remains the same: *You pick things up and put them down.* Here's an exhaustive analysis of the most magnificent move in all of resistance training and how you can start moving some heavier metal in eight weeks.

Deadlifting for Strength

Ripping a heavy barbell off the floor requires a serious commitment. To get stronger, the idea is to develop the confidence to know a lift is complete before you even wrap your hands around the barbell, every time you deadlift. Come hell or high water, you have to keep pulling.

Though deadlifting seems simple, the lift has several technical aspects you'll need to master to make progress. By learning to use your body's natural leverages and finding your groove, you'll both lift heavier weights and prevent injuries.

Proper technique starts with your stance. To find yours, perform a standing vertical jump, noting the width of your feet at the start. This foot position, with your toes pointed out slightly, is your new deadlift stance. From here, descend into a half squat with the barbell — which sits over the centers of your feet —

3-Inch Deficit Deadlift

Your shoulder blades should be over the bar, with your shoulders in front of it. Position your hands slightly outside your thighs. The middle of your foot should be directly under the bar, with your shins touching the bar.

Front Squat

Front squats will help build the quad strength you'll need for the initial pull of a deadlift. **Deadlifting** will make you stronger in all squat variations and vice versa.

touching your shins and your arms fully extended.

Your workouts for this strength cycle are designed to develop two cornerstones of correct deadlifting technique. First, you'll be using compensatory acceleration training (CAT) every time you perform a deadlift. This means every rep will be done as fast and explosively as possible — even your warm-up sets. Next, with every rep, focus on pushing your heels through the ground while making sure your hips don't rise faster than your shoulders. Keeping your hips down will prevent your legs from locking out before your hips — a mistake that will take away significant amounts of power, and leave your hamstrings and lower back vulnerable to injury.

The workout template provided is an eight-week cycle designed to increase your deadlift max by as much as 10%. On Day 1, you'll deadlift. On Day 2, you'll perform a series of accessory squat variations with direct carryover to your deadlift strength.

Once your technical proficiency improves and you're adding more weight to the bar, you'll notice that deadlifting works virtually every muscle in your body, with an emphasis on the muscles of your posterior chain: your glutes, hamstrings, and lower back. Working these muscle groups independently with your assistance exercises is

crucial to developing the lower-body strength you'll need for a powerful pull.

Shrugs, barbell rows, and weighted chins will add mass to your upper back and allow you to pull heavier weight to the standing, locked-out top position of the deadlift. Rows and chins also provide your workouts with balance by having you perform pulling movements in both the vertical and horizontal planes. For your glutes and hamstrings, there's no better movement than the glute-ham raise, a movement requiring a powerful co-contraction of these two massive muscle groups.

Deadlifting for Size

Ronnie Coleman has a big back. Big enough for eight Mr. Olympia titles, big enough that calling it big qualifies as an understatement and big enough for you to pay close attention to how he built it. Brian Dobson, Coleman's longtime trainer, attributes Big Ron's massive back to one factor that's remained constant in his training programs through the years. "Deadlifts," Dobson says, "are the king."

Deadlifting forces you to use virtually every muscle in your body to take the bar from the floor to waist height. In the chain of muscles involved in this process, nothing is left behind and everything kicks in eventually.

Everything starts with your lower back. Nothing builds your spinal erectors like the repetitive action of bearing and moving a massive load. The deadlift isn't just a lower-back exercise, though. As you move through your range of motion and transition from the lower part of the lift to the upper lockout phase, your lats, traps and other upper-back muscles take over. At the top of the movement, you're holding a very heavy weight in a dead-hang position — which places immense pressure on your traps. This is a very efficient combination of movements for building thickness in your upper back and shoulders.

In the bottom position, proper deadlift technique entails pushing through your heels to move the bar

Olympic Pause Squat

Descend to a position below parallel, pause for a second, then explode back to the top.

THE "GET STRONGER" DEADLIFT PROGRAM

WEEK 1

EXERCISE	WEIGHT*	SETS	REPS
DEADLIFT	75%	1	3
DEADLIFT[1]	60%	3	6
3-INCH DEFICIT DEADLIFT	65%	2	5
BENT-OVER ROW		3	8
SHRUG		3	12
GLUTE-HAM RAISE (OR 45-DEGREE BACK)		3	8

*Percentage of your one-rep max
[1] Rest 60 seconds between sets.

WEEK 2

EXERCISE	WEIGHT	SETS	REPS
DEADLIFT	80%	1	3
DEADLIFT[1]	60%	3	8
3-INCH DEFICIT DEADLIFT	68%	2	5
BENT-OVER ROW		3	7
SHRUG		3	12
GLUTE-HAM RAISE (OR 45-DEGREE BACK)		3	8

WEEK 3

EXERCISE	WEIGHT	SETS	REPS
DEADLIFT	85%	1	3
DEADLIFT[2]	70%	3	6
3-INCH DEFICIT DEADLIFT	75%	2	4
BENT-OVER ROW		3	6
SHRUG		3	12
GLUTE-HAM RAISE (OR 45-DEGREE BACK)		3	8

[2] Rest 90 seconds between sets.

WEEK 4

EXERCISE	WEIGHT	SETS	REPS
DEADLIFT	60%	6	1
LAT PULLDOWN		3	8
SHRUG	LIGHT	3	12
GLUTE-HAM RAISE (OR 45-DEGREE BACK)		26	

WEEK 5

EXERCISE	WEIGHT	SETS	REPS
DEADLIFT	90%	1	2
DEADLIFT[3]	75%	4	2
3-INCH DEFICIT DEADLIFT	80%	3	3
DUMBBELL ROW		3	6
SHRUG		3	10
GLUTE-HAM RAISE (OR 45-DEGREE BACK)		3	8

[3] Rest 120 seconds between sets.

WEEK 6

EXERCISE	WEIGHT	SETS	REPS
DEADLIFT	95%	1	1
DEADLIFT[3]	80%	3	2
3-INCH DEFICIT DEADLIFT	82.5%	3	
DUMBBELL ROW		3	6
SHRUG		3	10
GLUTE-HAM RAISE (OR 45-DEGREE BACK)		3	7

WEEK 7

Repeat Week 4, then attempt a new deadlift max in Week 8.

Chapter 13

out of a static position. By focusing on this leg drive, you're applying a tremendous amount of force to your quads, hamstrings and calves. Dropping your glutes and pushing through your heels with every rep will add mass throughout your lower body.

At the top of the deadlift, when you lock out your hips, your glutes act as the movement's agonist — its prime mover — while your hamstrings are targeted as the synergists, or assisters. When it comes to developing your glutes and hamstrings through the application of force, there's no better exercise than the deadlift.

The benefits aren't limited to your lower body. Your arms come into play throughout your range of motion. When you're both trying to hang onto a heavy load and move it upward, all the muscles in your arms are forced to contract, in addition to the obvious necessity for grip and forearm strength and mass development.

The routine provided here targets muscular hypertrophy with reps in the 6–15 range, as opposed to our strength routine, which focuses more on heavier sets for lower reps. Research by Dr. Eric Serrano has shown the importance of prolonging the time muscles are under tension during a set. Keeping your time-under-tension to 30–60 seconds — especially in the deadlift, where so many muscle groups are in play — will elicit the greatest muscle-building response from your resistance training. Keep your rest periods at two minutes or less for your main exercises each day, and take full advantage of the incredible growth hormone response deadlifting can produce.

Plank

 Keep your body in a straight line from your head to your feet.

Barbell Side Bend

THE "GET BIGGER" DEADLIFT PROGRAM

M&F TIP
—
Don't deadlift in front of a mirror. Even the slightest adjustment in form can cause serious injury.

WEEK 1

EXERCISE	WEIGHT(%)	SETS	REPS
STIFF-LEG DEFICIT DEADLIFT	30, 35, 40, 45 35	5	10
SHRUG		4	25
BENT-OVER ROW		4	10
WIDE-GRIP PULL-UP		3	6
NARROW-GRIP PULL-UP		3	6
INCLINE SIT-UP		3	15

WEEK 2

EXERCISE	WEIGHT(%)	SETS	REPS
STIFF-LEG DEFICIT DEADLIFT	30, 40 45, 50 37.5	5	10
SHRUG		4	25
BENT-OVER ROW		4	10
WIDE-GRIP PULL-UP		3	6
NARROW-GRIP PULL-UP		3	6
INCLINE SIT-UP		3	15

WEEK 3

EXERCISE	WEIGHT(%)	SETS	REPS
STIFF-LEG DEFICIT DEADLIFT	30, 40, 47.5, 52.5, 40	5	10
SHRUG		4	25
BENT-OVER ROW		4	10
WIDE-GRIP PULL-UP		3	6
NARROW-GRIP PULL-UP		3	6
INCLINE SIT-UP		3	15

WEEK 4

EXERCISE	WEIGHT(%)	SETS	REPS
REGULAR DEFICIT DEADLIFT	45, 50 55, 60 50	5	6
SHRUG		4	15
BENT-OVER ROW		3	8
WIDE-GRIP PULL-UP		2	9
NARROW-GRIP PULL-UP		2	9
INCLINE SIT-UP		3	15

WEEK 5

EXERCISE	WEIGHT(%)	SETS	REPS
REGULAR DEFICIT DEADLIFT	50, 55, 60, 70, 55	5	6
SHRUG		4	15
BENT-OVER ROW		3	8
WIDE-GRIP PULL-UP		2	9
NARROW-GRIP PULL-UP		2	9
INCLINE SIT-UP		3	15

WEEK 6

EXERCISE	WEIGHT(%)	SETS	REPS
REGULAR DEFICIT DEADLIFT	50, 55, 65, 75, 60	5	6
SHRUG		4	15
BENT-OVER ROW		3	8
WIDE-GRIP PULL-UP		2	9
NARROW-GRIP PULL-UP		2	9
INCLINE SIT-UP		3	15

Chapter 14

Backup Plan

For massive gains up front, you need to train your posterior chain

You're on the beach, showing off a winter's worth of gym work, when you approach a smoking-hot, bikini-clad bit of talent with a gleam in your eye. You break out your best game but she turns you down flat. Hey, it happens. But when you find yourself in this situation, there's only one thing you need to ask yourself: Do you look good enough walking away to make her reconsider?

Enter the posterior chain. Working the p-chain — the often-neglected muscle groups comprising the back of your body — will vastly improve your athletic performance, make your gym lifts stronger across the board and have you looking, from the back, like someone she may just want to chase.

The Links

By definition, the p-chain consists of the hamstrings, glutes, adductor magnus and lumbar erectors. To this we're adding some major upper-body muscle groups: the lats, rear delts and traps. Let's face it: Most guys lift weights because they want to look better in the mirror, from the front. They'll bench and squat every week but typically ignore the muscles in back. This is a critical mistake, because the p-chain muscles provide the most support and stability for the lifts that make your front side look and perform its best.

"When I assess new clients, I see the same posterior-chain weaknesses over and over," says strength and conditioning coach Jason Ashman, PFT, owner of Strong Island Strength and Conditioning in Amityville, New York. "They're always what I call 'front heavy,' with weak hamstrings, lats and [overall] support from the back of their bodies."

Posterior Performance

If you're an athlete, you need a strong lower back and hams to perform your best. From a biomechanical standpoint, when you run, jump or do anything requiring lower-body strength, your hamstrings and lumbar erectors — the "stovepipes" in your low back that hold you upright — are significantly activated, even more so than you think. If they're weak and underdeveloped, you can tap into only a fraction of your lower body's potential.

Strengthening your core is essential, too, but don't forget the strength and size balance you need between your abs and lower back. In other words, think of your core as a belt that goes all the way around your body from head to toe. "When I see an athlete miss a squat, it's usually not because his quads are weak," Ashman notes. "When you squat heavy, the idea is to sit back to activate your hamstrings. Most guys have weak hams and their lower backs can't support the weight, so they'll pitch forward. When you address that core imbalance, it makes a world of difference."

In the upper body, your lats, rear delts and traps provide the foundation from which you move objects or opponents forward. If you're after a bigger bench press, think in terms of improving the base from which you're pushing. If you don't have enough in back, you won't be able to stabilize increasing weights as you get stronger, much less powerfully push them to lockout. Focus on beefing up these supporting muscle groups and you'll smash through your upper-body sticking points in short order.

84

Percentage of total-body power contributed by the posterior chain during the crucial hip-extension portion of a two-leg vertical jump

THE PROGRAM

Our six-week upper-/lower-body split contains moves that specifically target the posterior chain. If you currently use a bodypart split for your weekly workout plan, simply add or substitute the exercises here on days when appropriate.

MONDAY

EXERCISE	SETS	REPS
BOX SQUAT	5	5
GLUTE-HAM RAISE		30 TOTAL
BAND 45-DEGREE BACK EXTENSION	3	10
TWO-HAND HEAVY DUMBBELL SWING	3	10
WEIGHTED DECLINE SIT-UP	3	10

TUESDAY

EXERCISE	SETS	REPS
BENCH PRESS	5	5
PUSHDOWN	3	10
FACE PULL	3	10
SHRUG	3	10
ONE-ARM REAR-DELT RAISE	3	10

THURSDAY

EXERCISE	SETS	REPS
RACK-PULL DEADLIFT	5	5
GLUTE-HAM RAISE		30 TOTAL
ONE-LEG BACK EXTENSION	3	10
CHAIN-SUPPORTED GOOD MORNING	3	10
WEIGHTED DECLINE SIT-UP	3	10

FRIDAY

EXERCISE	SETS	REPS
BENCH PRESS	3	10
PUSHDOWN	3	10
FACE PULL	3	15
SHRUG	3	15
ONE-ARM REAR-DELT RAISE	3	15

Glute-Ham Raise

FOCUS: Hamstrings

START: On a dedicated glute-ham raise unit, position the platform and rollers so the half-moon pad rests just above your knees. Lie facedown, extending your legs and torso so your body is nearly parallel to the floor. Arch your lower back and cross your arms over your chest.

EXECUTION: Contract your hams and glutes, and raise your torso until your thighs and upper body are nearly perpendicular to the floor. Keep your lower back arched. Slowly return to the start position.

One-Leg Back Extention

FOCUS: Hamstrings

START: On a back extension or 45-degree back extension unit, begin in the traditional bent-over start position, then remove one foot from under the roller and place it on top. Lightly touch your fingertips to the sides of your head.

EXECUTION: Keeping your lower back arched, contract your working hamstring and raise your torso until your body forms a straight line from head to foot. Slowly return to the start position.

Band 45-Degree Back Extention

FOCUS: Hamstrings, lower back

START: On a dedicated 45-degree back extension unit, place your feet on the platform with your ankles against the rollers so the main pad rests just below your waist. Attach a MUSCLE & FITNESS Strength Band to the base of the unit and grasp the band at chest level or loop it behind your neck. Lean forward as far as is comfortable, keeping your lower back arched.

EXECUTION: From the bottom position, contract your hams and low back to raise your torso until your body forms a straight line from head to feet.

The Look

Next time you're in the gym, take a look at the hamstring and lower-back development of the people around you. You'll likely see a disturbing pattern: Even with veteran gym members, the p-chain muscles simply aren't very visible. Once you start to notice this lack of symmetry, you'll quickly realize it's not the look you want for yourself.

The same appreciation applies to the p-chain muscles in your upper body. Trap-less, lat-less and rear delt-less is no way to go through life. "Even if you're not concerned about athletic performance, you still want that full-bodied look of muscles popping out of the back of your shirt and shorts, and a dedicated posterior-chain regimen will give you that," explains strength and conditioning coach Harry Selkow, CSCS, owner of Re-Active Gym in Pleasanton, California.

Chained Up

Think about p-chain training from the ground up, in order, from your hamstrings through your traps. On your lower-body lifting days you'll train hams, glutes and low back. On upper-body days you'll work lats, rear delts and traps. This program contains compound, multijoint lifts such as the box squat and rack-pull deadlift to engage your posterior chain with heavy weights and strengthen it all around. You'll also perform assistance exercises at higher reps that target various sections of your p-chain to add muscle mass.

"You need a combination of lifting styles to really get in there and nail your posterior chain," Selkow points out. "Compound lifts such as the bench and squat engage these muscle groups more than you think, which is something you'll realize when the back of your body starts getting stronger and your lifts take off."

Rack-Pull Deadlift

FOCUS: Hamstrings, lower back

START: In a power rack, set the spotter bars to about mid-shin level and place a loaded bar on them. With your feet shoulder-width apart and low back arched, grasp the bar with an alternating grip as close to your shins as possible.

EXECUTION: Keeping your hips down, contract your lower back, hams and quads. Raise the bar in a straight line as you stand up and extend your hips to lockout. Keep your lower back tight as you return to the start.

M&F TIP

When you're comfortable with the technique, take full advantage of this exercise by going heavy

M&F TIP

On the concentric portion of the movement, explode upward for maximal effect

Two-Hand Heavy Dumbbell Swing

FOCUS: Hamstrings, lower back

START: With your feet wider than shoulder width, squat down and grasp a heavy dumbbell by one end with both hands. The weight should hang between your legs and slightly behind you. Keep your low back arched.

EXECUTION: Extend your ankles, knees, hips and low back, and swing the dumbbell in front of you. Keep your arms loose but straight until the weight reaches eye level, then let it swing back down. Reverse the motion without dropping the dumbbell to the floor.

Face Pull

FOCUS: Lats

START: Attach a rope or strap to the high-pulley cable at a lat pulldown station. Stand erect with your feet shoulder-width apart and, using an overhand grip, grasp the rope at arm's length above head level so there's no slack in the cable. Lean back about 45 degrees and place one foot on the seat.

EXECUTION: Keeping your elbows at shoulder level, pull the rope or strap as close to your upper chest as you can. Slowly return to the start position.

Weighted Decline Sit-Up

FOCUS: Abs

START: Hook your feet under the foot-pads of a dedicated decline bench and lie faceup holding a weight plate — a 10, 25 or 45 — just above your forehead.

EXECUTION: Bend at the hips and crunch your abs to raise your torso as high as you can, then slowly return to the start.

Chain-Supported Good Morning

FOCUS: Lower back, hamstrings

START: In a power rack, loop two lengths of chain or a heavy strap around the high crossbar and use the loops to support a loaded bar, which should sit roughly where your upper torso would be parallel to the floor at the bottom of the movement.

EXECUTION: With your feet shoulder-width apart and the bar across your upper traps, bend forward at the hips while keeping your lower back tightly arched until the bar touches the bottom of the loops. Contract your hams and low back to raise the bar back to the start position.

One-Arm Rear-Delt Raise

FOCUS: Rear delts

START: Stand alongside a power rack with your feet close to its base. Grasp the post at chest level and lean out to the side, supporting your weight with the hand grasping the rack. Grasp a dumbbell behind your thigh in your outside hand using a neutral grip.

EXECUTION: Keeping your arm straight, raise the weight out to your side to roughly shoulder level. Slowly return to the start position.

Box Squat

FOCUS: Quads, hamstrings, lower back

START: Find a sturdy box tall enough so that when you sit on it, your thighs are parallel to the floor. Place it in a power rack about 2 feet behind the j-hooks. With the bar across your upper traps, unrack it and take two steps back. Stand erect with your feet slightly wider than shoulder width.

EXECUTION: Squeeze the bar hard and tighten your entire back. Take a deep breath and sit back onto the box, leading with your hips. Don't allow your knees to pass your toes; your shins should be perpendicular to the floor. Keeping your lower back tight, reverse the motion by firing your hips, contracting your hams and standing up forcefully.

Fine-Tune Your Abs

Build a better six-pack and get stronger in all your big lifts with this comprehensive ab routine

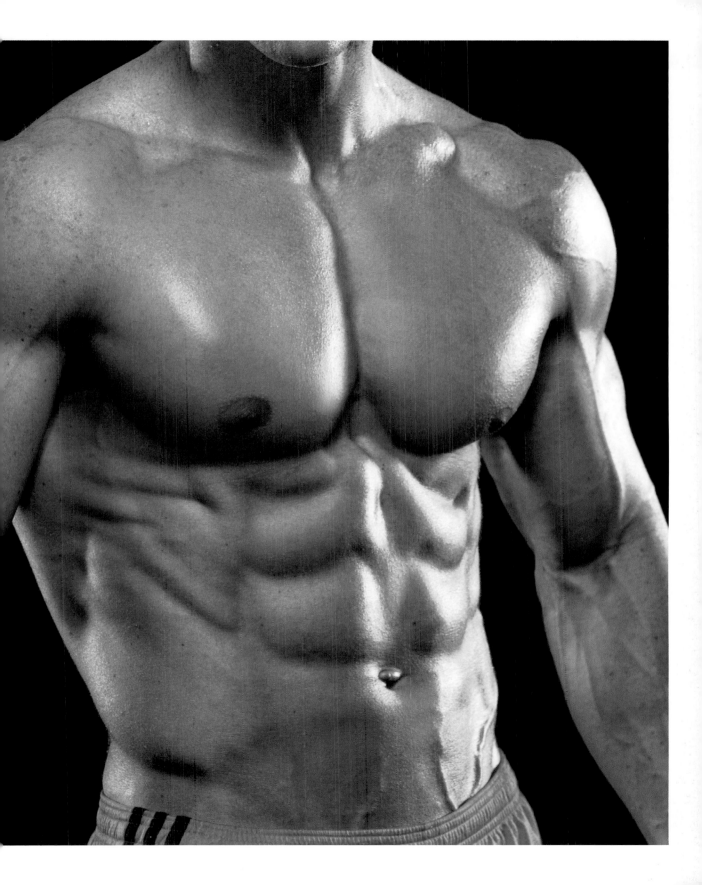

These days, saying you're training abs is sort of like stating, "I'm training my pec minors today," or "It's middle traps and brachialis day." It's an incomplete workout that falls short of any reasonable goal. You don't hit your abs anymore; you train your core. And why would you want to train only the rectus abdominis when you have the obliques, transverse abdominis and erectors (to name a few) that help rotate, extend and stabilize your trunk?

"Think about your core as being composed of four sections," says Mike Robertson, MS, CSCS, president of Robertson Training Systems (robertsontrainingsystems.com) and co-owner of the gym Indianapolis Fitness and Sports Training. "You have a front, two sides and a back. You want to train all four sections so you have a nice solid 'belt,' so to speak."

The way many people train their midsections — with the same predictable collection of crunches and sit-ups — won't cut it. Maybe the chest will continue to grow and get stronger through progressive resistance with barbell and dumbbell bench presses, but the abs are much more multidimensional and require constant variety in exercise selection. This is implemented in this core routine Robertson designed.

"Another thing you'll see people doing wrong is always moving in the same planes," he says. "One thing you'll notice about these exercises is there are many different components. You resist extension, resist rotation and do moves in planes you're probably not used to training in."

Outside of its exotic menu of exercises, Robertson's workout flies in the face of the typical paint-by-numbers ab routine you see at commercial gyms. Absent are high rep ranges since, according to Robertson, exercise technique "gets really sloppy really fast" when you start moving beyond 8–12 reps. He also discounts the notion that abs should be trained more frequently than other bodyparts. Due to the intensity of the routine, he recommends performing it only twice a week, either after training larger muscle groups or on its own if the core is a weak point.

And if you think only elite athletes trying to avoid injury need a well-rounded core-training program, think again. Having a strong core will benefit the serious gym rat just as much as it helps a football player or MMA fighter.

"A lot of people don't realize the core helps transfer the strength, energy and power that your hips and thighs produce," Robertson says. "If you have a weak midsection, you're not going to transfer as much energy up to the bar when you squat. The core is the weak link in a lot of lifters' bodies. If people just strengthened their cores, their squats and deadlifts would improve, and from an aesthetic standpoint it's fantastic for leg development."

48

Percent gain in transverse abdominis activation in individuals who performed core stabilization exercises twice a week for six weeks, according to a 2010 study out of São Paulo, Brazil

THE WORKOUT

EXERCISE	SETS	REPS/TIME
KETTLEBELL/DUMBBELL	2–3	5
WINDMILL		EACH SIDE
AB-WHEEL ROLLOUT	3	8–12
BAND-RESISTED JACKKNIFE	3	8–12
PALLOF PRESS (ISOMETRIC)	2	25–30 SEC.
		EACH SIDE

Rest 60–90 seconds between sets.

Working your lateral stabilizers will help you both in and out of the gym.

QUICK TIP

"With windmills, you're training what I call the lateral stabilizers — your external and internal obliques and your quadratus lumborum, a big core and lower-back stabilizer."

Kettlebell/ Dumbbell Windmill

START: Stand erect with your feet shoulder-width apart and hold a kettlebell or dumbbell near your chin in your right hand, with the weight resting against your forearm. Point your feet to the left at roughly a 45-degree angle, and extend your right arm toward the ceiling and point your left arm down.

EXECUTION: Keeping your eyes locked on the kettlebell, slowly bend at the waist to the opposite side, keeping your legs straight and pushing your hip to the right. Your left hand will slide down your leg until your fingers touch the floor or your foot. Your arms should form a straight line here, more or less perpendicular to the floor, with the weight directly above your shoulder. Slowly reverse the motion to return to the start position. Repeat for reps, then switch sides.

ROBERTSON'S TIP: "Keep your right leg straight [when the weight's in your right hand] and think about pushing into your hip. When you do this vs. just letting your lower back rotate or twist over, it keeps your lower back healthy and enhances hip mobility."

Ab-Wheel Rollout

START: In an almost-prone position, grasp the handles of an ab wheel directly below your shoulders at arm's length with your knees on the floor, and your torso and thighs in a straight line.

EXECUTION: Keeping your back flat (don't allow your hips to bend) and arms extended, slowly roll the wheel out as far in front of you as possible, then contract your midsection to pull yourself back to the start position.

ROBERTSON'S TIP: "Roll out just far enough so you start to feel increased pressure in your lower back — you want to stop just before that point and pull yourself back in. A lot of people go out too far and say, 'Oh, this exercise hurts.' But it's not so much the exercise that's the problem; it's how they execute it."

QUICK TIP

"Here we target the rectus abdominis and external obliques, and teach the body to resist extension. I try to convey that we're not just training motion around the core — we're training stability as well."

Jackknives with bands effectively target the stubborn lower abs.

Band-Resisted Jackknife

START: Loop an elastic band several feet up on a stable structure like a cable crossover station. Get in push-up position on the floor with the band supporting your feet. Keep your body in a straight line from head to heels.

EXECUTION: Contract your abs and bend your knees to pull them forward and down against the band resistance until your hips and knees form roughly 90-degree angles, then return to the start position under control.

ROBERTSON'S TIP: "Imagine there's a pipe balancing on your spine and you have to pull your knees to your chest without moving the pipe. That way, you focus on trying to control the motion by using your abs, not just your hip flexors and lower back."

QUICK TIP

"This move trains the same core function as leg raises. I describe it as promoting hip flexion without losing your lower-back position. If you want to squat deep without losing your back position, this is one exercise that'll help you do that."

Isometric core moves can help minimize gym-related injuries.

Pallof Press (isometric)

START: With a D-handle attached to a low-pulley cable, stand erect a few feet away from the weight stack with your feet shoulder-width apart. Grasp the handle with both hands, turn your body so your right side faces the stack and begin with your hands in front of your upper abs.

EXECUTION: Extend your arms parallel to the floor so your hands are straight out in front of you. Hold this position for 25–30 seconds, then return to the start. Repeat for reps, then switch sides.

ROBERTSON'S TIP: "Your arms should be straight [at the finish], but the real focus of the exercise should be on staying tall and keeping your glutes tight. That'll prevent you from rotating back toward the weight stack."

Chapter 16

Lift to Get Lean

Get ripped without the treadmill. This iron-only training plan is all you need.

We're gonna come right out and say

it: You don't have to do cardio to lean out and look like a bodybuilder. Sure, it helps. A lot. But if you're the type of guy who can't handle the boredom of the treadmill or you just don't have time for additional workouts during the week, you still have more than a sporting chance of getting the cut-up physique you desire.

We admit that cardio burns calories, and when it's done at a moderate intensity, most of those calories come from fat (it's also healthy, but, hey, this chapter is about getting ripped, so we'll keep the focus on that). For these reasons, it's no wonder bodybuilders have adopted it to help them cut up for contests. But it wasn't always that way. Do you remember any scene in *Pumping Iron* in which Arnold and Lou Ferrigno are jogging or using an elliptical...or a stairclimber?! We don't either. That's because old-school bodybuilders relied on a tight diet to shed the fat, and they tweaked their workouts to become fat furnaces before a contest.

Train to Maintain

In lieu of cardio, your weight workouts are going to double as conditioning sessions. Don't worry, they won't be boring like the treadmill. In fact, they'll be very intense. You'll be forced to perform supersets and use higher rep schemes than you're probably used to. The rest periods will be short. This strategy won't get you significantly stronger, but it will elevate your heart rate so you burn more fat during each session. Since muscle maintenance is the main goal during any cutting phase, we threw in some classic bodybuilder intensity techniques such as slow negatives and peak contractions. This will make sure your muscles work hard on each rep and you don't get assistance from the momentum of the stretch reflex. If you're wondering why abs and hamstrings are trained first on their respective days when they're usually an afterthought, it's for safety's sake. Training those areas first warms you up and can make for more joint-friendly training.

TRAINING PROGRAM

SPLIT
You'll train four days per week. You can perform the first two workouts on back-to-back days, but rest a day between Day 3 and Day 4.

DIRECTIONS
Perform the exercise pairs (marked "A" and "B") as supersets. So you'll do a set of one move and then go on to the next without rest. Afterward, rest as prescribed and repeat for all the prescribed sets. Perform the remaining exercises as straight sets.

Chest-Supported Row (Day 3)

Using a bench for support, you can focus solely on lats.

Barbell
Shrug (Day 3)

A heavy shrug will activate muscles throughout your body.

DAY 1 - Quads | Hams | Calves

3A Dumbbell Walking Lunge

SETS: 4 **REPS:** 10 **REST:** 0 sec. Perform all your reps with the same leg and then turn around and use the opposite leg to go back to where you started.

Pinch your shoulder blades back before descending.

2B Dumbbell Stiff-Leg Deadlift

SETS: 3 **REPS:** 8 **REST:** 90 sec. Focus on the hamstring stretch on every rep.

1A Lying Leg Curl

SETS: 4 **REPS:** 15 **REST:** 0 sec. Take two seconds to lower the weight on each rep.

1B Leg Extension

SETS: 4 **REPS:** 12 **REST:** 60 sec. Squeeze your quads at the top of each rep for three seconds.

2A Leg Press

SETS: 3 **REPS:** 12 **REST:** 0 sec. Place your feet high on the plate to target the hamstrings more. Perform sets of 12 with increasingly heavier weights until you reach a load that allows you 12 very hard reps. Stay with that weight and perform three work sets.

3B Machine Hack Squat

SETS: 4 **REPS:** 20 **REST:** 120 sec. Position your feet close together, in the middle of the platform.

4 Seated Leg Curl

SETS: 2 **REPS:** 25 **REST:** 90 sec.

5A Standing Calf Raise

SETS: 4 **REPS:** 12 **REST:** 30 sec.

5B Seated Calf Raise

SETS: 4 **REPS:** 15 **REST:** 30 sec. Get a deep stretch in your calves in the bottom position on every rep.

DAY 2 - Chest | Shoulders | Abs

1B Hanging Leg Raise

SETS: 4
REPS: 15 **REST:** 30 sec.
If it's too hard to hold your legs out straight, bend your hips and knees 90 degrees.

1A Cable Crunch
SETS: 4 **REPS:** 15
REST: 30 sec.

2A Incline Dumbbell Press
SETS: 4 **REPS:** 8
REST: 0 sec.
Do two to three warm-up sets of 10 to 15 reps and then begin working sets with eight reps. Hold the contracted (top) position for one second on each rep.

2B Pushup
SETS: 4 **REPS:** to failure
REST: 60 sec.

3A Pec-Deck Flye
SETS: 4 **REPS:** 12
REST: 0 sec.
Hold the top position for two seconds on each rep.

3B Machine Chest Press
SETS: 4 **REPS:** 10
REST: 45 sec.
Stop the press a few inches short so you don't lock out your elbows.

4 Dumbbell Lateral Raise
SETS: 4 **REPS:** 15
REST: 30 sec.

5A Machine Overhead Press
SETS: 4 **REPS:** 8
REST: 0 sec.
Hold the top position of each rep for two seconds, flexing your shoulders and arms.

5B Bentover Dumbbell Lateral Raise

SETS: 4
REPS: 20
REST: 45 sec.
Don't swing the weights up.

DAY 3 - Back | Traps | Calves

1A Seated Cable Row
SETS: 4 **REPS:** 10 **REST:** 0 sec.
Perform two to three warm-up sets and then do four working sets. Hold the contracted position for one second on each rep.

1B Wide-Grip Pulldown
SETS: 4 **REPS:** 10 **REST:** 60 sec.
Pull the handle to your neck. Hold the contracted position for one second.

2A Chest-Supported Row
SETS: 1 **REPS:** 12 **REST:** 0 sec.
Raise your elbows out wide as you lift the weights so that your upper arms form a "T" with your body in the top position.

4 Barbell Shrug
SETS: 3 **REPS:** 20
Hold the top position of the shrug for one second on each rep.

5A Standing Calf Raise
SETS: 4 **REPS:** 8 **REST:** 0 sec.

5B Seated Calf Raise
SETS: 4 **REPS:** 12 **REST:** 15 sec.

2B Dumbbell Pullover
SETS: 1 **REPS:** 12
REST: 60 sec.
Keep continuous tension on your lats by not pulling the dumbbell over your face.

Squeeze your abs to stabilize your spine.

3 Dumbbell Row
SETS: 3 **REPS:** 8
Add 10 pounds each set. Do not use momentum.

Keep your hips thrust toward the ceiling.

DAY 4 - Arms | Abs

1A Cable Crunch
SETS: 4 **REPS:** 15
REST: 0 sec.

1B Hanging Leg Raise
SETS: 4 **REPS:** 15
REST: 30 sec.

2 Rope Pushdown
SETS: 4 **REPS:** 15, 12, 10, 8
REST: 30 sec.

3A Dip
SETS: 4 **REPS:** 12
REST: 0 sec.
Flex your triceps at the top of each rep for one second.

3B Alternating Dumbbell Curl
SETS: 4 **REPS:** 10
REST: 45 sec.
Flex at the top of each rep for one second.

4B Preacher Curl
SETS: 4 **REPS:** 6
REST: 30 sec.
Squeeze for one second at the top and take three seconds to lower the weight on each rep. Don't lower your arm all the way—stop a few inches short.

5B Hammer Curl
SETS: 2 **REPS:** 8
REST: 60 sec.
Take two seconds to lower the dumbbells on each rep.

The reverse curl will give you unique grip work.

5A Reverse Curl
SETS: 2
REPS: 12
REST: 0 sec.
Hold the contraction for one second at the top.

Keep your elbows pointed toward the ceiling.

4A Lying Skull Crusher
SETS: 4 **REPS:** 12
REST: 30 sec.
Lower the weight to your forehead.

Chapter 17

Eat for Strength

Seeing maximum results from heavy training requires a strong diet like this one

Red meat is packed with protein, creatine and zinc, which will pay huge dividends with the iron.

Strong Meal Plan

This weekly strength-building nutrition schedule will have you throwing huge weight around in the gym

The Jack in the Box around the corner from your house shouldn't suddenly see an increase in sales when you start a strength-gaining lifting program. The notion that a guy training for strength can eat whatever crappy foods he wants is bunk (not to mention fattening). If you don't mind adding a spare tire and an increased risk of coronary artery disease to your big bench and squat, then by all means, eat a greasy burger every night for dinner. But gaining a gut is never acceptable — outside of maybe Matt Damon in *The Informant* or Sylvester Stallone in *Cop Land* — which is why every strength plan should be complemented by a hearty yet sensible meal plan.

Table Manners

First off, getting stronger in the gym means meeting your protein quotient outside of it. Strength training requires a higher protein intake because hoisting big weights puts a lot of stress on muscle fibers, and protein is the main nutrient that rebuilds and repairs that damage. You'll require at least 1.5 grams of protein per pound of bodyweight daily. Believe it or not, you won't need a high carb intake because training for strength uses relatively less volume (sets and reps) than your typical mass-building program. Less volume takes less energy and thus fewer carbohydrates. A good target is 1.5–2 grams of carbs per pound of bodyweight per day. But you'll want to keep a close eye on the mirror: If you gain a significant amount of bodyfat, decrease your carb intake slightly; if you aren't gaining bodyfat, try increasing your carbs. The majority of these carbs should be slow-digesting; if you aren't already, get acquainted with oatmeal, whole grains, sweet potatoes and fruit (except postworkout when you want fast-digesting carbs to drive up your body's natural insulin levels).

Fat intake is the component of a strength-training nutrition plan that'll deviate a bit from the standard bodybuilding meal. When muscular strength is the primary goal, you need more dietary fat to lubricate joints and enhance the production of testosterone, the male

MONDAY

BREAKFAST
2 whole eggs, scrambled with
  6 egg whites
1 slice low-fat cheese
2 slices whole-grain bread
2 Tbsp. low-sugar jam

MORNING SNACK
20 g whey protein
  mixed in water
1 low-fat granola bar
  or 1 cup oatmeal with
  Splenda or other noncaloric
  sweetener (if desired)

LUNCH
6 oz. lean red meat
1½ cups brown rice
1 small salad + 2 Tbsp. olive oil/
    vinegar dressing

❮ Whole-grain bread will provide energy for the gym

AFTERNOON SNACK
2 slices whole-grain bread
4 slices roast beef
Dijon mustard, lettuce, tomato

PREWORKOUT
1 scoop whey protein mixed in water
1 medium banana

POSTWORKOUT
2 scoops whey protein mixed
  in water
1 medium bagel

DINNER
8–9 oz. fish*
1 large sweet potato
1 cup mixed vegetables

BEDTIME SNACK
1 scoop casein protein mixed
  in water

DAILY TOTALS:
3,250 calories, 305 g protein,
315 g carbs, 85 g fat

TUESDAY

BREAKFAST
6 egg whites, scrambled with
  2 oz. (about 2 slices) Healthy
  Choice low-fat ham, chopped
  1 slice low-fat cheese
1 whole-wheat English muffin
2 Tbsp. peanut butter

MORNING SNACK
12 oz. low-fat milk
1 scoop whey protein
1 banana

LUNCH
6 oz. lean red meat
1 large sweet potato
1 cup green beans

AFTERNOON SNACK
2 slices whole-grain bread
1 can white tuna, packed in water
1 Tbsp. light mayo

PREWORKOUT
1 scoop whey protein mixed
  in water
1 large apple

POSTWORKOUT
2 scoops whey protein mixed
  in water
32 oz. Gatorade

DINNER
8 oz. chicken breast
1 cup whole-wheat pasta
¼ cup marinara sauce
2 cups mixed green salad
2 Tbsp. olive oil/vinegar dressing

BEDTIME SNACK
1 cup low-fat cottage cheese
1 oz. mixed nuts

DAILY TOTALS:
3,320 calories, 330 g protein,
320 g carbs, 80 g fat

WEDNESDAY

BREAKFAST
2 whole eggs, scrambled with
  6 egg whites
  1 slice low-fat cheese
2 slices whole-grain bread
2 Tbsp. low-sugar jam

MORNING SNACK
1 scoop whey protein mixed
  in water
1 low-fat bran muffin

LUNCH
6 oz. 90% lean ground beef
1 slice low-fat cheese
1 whole-wheat hamburger bun
1 Tbsp. ketchup

AFTERNOON SNACK
4 oz. (about 4 slices) turkey
  breast
2 slices whole-grain bread
1 large orange

PREWORKOUT
1 scoop whey protein mixed
  in water
1 medium banana

POSTWORKOUT
2 scoops whey protein mixed
  in water
1 medium bagel

DINNER
8–9 oz. fish*
1 large sweet potato
1 cup mixed vegetables

BEDTIME SNACK
1 scoop casein protein mixed
  in water
2 Tbsp. peanut butter

✳ **We recommend eating salmon 2–3 times a week; other fish can include halibut, kingfish, mackerel, scallops or snapper.**

DAILY TOTALS:
3,300 calories, 305 g protein,
305 g carbs, 95 g fat

hormone most closely associated with strength increases. Very low-fat diets are actually counterproductive to gains in strength.

It's important to include red meat in your diet because it's packed with zinc, a mineral that helps promote higher testosterone levels, and creatine, which can help provide immediate energy and boost strength levels. Nearly every great powerlifter says he feels stronger on a diet that includes red meat and doesn't restrict dietary fat. Make sure your total daily calories are made up of at least 20% fat, with the majority coming from healthy sources such as avocado, nuts, olive oil, peanut butter, salmon and tuna.

Energy to Burn

Many lifting programs — like the "Stronger in 2 Months" program in chapter 2 — call for training five days a week, so the nutrition regimen you see in this chapter alters nutrient totals based on whether it's a training day. On days you lift, you'll consume slightly more calories than you burn in the gym, which is the only way to get stronger. You'll burn roughly 17–18 calories per pound of bodyweight per day on training days, so you should consume just above that, or about 3,300 calories daily for a 180-pound guy.

Rest days are a bit different, as you'll likely burn only about 13 calories per pound of bodyweight. Consuming 14–16 calories per pound (2,500–2,800 calories for a 180-pounder) on these days will do the trick, allowing you to get stronger without adding much bodyfat. Protein stays the same on rest days, because you still want to get a minimum of 1.5 grams per pound of bodyweight, or about 270 grams for a 180-pounder.

Carbohydrates drop to about 1 gram per pound of bodyweight (180 grams for a 180-pound guy) on rest days. Unless you do manual labor for a living, that 1 gram should cover your sedentary needs. Fat stays above 20% of your total daily calories, though you'll eat a bit less fat as you keep calories in check.

Of course, you may have to do some math depending on your current weight — this program is adaptable to any size if you follow the aforementioned guidelines. Just don't forget to adjust your intake based on the new lean bodyweight you're sure to amass.

THURSDAY (OFF DAY)

BREAKFAST
2 whole eggs, scrambled with
6 egg whites
1 slice low-fat cheese
2 slices whole-grain bread
1 Tbsp. peanut butter

‹ Almost all of peanut butter's fat is unsaturated (healthy)

MORNING SNACK
2 scoops whey protein mixed
in water
1 low-fat granola bar
or 1 cup oatmeal with
Splenda or other noncaloric
sweetener (if desired)

LUNCH
6 oz. lean red meat
1 cup brown rice
2 cups mixed green salad
2 Tbsp. olive oil/vinegar dressing

AFTERNOON SNACK
2 slices whole-grain bread
1 can white tuna, packed in water
1 Tbsp. light mayo

SNACK
2 scoops whey protein mixed
in water

DINNER
8–9 oz. fish*
1 medium sweet potato
1 cup mixed vegetables
2 scoops whey protein mixed
in water
2 rice cakes

BEDTIME SNACK
1 cup low-fat cottage cheese
1 oz. mixed nuts

DAILY TOTALS:
2,760 calories, 320 g protein,
190 g carbs, 80 g fat

FRIDAY

BREAKFAST
6 egg whites, scrambled with
- 2 oz. (about 2 slices) Healthy Choice low-fat ham, chopped
- 1 slice low-fat cheese
1 whole-wheat English muffin
2 Tbsp. peanut butter

MORNING SNACK
12 oz. low-fat milk
1 scoop whey protein
1 banana

LUNCH
8 oz. chicken breast
1 large sweet potato
2 cups mixed green salad
2 Tbsp. olive oil/vinegar dressing

AFTERNOON SNACK
2 slices whole-grain bread
1 can white tuna, packed in water
1 Tbsp. light mayo

PREWORKOUT
1 scoop whey protein mixed
- in water
1 large apple

POSTWORKOUT
2 scoops whey protein mixed
- in water
32 oz. Gatorade

> Eating veggies at dinner will help keep carbs in check

DINNER
8 oz. top sirloin
1 cup brown rice
1 cup mixed vegetables

BEDTIME SNACK
1 cup low-fat cottage cheese
1 oz. walnuts (14 halves)

DAILY TOTALS:
3,370 calories, 325 g protein, 285 g carbs, 103 g fat

SATURDAY

BREAKFAST
2 whole eggs, scrambled with
- 6 egg whites
- 1 slice low-fat American cheese
1 whole-wheat English muffin
2 Tbsp. low-sugar preserves

MORNING SNACK
1 scoop whey protein mixed
- in water
1 low-fat bran muffin

LUNCH
6 oz. 90% lean ground beef
1 slice low-fat American cheese
1 Tbsp. ketchup
1 whole-wheat hamburger bun
2 cups mixed green salad
2 Tbsp. olive oil/vinegar dressing

AFTERNOON SNACK
2 slices whole-grain bread
1 can white tuna, packed in water
1 Tbsp. light mayo

PREWORKOUT
1 scoop whey protein mixed
- in water
1 medium banana

POSTWORKOUT
2 scoops whey protein mixed
- in water
1 medium plain bagel

DINNER
8–9 oz. salmon
1 cup mixed vegetables
1 large sweet potato

BEDTIME SNACK
1 scoop casein protein mixed
- in water
1 Tbsp. peanut butter

> Slow-digesting casein and peanut butter will ensure you don't waste muscle overnight

DAILY TOTALS:
3,340 calories, 325 g protein, 285 g carbs, 100 g fat

SUNDAY (OFF DAY)

BREAKFAST
12 egg whites, scrambled with
- 1 whole egg
- 1 slice low-fat cheese
1 cup oatmeal with
- Splenda or other noncaloric
- sweetener (if desired)

MORNING SNACK
2 scoops whey protein mixed
- in water
1 banana

« Fruit is one simple carb you can get away with on an off day

LUNCH
8 oz. chicken breast
1 cup whole-wheat pasta
¼ cup marinara sauce
2 cups mixed green salad
2 Tbsp. olive oil/vinegar dressing

AFTERNOON SNACK
4 oz. (about 4 slices) sliced turkey breast
2 slices whole-grain bread

SNACK
2 scoops whey protein mixed
- in water

DINNER
8 oz. shrimp
1 medium sweet potato
1 cup chopped broccoli

BEDTIME SNACK
1 scoop casein protein mixed
- in water
1 Tbsp. peanut butter

DAILY TOTALS:
2,500 calories, 320 g protein, 180 g carbs, 55 g fat

Chapter 18

Power Pills

Get stronger, faster and more explosive with these five supplements

To get stronger, there are a few basic things you need to do:

Do basic exercises like bench presses, squats and deadlifts; lift heavy weights for relatively low reps; and support your hard-training efforts with sufficient calories and protein. Fortunately, a handful of dietary supplements can also improve physical strength as well as power output. Some are tried and true while others are newcomers to the iron game. Here are five of the most promising.

2-2.5

This is roughly how much caffeine (in milligrams) you'll need per pound of bodyweight

Caffeine

WHAT IT IS The most consumed psychoactive drug in the world.

HOW IT WORKS A ton of data support the ergogenic role of caffeine. For instance, athletes who took caffeine and then performed 60% of their one-rep maxes on the bench press and leg press lifted 11% and 12% more weight, respectively, compared to the placebo group. In addition, competitive athletes lifted more weight on the chest press with a moderate intake of caffeine, and caffeine has been shown to improve performance of prolonged intermittent-sprint ability in trained men.

DOSAGE Most scientists believe 2-2.5 mg of caffeine per pound of bodyweight is sufficient.

Beta-Alanine

WHAT IT IS Beta-alanine is a non-essential amino acid that has been shown to elevate intramuscular carnosine concentrations.

HOW IT WORKS Taking beta-alanine can significantly increase stored levels of intramuscular carnosine, which helps fight the fatiguing effects of low muscle pH. (These high acidity levels also affect the muscles' ability to contract, hindering power and strength.) By increasing carnosine levels, you can improve athletic performance, particularly in sports that require explosive work.

In a recent study, trained cyclists took 2–4 grams of either beta-alanine or a placebo per day for eight weeks, then performed a 10-minute time trial and a 30-second sprint following a 110-minute simulated race. Researchers found that the mean power output during the time trial was similar in both groups, but in the final sprint those taking beta-alanine increased peak power output by more than 10%.

In another study, researchers gave college athletes 1.5 grams of beta-alanine and 15 grams of dextrose or a placebo. Beta-alanine supplementation further enhanced test subjects' ability to perform high-intensity interval training, improved endurance performance and increased lean body mass. When college football players were given a daily dose of 4.5 grams of beta-alanine for 30 days, they could train at a higher volume and experienced less fatigue.

DOSAGE Take 3 grams of beta-alanine with each of your pre- and postworkout shakes. After three weeks, drop the dose to 1–2 grams in each pre- and postworkout shake.

Creatine

WHAT IT IS Creatine is a nitrogen-containing organic acid that's made from the amino acids arginine, glycine and methionine, and is typically found in fish and other meats.

HOW IT WORKS Hundreds of studies prove that creatine is the single most effective supplement for increasing muscle mass, power and strength, and it provides a performance benefit in as little as five days. In one study, subjects given 20 grams of creatine a day for five days increased their average anaerobic power as measured by the Wingate test (a power test on a bicycle involving all-out sprints) and back squat strength compared to just training. In addition, five days of creatine supplementation enhanced lower-body maximal strength, and maximal repetitive upper- and lower-body high-power exercise bouts; it also increased total reps to fatigue and improved repeated sprint performance in highly trained athletes.

DOSAGE Take 3–5 grams with each of your pre- and postworkout shakes.

Chapter 18

Betaine

WHAT IT IS Betaine, or trimethylglycine, is found in foods such as beets, shellfish, spinach and wheat.

HOW IT WORKS Betaine can act as a methyl donor, which helps synthesize creatine. The data on betaine's ergogenic effects are sparse, but one recent study published in the Journal of the International Society of Sports Nutrition is worth noting. Researchers had 24 men consume 1.25 grams of either betaine or a placebo twice a day, and found that the betaine group could perform significantly more squat reps than those taking a placebo after two weeks of supplementation. The number of squats the betaine group could perform at a peak power of 90% or greater was also significantly higher than the placebo group.

DOSAGE Take 635 mg of betaine with each of your pre- and postworkout shakes.

635

Take this many milligrams of Betaine both before and after workouts to aid creatine synthesis

Arginine-AKG

WHAT IT IS A-AKG is a combination of the conditionally essential amino acid arginine and alpha-ketoglutarate, a byproduct of aerobic metabolism.

HOW IT WORKS Arginine plays a role in the production of nitric oxide, which increases blood flow as well as the delivery of nutrients to working muscles. In one study, 35 trained men were given 4 grams of either A-AKG or a placebo three times a day and performed a standard resistance-training program four days a week. The researchers discovered that the A-AKG group had a greater one-rep-max bench press and Wingate peak power than the placebo group.

DOSAGE Take 4 grams of A-AKG three times a day on an empty stomach.

POWER SUCKER

If you want to become less powerful, do a ton of cardio. Not only does excess endurance training cause muscle loss, but it also decreases your ability to move quickly and powerfully. So if you're a power athlete, you're better off doing high-intensity interval training than hours of endurance work.

In one study, 16 Division I college baseball players were divided into two training groups: One did moderate-to high-intensity cardio 3–4 days a week, and the other did speed/speed endurance training. The endurance group experienced a decrease in lower-body power while the speed group improved.

The only thing endurance training will do for you is increase endurance. If you play a sport in which power or strength is important, don't waste time mindlessly jogging on a treadmill.

Exercise Index

Abs

CRUNCH

Lie faceup on the floor with your knees and hips bent about 90 degrees, feet in the air, and either cross your arms over your chest or place your hands lightly behind your head. Contract your abs to lift your shoulder blades off the floor, then lower slowly. The range of motion is very short; the goal is to press your lower back into the floor to bring your sternum closer to your pelvis.

DOUBLE CRUNCH

Lie on the floor with your hands cupped gently behind your head and your legs almost completely straight and raised a few inches off the floor. Simultaneously bring your knees to your torso while crunching your upper body toward your legs. Squeeze in the middle, then return to the start and repeat. Don't let your feet touch the floor between reps.

HANGING LEG RAISE →

Hang from a pull-up bar or vertical bench with your legs straight and perpendicular to the floor. Keeping your knees extended but not locked out, raise your legs in front of you until they're parallel to the floor. Concentrate on contracting your abs, not your hip flexors, throughout the movement. Slowly lower your legs back to the hanging position.

REVERSE CRUNCH

Lie faceup on the floor with your hands at your sides or under your glutes. Begin with your legs extended and your feet a few inches off the floor, suspended in the air to put tension on your abs. Contract your abs to slowly raise your legs, keeping them straight, until they're roughly perpendicular to the floor. (As with the hanging leg raise, your abs are the focus, not your hip flexors.) Slowly lower your legs back to the start position without letting your feet touch the floor.

CABLE CRUNCH ↑

Kneel a couple of feet in front of cable weight stack with a rope attached to a high-pulley cable. Grasp the ends of the rope and hold it at the sides of your head. Begin slightly bent over, then contract your abs to lower your torso toward the floor. As with the crunch, the range of motion here is slight; your head shouldn't reach the floor. The key is a full contraction of the abs.

INCLINE SIT-UP

Lie back on an incline sit-up board or decline bench with your feet secured under the pad and your hands either behind your head or your arms crossed over your chest. Begin with the backs of your shoulders on the bench. Contract your abs to initiate a full sit-up, then slowly return to the start position.

PLANK

Assume a position similar to a push-up, only with the pinky side of your forearms (the ulna bones) on the floor — a padded surface may be preferred for comfort. You should be supported only by your forearms and your toes, with your body in a straight line from head to feet, head facing the floor. Hold this position for a length of time. The key is to keep your core tight to avoid letting your pelvis drop toward the floor. As you get stronger on this static exercise, increase the amount of time you hold the plank.

SIDE PLANK

Assume a modified plank position on the floor where, instead of facing down with your weight resting on both forearms, you're facing one side with your weight resting on only one arm with your forearm perpendicular to your torso. Keep your body in a rigid, straight line from head to feet. Hold this position for a length of time, then switch to the other side and repeat.

WEIGHTED DECLINE SIT-UP ↓

Lie back on a decline bench or incline sit-up board with your feet secured under the pads and hold a light weight plate either in front of your chest or on your head just above your forehead. (Start with a 10-pound plate and move to a 25-pounder if you're able to.) Begin with the

backs of your shoulders on the bench. Contract your abs to initiate a full sit-up, keeping the plate in the same position throughout. Slowly return to the start position and repeat for reps.

Weighted Roman Chair Sit-Up: Use the same form as above, only using a Roman chair, which is similar to a decline bench except that its back pad is considerably shorter. Because of this, the backs of your shoulders won't touch the bench; only your lower-middle back will.

WOODCHOPPER ↑

Stand sideways to a cable weight stack with a D-handle or rope attached to the high pulley. Grab hold of the attachment with both hands and begin with your arms extended up toward the high pulley, hands just above shoulder height. Your torso should be twisting slightly toward the weight stack. Keeping your arms extended, twist your torso the opposite way (away from the weight stack) and downward to pull your hands to the outside of the thigh further away from the stack — all in one fluid motion. Hold the end position for a count, then slowly return to the start position by twisting back the other way. Do all reps to that side, then switch sides and repeat.

Back

PULL-UP

Take a wide grip on a pull-up bar (hands outside shoulder width) and start in a hanging position, arms fully extended. Pull yourself up explosively by contracting your lats until your chin clears the bar. Slowly lower yourself to the start position.

LAT PULLDOWN ↓

Adjust the seat of the machine so your knees fit snugly under the pads. Grasp the bar outside shoulder width, arms fully extended overhead. Contract your lats to pull the bar down past your chin, squeeze your back muscles and slowly return the weight to the start position.

REVERSE-GRIP LAT PULLDOWN

Sit in a lat pulldown machine and grasp the bar with a reverse (palms facing you), shoulder-width grip, maintaining an erect posture and starting with your arms extended above you. Contract your lats to pull the bar down to your upper chest, bringing your elbows straight down and as far behind you as possible. Squeeze your shoulder blades together at the bottom, then slowly return to the start position.

BARBELL BENT-OVER ROW →

Stand holding a barbell with a shoulder-width, overhand grip. Bend your knees slightly and lean forward at the waist so your torso is angled roughly 45 degrees to the floor; maintain this position throughout. Start with your arms extended, hanging straight down, and

bend your elbows to pull the bar into your midsection. At the top of the move, squeeze your shoulder blades together for a count to fully contract your back muscles, then slowly return to the start position. For a reverse-grip bent-over row, the technique is the same, except that your hands will hold the bar in an underhand (supinated) grip.

Dumbbell Bent-Over Row: Use the same form as above, only holding a pair of dumbbells instead of a barbell.

SEATED CABLE ROW ↗

Sit on the bench of a cable-row station with your feet flat on the platform. Bend at your waist to grasp the attachment with both hands and sit upright (back flat, not bowed), arms extended in front of you. Bend your

toward your thighs, keeping your elbows extended to isolate your back muscles.

One-Arm Straight-Arm Pulldown: Use the same form as on the two-arm version, only with one arm at a time holding a D-handle or rope attachment.

elbows to pull the handle straight toward your midsection by contracting your back muscles; de-emphasize the amount of work your biceps do to keep maximal tension on your back. When your hands reach your abs, squeeze your shoulder blades together and hold before slowly returning to the start.

ONE-ARM DUMBBELL ROW

Place one knee and the same-side hand on a flat bench, bent at the waist. Keep your other foot on the floor and hold a dumbbell in the same-side hand hanging straight down with your arm extended. Pull the weight up into your side, keeping your elbow in close. Pull your elbow as high as you can, squeezing your shoulder blades together for a full contraction, then lower.

STRAIGHT-ARM PULLDOWN

Stand facing a cable stack and attach a straight bar or rope handle to a high-pulley cable. Grasp the attachment with both hands and begin with your arms extended in front of you and your hands at roughly head height. (Make sure the weight isn't resting on the stack.) Contract your lats to pull the weight down

45-DEGREE BACK RAISE ↑

Secure your feet in a back-extension apparatus and allow your upper body to hang down freely, keeping your back flat. Cross your arms over your chest, squeeze your glutes and slowly raise your torso until your body forms a straight line. Slowly return the way you came. To add resistance, hold a weight plate across your chest or use and elastic band, as pictured.

INVERTED ROW

Position the bar of a Smith machine or a barbell on a squat rack so that it's a foot or two above arms length from the floor. Position yourself underneath the bar with a shoulder-width grip on it, the backs of your heels on the floor in front of you and your arms extended, shoulders below your hands. Pull your body up in a rowing motion until your chest touches the bar, then lower back down and repeat.

Biceps/ Forearms

BARBELL CURL ↑

Stand holding a barbell in front of your thighs, arms extended and knees slightly bent to relieve pressure on your lower back. Keeping your elbows at your sides, bend them to curl the weight as high as you can. Squeeze your biceps for a count at the top, then slowly return the bar to the start position.

DUMBBELL CURL

Hold a pair of dumbbells outside your thighs, palms up. Using one arm at a time, curl each dumbbell up toward your shoulder without swinging the weight or rolling your shoulder, making sure your upper arm is locked at your side. Squeeze your biceps at the top, then slowly lower to the start.

PREACHER CURL ↓

Adjust the seat of a preacher bench so the top of the pad touches your armpits. Sit down and grasp a straight bar or EZ-bar with a shoulder-width grip, arms extended but not locked out. With your upper arms flush against the pad, curl the weight as high as you can and squeeze the contraction. Lower the bar under control, again stopping just shy of locking out your elbows.

DUMBBELL INCLINE CURL

Adjust an incline bench to 45–60 degrees and lie faceup on the bench with your feet flat on the floor. Hold a pair of dumbbells with your arms hanging straight down, palms forward. Keeping your shoulders back and upper arms fixed perpendicular to the floor, curl the dumbbells toward your shoulders. Squeeze your biceps hard at the top before slowly returning to the start position.

HAMMER CURL ↓

Stand holding a pair of dumbbells at your sides with your wrists in a neutral position (palms facing in). Flex your elbows to curl both dumbbells up without turning your palms up — keep them in the neutral position. Squeeze your biceps and forearms at the top, then lower the weights to the start position.

ROPE HAMMER CURL (CABLE)

Stand in front of a cable weight stack and grasp a rope attachment from the low pulley with your palms facing each other (neutral grip) and your arms extended toward the floor. Flex your elbows to curl both dumbbells up without turning your palms up — keep them in the neutral position. Squeeze your biceps and forearms at the top, then lower the rope to the start position.

BARBELL WRIST CURL ↑

Straddle a flat bench with your feet flat on the floor. Hold a straight bar with a palms-up grip and rest the backs of your forearms on the bench with your hands past the end of it so they aren't supported. Start with your wrists extended so your knuckles point toward the floor and only your fingers hold the bar. Flex your wrists by contracting your forearm muscles to raise the bar; the range of motion is only a few inches. Squeeze your forearms for 1–2 counts at the top, then slowly return to the wrists-extended position.

CONCENTRATION CURL

Sit at the end of a flat bench. Bend over and grasp a dumbbell with an underhand grip, locking your working arm against your same-side inner thigh. Place your non-working arm on the same side leg for balance. Moving only at your elbow, curl the weight as high as you can. Squeeze your biceps at the top before lowering the dumbbell back to the start.

Cable Concentration Curl: Use the same form as above, curling a D-handle attached to the low pulley while either sitting on a bench or bent over at the waist in front a cable stack.

Chest

BENCH PRESS ↑

Lie faceup on a flat bench with a rack and grasp the barbell just outside shoulder width. Carefully lift the bar off the rack and slowly lower it toward your chest. Lightly touch the bar to your lower pecs, then forcefully press it up to an arms-extended position without locking out your elbows. The bar should be directly over your face. The path of motion here is a slight backward arc rather than a straight line up from the lower pecs.

FLAT-BENCH DUMBBELL PRESS

Lie on a flat bench and hold a set of dumbbells just above chest level with your palms facing forward and your wrists directly over your elbows. Press the dumbbells up and inward toward each other over your midchest until your elbows are almost locked out. Bring the weights back down until your elbows form 90-degree angles.

BARBELL INCLINE PRESS

Lay back on a 45-degree inclined bench with a rack and grasp the bar with a slightly wider than shoulder-width grip. Start with the bar straight over your upper pecs and your arms extended but not locked out. Lower the bar to your chest, then press it up forcefully to the start position.

DUMBBELL INCLINE PRESS

Lie faceup on an adjustable incline bench and start with the dumbbells just outside your shoulders. Press the weights straight above you until your elbows are extended but not locked out. Slowly return to the start position.

DUMBBELL DECLINE PRESS ↑

Lie faceup on a decline bench with your feet secured beneath the pads and start with the dumbbells just outside your lower pecs. Press the weights straight up until your elbows are extended but not locked out. Slowly return to the start position.

DUMBBELL FLOOR PRESS

Lie on your back on the floor and hold a pair of dumbbells with the backs of your upper arms on the floor (being on the floor, not a bench, will limit your range of motion), your palms facing forward and your wrists directly over your elbows. Press the dumbbells up and inward toward each other over your mid-chest until your elbows are almost locked out. Return to the start position.

FLAT-BENCH DUMBBELL FLYE

Lie faceup on the bench with your feet flat on the floor. Hold a dumbbell in each hand with a neutral grip and extend your arms above your chest. Bend your elbows slightly. Slowly lower the dumbbells in a wide arc out to your sides. Keep your elbows locked in the slightly bent position throughout the range of motion. Stop when your elbows reach shoulder level, then contract your pecs to reverse the motion and return to the start position.

DUMBBELL INCLINE FLYE

Lie faceup on an adjustable bench set to 45 degrees, holding a pair of dumbbells over your chest with your arms extended and palms facing each other. With a slight bend in your elbows, lower the weights out in an arc to your sides until you feel a good stretch in your pecs. Contract your muscles to return the dumbbells to the start position, maintaining the slight bend in your elbows throughout.

DUMBBELL DECLINE FLYE

Lie faceup on a decline bench, holding a pair of dumbbells over your lower pecs with your arms extended and palms facing each other. With a slight bend in your elbows, lower the weights out in an arc to your sides until you feel a good stretch in your pecs. Contract your muscles to return the dumbbells to the start position, maintaining the slight bend in your elbows throughout.

DIP →

Start by holding yourself between the bars of a dip apparatus with your arms extended. Lower yourself under control until your upper arms are parallel to the floor and you feel a good stretch in your chest, then push with your chest and triceps to lift yourself back to the start position. To do weighted dips, hang weight in the form of a weight plate or dumbbell from a chain attached to a lifting belt.

CABLE CROSSOVER

Stand in the middle of a two-sided cable station with D-handles attached to both high-pulley cables. Begin with your arms extended out to your sides and elbows slightly bent. Step forward to make sure the weights aren't resting on the stacks, then contract your pecs to pull your hands together, maintaining the slight bend in your elbows. At the end of the motion, cross your hands and squeeze your pecs for a count.

MACHINE FLYE/PEC DECK

Sit in the machine with your lower back fully supported and your feet flat on the floor. If using a traditional pec deck machine, place your forearms flush against the pads and grasp the handles; if using a more modern flye machine, grasp the handles and begin with your arms extended out to the sides with a slight bend in the elbows. Bring the handles together in front of you, squeezing your chest hard at the top of the movement, then slowly return to the start.

"CLAPPER" PUSH-UP

Assume a standard push-up position. Slowly lower your body down, and when your elbows pass 90 degrees explode back up by contracting your pecs and extending your elbows to that your hands leave the floor at the top. Clap your hands in midair if possible and land back down with soft (not locked out) elbows.

Legs

SQUAT ↑

Stand with a barbell resting across your upper traps, grasping it with your hands to keep it stable. With your feet about shoulder-width apart and head facing forward, push your chest out slightly so your back arches naturally. Squat down with the weight as if sitting in a chair, keeping your feet in full contact with the floor and maintaining the arch in your back. When your thighs reach parallel to the floor, press through your heels, extending your knees and hips to return to standing.

FRONT SQUAT

Stand inside a power rack with the barbell across your front delts and upper chest. Cross your arms over your chest to build a shelf for the bar, unrack it and step back so you clear the rack. Keep your chest up and back flat, eyes focused forward. With your abs tight, bend your knees and hips as if to sit in a chair until your thighs are well past parallel to the floor. Reverse direction by driving through your heels and pressing your hips forward.

SMITH MACHINE FRONT SQUAT

Stand in a Smith machine with the bar resting across your front delts, holding it in your hands with your arms crossed over each other. Position your feet about shoulder-width apart and a foot or so in front of the bar. Face forward and push your chest out slightly so your back arches naturally. Undo the safety hooks, then squat down as if sitting in a chair, keeping your feet in full contact with the floor and maintaining the arch in your back. When your thighs reach parallel to the floor, push yourself up through your heels, extending your knees and hips, to return to the standing position.

LEG PRESS ↓

Sit on a leg-press machine and place your feet hip- to shoulder-width apart on the foot platform above you. Press the weight up with your legs to a point at which your knees are extended but not locked out. Release the machine's safety catches. Lower the weight under control until your knees form 90-degree angles or

slightly less. Push the weight back up explosively to the start position, again without locking out your knees at the top.

One-Leg Press: This exercise can also be done unilaterally, using the same form described above, only with one leg.

HACK SQUAT

Step inside a hack squat machine, placing your shoulders and back against the pads with your feet shoulder-width apart on the platform and your legs extended. Maintain good posture, with your chest up and abs pulled in tight. Unhook the safety bars and bend your legs to slowly lower yourself until your knees are past 90 degrees. Pause, then forcefully press yourself up to the start position without locking out your knees at the top.

DEADLIFT ↑

Stand in an open space with a loaded barbell on the floor in front of you, feet hip-width apart. Keeping your back flat and head up, bend your knees and hips to grasp the bar with a shoulder-width staggered (one palm facing forward, the other backward) grip. This is your start position. Stand up with the bar in one explosive motion by extending your knees and hips. Never round your back. Return to the start position, weight touching the floor, under control.

PUSH PRESS

Take a barbell from a power rack with a shoulder-width overhand grip, resting it across your upper chest, and step back. With your head up, chest out and the feet shoulder-width apart, initiate the movement by flexing your ankles, hips and knees slightly so your body descends about 4 inches. Rapidly extend your hips, knees and ankles to fully extend your body, then quickly press the bar in front of your face to elbow lockout at the top. Lower the bar back to your upper chest, bending your hips and knees slightly to cushion the weight before starting the next rep.

DUMBBELL STEP-UP

Select a bench or box that's 12–18 inches high. Start by standing upright holding a pair of dumbbells, keeping your head up and chest out for proper back alignment. Step up so that your entire foot is on the bench, then stand up, pressing into the bench and pulling your trailing leg upward. After both feet are on the bench, slowly move your trailing leg back down, emphasizing the negative motion. Alternate legs every other rep, or do all your reps with one leg and then switch.

LUNGE

Hold a dumbbell in each hand and stand with your feet hip-width apart and your arms down at your sides. (Lunges can also be performed holding a barbell across your upper traps.) Step forward a comfortable stride length with one foot, lift the back heel, and lower your back knee straight down toward the floor. When your front thigh is parallel to the floor, press off the heel of your front foot, raising your body straight back up to the start position. Step forward and repeat with the other foot. Continue alternating legs until you've completed all the reps for one set.

Lunges can also be performed walking, where instead of stepping back to the start position on each rep, you step forward with your back foot so that it meets your front foot, gaining ground with each rep. Either variation of lunge can also be performed with a barbell resting across the upper traps.

Legs, cont.

REVERSE LUNGE

Hold a dumbbell in each hand — or hold a barbell across your upper traps — and stand with your feet hip-width apart. Step backward with one foot and lower that knee toward the floor; only the ball of foot you step back with will land on the floor, not the heel. When your front thigh is parallel to the floor, press off the back foot to lift your body back to the start position. Repeat with the opposite leg. Continue alternating legs until you've completed all the reps for one set.

SMITH MACHINE LUNGE

Stand in a Smith machine with the bar resting across your upper traps and your feet together. Unhook the latches and step a few feet forward with one foot, keeping both legs extended. Bend your front knee and drop your back knee to the floor until it's a few inches from touching. (Your front knee should not extend past your toes; if it does, step out further.) Contract the quad and glute of your front leg to press yourself back up to the standing position. Perform for desired number of reps, then switch leg positions and repeat.

LEG EXTENSION

Adjust the seat of a leg-extension machine so that your lower back is flat against the seatback and your knees line up with the machine's axis of rotation. Begin with your legs bent 90 degrees and the weight lifted a few inches off the stack. Contract your quads to extend until your legs are completely straight. Squeeze your quads at the top, then return to the start position. One-Leg Extension: This exercise can also be done unilaterally, using the same form described above, only with one leg.

ROMANIAN DEADLIFT ↗

Stand upright, holding a barbell in front of your thighs with a shoulder-width grip. With your back flat and knees slightly bent, bend at the waist to slide the bar down your legs as you lower it straight toward the

floor. Keep your knees slightly bent and your arms straight throughout the movement. When the bar reaches about mid-shin level (how far you can lower it depends on your flexibility), contract your hamstrings and glutes to pull yourself back up to the start position. Dumbbell Romanian Deadlift: Use the same form as above, only holding a pair of dumbbells instead of a barbell.

SMITH MACHINE ROMANIAN DEADLIFT

Stand upright holding the bar in front of your upper thighs with an overhand grip. Keep your feet shoulder-width apart and a slight bend in your knees. Rotate and unrack the bar.

Keeping your abs pulled in tight while maintaining the natural arch in your low back, lean forward at your hips, pushing them rearward until your torso is roughly parallel to the floor. As you lean forward, keep your arms straight as the bar travels toward the bottom of the guide rods. At the bottom, keep your back flat and head neutral, then flex your hamstrings and glutes to lift your torso while pushing your hips forward until the bar reaches the start position.

GOOD MORNING ↓

Set a lightly weighted barbell across your upper back/traps and position your feet shoulder-width with your knees slightly bent. With your torso high and eyes straight ahead, start the movement by pushing your glutes back and bending forward at the waist. Descend forward until your torso is parallel to the floor. Pause deliberately at the bottom before contracting your lower back, glutes and hamstrings to raise your torso back to the start position.

LYING LEG CURL

Adjust the machine so the roller pad fits on the backs of your ankles. Lie facedown and grasp the handles. Start with your legs straight and the weight lifted a few inches off the stack. Bend your knees to curl the roller pad toward your glutes. Squeeze your hamstrings for a

count at the top and slowly lower to the start position. **One-Leg Lying Leg Curl:** This exercise can also be done unilaterally, using the same form described above, only with one leg.

SEATED LEG CURL

Adjust the seat so your knees line up with the machine's axis of rotation. Sit squarely in the machine, placing the backs of your ankles on the rollers and securing the pad across your lower quads. Begin with your legs extended, then contract your hamstrings to flex your knees as far as possible. Hold for a count, then slowly return to the start position.

STANDING CALF RAISE

Step onto the platform so only the balls of your feet and toes touch it and your heels are suspended. Place your shoulders snugly underneath the pads. Start with your knees slightly bent (keep them this way throughout the range of motion) and your heels dropped toward the floor below the level of the platform. Flex your calves to extend your ankles as high as possible. Squeeze your calves for 1–2 counts at the top, then lower back to the start position, feeling a stretch at the bottom.

SEATED CALF RAISE

Sit on the seat and adjust the pads so they fit snugly on your lower thighs. Place the balls of your feet and toes on the platform so your heels are suspended. Release the safety catch and begin with your heels below the level of the platform so you feel a stretch in your calves. Extend your ankles to push the pads up as high as you can — you should be almost on your tiptoes at the top. Squeeze your calves, then lower back down.

LEG PRESS CALF RAISE

Sit in a leg press machine and put the balls of your feet at the bottom of the platform. Do NOT unrack the safety bars. Flex your calves to extend your ankles as high as possible, squeeze them at the top, then lower back down until you feel a stretch.

Shoulders/ Traps

MILITARY PRESS

Stand holding a barbell with an overhead grip just out-side shoulder-width. Begin with the bar just over your upper pecs and below your chin with a slight bend in your knees. Keeping your lower body stationary, press the bar straight up overhead without locking out your elbows at the top. Slowly lower the bar back to the start position.

↙ BARBELL OVERHEAD PRESS

Sit on an upright bench or low-back seat with a barbell racked overhead. Grasp the bar just outside shoulder width, lift it off the rack (preferably with the help of a spotter) and begin with it overhead, arms extended. Slowly lower the bar in front of your face until it reaches about chin level, then explosively press it back up without locking out your elbows.

DUMBBELL OVERHEAD PRESS

Sit on an upright bench or low-back seat and hold a set of dumbbells at shoulder level, elbows and wrists stacked. Press the weights simultaneously up and in over your head until the dumbbells nearly touch, then reverse the motion to return to the start.

UPRIGHT ROW

Stand holding a barbell in front of you with a shoulder-width grip and your arms extended down. Lift the bar straight up along your body by bending your elbows and contracting your delts until it reaches chest level. Hold the contraction for a count, then slowly lower the bar to full elbow extension. Upright rows can also be performed with dumbbells using the same technique. Dumbbell Upright Row: Use the same form as above, holding a pair of dumbbells instead of a barbell.

DUMBBELL LATERAL RAISE ↑

Stand holding a pair of relatively light dumbbells at your sides, arms extended. Lift the weights straight out to your sides in an arc until your arms are parallel to the floor. Hold the contraction for a count, then slowly lower the dumbbells back to your sides.

CABLE LATERAL RAISE

Stand sideways to a cable weight stack and grasp a D-handle attached to the low pulley with your hand further from the stack (if your left side is facing the stack, your right arm is working). Start with your working arm at your side, elbow slightly bent, and your non-working hand grasping onto the machine for stability. Lift the handle straight out to the side in an arc until your arm is parallel to the floor. Slowly lower back to the start position. Rep out with that arm, then switch arms and repeat.

MACHINE OVERHEAD PRESS

Adjust the seat so that your upper arms are just past parallel to the floor, and grab the handles slightly outside shoulder-width. Press the weight up just shy of locking out the elbows, then slowly return the weight to the start position without letting the weight rest on the stack between reps.

BENT-OVER LATERAL RAISE

Hold a pair of dumbbells and lean forward at the waist so your torso is nearly parallel to the floor. Let your arms hang straight down, elbows extended and palms facing in; keep your chest up and back flat to avoid injury. Simultaneously lift the dumbbells in an arc out to your sides until your arms are roughly parallel to the floor. (Keep your elbows relatively straight; bending them excessively takes tension off your rear delts.) Lower the weights under control back to the start position; don't simply let them drop.

REVERSE PEC-DECK FLYE

Sit backward at a pec deck machine and grasp the handles in front of you with a neutral grip (palms facing each other). Keep your abs tight and your chest up. Flex your rear delts, keeping a slight bend in your elbows, to pull the handles back until your upper arms are just past perpendicular to your torso. Hold briefly, then return to the start position.

FACE PULL ↑

Stand facing a lat pulldown machine with a rope attached to the cable instead of a bar. Grasp the rope with both hands, palms facing downward. Start by leaning back slightly with one foot up on the edge of the seat and the other on the floor in a stable position and your arms extended in front of your face. Pull the rope toward your face be leading with your elbows so that they point out to the sides while your hands still face down. Pull the rope to your face, then return to the start position.

BARBELL SHRUG →

Hold a barbell at arms' length in front of your thighs. Keeping your elbows extended, simply elevate ("shrug") your shoulders as high as you can — straight up and down, not backward or forward — and squeeze at the top. Lower back to the start position, depressing your shoulders, then repeat for reps.

Barbell Behind-the-Back Shrug: Stand directly in front of a barbell resting on low bars of a power rack with your feet spaced about shoulder-width apart. Grasp the bar with an overhand grip and your hands just outside your hips and unrack it. Keeping your arms straight, chest up and eyes facing forward, shrug your shoulders upward, bringing your delts toward your ears. Hold the peak contraction and squeeze for a count before lowing the bar to the start position. Repeat for reps.

Triceps

PUSHDOWN ↑

Stand facing a cable stack and attach a straight-bar, EZ-bar, V-bar or rope handle to a high-pulley cable. Grasp the attachment with both hands and begin with your elbows tight at your sides and your forearms just shy of parallel to the floor. Keeping your elbows in, extend your arms until they're straight, squeezing your triceps at the bottom of the rep.

CLOSE-GRIP BENCH PRESS

Position yourself as you would when benching, but grasp the bar (loaded with a lighter weight than you'd use for wide-grip benching) with your hands 6–12 inches apart. Lower the bar to your mid-to-lower chest, then press it back up explosively, keeping your elbows as close to your sides as possible. This exercise can also be performed on a Smith machine using the same technique.

LYING TRICEPS EXTENSION

Lie faceup on a flat bench, holding a weighted EZ-bar at arm's length over your face. Keeping your elbows pulled in, slowly lower the bar toward the top of your head. Before it touches, pause, then contract your triceps to press back up to the start position. This exercise can also be performed on an incline bench using the same technique.

DUMBBELL OVERHEAD TRICEPS EXTENSION

Sit on a low-back seat with your feet flat on the floor. Grasp the inner plate of a dumbbell with both hands and hold it overhead with your elbows extended. Bending only at your elbows, lower the weight behind your head until your arms form 90-degree angles. Press back up to full arm extension and squeeze your triceps hard at the top.

CABLE OVERHEAD TRICEPS EXTENSION

Attach a rope to a high pulley on a cable apparatus. Stand facing away from the stack, grasp the rope near the knots and hold the attachment behind your head. Bend forward at your waist so your torso is at approximately a 45-degree angle to the floor and start the move with your elbows bent less than 90 degrees and your hands still behind your head. Keeping your elbows pressed together, extend your arms so your hands move forward in front of your head. Squeeze your triceps at full elbow extension by turning your palms out, then return to the start position.

DUMBBELL LYING TRICEPS EXTENSION

Lie faceup on a flat bench and hold a pair of dumbbell at arms length straight above you. Keeping your elbows pulled together, lower the dumbbells slowly toward your forehead. When your elbows slightly beyond 90 degrees, immediately press the weights back up to the start position by contracting your triceps.

Exercise Log

Track
Your
Progress

Keeping a journal of your training and diet will help you stay on track. Here are three blank journal pages you can photocopy to get you started

Date _____

Weight Training Session

Warm-Up	EXERCISE	DURATION

Bodypart	Exercise	SET 1 REPS	WT	SET 2 REPS	WT	SET 3 REPS	WT	SET 4 REPS	WT

Cardio Training Session

EXERCISE	Notes
DURATION	

Nutrition Journal

Meal 1	CAL	PROTEIN	CARBS	FAT	Meal 4	CAL	PROTEIN	CARBS	FAT

Meal 2	CAL	PROTEIN	CARBS	FAT	Meal 5	CAL	PROTEIN	CARBS	FAT

Meal 3	CAL	PROTEIN	CARBS	FAT	Meal 6	CAL	PROTEIN	CARBS	FAT

DAILY TOTALS	CALORIES:	PROTEIN:	CARBS:	FAT:

Exercise Log

Date _____

Weight Training Session

Warm-Up	EXERCISE	DURATION

Bodypart	Exercise	SET 1 REPS	SET 1 WT	SET 2 REPS	SET 2 WT	SET 3 REPS	SET 3 WT	SET 4 REPS	SET 4 WT

Cardio Training Session

EXERCISE	Notes
DURATION	

Nutrition Journal

Meal 1	CAL	PROTEIN	CARBS	FAT	Meal 4	CAL	PROTEIN	CARBS	FAT

Meal 2	CAL	PROTEIN	CARBS	FAT	Meal 5	CAL	PROTEIN	CARBS	FAT

Meal 3	CAL	PROTEIN	CARBS	FAT	Meal 6	CAL	PROTEIN	CARBS	FAT

DAILY TOTALS	CALORIES:	PROTEIN:	CARBS:	FAT:

Date _____

Weight Training Session

Warm-Up	EXERCISE		DURATION	

Bodypart	Exercise	SET 1 REPS	WT	SET 2 REPS	WT	SET 3 REPS	WT	SET 4 REPS	WT

Cardio Training Session

EXERCISE	Notes
DURATION	

Nutrition Journal

Meal 1	CAL	PROTEIN	CARBS	FAT	Meal 4	CAL	PROTEIN	CARBS	FAT

Meal 2	CAL	PROTEIN	CARBS	FAT	Meal 5	CAL	PROTEIN	CARBS	FAT

Meal 3	CAL	PROTEIN	CARBS	FAT	Meal 6	CAL	PROTEIN	CARBS	FAT

DAILY TOTALS	CALORIES:	PROTEIN:	CARBS:	FAT: